Limited Collectors' Edition made possible by the

*Anchorage Museum of
History and Art*

CRUDE DREAMS

*A Personal History
Of Oil & Politics
In Alaska*

JACK RODERICK

CRUDE DREAMS

*A Personal History
Of Oil & Politics
In Alaska*

JACK RODERICK

Epicenter Press
Fairbanks/Seattle

Epicenter Press, Inc. is a regional press founded in Alaska whose interests include (but are not limited to) the arts, history, environment, and diverse cultures and lifestyles of the North Pacific and high latitudes. We seek both the traditional and innovative in publishing quality nonfiction trade books, contemporary art and photography gift books, and destination travel guides emphasizing Alaska, Washington, Oregon, and California.

Cover photos:
(background) Kanatak village on the Alaskan Peninsula (Fred Henton Collection)
(clockwise from upper left): Trans-Alaska Pipeline construction (Alyeska Pipeline Service Company); Union Oil's Cook Inlet Monopod (*Anchorage Daily Times/Anchorage Daily News*); Bill Egan (Steve McCutcheon/Anchorage Museum of History and Art); Prudhoe Bay Drillers (Joe Rychetnik)

Project Editor: . . . . .Don Graydon
Typesetting and Design: . .Doug Belew, Paragon Communications Group, Tulsa OK
Production Editor: . . . . . . .Sue Rhodes Sesso
Maps: . . . . .Rusty Nelson
Index: . . . . .Carolyn Embach
Proofreaders: . . . . .Jennifer Luitwieler, Sue Rhodes Sesso, Phylinda Moore

Printed in Canada

First printing, August, 1997
ISBN 0-945397-62-3

10 9 8 7 6 5 4 3 2 1

To
Martha

Alaska

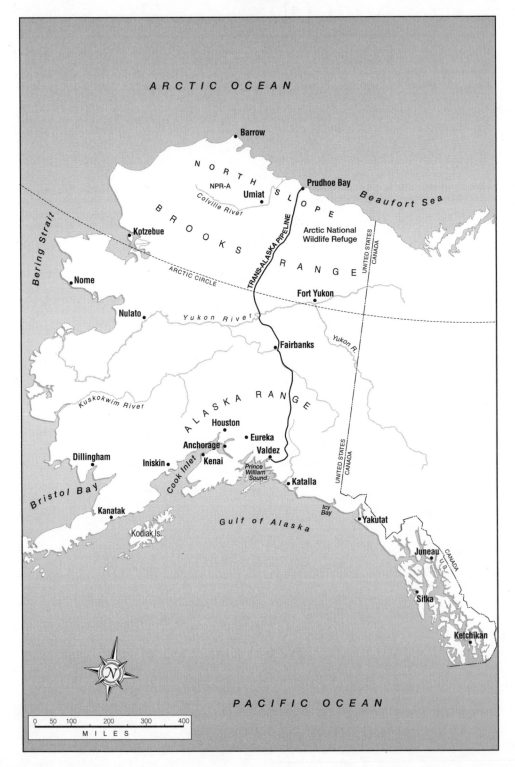

ARCTIC OCEAN

Barrow

NORTH SLOPE

NPR-A

Colville River

Umiat

Prudhoe Bay

Beaufort Sea

BROOKS

Kotzebue

Arctic National
Wildlife Refuge

TRANS-ALASKA PIPELINE

RANGE

UNITED STATES
CANADA

Bering Strait

ARCTIC CIRCLE

Nome

Fort Yukon

Nulato

Yukon River

Yukon R.

Fairbanks

Kuskokwim River

ALASKA RANGE

Houston

Eureka

Anchorage

Valdez

UNITED STATES
CANADA

Dillingham

Iniskin

Kenai

Prince
William
Sound

Cook Inlet

Katalla

Bristol Bay

Kanatak

Icy
Bay

Yakutat

Kodiak Is.

Gulf of Alaska

Juneau

CANADA
U.S.

Sitka

Ketchikan

N

PACIFIC OCEAN

0   50   100   200   300   400

MILES

CONTENTS

Part III: An Oil State

Part IV: Riding the Tiger

FOREWORD

If you're searching for the defining moment in Alaska's relationship with the oil industry, Jack Roderick's careful chronicle offers ample choices for consideration.

Perhaps you think it was one of the "Eureka" moments that came with discovery at Swanson River in the 1950s; maybe the decisive time came the instant geologists knew their hunches about a massive field at Prudhoe Bay would actually pay off. We could propose the 1969 North Slope lease sale, when the then-unimaginable sum of $900 million vaulted Alaska out of its adolescent poverty once and for all; we could argue for the moment of "oil in" at the wellhead of the trans-Alaska pipeline.

But those events relate mainly to the industry itself. Some of us would argue that to understand how permanently the state is now entwined with Big Oil, a better reference point is the moment the Exxon Valdez fetched up against Bligh Reef and began spilling Prudhoe crude into Prince William Sound. It was that massive oil spill—and, more tellingly, Alaskans' reaction to it—that proved Alaska was fundamentally oil country, as surely as Tulsa or Abu Dhabi. Looking back, the spill and its aftermath made it clear that there could be no turning back.

How did Alaska reach that point? Gradually but inexorably—and you can follow the journey step-by-step through the chapters that follow in *Crude Dreams.* Alaskans' attitudes toward the oil industry have evolved markedly over the years outlined in the book, ranging from wide-eyed enthusiasm to wary partnership and back again, but in the end the fortunes of the state have become so dependent on the industry that the marriage seems sure to hold together—if only "for the sake of the kids."

Before construction of the trans-Alaska pipeline, debate about oil development in the state centered almost entirely on environmental concerns. Alaskans worried that the oil line would leak, that it would melt the permafrost, that caribou would be scared away. After substantial reengineering to address those and other concerns, the industry proved that it could build a pipeline that essentially avoided those pitfalls.

Few Alaskans thought to worry in those relatively halcyon days about how oil would reshape the state's sociological landscape. In retrospect—even considering the spill of the Exxon Valdez—the

9

effects on people and attitudes in the state have been far greater than any environmental impacts.

To understand why Alaskans in 1997 have come to think of an annual dividend check from oil as a natural birthright, it helps to understand where Alaskans were in 1957. On the threshold of both statehood and bankruptcy, those pioneer Alaskans looked at the oil potential they could almost smell under the muskeg as a bankbook for the future. When the 1980s oil boom pushed crude prices to $30 a barrel and the state had budget surpluses in the billions, Alaskans launched capital projects that seemed designed "to buy themselves a Houston off the shelf." When the state income tax was repealed—replaced with revenues from Big Oil—a lot of Alaskans vowed they'd never go back.

As Alaskans came to expect oil to pay for their government, something fundamental about the state's pioneer spirit changed forever. The mystique of the rugged individualist lives on in Iditarod posters and tourists brochures, but there is less of it these days on Fourth Avenue or Front Street.

How that came to be is the story told between the lines in *Crude Dreams.* Anybody who cares about where Alaska was and where it's going will want to spend the time to understand it well.

Howard Weaver
Editor, *Anchorage Daily News, 1983-1985*

PREFACE

Alaska radiated opportunity and adventure when I first arrived in 1954. I was a graduate of Yale, with a Teamsters card and one year of law school, and I reveled in Alaska's openness to newcomers and its absorption with self-determination.

In my first job, I moved furniture and drove a truck between Anchorage and Fairbanks. A year later, when my employer went bankrupt, I had to do something in a hurry to survive. Charlie Barnes, a friend of mine at Shell Oil, suggested I start a scouting service. "What's that?" I asked.

He directed me to Joe McCusker, who owned a scouting service in Portland, Oregon, where I spent several weeks getting a detailed answer to my question. When I returned to Anchorage, I was ready to publish the Alaska Scouting Service, a periodic mimeographed report on oil drilling and leasing activity.

Several major oil companies were exploring in the Territory of Alaska at the time. Phillips was drilling at Icy Bay on the Gulf of Alaska; Chevron, Shell, and Richfield were filing for leases on the Kenai Peninsula, in the Cook Inlet, and on the Alaska Peninsula. The "little guys" were competing in the oil game by drilling in several of Alaska's sedimentary basins, including far off to the west toward Nome.

At the same time, the Territory with its tiny population was loudly calling on the U.S. Congress to grant statehood—the political equivalent of the little guy challenging the big guy. Alaskans wanted their own state. We (I adapted quickly) wanted a place to flex our political muscle. We wanted to get the "outsiders" off our backs. We wanted to elect our own governor, not have one appointed by the president of the United States.

I was from a middle-class Seattle family and grew up with children from some of the families who had made fortunes extracting Alaska's resources. Now it felt good to do battle with these families who had exploited my new country. My father was a former Presbyterian minister turned failed small-businessman because of alcohol, but he had imbued in me the notion that the businessmen who appeared so pious on Sundays were hypocrites. I was angry, and Alaska's battle with the "big guys" who were exploiting and controlling her felt like my fight. Later, of course, I learned that the history of the Territory is not quite as simple as I wanted to make it.

Some of the big oil companies sent me checks for $385 to subscribe to my scouting service. Along with technical data, I reported rumors about who was seen in town and who might be doing what to whom and where. It didn't bother me that I knew almost nothing about the oil business. I had energy and was ready to be an entrepreneur. I simply learned as I went along.

One thing I learned was that I wasn't going to get rich quick. At the end of my first year of reporting I had eight subscribers and a wife. Growth prospects for the business weren't great, and I decided I'd better finish law school. So I took my mimeograph machine with me and began publishing the Alaska Scouting Service in Seattle, returning to Anchorage during the summers.

The discovery of oil at Swanson River in 1957 renewed my entrepreneurial spirit. Back in Alaska to stay, Charlie Barnes joined me in a series of oil-related small businesses, including leasing land and looking for oil. Those early days were exciting. Each morning brought new prospects, and with them the vision of finding the mother lode of Alaskan oil.

Alaska became a state in January 1959, as I was about ready to finish law school. With statehood, Alaskans suddenly became owners of the state's oil and gas lands. Lease terms could be set, rents and royalties charged, oil companies taxed. But unlike Texas, Oklahoma, and Louisiana, where thousands of farmers, landowners, and businessmen influenced politics by owning oil royalties, as independent operators or as oil company employees, only a small handful of Alaskans—the "little guys"—got a piece of the action dominated by the big oil companies. And after the Prudhoe Bay discovery in 1968, even these few Alaskans faded from the game.

Though the discovery at Prudhoe Bay on the North Slope was a boon to Alaska's economy, it actually extinguished much of the early entrepreneurial spirit I found so attractive. Even before Prudhoe Bay, the smaller operators had begun to withdraw, due mostly to changes in the leasing laws. But Prudhoe was the beginning of the end for us "little guys" as the major operators took charge. I moved on to careers in politics, public administration, and teaching, but my work always seemed to bring me back to this immense factor in Alaskan life, the multibillion-dollar treasure in oil.

From 1968, when the world price of oil was around $3 a barrel, to 1977, when North Slope oil first flowed to Valdez, the world price had risen to about $11 a barrel. Two years later, when the Shah of Iran was dethroned and Prudhoe Bay oil production stood at 1.5 million barrels a day, the price jumped to over $30 a barrel. From 1969 to 1979, the state of Alaska's income from oil increased tenfold, and by 1982 the state's annual budget grew to more than $4 billion—making the share of public wealth owned by each Alaskan more than that of a citizen of Saudi Arabia.

I wrote this book to provide an inside view of the personalities and politics that led up to and swirled around the Prudhoe Bay discovery, the largest oil reserve in U.S. history. The book is as objective as possible—and at the same time terribly subjective. I interviewed more than 100 people intimately involved in the oil business in Alaska, hoping to achieve a measure of objectivity by including many voices. But the book also is the chronicle of Alaska oil as witnessed by me during my forty years on the edges of this great story.

This book will mostly tell about the actions and recollections of people who were white and male, because I have chosen to focus on the political and corporate parts of the story. There are very different versions that could and should be written about the impact of the oil industry on Native Alaskans, the environment, and the Alaskan way of life, but I would not be the best person to write those stories.

From my perspective, the story of oil in Alaska is largely a tale of the "little guys"—the early, independent explorers—competing with the multinational oil companies, the "big guys." This perspective is in line with a well-established Alaskan attitude that financial interests from "outside" have had an economic stranglehold on Alaska. I have focused on what I know best, and thus this book represents, to some extent, the story of my life in Alaska.

COMPANY NAME CHANGES

PRESENT COMPANY NAME	PREVIOUS COMPANY NAME
Amoco	Pan American Petroleum Corp.
ARCO (Atlantic Richfield)	Atlantic Refining Co. Richfield Oil Co. Sinclair Oil & Gas Co.
British Petroleum	Standard Oil Co. of Ohio (Sohio)
Chevron	Standard Oil Co. of California (Socal)
Exxon	Humble Oil & Refining Co.
Marathon	Ohio Oil Co.
Mobil	General Petroleum Corp.

ACKNOWLEDGMENTS

I want to thank some of the people who contributed to the writing of this book. Friend Vic Fischer suggested I attend the Kennedy School of Government at Harvard in 1980, where I met Dan Yergin and Professor Raymond Vernon, whose writings on oil inspired me to write a book on Alaska's oil experience.

Friends Kay Fanning, Jim Atwater, John Strohmeyer, Hugh Gallagher, Bryan "Tim" McGinnis, Charles Hayes, and the Elizabeth Tower family in Anchorage all read portions of the various drafts.

Charles Towill, BP's Alaska public affairs officer during the pipeline construction days, gave me important materials, as did Wilson Condon, whose Anchorage law firm handled the oil royalty lawsuit for the state.

Librarian Bruce Merrell at the Anchorage Loussac Library gave me early important help. Librarians Diane Brenner and Mina Jacobs at the Anchorage Museum of History and Art helped locate photos, as did Michael Carey, Fran Durner, and librarian Sharon Palmisano at the *Anchorage Daily News*. Special thanks to Anchorage lawyer John McKay, who helped me with my publisher's contract.

Charles Wohlforth edited my early scribblings, and longtime Alaska newsman Cliff Cernick helped take off some of the rough edges. Editor Don Graydon, of Index, Washington, made my manuscript reader-friendly. His hard work reordered many of my thoughts, and even some of my words. And, finally, the one editor who read through all the many drafts looking to simplify was my wife, Martha. Without her help and encouragement and that of our daughters, Selah and Libby, I could not have finished this book. At times, it seemed like an endless journey over dark and stormy waters, but for the early "little guys" like Earl Grammer, Charlie Barnes, Locke Jacobs, and others, it now seems worthwhile.

Interviews of former ARCO employees Harry Jamison, Marvin Mangus Charles "Gil" Mull (now with the state), Charlie Selman, and Armond Spielman took place in Anchorage. I spoke with former ARCO chairman Robert O. Anderson in the coffee shop at the Anchorage Sheraton Hotel. My interviews with BP personnel, in addition to Charles Towill, were with Geoff Larminie, Mike Savage, Roger Herrera, and Tim Bradner. Union's Dick Lyon, Alyeska's Harry Brelsford, Chevron's Howard Vesper, John Carson, and Clarence "Chat" Chatterton, and Sinclair's Zed Grissom and Phillips' Don Buelow spoke with me. Cliff Burglin, Jack Walker, Frank Shogrin, Jerry Ganopole, Lum Lovely, and Dan Pickerell were the "little guys" who gave their thoughts.

Elected officials interviewed included Senator Ted Stevens, Jay Hammond, Chancy Croft, Irene Ryan, John Rader, Willie Hensley, Mike Bradner, Cliff Groh, Sam Cotton, Hugh Malone, and Steve Cowper. State administrators included Phil Holdsworth, Charles Herbert, John Havelock, Tom Marshall, Alex Miller, Joe Rothstein, Tom Kelly, and Robert Maynard. Information otherwise not available through interviews came from affidavits, depositions, and documents produced from state-versus-oil industry lawsuits, and from TV interviews.

Neva Egan, Arlon Tussing, Peter Zamarello, Ralph Whitmore, Frances Richins Clark, John Buchholtz, John Grames, Don Mitchell, and Richard Fineberg talked with me. Locke Jacobs, John McManamin, and Bob Atwood edited portions of the manuscript (Swanson River). And, at a course on oil I taught at Alaska Pacific University in the mid-1980s, Emil Notti, Bill VanDyke, Roger Marks, Milton Lipton, Frank Shogrin, and Tom Williams gave their particular views on oil in Alaska.

Jack Roderick
Anchorage, Alaska
June 20, 1997

PART I: BEGINNINGS

The meek shall inherit the earth,
but not its mineral rights.
— J. Paul Getty

Kanatak

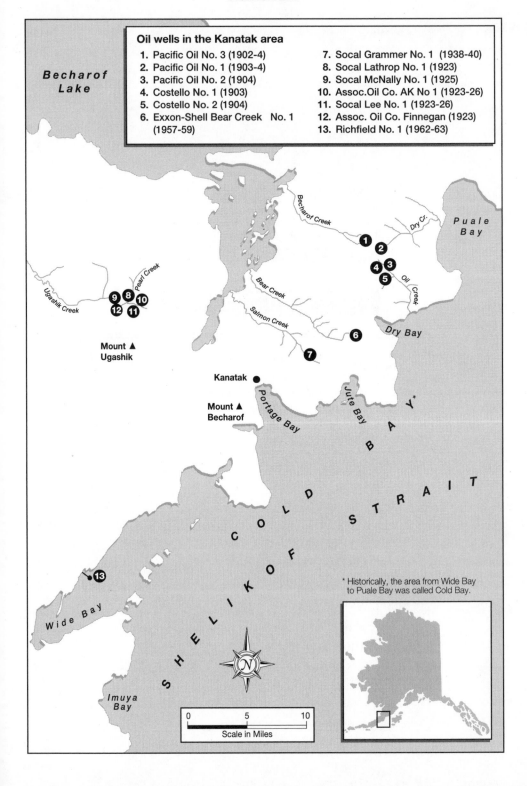

Oil wells in the Kanatak area

1. Pacific Oil No. 3 (1902-4)
2. Pacific Oil No. 1 (1903-4)
3. Pacific Oil No. 2 (1904)
4. Costello No. 1 (1903)
5. Costello No. 2 (1904)
6. Exxon-Shell Bear Creek No. 1 (1957-59)
7. Socal Grammer No. 1 (1938-40)
8. Socal Lathrop No. 1 (1923)
9. Socal McNally No. 1 (1925)
10. Assoc.Oil Co. AK No 1 (1923-26)
11. Socal Lee No. 1 (1923-26)
12. Assoc. Oil Co. Finnegan (1923)
13. Richfield No. 1 (1962-63)

Becharof Lake

Becharof Creek

Dry Cr.

Puale Bay

Pearl Creek

Ugashik Creek

Bear Creek

Salmon Creek

Oil Creek

Dry Bay

Mount ▲ Ugashik

Kanatak ●

Mount ▲ Becharof

Portage Bay

Jute Bay

COLD BAY*

SHELIKOF STRAIT

Wide Bay

Imuya Bay

* Historically, the area from Wide Bay to Puale Bay was called Cold Bay.

N

0   5   10
Scale in Miles

Chapter 1

"Little Guy" Earl Grammer

L ike the gold prospector, the oil explorer has a peculiar mind-set. He or she believes that tomorrow the "mother lode" will be found. Even with more sophisticated technology and tools than the hard-rock miner had, the modern explorer needs this kind of optimism. Tomorrow, the strike will come. Tomorrow, the discovery will be made!

My choice for Alaska's most persistent oil prospector has to be Lewis Earl Grammer. A wisp of a man, less than five feet tall and weighing about 100 pounds, he dressed in a gray wool twill "Alaska tuxedo," always looking like a shy but friendly ferret.

Our first contacts in the early 1950s were in the Anchorage land office in the old federal building. I would be checking lease records to print in my scouting service; he would be filing for oil and gas leases or appealing rejected lease applications. Our conversations were short, but from people in town I knew he was considered the expert. When oil company landmen needed to double-check leasing information, they went to Earl Grammer. His maps were always up-to-date, he kept confidences, and his word was his bond.

I suddenly got to know him in the summer of 1957 after coming up from Seattle between semesters of law school, still publishing my scouting report. I was in the land office when news came of Richfield's major oil discovery on the Kenai Peninsula at Swanson River. I immediately recalled that I had earlier reported that some of the oil and gas leases on Kalgin Island, offshore

19

from the Kenai in Cook Inlet, had expired due to failure to pay lease rentals. Here was my chance to file on land in the area of the Richfield discovery. But I didn't know anything about filing for leases.

I hurried down the street to Earl Grammer's one-room log cabin in the alley behind a laundry and told him about the lease expirations. Should we file on Kalgin?

On his advice, I decided to use every cent I had saved for law school to file for two leases on Kalgin Island. Grammer filed on the rest of the 17,000-acre island in his own name and in the name of his sister Elsie and several local friends. There, in that tiny room, we frantically filled out lease applications in order to be the first to file them in the federal land office.

After filing, we went back to Grammer's cabin to celebrate. From behind a curtain at the back of the cabin, he brought water heated on a hot plate, tea bags, sugar in a jar, milk in a can, and crackers from a tin. Always crackers. And several months later, I had my first Alaska oil and gas leases. I later optioned them to oil companies, giving me enough money to finish law school and to start several businesses.

JACK RODERICK

ALMOST FROM THE DAY he arrived in Anchorage in 1918, Earl Grammer was convinced there was oil all over Alaska. He knew Eskimos had burned oil on the Arctic North Slope, as they said, "since time immemorial." He read that Peters and Schrader, the first white men to traverse the Brooks Range, told of oil seepages on the Arctic coastal plain in 1901. He knew that geologist Ernest de Koven Leffingwell had written in 1908 of oil seeps lying only one third of a mile from the Arctic Ocean and twenty feet above tidewater at Smith Bay on the North Slope.

In 1920, Alaska oil pioneer Earl Grammer began his solitary explorations of the wet and windy Kanatak area on the Alaska Peninsula. (1957 photo)

The plank shelves on the walls of Grammer's cabin held stacks of *National Geographic*, rocks, sea shells, and oil seepage samples from the Alaska Peninsula. A report from a Hudson Bay Company agent, dated "around 1830," told of "oil seepages at Cape Simpson" on Alaska's North Slope.

Next to it was an 1870 U.S. Geological Survey report that read: "Petroleum floating on the surface of a lake near the bay of Katmai, in its crude state was an excellent lubrication for machinery."

Another USGS report noted that the Russians had discovered oil seeps on the Iniskin Peninsula on the west side of lower Cook Inlet "around 1853," following which the U.S. government had given the names of Oil Bay and Oil Point to an inlet and promontory on the peninsula. Grammer knew it was at Iniskin that the first drilling for oil had taken place "around 1900." From these files and from stories told in Earl Grammer's little log cabin, I learned the history of oil exploration in Alaska.

Grammer had come to Anchorage three years after the city was founded as a railroad town and just as the original town site was being surveyed. A surveyor himself, he went to work for the federally owned Alaska Railroad then being built.

In early 1920, rumors began circulating in Anchorage about big money being made in oil leases out at "Cold Bay" on the eastern shores of the Alaska Peninsula, in an area centered at the old Native village of Kanatak. Congress had passed the Mineral Leasing Act, and now you could simply lease oil and gas land, a much less cumbersome procedure than the old requirement of staking the land for

> *This petroleum residue—sour, pungent-smelling, putty-like stuff, strong enough to bear his weight yet soft enough to yield to his foot—convinced Earl Grammer that commercial oil lay somewhere below.*

mineral claims and working on it each year. With a lease in hand, you could assign or option it to an oil operator for cash and perhaps a small royalty interest in any oil that is found. Just as importantly the new law reopened land that had been withdrawn while Congress examined U.S. mineral leasing policy.

Nearly all of Alaska's land was now thrown open for oil and gas filings under "race-to-the-counter" leasing. The first U.S. citizen over twenty-one years of age, or U.S. oil company, who filed an oil and gas lease application in the federal land office and who paid a $10 filing fee and rental of twenty-five cents an acre got an exclusive ten-year right to that land.

This first-come-first-served method of leasing gave everyone, including the little guys, a chance to play in Alaska's oil and gas leasing game. There was no bidding and no work requirements, just the chance to reach the counter first with a modest payment and get your hands on a lease that could net a fortune if the holder found oil or managed to sell the rights to an oil operator.

A 1920 editorial in the *Seattle Post-Intelligencer* excitedly exclaimed that passage of the Mineral Leasing Act had "unlocked the oil fields of Alaska, which the conservationists had put the padlock upon. It had thrown it open to those who were qualified and financially able to exploit, explore and develop the land and put it in the way of productiveness. . . ."

Seasoned gold miners, bootleggers, railroaders, painters, even conservative bankers, took leave of their senses, and jobs, to join the "oil rush" to Cold Bay, on the Alaska Peninsula across Shelikof Strait from Kodiak Island.

EARL GRAMMER'S CASUAL INTEREST in minerals turned to full-fledged oil fever. His old friend Ray McDonald, manager of Anchorage's Empress Theater, readily agreed to help finance him in a venture into Cold Bay petroleum prospecting. Grammer caught the train for Seward, where he boarded the steamer *Starr* bound for the Cold Bay "oil fields."

On March 15, 1920, beneath the looming shadow of Mount Becharof, Earl Grammer stepped off onto the beach at Portage Bay and into a cauldron of rough weather. Like everyone else at Cold Bay, he hastily put up a canvas tent.

The next morning, soaked to the skin by incessant rain, he heated water for tea, ate some hardtack, and hiked up to Oil Creek, where he knew claims had been staked in 1901 and 1902. Large oil seepages had attracted early drillers to put down several shallow holes, in what Grammer called the "east field."

But Grammer found his first promising land closer to the Native village of Kanatak, around Bear Creek and Salmon Creek. He found oily residue two to ten feet deep mixed with vegetation spread over several acres, and it was here he decided to concentrate his efforts.

His first Cold Bay oil and gas lease applications were filed, as promised, in theater manager McDonald's name. Before the next season, however, sister Elsie had rounded up a bunch of her brother's friends in Indiana, had them sign blank lease applications, and sent them to Earl. When he returned to Salmon and Bear creeks a year later, he leased for his sister, himself, and his friends back in Terre Haute. (Under federal law, an individual could hold no more than 15,360 acres, so Grammer increased his odds, as did everyone else filing, by involving friends and relatives.)

EACH SPRING for the next several years, Grammer would "just walk off," as he liked to say, out from the Native village of Kanatak on the shallow, crescent Portage Bay beach. With only a bedroll and a canvas tent, he would face the cold, incessant wind and rain.

During his walkabouts, Grammer examined five giant Oil Creek seepages, where oil had been oozing onto the creek and then into the saltwater at Dry Bay for centuries. He found signs of the earlier drilling near the largest seep, which still flowed about half a barrel of oil a day.

In 1902, speculator J. H. Costello had staked several oil claims along Oil Creek. Costello had been convinced by a local sea captain and sometime gold prospector, Austin "Cap" Lathrop, that Cold Bay was the place to look. Lathrop had been told in 1900 by crewman Jack Lee of a visit to Cold Bay during which he saw pools of an oily substance several feet deep simply running out onto the ground. Lee told of Aleut Natives cleaning their guns with this "tar" and saying they had seen bears covered with the stuff.

Oil exploration brought immense change to the old Native village of Kanatak, shown here in 1923 at the head of Portage Bay on the Alaska Peninsula.

As trustee for seven groups of oil claim owners, including Lathrop and Lee, Costello used his steam-powered cable-tool rig between 1902 and 1905 to pound down two shallow holes at Oil Creek, one of them a quarter mile deep. Another group of promoters, calling themselves the Pacific Oil & Commercial Company, drilled three shallow holes on Trail, Dry, and Becharof creeks in the "east field" during the same period, but no one came up with any commercial oil.

COLD BAY BECAME the area Earl Grammer knew best. Seeps were everywhere, oozing several feet deep into great dark black-green pools of goo into the streams and bays. The mountains at Cold Bay seemed to have been exposed, like elephants baring their bellies to the sun, by giant geologic forces. The sedimentary beds had been thrust up into what appeared to be anticlines—geological "traps"—an ideal place to contain oil. With the presence of such seepages, this was oil country.

But the oil doesn't simply lie within the earth like a lake or river. Instead, it is in porous rock—sandstone or lime-stone—made up of millions of individual sand grains. Crude oil, gas, or water can flow through these interconnected porous spaces. The permeable upward pressure from natural gas and water beneath the oil often produces a foamy natural gas or crude oil mixture at the surface. It seemed to early explorers like Earl Grammer that it was

A severe winter storm in 1923 drove buildings off their foundations in the new oil town of Kanatak.

24

only a matter of drilling straight down through the petroleum residue— maybe as deep as two miles—to locate commercial quantities of oil.

This petroleum residue—sour, pungent-smelling, puttylike stuff that he could scoop up with his hands, strong enough to bear his weight yet soft enough

The Associated No. 1 well, drilled in the early 1920s, looked at first like a promising find in the Pearl Creek area northwest of Kanatak.

to yield to his foot—convinced Earl Grammer that commercial oil lay somewhere below. This goo was more than just a hint that oil was nearby. It had actually been burned as fuel in Costello's steam-powered rigs at Cold Bay just after the turn of the century.

EARL GRAMMER KEPT A DIARY, which he later gave to me. He always kept his diary and records in neat files. Over the years as he examined land records in U.S. Commissioner offices in Kodiak and Anchorage, he made detailed notes on his maps, driller's logs, lease application appeals, and so forth. Always in tiny, precise script. Always in pencil.

On a small sheet of transparent paper—again written in pencil, as if later he might be able to erase them—he recorded the deaths of friends at Cold Bay. At the top of the page on which he listed the fifty deaths that occurred between 1920 and 1926 he had written "Dead Men."

"Thompson, Curry and Boudin, froze," he wrote. "Swede" committed suicide with a shotgun. "Gordon Gust died from inhaling gas. Three froze, five drowned, five were murdered, five committed suicide, and nine died natural deaths. Demion, second Chief Fred Kalmakoff and the Chief Ruff Kalmakoff, Chief of the Kanatak Natives—all died of T.B."

AS GRAMMER CONTINUED HIS EXPLORATIONS in the early 1920s, two small investor-financed companies joined forces to drill the first well on the Pearl Creek anticline in the west field at Cold Bay. Associated Oil Company of California and Alaska Oil Company dug their Associated No. 1 well down to 800 feet amid tremendous excitement. A small amount of oil had been seen flowing freely from the well bore.

Excitement turned to disappointment because, as the well was deepened to 3,033 feet during the next two drilling seasons, no commercial oil was found. A second well, drilled to only 560 feet, was also dry.

Despite this inauspicious start, the new oil town at Kanatak had taken shape alongside the old Native village. The northern boundary of the Native old town was separated from the new oil town by a fence, so to go from one town to the other, it was necessary to cross a rope-railed plank bridge spanning the narrow Kanatak Creek.

A particularly severe winter storm in 1923 drove buildings off their foundations in the new town. Grammer was there to record the judgment of Kanatak Chief Ruff: "White man drink whiskey, no go church, stay up all night, water come, take houses away. Native go church all time, water come, no touch Native house."

Grammer was disappointed that Associated's drilling had not proven the area's oil potential. But he also knew that Standard Oil Company of California (now Chevron) was planning to drill a well of its own at Cold Bay, and he realized that any real test of the region would have to be made by a company as large as Chevron.

EARL GRAMMER COLLECTION, ANCHORAGE MUSEUM OF HISTORY AND ART

Standard Oil Company of California (now Chevron) pinned its earliest hopes of an oil discovery in the Kanatak area on this 1923 well, the Lee No. 1.

CHEVRON HAD BEEN BARG-
ING DIESEL FUEL from its California refineries to western Alaska villages and the Anchorage-Fair-
banks rail belt since 1898, being
the principal marketer of refined
products in the Territory. The
Mineral Leasing Act of 1920
opened the door to leasing of large
tracts of federal land at relatively
low cost, so exploration in Alaska
now made good business sense
for Chevron.

Chevron's explorationists studied most of the Territory's sedimentary basins and concluded that Cold
Bay was the best bet for large oil
reserves. Chevron teamed up in
1921 with General Petroleum (now
Mobil) to explore Cold Bay.

Drilling on Pearl Creek Dome in 1925.

Chevron put geologist G. Dallas Hanna in charge of the Cold Bay-
Kanatak district program. He was fascinated with the prolific oil seepages in
the area, reminiscent of those along the California coast. Cold Bay, with its
huge, exposed anticlines, gave every indication of large oil reserves, and
Hanna decided the best place for Chevron to drill was in the west field on the
Pearl Creek Dome (anticline). He said he decided to put his drilling rig on the top
of the dome partly "because a surveyor named Earl Grammer" had identified
the precise location of the three largest seeps.

By then, Chevron and Mobil had each acquired the use of 10,000 acres
near the three seepages, and Hanna had struck a deal with Associated and
Alaska Oil for their acreage. He also had assembled claims and leases held by
"friendly parties" like W. E. Lee, J. J. Finnegan, Jane McNally, and "Cap"
Lathrop. With no other large companies interested in drilling at Cold Bay,
Hanna reported to San Francisco that these individuals "were eager to assign
their claims and leases to Chevron"—in hopes, of course, that Chevron would
hit oil and they would reap part of the reward.

Geologist G. Dallas Hanna (right) was in charge of Chevron's 1938 effort to find oil on land leased by Earl Grammer (left) at Bear Creek on the Alaska Peninsula.

Hanna warned that the location would demand a lot from the men who worked there. A Chevron geologist at the time described Cold Bay as "barren, desolate country with no sign of shelter or human habitation. We managed to set up three tents on the wet ground, and spent a thoroughly miserable night. It wasn't the cold that bothered us so much as it was the terrific winds.

"The climate is generally disagreeable, always windy, usually raining. At first the ground was frozen so solidly as to be unworkable. Later, when the thaw set in it was so swampy as to be almost unworkable. Temperatures fell well below zero. Blizzard conditions prevailed."

As Chevron prepared to drill, the new town of Kanatak grew up on the shore at Portage Bay. Where previously there had been only a few small huts in the Native village, by 1923 the "old" village had seventy-three permanent buildings. The new oil town across the bridge over Kanatak Creek had fifty-nine, one of them two stories high. Earl Grammer had surveyed the 100-acre site and was present in 1923 when the town was officially dedicated.

Chevron's cable-tool rig on the top of the Pearl Creek Dome began drilling the Lee No. 1 well in March 1923. In the first thousand feet, the casing broke eleven times as it was driven into the hole. The rig then stood silent for thirty-four days while crews waited for needed tools to arrive from San Francisco by boat.

Chevron didn't have any more luck than the earlier drillers. Hanna abandoned the Lee No. 1 in 1926 at 5,033 feet. Only a few crude oil shows had been seen in the well cuttings. After analyzing data from Lee No. 1 and the shallow-well results from two other wells, Hanna reported that Chevron should pull out of Cold Bay. It was more bad news for Earl Grammer and his hopes for a big strike at Cold Bay.

EARL GRAMMER RETURNED TO HIS CABIN in Anchorage when drilling at Cold Bay ended in 1926. During the following decade he would continue to "walk off" to Cold Bay each spring, taking more seepage samples and plotting and filing new lease applications. He assembled a solid forty-thousand-acre block of leases on the Salmon Creek and Bear Creek anticlines in the names of his sister Elsie, geologist Carlton H. Beal of Midland, Texas, Los Angeles wildcatter Russell E. Havenstrite, and three of Havenstrite's Hollywood investor friends: Walt Disney, Darryl Zanuck, and Hal Roach.

Grammer worked tirelessly to attract another operator to dig for oil at Cold Bay, but by 1937 he had about given up. Just then, Chevron announced it would return to Cold Bay with its new partners, Union Oil of California and Tidewater Associated Oil. And geologist G. Dallas Hanna would again be in charge. Hanna now believed the best place to drill was at Bear Creek in the West Field, on land leased by Earl Grammer.

During spring 1938, Chevron crews unloaded four thousand tons of drilling equipment and supplies onto the beach at Jute Bay. Drilling began on the Grammer No. 1 well, across Salmon Creek from Chevron's base camp. After several weeks, the bit encountered minor gas shows and free light oil in fractured shale at 2,000 feet. At about 7,000 feet, drillers

The mountains at Cold Bay seemed to have been exposed, like elephants baring their bellies to the sun, by giant geologic forces. This was oil country.

recovered tarry oil and oil residue, and Hanna began to feel more encouraged. But drill stem tests at depths below 2,000 feet, though showing a few spots of oil, produced only saltwater. Hanna knew saltwater below 2,000 feet meant no commercial oil could be expected, so at 7,596 feet he called it off.

Chevron assigned its operating rights back to Earl Grammer and Carlton Beal. A disappointed Grammer was forced to accept the fact that Chevron's Grammer No. 1, the first truly deep well in all of Alaska, was a bust.

EARL GRAMMER WAS NO QUITTER. He kept his Bear Creek leases alive, and more than a decade after Chevron abandoned its Grammer No. 1 well, Shell Oil began exploring there in the 1950s. Shell had looked at the North Slope and other sedimentary basins and now decided to concentrate most of its efforts on Bear Creek and nearby Wide Bay.

Shell ended up acquiring most of the leases at a 1954 federal lease drawing for land the U.S. Navy was restoring to public domain at Wide Bay. The leases were actually won by a number of individual Alaskans, who then assigned them to Shell for cash and a royalty interest. The man in charge of seeing that Shell got the leases was Charlie Barnes, my future business partner.

Leaseholders who assigned their rights to Shell included some people who figure prominently in the story of Alaska oil, including petroleum consultant Irene Ryan, shoe clerk/leasehound Locke Jacobs, and barber Jack Walker. And Charlie Barnes made very sure that Shell got Grammer's leases at Bear Creek.

Shell then looked for a partner at Cold Bay, and found Humble Oil and Refining Company (now Exxon). Both companies knew, of course, of Chevron's 1930s' dry hole at Bear Creek, but with Shell's thorough geologic data and Exxon's desire to find an oil reserve in this vast, nearly unproven province, executive minds merged. By April 1957, Shell had drilling units at Bear Creek, Ugashik, and Wide Bay, and Exxon had promised to drill a 12,000-foot well at Bear Creek. In exchange, Shell would assign half interest in the drilling units to Exxon.

CHEVRON

Gasoline, oils, and supplies on beach at Kanatak for drilling at Pearl Creek in 1922.

Exxon built a first-class port and a five-mile road to the drill site, then floated an entire "city" to Jute Bay. By late September 1957, drilling began on the Bear Creek No. 1 well on a lease held in the name of Earl Grammer's sister Elsie.

It was another deep disappointment. Exxon abandoned the well at 14,000 feet on March 1, 1959, two months after Alaska became a state. The drilling had cost Exxon over $7 million—by far the costliest well drilled in Alaska before the Prudhoe Bay discovery, and more than the United States paid Russia for all of Alaska.

The bad news was an old story for Earl Grammer. With no oil to be found, Exxon reassigned its leases to Shell, who transferred them back to Grammer and Carlton Beal. This was the second deep dry hole drilled at Bear Creek and the latest in a string of failed attempts during Grammer's years of exploration.

> *"Thompson, Curry and Boudin, froze. . . Gordon Gust died from inhaling gas. Three froze, five drowned, five were murdered, five committed suicide, and nine died natural deaths."*
> —From Earl Grammer's diary

31

Iniskin

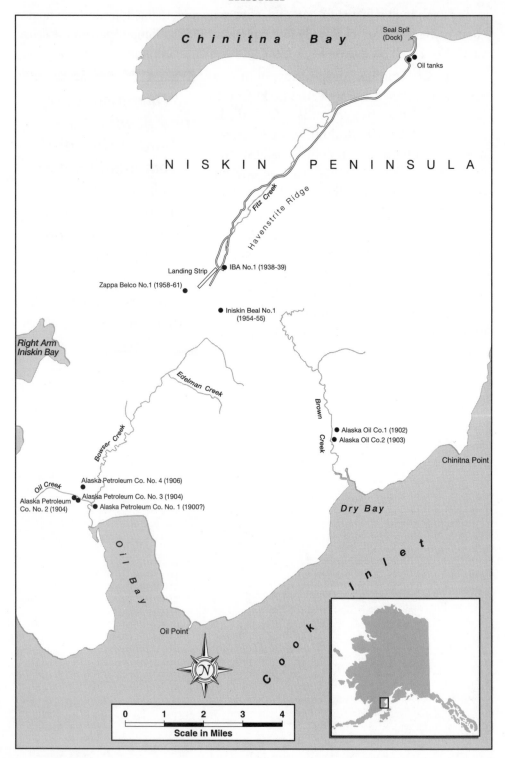

PROFILE

THE RUSS HAVENSTRITE STORY

While the lengthy Earl Grammer saga was playing itself out, a wildcatter from Los Angeles was doing his best to find oil farther north on the Alaska Peninsula. In the early 1920s, Russell E. Havenstrite, wife Edith, and their parrot moved from Lovell, Oklahoma, to Los Angeles to live in a log cabin alongside his drilling rig located on Signal Hill. The story is that one day a stranger, stopping to admire the parrot, which liked to slip out through the cabin logs to freedom, told Havenstrite of huge oil fields recently discovered in Alaska. Havenstrite went north in 1932 to see for himself.

His excitement grew when he got to Alaska and heard about the oil seepages on the Iniskin Peninsula, across Cook

Russ Havenstrite

Inlet from Homer. What stuck in his mind were stories of several shallow wells drilled around 1900 at Iniskin, up on the southeast flank of what people called the Fitz Creek anticline. A prospector named Edleman in 1892 was said to have staked claims on oil seepages at Bowser Creek, and about six years later two men named Pomeroy and Griffin, having staked claims near Oil Bay, promoted Alaska Petroleum Company to drill a 1,000-foot well at Bowser Creek.

Although several more shallow holes were drilled at Bowser Creek, plus two more at Brown Creek by a group called the Alaska Oil Company, no commercial oil was found. But Havenstrite learned that crude continued to run out onto the waters of Oil Creek and Oil Bay, and word was that the early drill sites had not been located on top of the anticline, the best place to drill.

In 1936, Havenstrite put together the Iniskin Bay Associates, with partners geologist Carlton Beal and Hollywood's Walt Disney, Darryl Zanuck, and Hal Roach. Two years later, Iniskin Bay Associates began drilling its IBA No. 1 well. Drilling continued during several seasons to 8,700 feet, but the well was abandoned in 1939 after producing what the USGS reported was "substantial quantities of petroleum, but not less than twenty barrels saved." Havenstrite's group

ANCHORAGE DAILY TIMES/ANCHORAGE DAILY NEWS

had no better luck in its drilling than Earl Grammer had at Salmon and Bear creeks, where Chevron came up with its dry hole in the late '30s.

Havenstrite returned to California, where he hit the jackpot in 1941 when he discovered the Del Valle oil field near Newhall. Polo ponies, society bashes, and private airplanes followed. After World War II, the moviemakers and Chicago banker Hugo Anderson backed him in another try at Iniskin. (Anderson was the father of Robert O. Anderson, later chairman of the Atlantic-Richfield Oil Company.) Havenstrite still had his Iniskin leases, although his operations at Iniskin had to cease during the war because Secretary of Interior Harold Ickes refused to let them continue, possibly due to animosity between Havenstrite and the Roosevelt administration.

STUART HAVENSTRITE

IBA No. 1 well in 1938.

Havenstrite despised Ickes. Knowing Ickes insisted on having limes in his gin and tonics, Havenstrite sent his drilling crew to buy every lime in Anchorage during an Ickes wartime visit to Alaska. After Ickes disembarked from his private Alaska Railroad car, settled into his hotel suite, and asked for a lime in his drink, he was told none could be found in all of Anchorage. When he looked out on the sidewalk beneath his hotel window, he saw neat piles of all the lime peels in Anchorage—perhaps in the entire Territory.

After the war, Havenstrite was eager to make up for lost time. He still believed that a huge oil field might lie beneath Iniskin's Fitz Creek anticline. To keep his investors interested, Havenstrite brought them to Alaska in the summer of 1946. He flew banker Hugo Anderson, Mrs. Anderson, the

Disneys, and the Zanucks out near the Native village of Kotzebue in western Alaska to see his jade mine at Kobuk and his gold mine at Candle. They traveled in Havenstrite's luxury DC-3, the "Blue Nose," moving about on oriental and tiger-skin rugs and being offered a stream of martinis.

In August 1954, Havenstrite began his second well at Iniskin—Unit Operator No. 1 (sometimes known as the Beal No. 1). By then I had been in Alaska just four months, and by the time the new Iniskin well was several thousand feet deep, I had started the Alaska Scouting Service. My first chance to meet a "real wildcatter" was when Havenstrite's manager, Frances Richins Clark, invited me to have breakfast with the oilman in his office-apartment atop the McKinley Building in Anchorage. Quickly agreeing, I waited with great excitement. Richfield geologist Ray Arnett was there that morning also, but what I recall most was being offered martinis at 10 in the morning.

Drilling on the Iniskin Unit No. 1 was suspended in October 1955 below 9,000 feet, but it continued to be "tested" during the next two years. I remember reporting the well as "suspended" in my reports, but I didn't know what that word really meant in the oil business. Later I realized Havenstrite had been trying to stall until he could raise enough money to continue. Ironically, he would abandon his last try in Alaska only two weeks after Richfield announced its big discovery at Swanson River, less than a hundred miles northeast of Iniskin. But short distances are what the oil business is all about.

Katalla

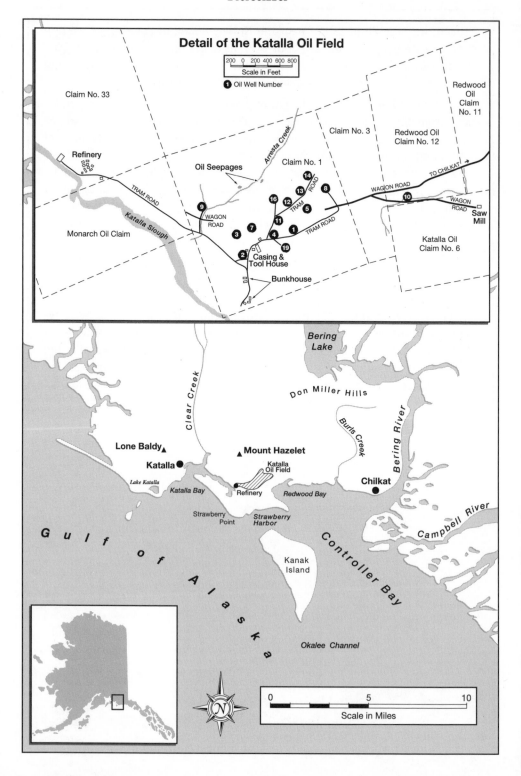

Detail of the Katalla Oil Field

200 0 200 400 600 800
Scale in Feet

1 Oil Well Number

Claim No. 33

Redwood Oil Claim No. 11

Arresta Creek

Claim No. 3

Redwood Oil Claim No. 12

Refinery

Oil Seepages

Claim No. 1

TO CHILKAT

WAGON ROAD

14

TRAM ROAD

13

8

WAGON ROAD

16 **12**

10

5

WAGON ROAD

Saw Mill

TRAM ROAD

9

WAGON ROAD

11

Katalla Slough

3 **7**

4 **1**

TRAM ROAD

Monarch Oil Claim

2

19

Katalla Oil Claim No. 6

Casing & Tool House

Bunkhouse

Bering Lake

Don Miller Hills

Clear Creek

Burls Creek

Bering River

Lone Baldy▲

▲ Mount Hazelet

Katalla●

Katalla Oil Field

Campbell River

Lake Katalla

Katalla Bay

Refinery

Chilkat●

Redwood Bay

G u l f   o f   A l a s k a

Strawberry Point

Strawberry Harbor

Controller Bay

Kanak Island

Okalee Channel

0   5   10
Scale in Miles

N

Chapter 2

Gulf Coast Explorers

The remarkable, sometimes bizarre, story of oil exploration along the shores of the Gulf of Alaska begins at the turn of the twentieth century, when the oil-thirsty British became the first to drill at Katalla.

In 1900, British oil expert Sir Thomas Boverton Redwood painted a bright picture of the oil potential at Katalla, on the shores of Controller Bay on the northerly coast of the Gulf. "In the whole course of my thirty years experience," he told directors of the British consortium known as Alaska Steam Coal and Petroleum Syndicate, Ltd., "I have not had occasion to arrive at a conclusion upon more promising data than petroleum prospects in the Kayak and Yakataga district, Alaska," which includes Katalla.

Author Daniel Yergin, in his best-selling book *The Prize,* says Redwood "saw the advantages to the Royal Navy of burning fuel oil rather than coal. Strongly suspicious of both Standard Oil and Shell, he wanted to see oil reserves developed by British companies from sources under British control."

Redwood urged the British syndicate to drill its first well in the Katalla Meadow, "where an almost immediate output of oil can probably be obtained by boring." The slight elevation of Katalla Meadow would permit the crude to gravity-flow through a pipeline to a wharf at Katalla, Redwood said. A steam launch could take the oil to Kayak Island, where it would go "directly into the Pacific Steam Whaling Company's steamer," thence to markets to the south.

The British began drilling at Katalla Meadow in 1901, and from a depth of 365 feet began pumping as much as fifty barrels a day from the No. 1 well. The No. 2 well was drilled in 1902-1903 and produced some twenty-five barrels a day from about 800 feet. The third meadow well, drilled deeper, produced about thirty barrels a day, while No. 4 turned out dry.

The next well, Redwood No. 1, was a producer, and several other wells looked promising. But by the end of 1910, only four wells were producing. The oil field was not living up to British expectations, and they abandoned the effort. A Washington state corporation, Amalgamated Development, paid the British syndicate $300,000 for its seventy-four oil claims at Katalla.

Amalgamated and four more small companies took unsuccessful cracks at Katalla over the next year or so, before Chilkat Oil Company acquired the claims and built a small topping refinery on the Katalla slough. But Katalla still failed to live up to its promise. By 1913, daily production had dropped to between forty and forty-five barrels. Production from the meadow well No. 1 had dropped to ten barrels a day; the No. 2 to five barrels. The high paraffin-based oil had clogged the small casing perforations, and almost no effort was made to clean out the wells.

Despite the problems, a Chevron geologist—hoping to encourage his company to do more exploration in the area—claimed in 1913 that the small

R. W. STONE/U.S. GEOLOGICAL SURVEY

Oil seeps like this one in 1904 spurred the hopes of oil explorationists in the Katalla area on the Gulf of Alaska.

A series of companies believed in the promise of the Katalla field, though the few wells at work in 1915 were turning out only tiny quantities of oil.

Katalla refinery was "processing about 60 barrels of oil per day, all of it from four shallow wells." He shipped fifty gallons of Katalla crude to be chemically analyzed at Chevron's Richmond, California, refinery, enthusiastically writing that, "A sample of the crude, which I burned in a large round lamp, compared favorable with our best oils."

Production at Katalla increased only slightly when additional wells were drilled after 1920. Between 1902 and 1934, when the refinery burned, only 154,000 barrels of crude were produced from the Katalla field. Most of the oil was fed into the refinery to be refined, then poured into wooden barrels and transported by horse-drawn railway about a mile to the Katalla wharf. The barrels then were put on small boats or barges for the 24-hour trip to Cordova, where the oil was used in Copper River Railway locomotives as a lubricant.

Despite a Toronto Imperial Oil Company geologist's warning in 1922 that "the odds against making a commercial success of oil production at Yakataga (Katalla) are too great," the Kennicott Copper Corporation bought Chilkat Oil Company's Katalla oil claims. After visiting Katalla in the summer of 1922, a Mobil geologic field party recommended drilling in the old Katalla oil field or on the shore of nearby Bering Lake. "If the same area with the same geology were located in California," said the Mobil geologist, "a deep well would unhesitantly be recommended."

Mobil never drilled in the area, but in 1925 the company established a well near a large oil seepage on Johnson Creek, far to the east of Katalla near Icy Bay. Though encouraging natural gas shows were encountered, the Sullivan No. 1 well was abandoned at about 2,000 feet.

Chevron geologist G. Dallas Hanna and Union Oil's John Hazzard visited Katalla during the summer of 1938, at the time they were drilling the Grammer No. 1 well on the Alaska Peninsula. Afterward, Hanna summed up Katalla's sorry story.

"The history of this region has been filled with countless blasted hopes and bitter disappointments," he reported. "Millions of dollars have been spent fruitlessly on projects which doubtlessly seemed commercially feasible at the time, but which were destined to fail for one reason or another. Probably no other equal area in Alaska has had so sad a fate."

Despite Hanna's glum report, Chevron, Union, and Tidewater Associated bought the old Katalla mineral claims, and in future years a fruitless search continued for commercial quantities of oil around Katalla.

WILLIAM T. FORAN WAS A LEADING CHARACTER in the Gulf of Alaska oil saga—a colorful explorer best known for leasing a moving glacier. Though failing to find the world-class petroleum reserves he felt certain lay somewhere beneath Alaska's soil, he put together several ventures that opened a new phase of oil exploration.

Foran's first mission in Alaska came during the 1920s, for the U.S. Navy. President Warren Harding was convinced that Navy ships needed a dependable supply of fuel oil so they would no longer have to rely on burning coal. In 1923 Congress set aside nearly half the North Slope of Alaska, the immense coastal area far north of the Arctic Circle, as Naval Petroleum Reserve No. 4—usually referred to as "Pet-4." The designated area comprised nearly 25 million acres, and soon after its cre-

> *"The history of this region has been filled with countless blasted hopes and bitter disappoint- ments. . . . Probably no other equal area in Alaska has had so sad a fate."*
>
> —*Chevron geologist G. Dallas Hanna, reporting on oil prospects at Katalla*

In 1928, the small refinery on the Katalla slough processed oil from wells in the area.

ation, three U.S. Geological Survey field parties set out for Pet-4 on behalf of the Naval Coal Commission.

Foran's party left Nome in July 1923, hoping to determine whether the stratigraphy and rock structure of Pet-4's western region might contain commercial oil. The government geologists found lots of coal, but little oil.

The following July, Foran headed a second North Slope geologic field party, this one to survey the Noatak area south of Cape Beaufort. The explorers spent most of their time fighting storms. Late in 1924, Foran reported "no gas or petroleum seepages or residue were observed in this area."

Despite these and many other inconclusive survey results, the U.S. Navy began drilling Pet-4 during World War II. Between 1945 and 1953, thirty-five wells were drilled to depths between 130 and 10,000 feet on eighteen geologic structures, plus forty-one core holes. Two small oil fields and two small gas fields were discovered. Foran was encouraged by this success on the North Slope, and wrote in his Field Note No. 479 that "vast commercial quantities of petroleum will someday be found in all these areas."

———

AFTER THE WAR Foran returned to Tacoma, Washington, convinced that Alaska had enormous oil potential. With the North Slope closed to private leasing, he began promoting the leasing of land in the Katalla-Yakataga district. He set his sights on the Sullivan anticline at Icy Bay, particularly in the Samovar Hills above the giant Malaspina Glacier.

Foran and his gregarious Tacoma neighbor Ben Gellenbeck talked virtually nonstop about the oil promise of Alaska. In 1950 they put together a mega-scheme which called for enticing a major oil company to explore the 300-mile glacier-infested, mountain-enveloped eastern shore of the Gulf of Alaska.

A big, good-natured man, Gellenbeck had for twenty years been western manager for Keystone Lubricating Company of Philadelphia. During World War II he got to know politically prominent Washington, D.C., land lawyers Nathaniel J. Ely and Jacob Wasserman. These lawyers had discovered a little-known federal statute that authorized the Interior Secretary to grant huge tracts of federal lease-land to help promote private oil and gas exploration. This power appeared to particularly favor "frontier" areas such as Alaska.

Ely, Wasserman, Gellenbeck, and Foran believed that if a large enough block of land—say 1 million acres—could be leased and offered to a major oil company, it might agree to spend enough exploration money for the Interior Secretary to award it a development contract. The company would be granted an exemption from the 15,360-acre federal acreage limitation—designed to keep large oil companies or individuals from monopolizing oil and gas lands—so that it would have a large expanse of land to explore.

In this grand plan, the four men were hoping for the help of U.S. Senator Robert Kerr (D-Okla), a major power in the Senate and owner of Kerr-McGee Oil Industries, which appeared interested in exploring for oil in Alaska.

Foran and Gellenbeck first had to round up enough people to do the leasing of a million acres. With individuals not permitted to hold more than 15,360 acres apiece, a large group had to be assembled. But once leases were issued, they could be pooled to make up a huge drillable block of acreage.

Foran and Gellenbeck then became attorneys-in-fact for the leaseholders, and on their behalf formed Northern Development Company. By 1951, they had gathered more than 100 applicants to file some 400 federal oil and gas leases covering more than a million acres in a block centered at Icy Bay, beneath the lonely magnificence of 18,008-foot Mount St. Elias, between Katalla and the Native village of Yakutat.

This much acreage, put together by such a prominent group, was enough to prompt Senator Kerr to help the Foran group convince Phillips Petroleum

Company to commit to spend $1.2 million prior to June 30, 1956, exploring for oil on Northern Development Company leaseholds.

The full deal was that Phillips and the senator's own company, Kerr-McGee, would receive a development contract covering a million acres and an exemption from the federal acreage limitation if they would drill two exploratory wells at Icy Bay. And if the results looked promising, they agreed to drill ten more during the following decade.

When the Katalla-Yakataga development contract was awarded in 1951—the first in the nation—Phillips took half of it and Kerr-McGee half. But a year later, when the cost of building a road on the inhospitable coastline skyrocketed, Kerr-McGee cut back its interest to one-eighth.

In April 1954, Phillips and Kerr-McGee began their Sullivan Stratigraphic No. 1 at Icy Bay. This "slim hole" would be drilled to 4,800 feet to see what the relatively shallow geological horizons beneath the Sullivan anticline looked like. Two months later, with stratigraphic results in hand, Phillips began the Sullivan Unit No. 1 well, its first deep test, five miles west and two miles north of the "strat test."

> *Foran and his gregarious neighbor Ben Gellenbeck put together a mega-scheme for enticing a major oil company to explore the glacier-infested, mountain-enveloped eastern shore of the Gulf of Alaska.*

As of early 1955, 300 feet of "good oil sands" had been encountered at about 8,700 feet in Sullivan Unit No. 1. The results showed some promise, but soon after, the well was abandoned after reaching below 10,000 feet.

Phillips moved the rig a quarter mile south, and in late January 1956 began drilling the Sullivan Unit No. 2 well. It also had good oil shows, but that was all; it was abandoned below 12,000 feet. Phillips told operations manager Phil O'Rourke to shut down the entire Icy Bay operation and prepare to return to Bartlesville, Oklahoma.

Dry holes at Icy Bay discouraged Phillips—but not William T. Foran and many Alaskans, who seemed to feel that the drilling effort only confirmed the existence of commercial oil somewhere along the barren eastern coast of the Gulf of Alaska. Geologist Foran believed that the largest seepage area was at Oily Lake in the Samovar Hills and that Phillips' two dry holes to the north had hardly condemned a geologic province larger than the North Sea.

Foran and Gellenbeck organized a new group of leaseholders, this time to lease land from Dry Bay (southeast of Icy Bay) up to the Native town of Yakutat. Individuals, mostly Alaskans, calling themselves the Yakutat Development Company, filed five hundred lease applications for another million acres, which they later assigned to Colorado Oil and Gas Corporation, a Denver independent. Colorado Oil and Gas began drilling its Yakutat No. 1 in March 1957, encountering good hydrocarbon shows at about 9,000 feet but no commercial oil. Its Yakutat No. A-1 well, three miles northeast of No. 1, also turned up dry.

THE GRANDEST SCHEME OF ALL was then hatched by Foran. He determined to lease acreage at the upper end of the immense Malaspina Glacier. Foran's former partner Gellenbeck wanted no part of this enterprise, because leasing on the largest glacier in the world—a piece of ice larger than the state of Rhode Island—made no sense to him.

Nevertheless Foran, with two of his Tacoma high school buddies, H.H. Rayburn and Morris D. Kennedy, organized the leasing of 400,000 acres east of Icy Bay in the names of Territorial Development Company and Acme Development Company. Foran told leaseholders that huge crude reserves lay beneath the Samovar Hills at the upper reaches of the glacier, and he declared

W. T. FORAN/U.S. GEOLOGICAL SURVEY

The Alaska oil adventures of William Foran (second from right) got under way in 1923 with a U.S. Geological Survey field party on the North Slope.

that as many as five hundred producing wells could be drilled there. What he didn't stress was that the glacier, as glaciers do, was moving, slowly inching its way to the open waters of the Gulf of Alaska.

Foran assured investors that cold-water jets could be set up on the glacier to melt the ice and that as many wells as needed could be drilled using streams of water to carve out stationary platforms. Although some glacier ice lay more than 700 feet below sea level, Foran claimed that wells could be drilled half a mile down through it. Most oilmen thought that was impossible.

I was in Seattle at law school at the time and remember being taken to lunch by Rayburn and Kennedy, who wanted to use my scouting report to lend credibility to their leasing venture. I wanted to find out what was going on. Foran, whom I had met earlier, hadn't come along to lunch. I got the very strong impression that neither Rayburn nor Kennedy knew anything about Alaska or the oil leasing business.

After applicants for leases in this new venture paid the Bureau of Land Management filing fees and first-year lease rentals, they paid an equal amount to Foran and his buddies. Glacier applications were filed in the spring of 1957, after which land office manager Virgil O. Seiser asked his Washington, D.C., supervisors if he should issue leases on top of a moving glacier. Seiser felt he was raising an important policy question: was the public being adequately protected in this matter?

Anchorage leasehound Locke Jacobs told several glacier lease applicants it was unlikely that the Malaspina Glacier would ever get drilled. In June 1957, Anchorage attorney Edgar Paul Boyko filed a $1 million lawsuit on behalf of Rayburn, president of Acme Development Company, and Kennedy, president of Territorial Development Company, charging Seiser, Jacobs, and *Anchorage Daily Times* publisher Bob Atwood with "libel, conspiracy and injurious falsehood."

The lawsuit alleged that Seiser had a "close collaboration with Jacobs," granting him special privileges in the land office, and that Jacobs was trying to get the Malaspina lease applicants to withdraw their applications. The lawsuit charged Atwood with using his newspaper "to cause panic, alarm and discontent" among Acme and Territorial investors. The lawsuit, however, was later dropped.

Washington directed Seiser to issue the glacier leases, but the vital grant of a development contract was denied. Most leaseholders continued to pay rentals through the fourth year, but stopped at the fifth, when the leases were allowed to expire. No oil wells were ever drilled on Malaspina Glacier.

INSIDE STORY

MY "SPY"

One of my first tasks after starting Alaska Scouting Service in early 1955 was to report the exact location of Phillips' well near Icy Bay off the Gulf of Alaska. To get the location for my subscribers, I went to Phillips' man in charge, Irishman Phil O'Rourke, a soft-spoken geologist from Oklahoma. O'Rourke agreed to give me the well location—but nothing else about the venture. Totally dependent on O'Rourke for my information, I found him less than cooperative. Hard as I tried I couldn't pry information out of him.

O'Rourke said he couldn't help me because the well at Icy Bay was "tight." I wasn't really sure at the time what "tight" meant, but what I did know was that I wasn't getting the information I needed. O'Rourke said he couldn't even tell me if the well was currently being drilled, much less the depth. I began asking other company men, local newspaper reporters, anyone who might know what was happening at Icy Bay. I also phoned Phillips' headquarters in Bartlesville, Oklahoma. No luck.

Information leaks are very much a part of oil exploration. In Alaska in the early 1950s, leaks added immense excitement to an already exciting time. Every major company had at least one oil scout whose job was to learn how deep a competitor's well was, or where the competitor planned to explore, or any other information that might help his company decide what to do next. By counting the number of thirty-foot drill stems in a well hole—sometimes with binoculars from afar—a scout might be able to estimate the depth of the drilling or the size of the casing in the hole. Thus the company doing the spying might better decide whether to lease surrounding acreage.

So it was only natural to me that a company would guard its investment. But what didn't make sense was why Phillips, with more than a million acres surrounding the Icy Bay well, felt it necessary to have a "tight" hole—that is, a well being drilled under tight security and an information blackout. Much later O'Rourke told me that the reason had to do with Phillips' partner in the drilling, Kerr-McGee Oil. O'Rourke said that U.S. Senator Robert Kerr, who owned Kerr-McGee, ordered all news from Icy Bay to come only from Bartlesville because he feared that if an oil discovery were made in such a remote, exotic place as Icy Bay, he might be accused by U.S. regulators of manipulating Kerr-McGee shares on the New York stock exchange.

Because the well was "tight," rumors flew around Anchorage about what had been "discovered." Laundry coming into Anchorage from Icy Bay was said to have been soaked with oil. "Special fluids" were seen being flown to Icy Bay to stop a "blowout." A group of high-level Phillips executives were said to have been seen rushing to Icy Bay from Bartlesville.

A little story will illustrate how seriously Phillips battled information leaks. The story involves one of Cordova Airlines' two stewardesses at the time, a recent Radcliffe College graduate in Alaska for the summer.

Each week, a Cordova DC-3 carrying mostly cargo would fly from Anchorage to Icy Bay, landing on the dirt strip and laying over for several hours before the flight back to Anchorage. The stewardess in question accepted a dinner invitation from a young Phillips geologist on one of the return flights from Icy Bay. The next morning, airlines President Merle "Mudhole" Smith called the stewardess into his office and told her he'd received a call from Phil O'Rourke, demanding that she be fired. O'Rourke had accused her of spying, claiming that when she was at Icy Bay, she spied for a local oil reporter.

In fear of losing Phillips, his best customer, Smith had easily been persuaded that the stewardess had indeed been spying. He had told O'Rourke he would fire her. But the stewardess told Smith she knew nothing about oil spying or about the Icy Bay operation and that nothing special was going on between her and the oil reporter. She told Smith that if he let her stay on, she would go directly into the Phillips mess hall on all future visits to Icy Bay and stay put until the plane left for Anchorage.

After checking with O'Rourke, Smith finally agreed, thinking he had silenced her with the threat of being fired. What he didn't know was that persuasiveness was her hallmark. It wasn't her job she wanted saved, it was her access to the great pastries at the Icy Bay mess hall. A mutual love of baked goods—particularly strawberry-rhubarb pies, and the way she made them—led me to ask Martha Brady Martin to marry me in September 1955. And she wasn't my spy. Honest.

Chapter 3
Dry Holes

Alaskans themselves were trying their hand at wildcatting beginning in the 1950s. Bill O'Neill, a local mining engineer and University of Alaska regent, and partner C. F. "Tiny" Shield, a giant of a man, believed they could find oil in the Copper River basin. Before coming to Alaska in the early 1920s, Shield had been a cable-rig "toolpusher" in Montana, Texas, and California.

While Anchorage newspapers rumored that oil had been discovered by Phillips Petroleum at Icy Bay, these two entrepreneurs formed Alaska Oil & Gas Development Company to drill at Eureka on the western edge of the Copper River basin, northeast of Cook Inlet. They planned to drill on federal leases near "mud volcanoes"—sulfuric residues bubbling up from the valley floor—and near where giant marine fossils had been discovered embedded in the mud cliffs of Sheep Mountain.

Early in the spring of 1953, O'Neill and Shield located their cable-tool rig several miles west of Eureka Roadhouse, just 200 feet off the Richardson Highway. Unlike a rotary drill rig, on which the entire drill stem with its diamond-headed bit rotates in the hole, a cable-tool rig simply pounds into the earth, crushing rock which has to be periodically bailed out of the hole.

By early 1954 the Eureka No. 1 well had been drilled down more than half a mile, but the antiquated equipment, making each day's going tougher, eventually forced O'Neill and Shield to shut down the operation. Shield traveled to Texas, and while looking up some toolpusher buddies, contacted Fort Worth independent James H. Snowden. As a result, Snowden sent geologist Waring Bradley up to Alaska, where he reported that by converting the cable-tool rig to a rotary, the Eureka well could be deepened to 5,500 feet.

With the rotary setup, the Eureka well was drilled an additional 3,000 feet, but no significant oil shows were found in it or in a second well. Both were plugged and abandoned in 1957, just as oil was discovered at Swanson River on the Kenai Peninsula.

TWO OTHER ALASKAN "LITTLE GUYS" drilled for natural gas on coal claims just off the right-of-way of the Alaska Railroad at Houston, about 40 air-miles north of Anchorage. The U.S. Bureau of Mines had discovered methane gas while drilling there, so claims-owners George Tucker and Ralph Peterson became convinced that commercial quantities of natural gas were just waiting to be uncovered.

Tucker was a stocky, silver-haired, gregarious man who looked more like a guard with the Chicago Bears than a master mechanic; his partner was a shy,

INA PETERSON

Ever-optimistic George Tucker (right) and his partner Ralph Peterson drilled wells at Houston, north of Anchorage, in the mid-1950s.

Houston drill site in the 1950s.

gentle carpenter who had helped build one of the two major office buildings in Anchorage in the 1950s. I remember climbing the stairs at the back of the Tucker and Peterson Building at Fifth and Denali to get the location of their well and whatever else I could turn up for my scouting report. Tucker was seated at his desk in the two-chair office, the picture of optimism. He was convinced, he said, that they would find huge reserves of natural gas at Houston. But I also recall seeing in Peterson's eyes what appeared to be a look of resignation. Perhaps he and his partner were just chasing a rainbow.

In May 1955, Tucker and Peterson brought a 10,000-foot rotary drill rig to their claims at Houston. Whenever they couldn't get parts, Tucker just made them in his own shop. He'd look at an equipment catalog, see a picture of a drilling tool, and make it himself. He made drill collars, sleeves, and all kinds of complicated "fishing" tools, and then used them successfully to drill.

While the Rosetta No. 1 (named for Tucker's wife) was being drilled in 1955, local news accounts gave regular reports on the well depth and findings. Advertisements appeared in Seattle newspapers offering "450,000 non-assessable common voting shares of Anchorage Gas and Oil Development Company, Inc., at $1.50 per share." Company shares also were sold locally over the counter. George Tucker's sister Grace, an Anchorage stockbroker, made regular trips to Seattle during the first drilling season and brought in enough money to keep the operation going.

EDNA MAE WALKER

Enterprising Anchorage barber Jack V. Walker, Jr., was tenacious in filing leases on potential oil lands. "Something big was going to happen," he said. "I just didn't know when." (1985 photo)

Tucker then turned to geologist Irene Ryan for advice. Ryan says that she, her husband, Pat, and Anchorage attorney Stanley McCutcheon "chartered an automobile-car on the railroad and went up at night. It was 20 degrees below zero."

"We took jars with us to get a sample," she recalls. "When the tests came back, they indicated that it wasn't just straight coal gas, but that it had some petroleum in it. I told Tucker the first thing to do, if he hadn't done it already, was to cover the area with oil leases."

As a result, Tucker filed for leases on 86,000 acres of federal oil and gas lands surrounding the coal claims. And he hired Ryan to prepare a subsurface map of the area.

"Sure enough," Ryan says, "I picked up a fault on the ground. There seemed to be a 'high' on the south side of the Castle Mountain fault. I suggested to Tucker that he should drill there. But he put his location right near the highway, just off the old coal mine road, because it was easier to get to."

Tucker then hired Ryan as the geologist on the well, and work got under way on drilling that sorely tested their patience. "Whenever we encountered any gas shows," Ryan relates, "the mud would blow out of the well. It was obvious that it was petroleum gas. I had lots of arguments with company geologists who thought it was only coal gas.

"The well was below 6,000 feet when Richfield discovered oil at Swanson River. On that July day in 1957, I was 'sitting' on the Rosetta well. One year later, when the bonfire was lit on the Anchorage Park Strip to celebrate the U.S. Senate's passage of statehood, I was still on the well."

The Rosetta No. 1 was suspended in October 1959, and the No. 2 and No. 3 were shut down at about the same time. Excitement surrounding the Swanson River discovery had overtaken Alaska, and George Tucker's and

Ralph Peterson's money and luck had run out.

———————

THE BULK OF OIL DRILLING ACTIVITY in Alaska during the 1950s was initiated by people from the Lower 48. A major effort was spurred by a consortium of thirty U.S. independents organized by Ray Thompson, a Denver geologist. In the late 1950s, this group began drilling near the Native village of Nulato on the western reaches of the Yukon River. The result was a dry hole.

New Yorkers were among the oil seekers. Three New York City siblings—Ted, John, and Caroline Zappa—drilled what turned out to be a dry hole a half-mile south of Russ Havenstrite's old IBA No. 1 well on the Iniskin Peninsula. The Zappas also came up dry at a drill site just a quarter of a mile west of Richfield's successful commercial production at Swanson River.

Two Bakersfield, California, wildcatters—John "Tex"

Geologist and legislator Irene Ryan, talking with Charlie Smith of Union Oil at a Kenai gas well in 1959, was one of the few Alaskans in the 1950s who was knowledgeable about oil.

Scarbrough and Chester Ashford—began probing for oil in Cook Inlet in late June 1955. Their deep test first pierced the earth near the old town of Knik, a half-mile north of Goose Bay and ten air miles north of Anchorage. Using capital obtained from the sale of shares in Alaska Gulf Oil and Gas Company of Anchorage, the partners set up their 6,000-foot-capacity rig smack dab on what turned out to be somebody else's lease. They began merrily drilling away on acreage owned exclusively by an enterprising Anchorage barber, Jack V. Walker, Jr.

Surprisingly, when Walker discovered Scarbrough and Ashford's rig on his lease, his thoughts turned to negotiation rather than retribution.

"I figured this might be my first chance to get my hands on a producing royalty in Alaska," he said. "My goal was always to get as close to the wells as I could, because the only way you get rich in this business is to be under a well that produces oil. I wanted to see drilling."

Walker could feel somewhat magnanimous. He had just sold leases on the southern Kenai Peninsula to Mobil, two more at $1 an acre to Chevron in the same area, and a lease to Shell for 75 cents an acre.

Negotiating with Scarbrough, Walker asked for no cash, but got a one-six-teenth royalty on the forty-acre drill site and a one-eighth royalty on the remainder of his federal lease. If Scarbrough struck oil, royalties would more than compensate Walker for the lack of an up-front cash payment.

But there was no bonanza at Goose Bay. Scarbrough abandoned the 4,000-foot Goose Bay dry hole in December 1955. Typically, Walker said he wasn't disappointed. "I was still convinced something big was going to happen, and it always did. I just didn't know when."

———

FROM 1941 TO 1942, JACK WALKER had been stationed with the 29th U.S. Engineer Battalion at Wasilla, Hope, and Moose Pass, Alaska. A decade later he returned to Alaska with his wife, Edna Mae, pulling a trailer up the Alcan Highway.

"I wanted to come back to get into the oil business," he said. "I saw film on the swamps, and sheen on the lakes, like those north of Rawlins, Wyoming. I was sure this was the place to be, because it looked and smelled just like where I grew up. I was sure there was oil here."

When he arrived in Anchorage in the early '50s, Walker brought his skill of barbering. He cut hair at the town's only sizeable hotel, the Westward (now the Anchorage Hilton), but soon opened his own barbershop on Fourth Avenue.

"It was right downtown, only a few blocks from the land office," he said. "I spent more time in those records—me, Locke Jacobs, Betty Thompson, and Earl Grammer—than even people who worked there. I was the first person there every day. All I ever talked about in the barber shop was filing leases."

Each morning without fail Walker would examine the land office records to see if anyone had applied for an oil and gas lease. Whenever an oil company landman, a lease broker, or anybody for that matter, had filed the day before and left an adjoining parcel "open," Walker immediately filed on that unleased tract, hoping to ride the applicant's coattails to oil profits in the event anyone eventually drilled on the leaseholds.

"Every time they filed, I filed," Walker fondly remembered. "And I had to file fast because others were ready to do the same." He was referring to Jacobs, Grammer, Monte Allen, Chuck Ledbetter, Bill Malcolm, and even a land office devotee from the Copper River Valley, Ed "Pappy" Devine. "I tried to beat them," said Walker, and he usually did.

> *"I saw film on the swamps, and sheen on the lakes, like those north of Rawlins, Wyoming. I was sure this was the place to be, because it looked and smelled just like where I grew up. I was sure there was oil here."*
>
> —*Oil "leasehound" Jack Walker*

On one of his regular morning land office checks in the spring of 1953, Walker's eagle eyes noticed that three lease applications filed by Mobil Oil for land on the southern Kenai Peninsula lacked sufficient postage on the envelope. A Mobil clerk in Los Angeles had apparently neglected to place enough postage, so an Anchorage land office employee, having dutifully noted the franking error on the office records, was sending the envelope back to Los Angeles.

Walker immediately filed three lease applications covering the same land. Land office adjudicators would later determine Walker's right to the land, because his application was accepted first—but before that determination, he already sold his lease rights to Mobil for $100,000 cash. Mobil had decided to acquire Walker's interest in the land rather than abandoning the drilling prospect. A few pennies in stamps would have saved Mobil $100,000. (Later, the "Elsie Walker No. 1" well on this land in the southern Kenai turned out to be a dry hole.)

"Tiny" Shield (left) and Bill O'Neill (center) help Robert Walker at Eureka, Copper River Valley in 1953.

PORTRAIT

LOCKE JACOBS

Earl Grammer gets my award for persistence, but the Horatio Alger of Alaska Award goes to Locke Jacobs.

The early memories of the man who became a prime figure in the Alaska oil story include Depression days in Oklahoma when he carried water to his ditch-digger father and when, at the age of nine, he worked in a service station. Later, at Gilchrist High School in Oregon, Jacobs slept near the school stage, cleaning floors at night. He enjoyed the books of Jack London, and he pored over accounts of boys who made good. He yearned to do the same.

A Gilchrist High teacher, Dorothy Huston, raised money to buy him some luggage, and in 1947, against his mother's wishes, he left for Alaska.

His first job, as a section hand at the Whittier railroad tunnel south of Anchorage, gave him time for reading. He became fascinated with the book *Practical Oil Geology,* loaned to him by Bob Bursiel of Girdwood, and took it with him when he went to work as a steward on the Yukon River sternwheeler *Nenana.* The captain, Howard Adams, was a graduate of the Colorado School of Mines, and he helped Jacobs learn about Alaska's mineral and oil potential.

Over the next few years, Jacobs was busy at various jobs, including staking mineral claims for others near Galena and working at the long-range navigation station in Kodiak. It was only when he came to the raw, dirt-street town of Anchorage (pop. 20,000) in 1952 that Jacobs started on the path that led to the realization of his childhood dreams.

Cook Inlet

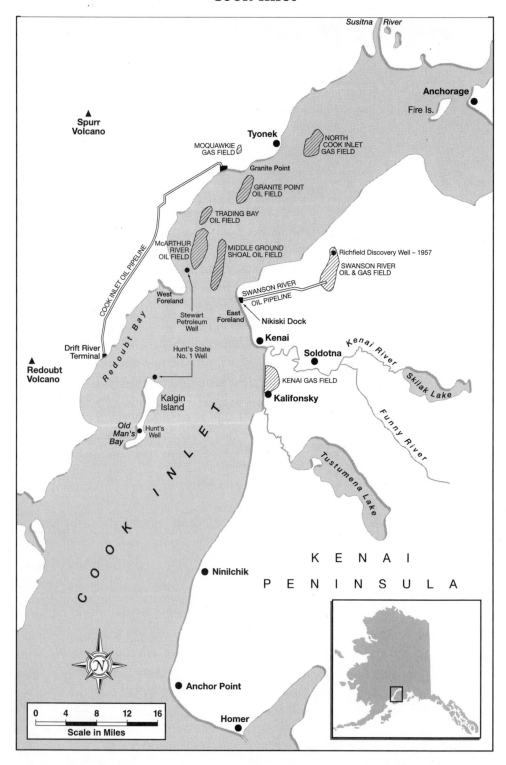

Susitna River

Spurr
Volcano

Anchorage

Fire Is.

Tyonek

MOQUAWKIE
GAS FIELD

NORTH
COOK INLET
GAS FIELD

Granite Point

GRANITE POINT
OIL FIELD

TRADING BAY
OIL FIELD

McARTHUR
RIVER
OIL FIELD

MIDDLE GROUND
SHOAL OIL FIELD

Richfield Discovery Well – 1957

SWANSON RIVER
OIL & GAS FIELD

COOK INLET OIL PIPELINE

West
Foreland

Stewart
Petroleum
Well

East
Foreland

SWANSON RIVER
OIL PIPELINE

Nikiski Dock

Drift River
Terminal

Redoubt
Volcano

Hunt's State
No. 1 Well

Kenai

Soldotna

Kenai River

Skilak Lake

KENAI GAS FIELD

Kalifonsky

Funny River

Kalgin
Island

Old
Man's
Bay

Hunt's
Well

Tustumena Lake

K E N A I

Ninilchik

P E N I N S U L A

N

Anchor Point

0   4   8   12   16

Scale in Miles

Homer

Chapter 4

Locke Jacobs and '50s Oil Fever

In Anchorage, Locke Jacobs started at the bottom, but he soon made his mark in the oil world. He began in the early 1950s doing rough and dirty work for contractor Kelly Foss, then was hired as a clerk and shoe-sorter at the Army-Navy Surplus store run by John "Mac" McManamin and Glenn Miller. During off hours, Jacobs bought reports and maps from the U.S. Geological Survey.

Jacobs obtained his first oil and gas map of southcentral Alaska from geologist Irene Ryan. It showed the area from Wide Bay to the Iniskin Peninsula in lower Cook Inlet, where some geologists believed petroleum sediments existed. In 1952, without knowing how to read land office records, he spent his $175 paycheck to file a lease application on the Iniskin Peninsula. It was rejected. The land was already under lease to Russell E. Havenstrite of Los Angeles.

Jacobs returned to Ryan for advice. He had heard about Bill Foran's big oil-lease ventures along the Gulf of Alaska. Would the Gulf be a good place for him to file for leases?

"I told Jacobs that a gap [of unleased land] of thirty to forty miles along the Gulf of Alaska shoreline was a granite exposure unlikely to contain oil," Ryan said. "He asked where lands were that might be valuable for oil and gas. I pointed to areas on the USGS map with favorable sedimentary basins."

Jacobs went to work with his USGS "trend map," with its regional "dips and strikes," and made a valuable observation. It appeared to Jacobs' still untrained eye that all the hypothecated geological structures in Cook Inlet lay in a northeast-southwest direction. He further noted that this trend seemed to go all the way from Wide Bay, on the Alaska Peninsula, through Cold Bay, through Iniskin, then farther north into Cook Inlet and perhaps into the Kenai Peninsula. If any oil lay under Cook Inlet, he mused, the structures or anticlines would have to lie in a northeast-southwest direction. The trend map also showed oil seepages in most of those areas, and the seep trend seemed to go that way too.

Jacobs continued his education by asking Ed Boyko, who was the attorney for the Bureau of Land Management at that time, about leasing procedures and the arcane knowledge of the business, such things as "unitization" and "well spacing." His questioning led to an important discovery: the federal bureaucracy in Alaska moved at a glacial pace. It sometimes took months for the lightly staffed land office to issue a lease. A person could tie up large tracts of valuable land for long periods of time simply by filing a lease application. Jacobs filed this information away in his mind for future use.

What Atwood, Wester, and other members of the leasing group were trying to accomplish was to gradually convert Anchorage, Alaska, into Tulsa, Oklahoma. It would never be the same.

Also keeping Jacobs' oil fervor alive were the encouragements of Irene Ryan and a favorable sign from the U.S. Congress. Congress had increased the oil and gas acreage an individual or company could hold in Alaska. Now the limit was 100,000 acres under lease and 200,000 acres under option. This sounded to Jacobs like the government was encouraging oil and gas leasing, and the only risk seemed to be that he might file on land nobody wanted. But that risk looked smaller and smaller as a growing number of oil company landmen and geologists headed north each year.

Jacobs watched as oil companies began to direct more attention to the Kenai Peninsula and Cook Inlet. Three companies began filing lease applications on the southern Kenai Peninsula: Chevron (then Standard Oil of

California), Union Oil Company of California, and Union's partner in Alaska, Marathon (then Ohio Oil Company). In 1953, the Interior Department granted Chevron a development contract on the southern Kenai Peninsula, binding the company to spend at least $450,000 over five years on exploration and to start drilling a well by July 1959. On the northern Kenai Peninsula, Union and Marathon combined had more than 250,000 acres under lease or option.

EVANGELINE JACOBS

Beginning as a shoe clerk in Anchorage in the early 1950s, Locke Jacobs went on to become a premier oil-leasing expert — the one everybody turned to for the full story.

JACOBS EMBARKED on a grinding program of fact-gathering that eventually made him one of the great fonts of oil-lease knowledge in Alaska—and one the oilmen went to for information. He began copying land office oil and gas "serial sheets" showing the name and address of each lease applicant, the filing date, a description of the land being applied for, the number of acres sought, and the date of lease if a lease had been issued. With this information, he would know where the action was hottest—and where the available unleased land was located.

He began copying the records in longhand. This took so much time that he started typing. Then he got a German-made Duplimat copier, which was soon to be replaced by a Kodak Verifax. He struck a deal with land office manager Virgil Seiser. If Seiser would allow him to leave his copier in the office overnight, he would let the staff use the valuable machine at no cost during office hours.

"The first week the machine was in the office was a disaster," Jacobs said. The employees "used up all the German-made copy paper and nearly broke me before I got started."

Using the land office records, Jacobs plotted lease descriptions on his own maps, coloring oil company leaseblocks in coded crayon hues. He was ready to get seriously into the oil leasing game.

Jacobs kept trying to persuade fellow employees at the Army-Navy Surplus store to join him in lease filing. Jacobs' boss Glenn Miller told him "to take it easy."

"You're into some pretty speculative stuff," Miller said, "and I don't want employees to get burned. Mac and I are only interested in the surplus business, not speculative oil leasing."

Finally, Miller asked him: "How much would it cost me to have you shut up about oil and gas?"

Jacobs quickly replied, "One thousand dollars." Just as quickly, Miller wrote him a check for that amount, hoping that everyone could then go back to work on surplus.

With that $1,000, several oil and gas lease applications were soon filed in the names of Glenn Miller and John McManamin. Jacobs also helped some Seattle people file lease applications on the Kenai Peninsula and areas in Cook Inlet that he figured would be right in the middle of the upcoming major oil company leaseplay.

THE '50s SAW FORMATION of a leaseholders' clique that used its position at the center of the Anchorage business world to boost the future of Alaska oil. The group was made up mostly of friends of John McManamin, Glenn Miller, and hotelman Wilbur Wester. *Anchorage Daily Times* publisher Bob Atwood was taken into the fold, as was banker Elmer Rasmuson, Atwood's brother-in-law.

Other members of the group included Willard Nagley, whose parents owned the land on which Wester's Westward Hotel was built; Fred Axford, an all-around entrepreneur who was a jeweler and an ice cream and office supply store owner; and accountant George Jones, whose clients included the *Times,* the Westward, and the Army-Navy Surplus store. The owners of the bar next to the surplus store, Phil and Ray Raykovich, were brought into the circle, as was contractor C. R. "Kelly" Foss and National Bank of Alaska vice president Rod Johnston.

And what about the surplus-store shoe clerk with the intense interest in oil leasing? Locke Jacobs didn't have the money or the connections of the businessmen, but McManamin and Miller insisted their enterprising clerk share fully in any of the group's profits from oil and gas leasing. It was an arrangement, Jacobs said, that "simply developed."

"I did the legwork, like filing applications, making maps, and copying records," he recalled. "Neither my bosses nor any member of the group ever questioned my participation. Mac and Miller always pitched in to help when I wasn't able to pay my share on oil-related travel."

THE BOYS IN THE LEASEHOLDERS' CLUB were situated just right for charting the temperature of the Alaskan oil fever. Major oil company geologists and landmen stayed at Wester's Westward Hotel when they came to town. They bought clothing and outdoor gear at McManamin and Miller's Army-Navy Surplus store. They were interviewed by publisher Atwood. Some opened personal checking accounts at Rasmuson's National Bank of Alaska. Two members of the club, Fred Axford and George Jones, were on the Anchorage City Council.

Most of these merchants met each week for lunch at the Elks Club the day after City Council meetings, so much of the discussion was about local politics. Atwood termed the group "a bunch of chippie guys trying to steal a nickel from each other." Most of these soon-to-be "golden boys" were children of the Depression. During the 1930s, the McManamin, Miller, Wester, Axford, Johnston, and Foss families were badly battered by the economic plunge. These men all served in Alaska during World War II, and after the war they stayed on.

> *"We found Anchorage a paradise and we did very well."*
>
> —*John "Mac" McManamin, businessman and oil leaseholder*

According to McManamin, "We found Anchorage a paradise and we did very well. We were aware that the military buildup couldn't last and we needed to develop Alaska's resources: such things as Talkeetna birch, mining, and oil."

Wester was "the catalyst who made the thing go since everyone else was busy running their own businesses," Jacobs said of the group. As part owner and manager of the Westward, which was then the center of the town's social activity, Wester had daily access to whatever oil exploration information was circulating.

It was rumored that Wester monitored Westward telephones calls, but Jacobs said that wasn't necessary. Wester's favorite spot was in the back corner of the Chart Room bar, where he presided at a circular table on which maps of Alaska's waterways were plasticized (thus the Chart Room). He bought drinks for company geologists and landmen in order to "swab" them for information.

Wester was good at trading oil stories and knew how to get the maximum amount of exploration information in return for giving as little as possible. Afterward, Wester would meet with McManamin or Atwood to compare notes on what they had gleaned. They wanted to learn where to lease.

McManamin admires Wester for his aggressive campaign to open the Kenai Peninsula to oil and gas leasing and drilling. Without his aggressiveness in Washington, D.C., Mac believes drilling on the Kenai never would have occurred.

JACK RODERICK

Leasehound Locke Jacobs (right) chats with oil reporter Jack Roderick in Anchorage in 1955. Roderick had started an oil scouting service, and Jacobs was becoming known as a font of oil information.

Wester's seemingly insatiable need for wealth seemed to some to make him brittle. Jacobs once accused Wester of trying to cut him out of a share of royalties, "but he mellowed in later years," Jacobs said, "and still liked trying to beat me at pinochle."

Though Wester was the oil group's catalyst, McManamin was the man who held it solidly together. He didn't mind sharing. Mac cultivated an "Aw, shucks" air with his quick and friendly humor, always with an unlit cigar dangling from his mouth. His Depression experiences made him sensitive to the plights of others. Jacobs had seen McManamin and

Miller hand out warm clothing to the ragged, jobless, and hopeless who often wandered off Fourth Avenue into the surplus store to escape the cold. The two men "knew how tough it was to survive an Anchorage winter," Jacobs said. "They helped the hard-up as much as they could whenever they could."

Publisher Bob Atwood kept churning up the oil excitement. Hardly anything of oil significance ever escaped the attention of the tall, husky, and very genial Atwood. No oilman got to town without Atwood noting it and printing it. Nobody filed a lease application without seeing it in the next day's paper.

Atwood's daily "Develop Anchorage" editorials were thoroughly oil-drenched, reflecting the sheer excitement of the oil "explosion." He regularly printed a column about oil events by a guy named Roderick.

Oilmen visiting Anchorage found themselves sitting right next to Atwood at Rotary Club and Anchorage Chamber of Commerce luncheons. More often than not they were called on to speak, while Atwood busily took notes. And Atwood was a reliable deliverer of oil speakers to the Elks Club, where luncheons were crowded with Alaska leaders of all persuasions.

What Atwood, Wester, and other members of the leasing group were trying to accomplish was to gradually convert Anchorage, Alaska, into Tulsa, Oklahoma. It would never be the same.

LOCKE JACOBS' FIRST BIG LEASING BREAK came in early 1954 when his friend Irene Ryan delivered a juicy tidbit. The U.S. Navy, she told Jacobs, was opening up, for leasing, 60,000 previously withdrawn acres at Wide Bay, near where Chevron had drilled in the early '20s and '30s. Shell Oil, she said, was ready to pay 75 cents an acre plus a 5 percent "overriding royalty" to any successful lease-drawing applicants who would assign their leases to Shell.

It even got better: Shell's senior geologist, M. C. "Max" Birkhauser, told Jacobs and his group that lease rental money accompanying unsuccessful applications would be immediately returned to the applicant. It was like being handed a money machine. Jacobs saw they could triple any money they put at risk in less than a month. And they stood a real chance of becoming rich from royalties on any oil found. It was like Christmas.

Ryan, a Territorial legislator at the time, put together her own leasing group consisting of fellow Democrats Stanley and Steve McCutcheon, Helen Fisher, and John Rader. "The more the merrier," she commented to Jacobs. "All Shell wants is to take assignments from any successful drawee."

Several members of Ryan's group won lucrative leases in the drawing, as did Jacobs and his Anchorage leaseholders' group, plus barber Jack Walker and Earl Grammer.

By the time of the Wide Bay drawing, Birkhauser was succeeded at Shell by Charlie Barnes, a young and ambitious Yale graduate (the same Barnes who was later to become my business partner). Barnes saw to it that all successful leases were dutifully assigned to Shell for the agreed-on price.

The consummate strategist, Barnes sought to ingratiate himself with Anchorage's business establishment. In dealing with Jacobs' group on the Wide Bay leases, however, he made a costly mistake. When Barnes spotted an error in one of Jacobs' Wide Bay applications, he refiled the application in Shell's name, thereby eliminating any payment or royalty to Jacobs and his group. When they learned of Barnes' action, they decided that any future leasing with Barnes would cost Shell "twice as much as the going market."

JACOBS' GROWING PROMINENCE as "the man in the know" drew him an invitation from Glenn Miller to speak at an Elks Club luncheon. Jacobs was neither a member of the club nor the social equal of downtown merchants— but he was by now the "oil leasing expert." The audience avidly lapped up Jacobs' discussion of oil leasing.

Wester and other members of the leaseholders group adjourned to the Westward, and Jacobs let them in on the latest tantalizing information: where major oil companies were leasing, how much they were paying for assignments and options, whose leases were being acquired.

The group then pledged more money for Kenai Peninsula leasing, at which point contractor Kelly Foss turned to Jacobs and declared, "Do you really know what you're doing? Last year you were digging ditches for me. Today you're spending my money and my banker's money."

"You're right," Jacobs replied. "I might not know much about oil and gas, but what I know puts me way ahead of the rest of the crowd up here."

Jacobs kept beating the bushes for people with cash to put on the line for leases. According to Atwood, anyone with money could have joined the group at that time.

By then, Jacobs was selling lease maps, record-check reports, and filing services as well as acting as a lease broker and consultant. He consolidated these activities into Western Lands and Leasing Corporation. He then sold shares in the firm to members of his leasing group.

JACOBS LIKED NOTHING BETTER than to twist the tails of the "big guys." In 1962, when Union Oil was the most aggressive oil explorer in Alaska, one of its wells was located just west of Nenana, about seventy miles southwest of Fairbanks. The 3,000-foot "slim hole" in the Middle Tanana basin was to be drilled with partners Pure, Sinclair, and Marathon. Before drilling, however, Union and its partners discovered to their chagrin that someone had leased inside their drilling block.

Most oilmen still think Jacobs had a "mole" inside the Fairbanks land office. Jacobs insists he didn't, and he points to British-American Oil Company geologist/landman Bob Kenyon as the one who hired him to engineer the scheme.

Here's what happened, as Jacobs tells it.

By the end of 1961, Union and its partners had filed for several federal oil and gas leases in the Middle Tanana basin and had engaged a truck-mounted rig to drill sometime the following year. Union's crew began brush-cutting seismic lines across the leased acreage so that small-tracked vehicles could drill shallow shot-holes in which explosives would be detonated to sound-record subsurface geology.

Kenyon flew over the area each day in a Cessna 180, plotting the seismic lines on a topographic map and photographing them from the air. He noticed the seismic lines gradually growing closer. Superimposing his photos onto his land map, he noted that where the lines converged was where Union intended to drill.

JACK RODERICK

Shell Oil's Charlie Barnes helped Locke Jacobs' investor group learn the leasing game and then joined Jack Roderick in oil scouting.

Kenyon tried to interest his company in joining the Union partnership, suggesting it pay part of the drilling costs in exchange for information from this first well in an entirely new geologic basin. Though his firm turned down his request for drilling money, Kenyon was given the go-ahead to acquire land leases in the Tanana basin—but only if he didn't tip his hand by using the company's name or by letting the Union partnership learn that someone was filing for British-American in the area.

But how do you file for leases inside another company's leaseblock without making it known? Filing applications in the Fairbanks land office would give immediate public notice. Kenyon contacted several lease brokers outside Alaska who said the task sounded impossible. He figured his last shot was to talk with Jacobs.

Jacobs came up with a way to file without the knowledge of Union or its partners. His applications, he told Kenyon, would be filed even before Union filed its own; so far, Union had applied for only a few leases within the leaseblock. Jacobs was about to twist the tail of the big guys.

Locke Jacobs embarked on a grinding program of fact-gathering that eventually made him one of the great fonts of oil-lease knowledge in Alaska—and one the oilmen went to for information.

First, he hired a young woman in Fairbanks whose sole job it was to phone Jacobs at his Anchorage office each morning at 8. He told her that if she failed to phone at 8 sharp, she would be immediately fired. He then completed lease applications in his own name for acreage surrounding Union's few leases and sent them to the woman in Fairbanks.

Jacobs knew that joint-venturing major oil companies would never trust one another. Any lease filings would be made as a group, by representatives of the companies flying together from Anchorage to the Fairbanks land office. He also knew that only two commercial airplanes regularly flew daily from Anchorage to Fairbanks, one in the morning, the other in midafternoon. Major oil company personnel would certainly not take the morning, propeller-driven flight to Fairbanks that stopped along the way at Clear. Most likely they'd take the afternoon prop-jet so they would have time to settle in at Fairbanks before going to the land office to make their filings the first thing the following morning. He also knew they would have to check land office records for any applications made the previous day before making their own filings.

> *Locke Jacobs liked nothing better than to twist the tails of the "big guys."*

Each day, after receiving his 8 A.M. call from Fairbanks, Jacobs would go to the Anchorage airport to sit and watch and wait . . . and wait and wait. After several weeks of daily phone calls and waiting, Jacobs saw three company landmen about to board the afternoon flight to Fairbanks. They represented three of the four Tanana basin joint-venturing oil companies. Jacobs felt that this was it.

The next morning Jacobs was in his office at 8 when his Fairbanks call came in. He told the woman to go immediately to the land office and slip his applications through the slot in the door. She was then to disappear. By putting the applications through the slot, Jacobs knew they would be hand-stamped by a land office employee as the first filings of the day. The office opened to the public at 10 A.M., so his applications would be recorded as having been filed exactly at 10 A.M.

About 9:40 A.M. Jacobs phoned the Fairbanks land office, asking if his lease applications had been received. He was assured they had, and that they had been hand-stamped with an official filing time of 10 A.M. He sat back and waited.

The company landmen arrived at the land office a few minutes before 10 A.M. They checked the index book to see if any filings had been made in their leaseblock during the previous day. There were none. And seeing no one at the counter, they felt sure the land on which they were about to file had no previous applicants. So they handed their applications to the clerk. Dutifully, she began stamping them in at 10:01 A.M., 10:02 A.M., and so on. The landmen retired to the Fairbanks hotel bar, returning to Anchorage that afternoon by jet, their task completed.

Meanwhile, Jacobs visited the Marathon Oil office in Anchorage that same day to ask if he could see the outline of the Tanana basin filings. He said he'd heard that Marathon and the other companies had filed and said he simply was interested in knowing where the land was. Marathon obliged. Now, with an outline of the companies' filings, Jacobs was able to mail more lease applications to Fairbanks—this time for acreage surrounding the land requested by the companies.

Several days passed before descriptions of all these filings were posted on land office records in Fairbanks. Another week would go by before the partnership companies realized Jacobs had not only filed applications for land within their leaseblock, but completely surrounding it. Even then they couldn't figure out whether Jacobs had filed for himself or for a competitor company.

Most oil people were convinced that Jacobs had planted a "mole" in the Fairbanks land office. He was barred from the offices of the partnership companies, and they demanded the Bureau of Land Management conduct an investigation of its land office procedures and personnel. Both the land office manager and Jacobs vehemently denied any insider information, and nothing ever came of the investigation, nor of the well later drilled by Union. Jacobs had been paid in cash by British-American, so again, Jacobs had beaten the big guys.

INSIDE STORY

QUICK PROFIT

The history of Alaska oil leasing is full of stories about the wheelings and dealings of Locke Jacobs. Here's another one. (His wild part in the Swanson River oil drama is told in the next chapter.)

After the big Prudhoe Bay discovery of the late '60s, Atlantic-Richfield Company (ARCO) needed to relinquish 150,000 acres in the South White Hills and Ivashak areas on the North Slope foothills to keep within acreage limitations—and to be free to acquire additional acreage on the more promising Arctic coastal plain.

The company not only wanted to rid itself of the acreage, but to reserve to itself a small overriding royalty on the land in case someone else eventually found oil. But because nearly $100,000 in rentals was due in six months, nobody was interested. Even after a discovery the mammoth size of Prudhoe Bay, the risk seemed too great.

ARCO landman Armand Spielman called Jacobs. Would Jacobs' leaseholder group take over the ARCO acreage?

"I decided to play poker," said Jacobs. "I told Spielman I'd take over the assignments myself."

He was assigned sixty leases covering about 150,000 acres in which ARCO reserved a 2 percent overriding royalty.

Jacobs paid $600 to file his assignments.

Within two weeks of filing, Cleary Petroleum Corporation offered him $25,000 cash for one lease.

"I think I can do better."

Cleary upped its offer to $50,000. Jacobs thought he could still do better. $100,000?

Still not enough.

At $200,000, Jacobs asked for "a little bit more," and at $250,000 he allowed as how it seemed "just about right."

Cleary paid Jacobs $100,000 cash with the balance in Cleary stock, the price of which immediately soared when Cleary merged with W. R. Grace & Co.

Jacobs sold other leases from the ARCO deal to Occidental Petroleum, H. L. Hunt, Bunker Hunt, Texaco, and Cities Service. Within six months—long before he paid out a cent of the $100,000 in rentals—Jacobs had made a $1 million profit.

Chapter 5

The Swanson River Discovery

I n the 1950s, Richfield Oil Corporation was considered a relatively small West Coast operation. Yet because of its aggressive exploration, it operated more like a much larger independent and became top dog in development of Alaska's first major oil field in Cook Inlet and later on the North Slope.

Richfield executive Frank Morgan had tried to get Richfield to explore in Bristol Bay during World War II, so management was aware of Alaska's huge petroleum potential. By studying USGS maps and records in the early 1950s, Frank Tolman, a Richfield geologist, had discovered a large topographic high in the middle of the north Kenai Peninsula, and the company lost no time filing on it.

The Richfield move was a stroke of luck for Locke Jacobs and his group of Anchorage leaseholders. One morning late in 1954, Jacobs noticed during his daily land office record-check that twenty-five lease applications had been filed by Richfield. Posted on the November 29 serial sheets, the applications were for 71,000 acres in the Swanson River area of the north Kenai.

He had noted earlier that on October 15, Union Oil's local consignees had filed for nearly 200,000 acres of the north Kenai. Richfield's filings lay to the east of Union's and were all within a game refuge, the Kenai National Moose Range.

Plotting Richfield's filings on his lease map, Jacobs discovered that several applications on the East Foreland area of the peninsula "top-filed" some of his group's leases. He immediately wrote Richfield's Los Angeles landman, George Shepphird, and pointed out the top filing. Would Shepphird like to discuss the overlap? Shepphird wrote back that he would.

Wilbur Wester from Jacobs' leaseholder group was dispatched to Los Angeles, armed with colored lease maps and a list of leases. He had an offer for Shepphird. His group would assign its leases on the East Foreland, on the West Foreland area on the other side of Cook Inlet, and on Kalgin Island at no cost to Richfield, in exchange for Richfield's commitment to drill a well anywhere in Alaska within two years. Shepphird, for his part, said Richfield would not accept a "free" acreage deal, but would pay them $2 an acre plus a 5 percent override for some of the acreage.

At this point Wester is reported to have asked, "What's an override?"

According to Bob Atwood, the group was so new at leasing it didn't know that an overriding royalty was what a leaseholder could reserve, after the government took its one-eighth royalty, when assigning a lease to someone else.

Wester tried to make it clear to Shepphird that his group's main interest was in seeing that Richfield drilled a well somewhere. Members of the group, all Anchorage businessmen, stood to benefit from an oil-boom economy.

"Everyone knew," said Atwood, "that they would profit from their existing businesses even without striking oil. We just wanted a well. We weren't out to make a quick dollar like so many people who play with oil leases, get in, buy 'em, and make a quick buck. The price of our leases, we told the oil company, was a drill hole."

Shepphird agreed Richfield would drill a well "somewhere in Alaska" beginning within two years, and he offered some up-front cash. And if Richfield failed to drill within the allotted time, Shepphird said, the company would make a penalty payment. But later, in an effort to make it as easy as possible for Richfield to drill, Mac McManamin persuaded the other members of the group to drop the penalty clause.

"That's the way the deal went together," Jacobs said.

74

ABOUT THIS TIME, a San Francisco oil and gas lease broker, Leroy Hines, filed on 40,000 acres on the north edge of Richfield's Swanson River leaseblock. Hines appeared to be filing not for some oil company, but simply as a speculator. He had become aware of what was happening on the Kenai Peninsula and throughout Alaska because Earl Grammer was helping with his leasing.

As he plotted the Grammer-Hines filings, Locke Jacobs realized he had to act fast or it would be too late to stake claims on the choicest acreage abutting the Richfield block. By now Jacobs was convinced a large oil field lay beneath the Kenai Peninsula.

He saw that Hines' lease descriptions were plotted in an intricate checkerboard pattern that sophisticated lease brokers use to confuse competitors and to tie up as much ground as possible for the least amount of money. But he also observed that Hines' leasing to the north of Richfield's block left an open

ARCO

Richfield brought in Alaska's first commercial oil well in mid-1957 at Swanson River on the Kenai Peninsula. The dramatic discovery set Alaska firmly on the road to eventually becoming a major oil state.

hole to the south. Jacobs knew that within days some oil company landman or a leasehound like himself would rush in to fill the hole. Unleased land adjoining a major oil company's lease-play cries for such action.

Anxious to file on the open acreage to the south, Jacobs contacted members of his leasing group. Most of them were out of the Territory. Those who remained in Anchorage weren't swayed by Jacobs' enthusiasm when they realized how much money it would require in rentals and filing fees to nail down a large amount of land. Discouraged, he looked around for anyone who would join him in a major filing effort, but he found no takers.

The July 23, 1957, front page of the Anchorage Daily Times *screamed "RICHFIELD HITS OIL." Within two days, Richfield common stock rose twenty points.*

Finally one member of the leasing group, Fred Axford, agreed to file—but only if Jacobs also filed the relinquishment forms that would let him get out of the leases if he wanted to. If the "winter birds," as Axford called the group members who were out of the Territory— McManamin, Miller, and Wester—declined to pay for a part of the rentals and filing fees when they returned, Axford could dump the filings.

The land office was all out of relinquishment forms, so Jacobs went to see Earl Grammer. Grammer gave him the forms, at which point Jacobs says he told Grammer where he planned to file. He said he told Grammer that he was welcome to file for any of the open acreage himself.

On January 21, 1955, Grammer did file three applications on the Kenai covering about seven thousand acres. One of Grammer's parcels abutted the southwest corner of Richfield's Swanson River leaseblock in the Soldotna Creek area and two others were farther to the north. They were filed in the name of a friend, S. J. Paradiso.

A week later Jacobs filed twenty-two lease applications in the name of Fred Axford. The applications, covering 52,500 acres, were accompanied by $14,000 in rental checks. Later that year, Richfield optioned the Axford leases. This eventually turned into a multimillion-dollar deal: five of these leases would produce most of the oil taken from the major Swanson River-Soldotna field.

Jacobs always contended that the story of how he hustled to file the Axford leases is true, but one is entitled to doubt. It's certainly possible that Wilbur Wester, in Los Angeles with Richfield's George Shepphird at the time, could have phoned Jacobs to advise him to file next to Richfield, with Richfield agreeing to option the land at a later date. All it would have taken was one phone call. However, Jacobs insists he did it all on his own.

"I simply filled the hole," said Jacobs. "Where I filed Axford was just pure luck. Had Grammer filed his Paradiso applications alongside Richfield's like we did instead of further south, he instead of us would have been the richer."

THE LAND UNDER THE AXFORD LEASES, like Richfield's block, lay entirely within the Kenai National Moose Range. Federal laws pertaining to wildlife refuges were murky, giving no guarantee to oil operators that any lease applications would be approved or issued.

Although issuance of Axford's leases remained in question, Richfield paid him $2.50 an acre—more than $130,000—for an option on the land. The option provided that the cash and royalty interests could be cross-assigned among Jacobs' leasing group. Thus Atwood, McManamin, and the other members of the select businessmen's leasing fraternity were cut in on what turned out to be an extremely lucrative deal.

In January 1955, Richfield filed for a 71,000-acre Swanson River exploration unit with the U.S. Geological Survey. The unit agreement required that all geophysical and drilling activity have prior approval of the U.S. Fish and Wildlife Service.

David L. Spencer, the local Fish and Wildlife supervisor, drafted regulations prohibiting use of dynamite in seismic work in the moose range. In August 1955, Richfield shot an east-west seismic line across the north end of the Kenai Peninsula using a helicopter-mounted drill rig. But after that one line, Spencer, reluctant to permit geophysical work for fear of harm to the moose, ordered Richfield to shut down the operation. Richfield now had to rely on surface geology and "creekology." It also borrowed a Shell seismic boat and ran an east-west seismic line between East Foreland and West Foreland in upper Cook Inlet.

By that time, leasing in all U.S. wildlife reserves was being examined by Congress, and hearings were held on several wildlife refuge protection bills. Alaska's Delegate to Congress Bob Bartlett and former Territorial Governor Ernest Gruening gave persuasive testimony in favor of opening the moose range to oil exploration before the House Merchant Marine and Fisheries Committee. On July 25, committee chairman Herbert C. Bonner, a North Carolina Democrat, said he had no objection to Richfield proceeding with the Swanson River Unit.

Several days later, Fish and Wildlife Service director John L. Farley and the U.S. Geological Survey authorized drilling inside the unit, prompting Richfield to announce it was proceeding with a well. After that, thirty-one leases were issued, effective September 1, 1956.

ANCHORAGE DAILY TIMES/ ANCHORAGE DAILY NEWS

Richfield's discovery at Swanson River, reported in the July 23, 1957, edition of the Anchorage Daily Times, *set off an oil-leasing frenzy.*

LEGEND HAS IT that the first Swanson River drill site was located by a Richfield geologist who unrolled toilet paper from a helicopter into the treetops between Sterling Highway and the river. This, it was said, was how geologist Bill Bishop traced the 21-mile pilot road from Soldotna to Swanson River. Bulldozers then blazed the surface along the paper trail.

The boots worn by Bishop as he

stomped his foot into the soft Swanson River soil in the fall of 1956 and exclaimed "Drill here!" became historical objects. They are now bronzed in the Anchorage Museum of History and Art.

On April 3, 1957, Richfield began its Swanson River No. 1 well. By early July, it was drilling below 10,000 feet. The well reportedly was nearly abandoned a few feet short of its target depth. Given instructions to shut it down at a predetermined depth, Bishop and his geologist assistant, G. Ray Arnett, are said to have ordered roughnecks to "drill just a few feet more."

Voila, there was oil!

Bishop decided to run a drill stem test to see what might come out of the hole. The test, on July 19, showed the well capable of producing two hundred to five hundred barrels per day of good quality oil. Four days later, a public announcement was made. There was jubilation in Anchorage.

The July 23, 1957, front page of the *Anchorage Daily Times* screamed "RICH-FIELD HITS OIL." Within two days, Richfield common stock rose twenty points to $70 a share.

With only one seismic line on a topographic high, Alaska's first commercial oil well was truly a "wildcat." The discovery seems even more remarkable decades later because, with drilling in most of the Kenai Moose Range still prohibited, Swanson River continues to be the only commercial field producing oil from the entire 2-million-acre Kenai Peninsula. The field was large, more than a quarter billion barrels in the ground.

The boost Richfield's gusher gave Alaska's fledgling economy was incalculable. Some say it convinced Congress to grant Alaska statehood.

ALL HELL BROKE LOOSE when Richfield struck oil. Landmen, leasebrokers, individual Alaskans—just about everyone wanted an oil lease. Land in all of Alaska's sedimentary basins suddenly became attractive. Leasehounds and ordinary citizens deluged the Anchorage land office.

Everyone knew that the northern portion of the Kenai Peninsula, inside the moose range, had probably all been leased. But were there any other areas available for leasing? What was still open? Where could someone file? There was pandemonium, confusion, and pure excitement.

Land office serial sheets showed where filings had been made, but days, perhaps weeks, would pass before recent filings could be posted. There was no way of determining where one could lease. The only person in Alaska who seemed to know where leases had been filed was a former shoe-clerk, Locke Jacobs.

The first thing Jacobs did after reading the *Anchorage Daily Times* headlines on July 23 was to call Betty Thompson, who had left the Bureau of Land Management, worked a year for Jacobs to help him copy land office oil and gas records, then decided to stay home and raise her kids. When Jacobs called, Betty's husband answered the phone.

"There is no way my wife's going back to work," he told Jacobs.

"How about ten dollars an hour?," Jacobs suggested.

"She'll be there first thing in the morning," he said.

"No way. I need her in an hour or sooner."

"No problem. I'm driving. She'll be there."

ANCHORAGE DAILY TIMES/ ANCHORAGE DAILY NEWS

Exploration site at Swanson River.

That night, all night, Jacobs and Thompson filled out oil and gas lease applications. The next morning they filed 100, covering 300,000 acres. All the next day they typed lease descriptions on application forms. By the morning of July 25 they had filed on another million acres, and Jacobs was on his way to cornering the market on leasable oil lands.

Nobody knew where Jacobs had filed because it would be days before the land office staff would post his lease descriptions. Paperwork swamped the staff. Until the land office could adjudicate any conflicts between Jacobs and other filers, no one could know for sure where anyone had filed. Nor were Jacobs and Thompson about to tell anyone what only they knew. And only they had a truly up-to-date set of maps. This was information Jacobs was about to start selling for a huge profit.

At the height of the filing frenzy, Jacobs had eighteen clerks and three draftsmen working for him. He estimated he brought in an average of $1,000 for every hour he could stay awake.

Before long, Jacobs ran out of blank lease application forms. Federal regulations required applications to be filed in quintuplet, so he needed a lot of them. He went to the land office, but was told that the office itself was out of forms. An employee had just been sent to the warehouse in the Alaska Railroad yards to bring back the remaining five thousand forms.

Jacobs went to the warehouse, saw the messenger fixing a flat tire on his truck, and offered to deliver the forms for him. The stranded employee reluctantly agreed. Instead of taking the forms to the land office, Jacobs rushed all five thousand to his own office.

When land office manager Virgil Seiser phoned at 8 the next morning and asked him to produce the lease forms, Jacobs said he would: "five at a time, and properly filled out."

Said Jacobs: "I'd never seen Seiser so fully pissed off."

By then Jacobs had not only monopolized where to lease, but how to lease. Until the land office came up with more application blanks, nobody but Jacobs could file.

WITHIN THREE WEEKS of the announcement of the Swanson River discovery, lease applications filed in the Anchorage land office totaled more than 4 million acres. Throngs of people continued to line up at the land office waiting to file. For most of them, however, the golden opportunity had passed.

Even more impressive was the line outside Jacobs' office. Major company landmen, lease brokers, ordinary citizens, all realizing they couldn't blindly top-file on earlier applications, packed Jacobs' hallway, clamoring for the leasing information only he possessed.

Landmen in the hallway surmised that Jacobs had made his first filings on the Kenai Peninsula, closest to the Swanson River discovery. But only Jacobs, Thompson, and a few members of the overworked land office staff actually knew the leading edge of the lease-play. All sedimentary basins in Alaska became of great interest. Landmen needed to know where filings ended and whether a competitor had gotten there first.

I was desperately trying to report what was going on. My wife, Martha, and I stayed up nights typing names of filers, the amount of acreage they filed on, and indications of the areas for which they filed. I ran off copies of the Alaska Scouting Service as soon as the pages filled up.

It was then that I had discovered the terminated leases on Kalgin Island, and hurried to Earl Grammer's log cabin to get his help in securing my first Alaska oil leases.

At the height of the filing frenzy, Jacobs had eighteen clerks and three draftsmen working for him. People paid him for the right to examine and copy his serial sheets and lease maps. Having filed enough for himself and his leasing group, Jacobs began filing lease applications for oil companies, lease brokers, and individuals.

Jacobs ensconced accountant George Jones in an office across the hall from his own on the second floor of the Loussac-Sogn building and told him to keep track of all the money that was rolling in. Jacobs estimated that during the next heady month he brought in an average of $1,000 for every hour he could stay awake.

JUST A WEEK after the Swanson River strike, Richfield's George Shepphird met in Anchorage with several members of Jacobs' leasing group. Shepphird was shown a map with the group's Cook Inlet leases colored yellow.

Shepphird was told Richfield could have any of the group's leases it wanted. Shepphird took assignments or options on most of its Kenai land, some as far south as Homer. Even though the group had originally offered its land free to Richfield if the company drilled anywhere in Alaska, Shepphird now paid $3 an acre—$1 an acre more than he'd paid for the original Forelands and Kalgin leases and 50 cents an acre more than for the Axford leases. As before, the group kept a 5 percent overriding royalty, in itself a bonanza.

"Richfield had taken the risk of drilling at Swanson River, and Richfield's success was our success," said Bob Atwood.

A few weeks later, Chevron paid Richfield $30 million for half interest in all of Richfield's Kenai Peninsula leases, including those at Swanson River and Soldotna Creek, and became operator of the oil field.

The boost Richfield's gusher gave Alaska's fledgling economy was incalculable. Some say it convinced Congress to grant Alaska statehood.

By now more than a hundred oil companies were actively leasing in Alaska, and a year after the July 1957 discovery more than 18 million acres in Alaska had been leased. A great land rush had occurred in the Great Land. No longer to be treated as the United States' future "storehouse of untapped natural resources," Alaska had become one of the world's great oil provinces, about to rival Texas as an oil state.

THE MOOSE CAPTURED a great deal of attention in the aftermath of the big oil discovery on their refuge. Although the Fish and Wildlife Service issued a permit to Richfield to drill a second well two miles south of the Swanson River discovery, further seismic and gravity-meter survey work in the moose range had been halted.

That fall, on behalf of the Anchorage Chamber of Commerce, Bob Atwood wrote his old friend General Nathan F. Twining, chairman of the Joint Chiefs of Staff, seeking support for continued exploration of the Kenai National Moose Range. He said the business community feared the government might shut down the entire Kenai oil operation.

"The discovery well," Atwood wrote to Twining, "is capable of producing 900 barrels daily, and oil company programs indicate $100,000,000 is available for further exploration immediately." Swanson River crude is ideal for making jet fuel, he claimed, and added that the military's fuel needs in Alaska could be met almost entirely by development of Kenai oil.

On January 8, 1958, Interior Secretary Fred Seaton suspended oil and gas leasing in the moose range but placed it in a category separate from the Lower 48 states. Henceforth, the Fish and Wildlife Service would determine which parts of the range were open and which were closed to further development.

Before Fish and Wildlife could announce its decision on the moose range, Congress suspended all oil and gas leasing in Alaska. It wanted to raise Alaska's 25-cent-an-acre lease rentals; federal lands in other states were bringing in 50 cents. A majority in Congress felt that after the Swanson River discovery, federal oil and gas lands in Alaska were worth at least as much as those in other states. A compromise was reached: Alaska's rentals would be raised to 50 cents after May 3, 1958, although by then nearly all the Kenai Peninsula had been leased.

Then Seaton announced the decision on open and closed areas of the moose range. He said he was opening the northern half of the range to oil and gas leasing but closing the southern half. This "Open and Closed" regulation was published in the *Federal Register* on August 2, 1958. The open area included the land on which Richfield had struck oil a year earlier.

Anchorage lawyer James Tallman took a look at the situation and came up with a remarkable scheme. He reasoned that if previously closed federal land was now open, it was therefore newly available. So he and a handful of Alaskans top-filed over the Richfield and Axford leases.

Tallman's lease applications were rejected on grounds that Richfield's leases had priority. Tallman's appeal of the rejection was denied in October 1959, and a long legal battle followed. It took a unanimous decision of the U.S. Supreme Court, written by Chief Justice Earl Warren, to settle the matter. Warren said in the March 1, 1965, decision that Richfield and Jacobs' group were to get the Swanson River leases once and for all.

Locke Jacobs was convinced that Alaska businessman and politician Wally Hickel had financed Tallman in an effort to wrest the Swanson River leases from his group. Henceforth, each time Hickel ran for governor during the '60s and '70s, Jacobs would walk the downtown sidewalks of Anchorage trying to persuade merchants and their employees to oppose Hickel. He chuckled in 1990 as he recalled the "Huck Fickel" bumper stickers he passed out.

———————

WHEN THE SWANSON RIVER FIELD was at its peak production in the 1970s, Jacobs and his brethren grossed a total annual income from their 5 percent over-riding royalty of about $1.5 million. After twenty-five years of royalty checks, each had received more than $3 million. And the checks keep coming in.

Locke Jacobs eventually relocated to the Lower 48 and from there put together several large North Slope leaseblocks. He jumped into California natural gas ventures, and he raked in another small fortune discovering uranium in extinct volcanoes on the border between Nevada and Oregon.

He and his wife, Evangeline, finally moved to Caldwell, Idaho, to raise thoroughbred racehorses. They became owners of one of the world's great horses, Shergar's Best, lone North American son of the Aga Khan's "horse of the century," Shergar. A few days before his death in October 1992, Jacobs told me: "Our horses are winning." It sounds like the great Jacobs luck stayed with him right to the end.

THE HAROLD KOSLOSKY STORY

Anchorage's leading clothier, Harold Koslosky, was the son of a merchant-settler from the earliest days of Anchorage. Inveterate gambler Koslosky decided he just had to take a hand in Alaska's oil and gas game. On the recommendation of oil promoter William T. Foran, he formed Koslosky Development Company to go after land on the Nushagak Peninsula in upper Bristol Bay, west of the Alaska Peninsula.

Foran told Koslosky that although Bristol Bay was not on top of his list of most promising geologic basins, "it has exceptional potential aspects not unlike the Wyoming, Montana, Alberta fields. The area is quite similar in structure and stratigraphic aspect to that of the long-productive provinces of the American-Canadian Rocky Mountain region."

Koslosky and his group filed for seventy-eight federal oil and gas leases on Nushagak Peninsula, with most of the leases being held by residents of Alaska. And in 1960, Koslosky began working out a deal with the Pure Oil Company.

Koslosky had been approached by Frank Shogrin, Pure's landman, in charge of securing land for the oil company's use. Koslosky listened attentively while Shogrin explained how Pure would get a development contract from the Interior Department if Koslosky would assign his group's leases to Pure. With this go-ahead from Interior, Shogrin said Pure would begin drilling the first of three wells south of the town of Dillingham on the Nushagak Peninsula.

Early the next year, after Koslosky accepted Shogrin's offer of $2 an acre plus a small overriding royalty on any oil found, the Interior Department awarded Pure a 200,000-acre development contract covering most of the peninsula. Koslosky's group received nearly $400,000 from Pure.

Shogrin had actually been authorized to pay Koslosky more than $2 an acre, so believing he had driven too hard a bargain, he now offered Koslosky an additional $300,000 for several more tracts.

Koslosky was characteristically prepared to roll the dice, so he summarily rejected Shogrin's offer.

"Kid," he said—he always called young men *kid*—"I have more money in my ass pocket than that."

But the Alaskan winter helped put a cold end to Koslosky's oil gamble as Pure moved ahead with its plans for drilling on the peninsula. Pure had arranged to barge a drill rig and equipment from its abandoned Canoe Bay well site (out toward the Aleutian Islands) north to the Nushagak Peninsula. The plan was to set up the rig on the peninsula before the annual ice freeze-up of the region's waters.

It was early October. Pure's division manager K. S. "Stu" Cronin, though realizing it was dangerously close to freeze-up in Bristol Bay, decided to go ahead with the move anyway. Cronin expected the four barges to reach Nushagak by early November, before freeze-up, and had attempted to obtain voyage insurance. But not even Lloyd's of London would touch such a hazardous trip. Despite the lack of marine insurance, and as ice formed on the saltwater of Bristol Bay, Cronin told the barge operator to go for it.

When the Alaskan winter sets in, everything stops. Immediately upon leaving shore, Pure's barges ran aground at Cape Lieskof, south of Port Moller, and became frozen in ice. Nothing could pull them free, and they would remain there throughout the winter.

Mother Nature and human miscalculation defeated Pure. The trapped barges, plus a major corporate restructuring, kept Pure from drilling on Bristol Bay, and no wells have ever been drilled on the Nushagak Peninsula. The following spring, what was left of the rig and equipment was freed from the ice and salvaged.

Koslosky was left holding less than a full deck of cards. Not having taken the extra cash from Shogrin, his group had $300,000 less than it could have had, and they would never see drilling on their leaseholds.

Pure's two top Alaskan officials, Cronin and Shogrin, were summarily fired. Management thought the decision to go forward without marine insurance inexcusable.

Getting the boot probably helped turn Frank Shogrin into a successful oilman. Made "independent" involuntarily, by the Pure fiasco, he leased state offshore land in Trading Bay in upper Cook Inlet in the early 1960s. When oil began flowing from Trading Bay, Shogrin became one of only a handful of "little guys" receiving monthly oil royalty checks from Alaska.

Chapter 6
"Little Guy" Bill Egan

I n the fall of 1955 Alaskans elected fifty-five delegates to draft a constitution for the state-to-be. Delegates at the November 8 opening session
of the Constitutional Convention on the University of Alaska campus at
Fairbanks heard some words of warning from E. L. "Bob" Bartlett, an
ex-Fairbanks gold miner who was the Territory's Delegate to Congress.

The pervading political rhetoric at the time was of "outsiders"—mineral
and fishing interests from Seattle and the eastern United States—controlling
Alaska's destiny, so Bartlett made them his principal target.

"Two very real dangers are present," Bartlett said. "The first, and most obvious, is that of exploitation under the thin disguise of development; the taking
of Alaska's mineral resources without leaving some reasonable return for the
support of Alaska governmental services. . . .

"The second danger is that outside interests . . . will attempt to acquire
great areas of Alaska's public lands in order NOT to develop them . . . . If large
areas of Alaska's patrimony are turned over to such corporations, the people
of Alaska may be even more the losers than if the lands had been exploited."
Bartlett believed, as did most Territorial officials, that the canned salmon and
mining "outside interests" might try to maintain control by monopolizing
any available land so that no one else could use it.

But unlike what many had expected, outside groups interfered very
little with the drafting of the constitution. What was drafted would become a

89

"model" constitution. Simple, direct, concerned as much with management of fish and game as with development of Alaska's mineral resources, it would give immense power to the new state's chief executive.

President of the convention was Bill Egan, the former mayor of Valdez who had served seven consecutive terms in the Territorial Legislature. During the winter of 1955 this unassuming man helped produce a consensus among convention delegates that led to the model constitution.

Bill Egan had an old-fashioned way of getting what he wanted politically: he worked hard.

On October 9, 1956, Alaskans went to the polls to elect three "Tennessee Plan" representatives, people who would walk the halls of Congress to persuade the nation's lawmakers to grant statehood. Tennessee had used this tactic in its drive to become a state. Alaskans elected former Territorial Governor Ernest Gruening as the six-year Tennessee Senator, ex-Fairbanks Mayor Ralph Rivers as the lone Tennessee Representative in the House, and kept Bartlett as Alaska's lone non-voting Delegate to Congress. To the four-year Tennessee Senator seat they elected Bill Egan.

The first time I met Egan was on the sidewalk outside the 4th Avenue Theater in Anchorage. He was there for a debate prior to the "Tennessee Plan" election. I recall thinking as I shook hands with the president of the Constitutional Convention: how could this shy, awkward-seeming man have led such an important event?

I was one of only a handful of Alaskans who heard the debate in the small theater atop the Reed Building involving Egan and publisher Bob Atwood (candidates for the four-year Tennessee Senator seat), and Ernest Gruening and Territorial legislator John Butrovich (candidates for the six-year seat). As a statehood supporter, I was heartened when all four men said it didn't matter who was elected because all of them supported statehood. After Egan beat Atwood in the October election, he and his wife, Neva, spent the next two years in Washington, D.C., lobbying Congress—successfully—for statehood.

Alaskans' attitude toward the oil industry after statehood would in large part be reflected by the outlook of the state's first governor. That person turned out to be Bill Egan. His view of the oil companies and his relationship with the key oil and gas administrators in the state would, again in large part, determine how the state reacted to the industry. That view was shaped by his upbringing in a tiny town at the head of Prince William Sound.

WILLIAM A. EGAN GREW UP in Valdez, an Alaskan town with the 1930s' Depression very much alive in the minds of its residents. One of seven children—five boys and two girls—Bill Egan was just six when his father was killed in a snow-slide east of the town. Several years later, he became an early provider to his family as he worked for ten cents an hour in the Valdez fish cannery. His mother took in washing, sold chickens, and became a matron in the local court system.

Growing up in Valdez meant the politics of Kennicott Copper. The copper mine, located deep within the Wrangell Mountains east of Valdez, shut down in the early 1930s when the world price of copper dropped from 35 cents to 5 cents a pound and the ore body became too

Governor Bill Egan and his wife, Neva, pose at the 1960 dedication of an oil pipeline from Swanson River to Nikiski on the Kenai Peninsula. Long before that time, Neva Egan says, her husband "knew Alaska would someday become a big oil state."

thin. About the same time, the Copper River Railroad closed, the oil refinery on the Katalla slough burned, and the old Katalla oil field ceased its small production. These events hit Valdez hard. The young Egan began to learn that the extraction of Alaska's natural resources held important political lessons.

Egan was awkward in public, with a voice ill-suited for TV or radio. Some said he was so shy that while waiting on customers at his Valdez grocery store, he couldn't look them in the eye. But Bill Egan loved politics.

"'Who is this can stacker?,' people would ask," recalls John Rader, the state's first attorney general. "'Who is this delivery boy?'"

"They all underestimated him, as did I," Rader said. "I didn't have any more ability than anybody else to see the depth of the guy, the ability of the guy. He was one of the brightest persons I have ever known."

"People sometimes underestimated him because he was such a soft sell," said his wife, Neva. Neva McKittrick first met Bill Egan in Valdez in 1937 when she arrived from Wilson, Kansas, to teach school. "I thought I was politically oriented, but, good grief, he is the only person I ever knew who read the Congressional Record.

"There were no 'good old days' in Alaska," she recalled. "We scrounged to make a living. Bill and I grew up in Depression days. I think it left its mark on us, but that's not all bad."

When Bill met Neva he was already serving on the Valdez City Council and had recently been elected to the Territorial House of Representatives. He learned quite early that Alaska had a vast oil potential.

"Two geologists came before the Ways and Means Committee in 1941," he later said in a public television interview, "and told us there were domes on the North Slope, even on the surface, like in the Middle East."

"Bill was always sure there was going to be oil under everything they were going to drill," said Neva Egan. "He knew Alaska would someday become a big oil state."

AS A STATE LEGISLATOR, Egan was in tune with Territorial Governor Ernest Gruening in the governor's harsh assessment of "outside" economic interests. Before statehood, Alaskans couldn't vote for their governor or for President of the United States. The governor of the Territory was appointed by the President. Alaska had to pay federal income taxes, but it was the bureaucrats in Washington, D.C., and the outside interests who decided if and when Alaska's resources would be developed. It was taxation without representation.

President Franklin Roosevelt appointed Gruening governor in 1941. One of Gruening's first acts was an attempt to pass a Territory income tax. He was thwarted by a group of interests he called the "Seattle monopolists": the Alaska Steamship Company; Alaska Canned Salmon, Inc., and its lobby group, the Alaska Packers Association; and the Alaska Miners Association.

Said Gruening: "Absentee controls, unique neglect, and downright discrimination is strangling Alaska."

Gruening lamented to the 1941 Territorial legislature:

"Take the conspicuous example of Kennicott [copper mine]. . . . some $200 million worth of copper was taken out in the course of a generation. What has the Territory of Alaska to show for these $200 million today? A hole in the ground."

Actions of the Seattle-based "monopolists" and Congress

NEVA EGAN

Governor Bill Egan was known as a hard worker. A campaign brochure for his 1966 reelection bid shows the lights burning late at night in his third-floor Capitol Building office.

and the federal bureaucrats left Alaska "a stepchild subject to distant bureaucratic domination," he said.

Gruening's words impressed freshman legislator Bill Egan. The closing of the Kennicott mine near his hometown in the 1930s by the Guggenheims of New York devastated Valdez and other Prince William Sound towns. Egan blamed big, outside economic interests for the local depression.

Publisher Bob Atwood agreed. "Outside interests owned everything in Alaska then. We were their peons. We were just working for them, and all the profits and everything went out to Seattle."

By the early 1950s, however, most Alaskans believed that the "colonialism" was about to come to an end. During World War II the U.S. military had invested heavily in the Territory's transportation and communication systems, greatly improving both. Many servicemen were deciding to stay in Alaska, and with statehood likely to come to Alaska it seemed a good place to live, a good place to build a permanent home. One could make dreams come true in the Last Frontier.

DEMOCRAT IRENE RYAN, one of the few Alaskans who really understood the oil business, got to know the man who would become the state of Alaska's first governor when she served with Egan in the Territorial Legislature in the 1940s.

Egan's distrustful attitude toward big business had nothing to do with the type of company he was dealing with, Ryan recalls.

"If it had been a big copper company instead of an oil company, it would have been the same. He didn't understand big business, so he was suspicious. He didn't want to move until he was sure he wasn't making a mistake.

"Although he probably never said so in his life or even would have admitted it to himself, Bill felt he didn't have a broad enough education." His graduation from Valdez High School in 1932 ended his formal education.

"I think Bill was just a very honest small-town businessman," Ryan said. "He was a grocer. He could empathize with the small businessman, because he had been a small businessman. The small businessman in Alaska was at the mercy of the banker, at the mercy of the navigation company, and the insurance companies, all owned by the same families."

Ryan was a remarkable woman who came to Alaska from Texas in the early 1930s with a degree in mining and petroleum geology from the University of New Mexico. She designed small airports in Alaska for the Civil Aviation Administration, then opened an Anchorage engineering and land surveying office. She knew oil and she knew the people in oil, people like Earl Grammer, Russ Havenstrite, Bill Foran, and Jack Walker. It was she who advised shoe-clerk Locke Jacobs on oil leasing in Alaska.

As a state legislator, Ryan advised Governor Gruening that commercial oil and gas would someday be found in Alaska and convinced him that Alaska needed a conservation law like that in Texas. Without it, she said, reckless oil drilling practices would waste precious natural reservoir pressures in oil fields and permit vast amounts of hydrocarbons to escape. The conservation law would compel landowners competing for oil in a field to coordinate drilling.

Egan was awkward in public, with a voice ill-suited for TV or radio. Some said he was so shy that while waiting on customers at his Valdez grocery store, he couldn't look them in the eye. But Bill Egan loved politics.

In the legislature, Ryan observed Bill Egan's education in the power of the "Seattle monopolists." One of Egan's most effective "teachers" was a man reputed to have single-handedly kept Alaskan statehood at bay for more than a decade: W. C. "Bill" Arnold— known not so affectionately as "Fish" Arnold—executive director of the Alaska Packers Association and longtime lobbyist for the canned-salmon industry.

"Egan was politically trained under the most powerful person to ever control the legislature, Fish Arnold," said Pat Ryan, Irene's husband. "He didn't vote with Fish Arnold, ever, but he was beaten by Arnold. Arnold would sit in the legislative gallery during the 1940s, and when something would come up in a hurry and some of the legislators didn't know which way to vote, they would look in the gallery and Arnold would motion up or down.

"That went on for years, and Egan was in those sessions," Pat Ryan said. "He was voting opposite from Arnold, so he knew where the control was. It was in the canned-salmon industry, the Guggenheim influence, the steamship influence.

"Egan didn't want the oil industry to have the power to do what Fish Arnold did against Bill Egan."

EGAN HAD AN OLD-FASHIONED WAY of getting what he wanted politically: he worked hard. After he became governor, the sight of the light burning late at night in his third-floor Capitol Building office became well known.

> *"I thought I was politically oriented, but, good grief, he is the only person I ever knew who read the Congressional Record."*
> —Neva Egan, speaking of her husband, Bill

"Our phone number at the governor's house was in the telephone book," recalls Neva Egan, "so people who couldn't get through to Bill would call the house. Often, it wasn't that important, but to them it was. . . . the fact that they could talk to somebody. I always made notes and showed them to Bill when he came home."

Egan's reputation for hard work became an integral part of his political campaigns. His 1966 campaign brochure featured a photo of the light shining in his third-floor office; no caption was necessary. Today, Egan would be considered a workaholic, but in those days he was simply seen as someone who really liked government and politics.

His success at politics was aided by a phenomenal ability to remember names, a talent that would become legendary in Alaska. Running into someone after a long time, he'd greet the person by name, ask about family members by name, and recall the discussion of long ago. Remembering names was good politics, but it was also what helped endear Bill Egan to most Alaskans.

SPOTLIGHT

THE TRUE BELIEVER

Chuck Herbert, a longtime friend and colleague of Bill Egan, describes Egan as "an absolutely true, true believer" in his devotion to the people of Alaska. "If he thought something was good for the people of Alaska there wasn't any political obstacle at all that would frighten him away from what he thought they should have."

Herbert recalls the time the governor of New Mexico advised then-Governor Egan to support an oil leasing system that would give ordinary citizens access to the state's mineral resources. "That populist idea seemed to impress Bill," Herbert said. "It also added to his natural instincts against giving large oil companies unlimited rights to explore in Alaska."

Alex Miller, a future legislative aide to Egan, says "No one even came close to knowing government the way Bill Egan did. Not only the technical parts, the human parts, too. . . .

"You know what he would do at 10 at night? He'd phone somebody in Bethel, in Barrow, in Kenai, in Homer. Every night. For a while, he'd say hello to friends. Then he'd take a phone book, and pick a name at random. He'd introduce himself on the phone, and say 'What do you think? How are things going? Do you have a family?'"

Chapter 7

Prelude to Statehood

Beginning statehood with a vast "storehouse of untapped natural resources" is great. Deciding what to bring out of the storehouse when, and how to package it, is critical when you need cash to finance that new state. Getting ready early is essential.

In 1955, several years before statehood, Territorial Governor Ernest Gruening became convinced that Alaska needed an oil conservation law. Territorial Commissioner of Mines Phil Holdsworth attended meetings of the 33-member Interstate Oil Compact Commission, although Alaska wasn't a member, and he came back armed with materials on the subject.

Territorial Senator Irene Ryan, working with Holdsworth, told the governor that a conservation law would "control things like well spacing and offset drainage [of oil]" from future state land lying next to federal land. It would help bring order to oil fields and require efficient cooperation among operators on adjacent lands.

During the 1955 legislative session, she and Holdsworth drafted the Alaska Oil Conservation Act that was introduced in the legislature, passed, and signed by Gruening in less than ten days. To prevent waste of oil or gas by careless or overly competitive drilling, legislators also established a maximum economic recovery policy.

Ryan and Holdsworth were up to date on the burgeoning activity in oil and gas leasing in the Territory, and it made them push all the harder for legislation and for membership in the Oil Compact Commission. The sharp increase in federal leasing in the Kenai National Moose Range and other areas of the Kenai Peninsula and on Gulf of Alaska uplands was beginning to occur in other sedimentary basins in the Territory. Federal lease drawings, notably the one at Wide Bay in July 1954, attracted major West Coast oil companies. (Senator Ryan herself and several other legislators were successful applicants in the Wide Bay drawing.)

Holdworth's goal was to go after big-company money by holding the state's first competitive oil and gas sale as soon as possible after Ike signed the Statehood Act.

Although no oil or gas had been produced in Alaska other than the small amount at Katalla, the 1955 legislature saw fit to pass a 1 percent gross oil and gas production tax. And, as was true in oil producing states in the Lower 48, to avoid a duplication the tax was to be in lieu of local petroleum taxes. The 1955 lawmakers also passed an eighth-cent-per-barrel "conservation tax," not to exceed $700,000 in any one year, to be levied on "any oil or gas which might be found in the Territory." The money was to pay for administration of a newly created Alaska Oil and Gas Conservation Commission.

Then in 1957, as Richfield was preparing to drill the well that would herald the Swanson River discovery, the legislature passed the Alaska Land Act, patterned on the U.S. Mineral Leasing Act. Legislators designated three classifications of Territorial oil and gas land to be offered only by competitive bid: the 1 million acres of Mental Health land which Congress had granted to the Territory in 1956, all University of Alaska land, and all land lying three miles seaward of mean high tide—the so-called tide and submerged lands. The Territorial Land Board had authority to classify oil and gas uplands as either competitive (cash bidding) or noncompetitive (first come, first served).

PHIL HOLDSWORTH could see an oil and gas land rush coming with the advent of statehood. As commissioner of mines and chairman of the Land

Board, he was instrumental in establishing the ground rules for leasing when statehood arrived. There would be a sixty-day filing period during which federal oil and gas lease applicants could convert to a state lease. A drawing would decide the winner in case of duplicate applications. Acreage limitations would be liberalized above the federal figure. An operator could hold up to 500,000 acres of tide and submerged lands through competitive bidding, plus up to 500,000 acres of state lands other than tide and submerged lands through noncompetitive application.

Holdsworth knew that a system of competitive cash bidding would increase an operator's initial exploration costs, but he believed it to be a more orderly, efficient way to manage natural resources. He knew that many of Alaska's "little guys" and most of the U.S. independents favored noncompetitive leasing because it gave them a chance against the big companies in the race for oil leases. Holdsworth, however, believed competitive bidding meant good land management, which increased the chances of good exploration.

But only four months after passage of the Land Act—and years before Holdsworth's expected "land rush"—Richfield discovered oil at Swanson River, setting off a leasing frenzy. By the end of 1957, major oil companies, independents, lease brokers, and Alaska's "little guys" had filed for more than 10 million acres in Alaska.

ON JUNE 30, 1958, CONGRESS PASSED the Alaska Statehood Act. Jubilant Anchoragites celebrated with a mammoth bonfire on the Park Strip. Campaigns began for Alaska's first gubernatorial election. Alaskans wanted to be ready with a governor the moment President Eisenhower signed the bill into law.

Oil was quickly becoming a key concern of leaders of the state-to-be. The Alaska Legislative Council, the legislature's between-session standing committee, met in Kodiak October 15 to discuss proposed oil and gas regulations. Phil Holdsworth reported to the council that the first shipment of Chevron's Swanson River oil was just then being trucked from Kenai to Seward to be tankered to the refinery at Richmond, California, for testing.

Things were moving too fast for at least one oil company, Superior Oil, which wired Holdsworth in Kodiak and asked that he defer making a policy on classification and selection of lands "because of its sweeping effect and possible ramifications . . . on future oil leasing and exploration."

Shell Oil came up with a list of worries of its own. Shell landman Roger Chaffin told Holdsworth in Kodiak that Shell feared its competitors might try to file for state oil and gas leases even before statehood. His company had spent millions of dollars at Cold Bay and didn't want competitors to get a jump on leasing. Shell was prepared to file for submerged lands at Wide Bay but didn't know when to do it.

Chaffin bombarded Holdsworth with questions and concerns: Could Shell get a state development contract, like the federal government had given other companies in Alaska? Did the state have to classify all its lands before they were offered for competitive lease? How soon could companies file for non-competitive oil and gas leases? And Chaffin—in common with landmen from other companies—made sure to put in a pitch to Holdsworth for the particular areas his company was interested in.

Holdsworth began assembling a staff to help oversee the Territory's transition into an oil state, though most of the new people knew little about oil leasing. Bureau of Land Management employee Evert Brown was hired as temporary director of the Land Board and charged with organizing the Territory's land and oil and gas records. Holdsworth also hired a former assistant Interior Department solicitor, Bill Dyer, whose first job was to see that all federal mining claims on state land were properly recorded. Unfortunately, Dyer knew even less about oil and gas leasing than Brown. Then Jim Williams, a hardrock miner who knew still less on the subject, was appointed Holdsworth's assistant.

Holdsworth and his people began looking for help. On a trip to San Francisco in November, Holdsworth met with Sig Nielsen, a partner in Chevron's San Francisco law firm of Pillsbury, Madison and Sutro, to discuss Nielsen's earlier offer to help the state draft its oil and gas regulations and lease forms. Meanwhile, Evert Brown visited Texas, Oklahoma, and California to pick up information about their regulations and forms.

STILL HARBORING MISGIVINGS about big oil companies coming to Alaska, Bill Egan on November 8 became Alaska's governor-elect. A week later, Holdsworth announced plans for Land Board hearings December 11 and 12 in Anchorage that would tackle a host of critical issues: leasing regulations, lease forms, competitive versus noncompetitive leasing, offshore leasing, and acreage limitations.

Brown and Dyer were putting together a proposed set of regulations and lease forms for Alaska. Holdsworth forwarded copies of the draft regulations to lawyer Nielsen in San Francisco and to the executive director of the Western Oil and Gas Association (WOGA) in Los Angeles, Henry Wright.

He told Wright that the Brown-Dyer lease form "would be similar to the present federal form now in use, but somewhat simplified." But in fact, the Brown-Dyer lease wasn't anything like the federal lease form.

On January 3, 1959, Ike signed the Statehood Act. Alaskans felt as if, suddenly, they'd been set free.

Brown and Dyer had taken provisions from ten Western and Southwestern state lease forms and thrown them all in the pot. They borrowed royalty provisions from Texas, Colorado, and Wyoming, and the preamble from the State of Washington. The cash consideration recital was taken from New Mexico and Colorado, while bonding provisions were from Utah. The royalty valuation paragraph eventually came from the State of Wyoming, and the verification royalty clause was taken from the Texas school lands lease.

All in all, the Brown-Dyer draft lease was a hodgepodge of disparate ideas and concepts.

As statehood approached, oil was looking bigger and bigger. Governor-elect Egan was publicly predicting oil and gas lease revenues from Alaska's tidelands would allow the new state to reduce its taxes. Chevron announced it would begin a $1 million geophysical study with other major oil companies of submerged lands in Cook Inlet. Almost as an afterthought, Chevron announced that the second well Richfield had drilled at Swanson River had come in with commercial quantities of oil.

EVERYONE EXPECTED A BIG TURNOUT at the Land Board hearings in December 1958. An *Anchorage Daily Times* headline read: "The Land Board Faces Impossible Task."

At the heart of things was the debate over competitive versus noncompetitive leasing. Should a lease on a piece of state oil land go to the person or company that offers the highest price per acre? Or should it simply go at a set price to the person or company that applies for it first?

Irene Ryan, now Senator-elect to the first State Senate, led off the testimony on December 11. Her remarks seemed to reflect the balance that everyone was seeking between what the people of the new state wanted and what the oil companies wanted.

Ryan pointed out that the legislature had agreed to give the Land Board discretion to put up acreage for competitive bid—just what most major oil companies had wanted. And the lawmakers had declined to adopt the Canadian system that let the government reap more of the riches of a successful oil field. Ryan had been resoundingly hooted down by oil company representatives at an earlier Land Board meeting when she suggested Alaska might use the Canadian system in which huge blocks of acreage are offered, half of which reverts to the Crown following a discovery.

But many Alaskans, herself included, wanted a continued opportunity to get in on oil and gas leasing, Ryan testified. They wanted noncompetitive leasing that would let the "little guys" have a chance, and the oil companies knew that, she said.

The oil companies indeed knew which way the wind was blowing. The companies had the cash, and the state needed it; Alaska's little guys didn't have cash, but they voted. The big guys were ready to pay good money for leases, but they didn't have a personal relationship yet with most Alaskans, other than officials like Phil Holdsworth. Most Alaskans, on the other hand, knew their elected officials personally and could make themselves heard. The oil companies knew it was best to tread softly.

Fred Bush, Union Oil's land manager, testified on behalf of twelve West Coast major oil companies on December 11. Bush acknowledged that noncompetitive leasing would encourage more local participation. The more Alaskans participating, the more acceptance of the oil industry by Alaskans, he said.

Bush argued that competitive leasing would probably lead to lower exploration costs. But Irene Ryan's testimony, he said, highlighted the political reality that local residents needed an opportunity to participate in oil leasing.

Richfield weighed in on the same side. "We believe that wildcat lands [unproven oil lands] of the State of Alaska should be leased on a noncompetitive basis to the first qualified applicant," said Richfield lawyer Gordon Goodwin. "We believe that competitive bidding for Alaska wildcat lands would retard development. Costs of operations are already very high and competitive bidding would only increase those costs."

Although most of the major companies came out in favor of noncompetitive leasing, some of them were less than enthusiastic. This first-come, first-served leasing meant that many different people would end up with leases. In most cases, these individual leaseholders weren't interested in drilling for oil; their goal was to assign their lease for cash and royalties to an oil company that

ALASKA STATE LIBRARY

Phil Holdsworth (center) is sworn in as state commissioner of natural resources in 1959 by Lieutenant Governor Hugh Wade as Governor Bill Egan watches. For more than a decade, Holdsworth was a key figure in Alaska's emergence as an oil powerhouse.

would. Not all companies looked forward to the tough chore of gathering individual leases into drillable blocks; some were better at this skill than others.

Exxon, the largest oil company in the world, was the main naysayer. Exxon's local landman, Bob Walker, said his company had neither the experience nor the inclination to bargain for enough individual leaseholds to come up with drillable blocks of acreage. Exxon believed competitive leasing to be more orderly and efficient, Walker said; it creates a more stable business climate. Negotiating directly with governments—rather than with an ungainly mix of individual small leaseholders—was preferable in finding giant-size oil fields. (Later, British Petroleum would say the same thing; its success in dealing directly with Alaska's government officials is an important part of the Alaska oil story.)

Some of Alaska's "little guys" stood up at the Land Board hearing to fight for noncompetitive leasing. They argued that only by increasing the number of participants in the hunt for oil could the state be assured of true competition. The more players, the greater the competition, the greater the public good. If the state offered any of its oil and gas lands competitively, they said, it should be only within the boundaries of a known geologic structure after an actual discovery.

> *Egan banned "fish traps"—the weirs that entrapped salmon at the mouths of streams. No longer would Seattle's fishing interests control Alaska's salmon catch.*

Ever since the discovery of oil in Pennsylvania in the late 1850s, the "big guy versus little guy" scenario had been played out in the Lower 48. Unlike the situation there, however, where the little guys found most of the oil but the big guys ended up owning almost all of it, in Alaska the big guys would find almost all of it and keep it.

At the close of the Land Board hearings, Holdsworth announced a plan that seemed to offer something for everyone. He told the gathering that all state tide and submerged lands would be leased competitively: the highest bidder would get a lease. State uplands, however, except within a known geologic structure, would be leased noncompetitively: anyone could apply for a low per-acre rental and get the lease by being the first in line.

Holdworth's goal was to go after big-company money by holding the state's first competitive oil and gas sale as soon as possible after President Eisenhower signed the Statehood Act, sometime in early 1959. Shortly after the Land Board hearing, Holdsworth told Land Board Director Evert Brown to alert the major oil companies that the state would be looking toward accepting competitive bids on offshore tracts in Cook Inlet, Wide Bay, Yakutat Bay, and Icy Bay.

ALASKANS HEARD TERRIBLE NEWS in mid-December 1958. Governor-elect Egan had been struck with severe abdominal pain and had undergone emergency surgery at the Juneau hospital. The day before Christmas an announcement was made that the governor's inaugural balls—a round of festivities scheduled January 8-22 in Nome, Fairbanks, Anchorage, and Juneau—would have to be postponed.

Egan was too sick to attend statehood signing ceremonies in Washington, D.C. Alaska's last Territorial lieutenant governor, Waino Hendrickson, went to the White House instead.

On January 3, 1959, Ike signed the Statehood Act. Alaskans felt as if, suddenly, they'd been set free. Now, having finally won their battle for independence, would they be able to pay the startup costs for their new government? Would they no longer have to depend on outside financial support? "Big Oil" was now expected to pay much of the bill.

On January 5, from his Juneau hospital bed, Governor Egan first did what he and all other statehood supporters had vowed to do: he banned "fish traps"—the weirs that entrapped salmon at the mouths of streams. No longer would Seattle's fishing interests control Alaska's salmon catch.

The following day, Egan underwent four hours of gall bladder surgery. Friends were no longer allowed to visit him in the hospital. He then suffered an acute pancreatic attack and was flown to Seattle's Virginia Mason Hospital on January 19.

Egan's doctors reported that "for full recovery he needs complete relief from responsibilities." They estimated he would be absent from Juneau for at least three months. Following two hours of emergency surgery to remove a bowel obstruction, doctors at first gave him less than a 50-50 chance of surviving. They didn't know if his heart, liver, and kidneys would hold up; peritonitis set in.

In succeeding days his condition improved, and on January 27 he was allowed to walk for brief periods. Released in a wheelchair from the hospital on February 25, Egan remained in his Seattle apartment for six weeks, when additional gallstone surgery was performed.

Egan returned to Juneau in late April, but further medical problems kept him from fully assuming his gubernatorial duties until the middle of the year. By that time, the major questions concerning oil and gas leasing had been answered by Phil Holdsworth, the state's first commissioner of natural resources, or by the legislature. These decisions were made largely without Egan's input and would add to tension between him and his key oil and gas administrators.

PORTRAIT

PHIL HOLDSWORTH

Probably the most important member of Bill Egan's cabinet was resources commissioner Phil Holdsworth. Congress had granted the state the right to select, within twenty-five years, up to 104 million acres of federal land—land that would become its only real asset. The selection of land and the generation of much of the revenue needed to organize the new government was the responsibility of the commissioner of natural resources.

The new governor and the new commissioner were not close. "Natural resources was the one department where Egan was never comfortable," says Gary Thurlow, Egan's administrative assistant in the days following statehood. "The governor was frustrated with Phil Holdsworth a lot of the time."

"Egan never trusted Phil," Thurlow said. "He was always suspicious of his loyalty." Thurlow thinks Egan distrusted Holdsworth because Holdsworth was a Republican. Egan didn't want to select Holdsworth as commissioner, but was pressured by Senator Irene Ryan and others, with the result that strong politician Egan and equally strong bureaucrat Holdsworth never felt comfortable with each other.

"Phil would come out of Egan's office, thoroughly frustrated," Thurlow said. "He would always ask me: 'What does the governor want?'" Thurlow himself was often frustrated with Egan "because of his Delphic style," a sometimes ambiguous manner.

Chuck Herbert, a close personal friend of Egan's, says the governor "was suspicious of both Phil Holdsworth and, later, Roscoe Bell," the former Bureau of Land Management official picked by Holdsworth as his director of lands.

"The reason for his suspicion was that he thought that the oil companies impressed Holdsworth and Bell too much," Herbert said. The governor believed "oil company executives had them wowed, if you want to put it that way; they could get anything they wanted out of them.

"That was the one reason he [Egan] wanted me to be deputy commissioner." (Herbert became Holdsworth's deputy in 1963 and served as commissioner of natural resources in a later Egan administration.)

Herbert says he didn't share Egan's concerns about Holdsworth and Bell. "Since both were friends of mine and, I think, thoroughly honorable men, I don't think his suspicions were at all well-founded."

John Rader, attorney general under Egan, says Egan's distrust of the state's oil and gas bureaucracy wasn't based on a suspicion that anyone was "double-dealing or feathering their own nests. . . . Instead, Egan would look at some people and think: 'This guy can be manipulated by the oil companies.'"

Holdsworth says the reason he and Egan didn't get along was that "all the commissioners were supposed to contribute $1,000 apiece to Egan's political campaigns, but I always refused. Bill felt I didn't play ball."

Holdsworth says people in the oil industry "respected me. They would all come to me, and I would listen. And if I thought it was right, I'd go to Bill Egan and explain it to him and see what he thought. Bill was so used to having people under him lobbied hard by the industry that he was always very hesitant, very suspicious. But what he did was always for the people of Alaska.

"I never was a guest at dinner hosted by oil companies or legislators," Holdsworth said. "They'd want to wine and dine me, but I refused." His alternative was to sometimes have major players over to his house for something to eat. "When it came down to a meal, I'd call [wife] Peggy and I'd walk in with about six guys. She'd have that spread out for them in no time at all. I don't know whether they really understood that was the way I did business."

One dinner guest at Phil and Peggy Holdsworth's Juneau home in January 1959 after a regulations hearing was Union Oil landman Bill Thompson. Thompson afterward wrote his boss, Fred Bush: "Phil Holdsworth is highly respected and very influential with the legislature. He also demonstrated his interest in cooperating fully with the oil industry."

In the letter to Bush, Thompson also advised on strategy for dealing with the legislature. He said he thought Chevron would make a serious mistake if it retained the Juneau law firm that represented lobbyist "Fish" Arnold and the canned-salmon industry. Statehood had been mostly about abolishing fish traps, Thompson said, and he sensed bitter feelings in the legislature toward outside fishing interests—feelings that could rub off on oil companies.

"This could possibly create a very serious problem for the entire oil industry," Thompson wrote.

"The oil industry should, at this particular time, tread very lightly and consider, very carefully, their every move in Alaska. I feel certain that at least some of the legislature, and possibly the Central Labor Council, would utilize this type of information [oil linked with salmon] in future attacks on the oil industry."

Chapter 8

Who's Minding the Storehouse?

n January 1959, Governor Egan had told resources commissioner Phil Holdsworth to get moving as quickly as possible with the first state oil and gas lease sale of submerged lands. The Swanson River discovery had greatly enhanced the value of Cook Inlet offshore lands, Egan believed, and now seemed the best time to take advantage of the momentum.

Holdsworth also hoped to move quickly. For him, managing public land meant making as much of it as possible available as early as possible. If the price was reasonable, he knew the mineral prospector could go about his business of finding an ore body, and oil seemed no different. The cornerstone of any mineral business was the availability of land. Without it, the exploration business in Alaska couldn't prosper.

Holdsworth thought the first sale might be held as early as July, but he soon realized there was a lot of work ahead in finalizing regulations and lease forms. The sale might have to wait until September. It would be December before the sale was held.

It became increasingly obvious to Holdsworth that he and his staff lacked the knowledge to draft the critical forms. Bill Dyer, on Holdsworth's staff, was working on the issues, but in February, Holdsworth began receiving a rash of confusing memos and questions from Dyer:

111

Where was the seaward boundary between federal and State of Alaska land? How did federal land regulations affect Alaska's right to select state land? Should the state issue geophysical permits? Would it be best if the Bureau of Land Management took over management of state oil and gas leasing, at least temporarily?

While Holdsworth considered these questions, the BLM each month began issuing 2 million acres of federal oil and gas leases in Alaska, effectively taking the land out of the selection reach of the state.

More questions: Senator Ernest Gruening of Alaska had introduced a bill in Congress that would give homesteaders on the Kenai Peninsula their mineral rights; should Holdsworth support the bill? What about the bill by Alaska's other U.S. senator, Bob Bartlett, to open the Navy's North Slope petroleum reserve area (known as Pet-4) to private exploration? Who should draft the state's oil and gas leasing regulations and lease forms? Certainly not Bill Dyer.

To Holdsworth—with a background in hard-rock mining, not oil—it seemed only logical to turn to the people who knew about oil and gas. The state government itself had no experts. What few petroleum geologists and petroleum engineers there were in Alaska were working for oil companies or in the federal bureaucracy. Holdsworth asked for money to hire a petroleum geologist and a petroleum engineer, plus a technical adviser for the state's Oil and Gas Conservation Commission. But progress was slow; he didn't get his first petroleum geologist until August 1960.

The fact of the matter was that Holdsworth knew little about the value of the resource he was about to sell or how to offer it for sale. He realized that only after a discovery might he have some idea of the value of the resource. Until then, the only way to know was by use of the competitive marketplace, and by drilling.

Holdsworth was well acquainted with people in the oil business. At Interstate Oil Compact Commission meetings since 1953, he had been meeting with employees of West Coast major oil companies and officials of WOGA. These companies, the likely primary bidders for Alaska's oil and gas lands, had the expertise the state lacked. Holdsworth decided to ask their advice on leasing. Why not have those who understand leasing provisions help to draft them?

Late the previous year, Holdsworth already had asked the opinion of the oil and gas association on regulations and lease forms drafted by Bill Dyer and Land Board Director Evert Brown. On March 11 the association's lease subcommittee came out with a report on the Brown-Dyer lease form. The group called for thirty-four changes.

Among its changes, the subcommittee inserted after the word "value" in the Brown-Dyer competitive lease form the phrase "at the well"; the revised form now read: "the Lessee [the oil company] hereby agrees to pay the Lessor [the state] the field market price or value *at the well* of all royalty oil produced or saved." The revised draft also directed the state to pay the cleaning and dehydration costs of all royalty oil. These changes, later incorporated by the state, would become central issues in a billion-dollar royalty pricing lawsuit filed by the state in 1977 against oil producers—the Amerada Hess lawsuit.

> *Holdsworth hoped to move quickly. For him, managing public land meant making as much of it as possible available as early as possible.*

In April, Holdsworth again turned to the oil companies for help. The state still had not finalized its lease documents. Holdsworth wrote to Paul Home, San Francisco land manager for Chevron and chairman of the public lands committee of WOGA.

It's imperative, he told Home, "that the regulations and lease form . . . be prepared by someone more familiar with the requirements and necessities of the industry than anyone presently available in Alaska." Did Home know anyone who could work with Holdsworth for two months to prepare for public hearings on the documents?

Home soon called to say Chevron and the oil and gas association would be happy to help and believed they had someone for the job.

CHEVRON'S LAW FIRM—Pillsbury, Madison and Sutro—could make available a lawyer named Jim Wanvig. If the State of Alaska could pay his transportation costs and $2,500 a month fees, WOGA member companies would pay his in-state personal expenses.

A graduate in philosophy and geology from the University of Minnesota, Wanvig had taught oil and gas law at the University of California at Berkeley. At the law firm, Wanvig had recently completed a draft for the oil and gas association of California's new offshore leasing regulations. He seemed a perfect choice for the Alaska job.

Holdsworth sent Paul Home a proposed Wanvig employment agreement. Wanvig, not a member of the Alaska bar, would be officially hired as a "technical consultant." The agreement said the hiring was based "upon recommendation and approval of WOGA." Chevron lawyer Sig Nielsen suggested deleting the phrase because "the words could have potential future adverse implications . . . ."

Wanvig's job description was straightforward: to write the state's first oil and gas leasing regulations and lease forms. On May 12 Holdsworth flew from Juneau to Anchorage to welcome Wanvig to Alaska.

> ### The fact of the matter was that resources commissioner Holdsworth knew little about the value of the resource he was about to sell or how to offer it for sale.

Wanvig hoped to complete a first draft of the regulations right away—by June 1. He told Holdsworth he felt his most important task was to make the documents explicit enough so the state would be saved from future revenue losses through voided leases and litigation.

On the advice of "technical consultant" Wanvig, Holdsworth made two far-reaching decisions that would affect the price the state would receive for its oil.

First, he said the state, not producers, should in effect pay for the cost of transporting oil from offshore Cook Inlet wells to land before it was tankered to West Coast refineries. The companies could deduct platform-to-shore charges before making their royalty payments to the state. Second, the point at which the value of the state's royalty oil should be determined was outside Alaska. It was to be "netted back" from the price paid at the refinery. This netting back—subtracting the cost of transporting the oil from the wellhead to the refinery—to determine the oil's value was realistic, Holdsworth believed, because most Cook Inlet oil would be refined on the West Coast.

By June 1, prodigious worker Wanvig completed his first draft of the regulations and the competitive lease form. He told Holdsworth he had drafted the documents to be "attractive to the oil industry and still protect the legitimate interests of the State."

Wanvig used aspects of the Brown-Dyer draft lease and the WOGA's royalty lease in coming up with his own form. From the State of Colorado's royalty pricing provision, he took the phrase "at the well"—which also was part of the association's proposed form. Wanvig said he included "at the well" in order to add "certainty and objectivity" in determining the value of Alaska's royalty oil; it would "reduce ambiguity and the risk of litigation in the future." In the end, however, it did anything but.

"In order to attract the oil industry and stimulate drilling and generate large bids for competitive leases," Wanvig told Holdsworth, "it was important to draft a lease form that the oil industry could understand and find reasonable."

IT WAS PERHAPS NOT SURPRISING that a lease form drafted by Wanvig would be one the oil industry "could understand and find reasonable." Wanvig had an obvious conflict of interest. On loan to the State of Alaska, he was an employee of a law firm that received 30 percent of its business from an oil company (Chevron) that would be subject to the lease forms he was drafting. WOGA, whose members thought Wanvig's draft should follow their own, were paying his expenses.

The association billed each of its members in September for a share of Wanvig's Alaska expenses. Association secretary Henry Wright told members that the group's support of Wanvig's work had been an "excellent opportunity to be of service to the State of Alaska, not to mention facing the possibility of having the rules and regulations drafted by less than competent personnel."

Ruling on Cook Inlet field costs in a 1978 royalty lawsuit, Alaska Supreme Court Justice Alan Compton said the state's hiring of Wanvig was like having "a fox in the chicken coop." Later, responding in a deposition to Compton's remark, Wanvig replied: "The state got exactly what it was looking for."

WHILE HOLDSWORTH was wrestling with the problems of preparing for lease sales, the state legislature had moved forward with amendments to the Alaska Land Act. The amendments unanimously approved March 19 would have an important bearing on who would get leases and how much they would pay.

The amendments provided for competitive leasing on known or producing geologic structures or on land located "in the same general area of a discovery well capable of producing commercial oil or gas." Also to be offered by competitive bidding would be lands lying seaward three miles of mean high tide, University of Alaska lands, and Mental Health lands. All other state land was to be leased by noncompetitive over-the-counter filing or noncompetitive drawings.

Existing federal oil and gas lease applications would be given a state priority. The term for both competitive and noncompetitive leases would be ten years.

Since the state couldn't take possession of the federal land it was selecting until it had been surveyed, the law created conditional leases that would go into effect when the state took title. Meanwhile, lessees could act on conditional leases as if they had been surveyed and issued.

And in order to encourage oil exploration in the new state, the Land Act promised an attractive incentive. Discoverers of commercial quantities of petroleum on state lease lands would pay a royalty of only 5 percent for the first ten years instead of the customary 12-1/2 percent.

ON JULY 9, EXACTLY AT 9 A.M., in the basement of Anchorage's Loussac Library at Fifth Avenue and F Street in Anchorage, public hearings on consultant Wanvig's oil and gas regulations and lease forms began. The hearing was called by Phil Holdsworth as chairman of the Alaska Oil and Gas Conservation Commission.

Entering through the F Street front door, people turned left past shelves partially filled with books and periodicals, went down a flight of broad linoleum-covered stairs, took a sharp right, and entered through double doors into a large unadorned room. The weekly meetings of the Anchorage City Council were held in the hall, which could comfortably seat about fifty people.

On the morning of the ninth, behind the long, wooden table across the far end of the room, were seated Phil Holdsworth, Jim Wanvig, and Roscoe Bell. As the new lands director, Bell's first task was to chair this oil and gas regulation hearing. "It was a full house of oil company representatives," Bell recalled later.

Exxon landman Bob Walker testified, as he had the previous year before the Land Board, that his company saw no need for noncompetitive leasing in Alaska. All state land should be offered by competitive bid. And once again, most other major oil company spokesmen went the other way, testifying that their outfits supported noncompetitive leasing. And, of course, the independents did too.

Random questions and comments came from individual audience members, interrupting as they saw fit. Is the state planning to classify its land? If so, how much will be classified? How will the state treat existing federal leases? How does it plan to survey tracts before they are offered for lease? What will the size of the tracts be? Can a company bid for multiple tracts? What kind of bids will be allowed—sealed? oral? royalty? sliding scale? What if a bidder fails to pay the balance of the bonus within thirty days? To whom can one appeal the land director's decision?

Lawyer Jim Wanvig had an obvious conflct of interest. On loan to the State of Alaska, he was an employee of a law firm that received 30 percent of its business from an oil company that would be subject to the state lease forms he was drafting.

Attending the session for my Alaska Scouting Service, I had a question of my own: Does the state plan to reproduce and publish the electric logs and other well drilling information? I hoped we could reproduce the drilling logs and sell copies to oil companies. And this is eventually just what we did.

For nearly eight hours, Wanvig, Bell, and sometimes Holdsworth tried to answers these and other questions. One important topic never surfaced. No comments were made and no questions asked about the royalty provisions in Wanvig's competitive lease form.

When the hearings ended, the oilmen emerged from the darkened basement into the bright evening sun and quickly repaired to the Club Paris on Fifth Avenue or to the Chart Room two blocks over for some serious drinking. The hardiest made their way east, out to the end of Fourth Avenue to the Last Chance for drinks with the "B-girls." Meanwhile, Bell recalls, he and Wanvig and Holdsworth "had some long sessions about the suggestions made at the hearing." They made few changes, however, in Wanvig's regulations and lease forms.

Before returning to his regular job in San Francisco, Wanvig again reviewed the state's lease forms and the other documents he had worked on. Later, he wrote to Holdsworth suggesting some further changes in lease language. Holdsworth sent copies of the revisions to the oil companies for comment. A few minor changes were made, and on September 15, 1959, Alaska's first oil and gas regulations and lease forms became effective.

On October 14, Assistant Attorney General Joe Rudd wrote to Wanvig, asking for advice on a matter involving navigable waters. Turner McBain, a partner at Wanvig's law firm, replied that Wanvig could no longer advise the state, "because of a potential conflict of interests."

BILL EGAN WAS FIRMLY BACK in the governor's chair by mid-1959. He had been too sick during the first part of the year to become involved in Holdsworth's hiring of his lands director, Roscoe Bell. Bell, former assistant director of the Bureau of Land Management in Washington, D.C., had come to Holdsworth's attention when he compiled a report in 1954 on the status of oil and gas exploration in the Territory. Egan's relationship with Bell, as with Holdsworth, turned out to be less than rosy.

"There was no love between Egan and Roscoe," Holdsworth says. "Bill Egan didn't want to move so fast. Although he was a good manager and a good land man, Roscoe was kind of a promoter type."

Bell would corral Egan at the Anchorage airport when the governor came to town. "This teed Bill off. Bell would jump the gun by going over my head, and this habit of going around me and getting publicity for himself annoyed Bill."

Herb Lang, then the state's real estate officer, thinks Bell was a good administrator. "When a policy determination had to be made, he would tell everyone about it, lay out all the alternatives, and send people out in all directions to come back with their recommendations. He ran it more like a private business. He and Holdsworth put all of Alaska's land system together."

It was Holdsworth's and Bell's oil and gas leasing policy all right, but it was Egan's personal relationship with them that shaped the attitude of the state toward the oil industry in those early years.

During the summer of 1959, eighteen oil companies opened offices in Anchorage. A Cities Service geological survey crew began operating in Alaska, and British-American Oil Company took leases in the upper Susitna Valley. By late 1959, Chevron's daily oil production at Swanson River had reached 650 barrels. If production expanded as expected, Chevron planned to put in a pipeline from the oil field to a marine terminal twenty-two miles away at Nikiski.

THE WAY WAS NOW CLEAR for the State of Alaska's long-anticipated first competitive sale of oil leases. Holdsworth told Egan the sale would probably

D.J. MILLER/U.S. GEOLOGICAL SURVEY

Phillips Petroleum Icy Bay drill site on the eastern shore of Gulf of Alaska in 1954.

bring in about half a million dollars. The new state government needed the money, and the oil companies were eager to spend it.

The big surprise at the December 10 sale came when bids were opened on offshore tracts at Wide Bay. For years, Shell geologists had studied and closely mapped the area. In 1954, the company had acquired federal land leases there, and now that offshore leases were being offered by the state, Shell was expected to be high bidder. But Phillips Petroleum, not Shell, picked up the tracts. Phillips bid more than $1 million. For the same tracts, Shell's bid was $56,000.

Union Oil and its partner, Marathon, were bidding on tracts along the eastern shore of Cook Inlet, just south of Kenai at Kalifonsky. In late May of that year, the partners had discovered a huge natural gas field at Kalifonsky, followed in October by a confirmation well. As the December sale approached, a third well was suspended so that Union and Marathon could keep the geologic information to themselves.

For the middle 2,000-acre parcel of the three Kalifonsky tracts, Union and Marathon jointly bid $1 million. For the same tract, Chevron and Richfield bid only $6,000. As oilmen would say, Union and Marathon left $1 million "on the table"—but in so doing they captured enough natural gas to be able to furnish Anchorage with marketable heat for the next half century. Each of the three gas wells turned out to be capable of producing up to 31 million cubic feet per day of natural gas unassociated with oil, ideally suited for domestic use.

Union's bidding had its funny side. Phillips Petroleum had added 66 cents on the end of each of its bids, calling attention to its "Phillips 66" trade name. With each Phillips bid, lands director Roscoe Bell dutifully called out the dollar amount, followed by "and 66 cents." When Bell began reading Union Oil's bids on the Kalifonsky tracts, he called out the dollar amount, then added "and no cents." After a while, Union's local manager, Charlie Smith, asked Bell if it "might be that the public would think Union's bids make `no sense?'" Henceforth, Bell read only the dollar amount.

Holdsworth turns out to have been way off in his estimate of proceeds from this first state sale. He had expected half a million dollars. The oil companies bid $4 million. Egan directed Holdsworth to plan a second sale as soon as possible. Bell announced shortly afterward that a sale would be held early in the new year.

PART II:
TRANSFORMATION

"I love exploration."
— Oilman Harry Jamison

North Slope

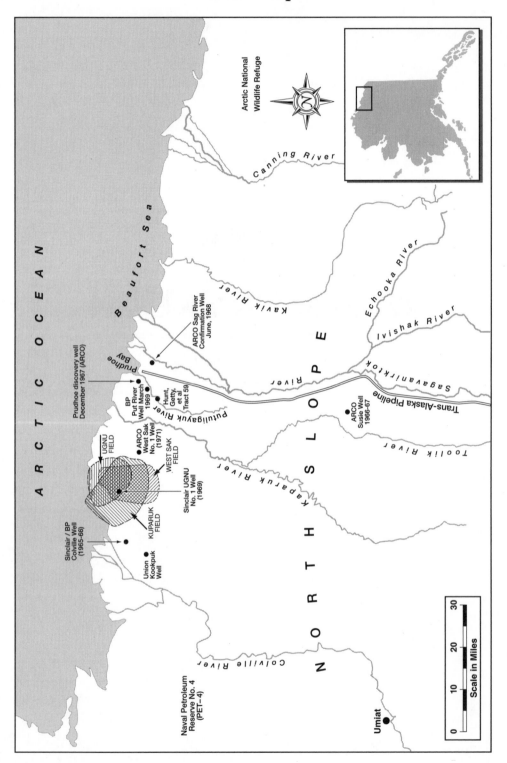

Chapter 9

British Petroleum Looks North

I n the summer of 1958, just six months before Alaska statehood, Anchorage had about 40,000 people (including those at the two military bases), three banks, two movie theaters, streets that were mostly unpaved, and a total of two buildings that stood higher than three stories. Visiting oilmen found entertainment at a number of drinking establishments or chose from the likes of the Oasis Club out on the Seward Highway or the Last Chance at the east end of Fifth Avenue. That summer, with the appearance of British Petroleum, the oil scene in Alaska changed permanently.

The chain of events leading to BP's examination of Alaska's oil potential began in March 1951 with the assassination of the prime minister of Iran, General Ali Razmara. A month later, Dr. Mohammed Mosaddeq nationalized the Iranian oil fields and rejected negotiations between British Petroleum and the National Iranian Oil Company. BP suspended its Iranian operations, terminated 70,000 Iranian employees, and pulled out. In so doing, it lost two-thirds of its worldwide production and refining capacity.

"Within weeks of being forced out of Iran," writes Bryan Cooper in his 1972 book *Alaska—The Last Frontier*, "a group of BP geologists . . . got together to prepare a world survey of oil prospects based on their knowledge of the sedimentary basins in various regions. These were graded according to the likelihood of oil being present.

123

"The survey was completed early in 1952 for consideration by Peter Cox, then head of BP's exploration department. . . . Amongst the several hundred places given a number one grading was the North Slope of Alaska, primarily because of the discovery of the Umiat oil field just announced by the U.S. Navy. BP's geologists noted that on Alaska's North Slope there were geologic structures of Middle East size, measuring 72,000 square miles, larger than BP's entire Iranian concession." Here was a place where "giants" might be found.

Retired BP geologist Roger Herrera tells a wonderful story about Peter Cox flying over the North Slope in the early 1950s. "It was one of those beautiful clear days," Herrera said. "He looked down, and what he saw below him was Persia [Iran]. Absolutely. He saw the foothills of the Zagreb mountains underneath him, and he couldn't believe it. He said, 'This is exactly the same. It's got to be the same. It's got to be full of oil.'"

But at that time, Bryan Cooper writes, "the area was too remote to be given serious attention, and in any case there were more worthwhile opportunities elsewhere. Alaska was for the time being forgotten."

The Iranian loss was temporarily remedied by increasing crude output in Iraq and Kuwait and building new refineries. Then the Shah of Iran regained his throne in 1954, and BP reentered the country as 40 percent owner of the Iranian Oil Consortium.

The 1956 Suez crisis and President Eisenhower's oil "import quotas" (to help U.S. independents) were reminders of BP's need to get its own crude oil reserves in the United States or stand to lose its prominent world position in oil. So, again, BP looked north.

DURING THE SUMMER OF 1958, a British Petroleum geologic field party surveyed surface indications of potential giant oil fields in the northern foothills of Alaska's Brooks Range. A report to London indicated huge anticlines on the North Slope. That fall, as Bill Egan campaigned to become the state's first governor, the BP geologists recommended acquisition of a modest amount of land on the Slope's foothills area, and London agreed.

Also that summer, BP geologist William Allan C. Russell and Sinclair Oil Corporation geophysicist Arthur L. Bowsher spent two weeks in Alaska to estimate the Territory's petroleum potential. Sinclair, a large U.S. independent that was short on crude oil, had already leased in Cook Inlet. To explore effectively on the isolated North Slope, it needed a partner. Sinclair's domestic exploration manager, Loren Ware, believed the North Slope could contain the crude oil reserves so desperately needed by his company. It could also give BP, then owner of nearly 20 percent of the world's crude oil supply, an entree into the U.S. market.

Following his joint survey with Sinclair's Bowsher, Russell recommended to London that BP share in Sinclair's cost of acquiring U.S. Geological Survey data on Naval Petroleum Reserve No. 4 (Pet-4) on the North Slope. A few months later the two companies signed a joint exploration agreement for Alaska.

OIL INTEREST FOCUSED ON THE NORTH SLOPE in 1958 with the Interior Department's plans to lease more than 4 million acres near Umiat in the central North Slope. In the late 1940s, the Navy had discovered a natural gas field at Gubik, near Umiat, and the U.S. government wanted the surrounding acreage to be offered to private operators.

The Interior Department planned to accept competitive bids on 16,000 acres at Umiat, but the bulk of the land would be offered through a subsequent non-competitive oil and gas lease drawing.

The competitive lease sale on 16,000 acres turned out to be a non-event. When the

A winning personal style boosted geologist Geoff Larminie in his work as Alaska manager for British Petroleum. Larminie credits BP's vast experience in seeking out big oil fields in isolated locations with much of the company's phenomenal Alaska success. (1991 photo)

envelopes were opened in early September, no major oil companies had bid. Only a few small companies and individuals put in bids, and they were low. Umiat was oil, but it was a small field. Everyone was waiting to get in on the lease drawing for the 4 million acres, where big oil prospects lurked.

One month later, the Interior Department held its drawing on 1,300 tracts. Major oil companies, independents, and individuals filed more than 7,000 applications in the 4-million-acre drawing. British Petroleum and Sinclair Oil were among the companies looking to pick up acreage.

Charlie Barnes and I filed applications in the drawing, as "nominees" for Sinclair. Charlie had made a verbal agreement with Sinclair's Loren Ware that we would file for as many parcels as possible and that we would assign to Sinclair any leases we won. The deal was that Sinclair would reimburse us for our filing fees and first-year rental charges and pay us 10 cents for every acre we won.

> *Nominees—the people who agreed to sell their leases—and the oil companies never put their agreement in writing. A simple handshake, a meeting of the minds, was all it took.*

It was a great situation. We stood to make good money on any leases we won in the drawing. And we couldn't be hurt much by applications of ours that weren't drawn, because our applications and certified rental checks would be returned to us immediately. We'd be out only a few dollars in interest on the money we would be borrowing to make the whole thing go in the first place.

With only Loren Ware's oral commitment, Charlie and I marched into the First National Bank to see our banker, Bill Renfro. Neither Charlie nor I had ever borrowed more than $5,000. Straight off, we asked to borrow to the bank's legal loan limit of $125,000. Evidencing no apparent surprise, Renfro quietly excused himself, probably to phone his good customer Loren Ware. Returning, he said we could borrow the full amount.

Renfro didn't even talk with the bank's president, Dan Cuddy. He knew Cuddy wanted to catch up with the oil loans being made by Elmer Rasmuson's National Bank of Alaska. When he learned about us, Cuddy said it was a "crazy deal," but he wanted to cooperate with Sinclair, so he let our loan go through.

We began preparing lease forms. The description of the land had to be typed on the outside of each application envelope, with a $10 check covering the filing fee attached. Inside was the certified check to cover the first-year rental fee of 50 cents an acre. By October 1 we had spent the entire $125,000. Applications were in my name and the names of our secretary Shirley Craig and local consulting petroleum geologist Tom Marshall.

At the drawing, forty of our lease applications were picked, and we assigned them to Sinclair, as agreed. We made more than $10,000! For two little guys in 1958, that was big money—enough to let us begin a title insurance company and some serious oil and gas leasing. (Charlie was a Yaleman, too, so we named our leasing company Ivy, Inc.)

British Petroleum also came out of the drawing with some lease land. Writing in BP's in-house publication *BP Shield,* chief geologist P. E. Kent says that George Jenkinson, an American and former vice president of Pan-American Oil, residing in Alberta, Canada, acted on BP's behalf at the drawing, serving as its nominee. Jenkinson won leases covering 55,000 acres and assigned them to BP.

THE 1958 LEASE DRAWING on the North Slope highlights the delicate and critical importance of the "nominee" system in Alaska's oil story. A nominee is simply a person who agrees before filing to assign his or her leases to an oil company at a prearranged price.

Major oil companies make these deals with individuals in order to increase their odds of acquiring certain acreage. They also use nominees in order to keep their acreage totals a secret from competitors. The main reason for using nominees, however, is to quietly exceed acreage limitations set by the government.

Bureau of Land Management regulations require full disclosure of all interests in a lease application when it is filed with the land office. This rule is meant to keep oil companies from exceeding acreage limits. Most major oil companies in Alaska used nominees in the '50s and '60s—and as far as I know, no nominee in Alaska ever bothered to observe the rule requiring disclosure of the oil company that would eventually get the lease.

The BLM never raised questions about the obvious infraction of the rules, even though land office personnel were well aware of who was leasing for whom. A quiet policy of "Don't ask, don't tell" seemed to suit everybody just fine.

Regulations also called for company and individual leaseholders to periodically report their total acreage to the government. A nominee's interest (usually a small overriding royalty) is not disclosed until the nominee turns the lease over to the oil company and the lease assignment is filed in the land office—often months after the original leasing has taken place. In the meantime, the company controls acreage long before the government officially knows about it.

Nominees, usually former company landmen turned lease brokers, used relatives, employees, and friends to file applications. (My partner Charlie Barnes was a former landman for Shell.) The nominee and the oil company never put their agreement in writing. A simple handshake, a meeting of the minds, was all it took. The nominee filed for leases and promised to sell resulting acreage to the company at a fixed price, usually plus a small royalty on any oil found, and the company promised to pay. The royalty was often so small—say, one quarter of 1 percent—that the company didn't mind making the nominee "rich" if oil was discovered later.

San Francisco lease broker Daniel J. Pickerell says Chevron used him in Alaska during the mid and late 1950s. He said his leaseholder group alone held more than a million acres in Alaska during that period, well over the statutory acreage limitation.

"My arrangement with Chevron was based on just a handshake, because they trusted me," Pickerell said. "I acted as their undercover agent. They paid me 25 cents an acre above my costs, plus a 1 percent overriding royalty. In return Chevron got an exclusive right to explore on my land." Like everyone else, Pickerell and Chevron ignored the disclosure requirements.

BRITISH PETROLEUM CAME TO ALASKA to stay in 1959. On April 1, 1959, BP made its first direct filings for open noncompetitive federal land on the North Slope, looking to add to the leases it had acquired the previous year from George Jenkinson. In November, BP opened its first office in Alaska, transferring geologist T. A. D. W. "Tim" Hillyard and secretary Ruby Reid Waterton from Calgary, Alberta, Canada, to Anchorage.

An archetypal "Brit"—a master of understatement, with great aplomb—Tim Hillyard quickly got to know Anchorage businessmen by inviting them to a cocktail party at his home near the corner of 10th and G Street. Roger Herrera claims Hillyard was so underpaid during his first year in Alaska that his family subsisted solely on the salmon Hillyard caught in nearby streams.

Wearing knickers and looking every bit like what Alaskans thought a British oilman should look like—worldly, but somewhat odd—Hillyard walked down the sidewalks of Anchorage wearing a deerstalker hat, carrying the *London Times,* and smiling graciously at curious onlookers. This glimpse of the "foreigner" suggested to Alaskans that here was someone different enough from Americans that he and his organization might help them in their struggle against a sort of "colonialism" still being practiced by the U.S. government.

> *Wearing knickers and looking every bit like what Alaskans thought a British oilman should look like—worldly, but somewhat odd—Tim Hillyard walked down the sidewalks of Anchorage wearing a deerstalker hat, carrying the* London Times, *and smiling graciously.*

"We used to talk about that," says one of Hillyard's Alaska successors, geologist F. G. "Geoff" Larminie. "There was a very significant degree of support for BP people in Alaska, because Alaskans were basically saying to the federal government, 'You have neglected Alaska for so bloody long and here comes a foreign operation, they move in, they are operating in a big way, nuts to you. If they can see what's happening, why can't you idiots in Washington realize just how important this state is?'

"It was a powerful weapon in the hands of many people. They could say: . . .'Look. You've got a foreign oil company here. It's operating in a progressively bigger way. It's investing in Alaska. Why is the bloody federal government still neglecting the place?"

By September 1960, BP and Sinclair's combined total North Slope acreage amounted to more than a quarter million acres. The following year—now with an office in the Denali Building on Fourth Avenue, down the hall from our Ivy, Inc.—BP and Sinclair began to assemble several huge drilling blocks on the northern flank of the Brooks Range in preparation for seismic surveys and drilling.

Richfield, Shell, Chevron, Amoco, and Texaco also were assembling large leaseblocks on the North Slope by the early 1960s. Most of them had placed geologic parties in the field. BP even tried to extend its survey to do geophysical work in the newly established Arctic National Wildlife Refuge in the far northeast corner of the state. Despite support from Alaska's Congressional delegation, the Interior Department said no.

GEOFF LARMINIE, as BP's manager in Alaska, had a winning style. Author Bryan Cooper describes him as "a shrewd, impish Dubliner who has been to many strange corners of the world in search for oil." A graduate of Dublin's illustrious Trinity College, Larminie thinks one of the reasons BP did so well in Alaska is that all its people were trained for foreign exploration.

"We were used to looking for oil in places where you had to bring in all your materials," he says. "You couldn't go down the road, or call up the service company to get your drill pipe, or get your mud and all the rest delivered to you. We were used to the long-range planning aspects of operating in an area with no communications, no sources of supply. Alaska was absolutely in that category. . . .

"Another reason I think we did so well," Larminie says, "was our tradition of looking for big oil fields. It was very clear that if we found a large volume high-pressure oil field on the Slope, we would have to go south to water, so we did a quick survey in 1962, drew lines on a map about where the pipeline would go from the Slope, and proceeded to drill."

Larminie won favor with an appealing manner of dealing with Alaskans. Unlike so many U.S. oil company employees, he was

> *"There was a very significant degree of support for BP people in Alaska, because Alaskans were basically saying to the federal government, 'You have neglected Alaska for so bloody long and here comes a foreign operation, they move in, they are operating in a big way, nuts to you.'"*
>
> —Geoff Larminie

130

open and fun to talk with. I remember a lunch at the Black Angus Meat Market restaurant on Fireweed Lane, where he delighted in showing me photographs of the northern foothills of the Brooks Range and placing them side-by-side with photos of Iran's Zagreb Mountains. Eagerly pointing to the striking similarities, he said confidently that "oil reserves on Alaska's North Slope will someday match those of Iran's." Larminie further endeared himself to Anchoragites by lecturing in Anchorage high schools on Charles Dickens.

With the wit and grace of people like Hillyard and Larminie (plus some luck), the Crown's Alaska success story was well on its way.

INSIDE STORY ▌

THE BP SEARCH

The oil explorers of British Petroleum were scouring the North Slope as the '60s began. Roger Herrera remembers the exhilaration of those days, when a series of crews kept the search going twenty hours a day, seven days a week. "I thrived on it," he said. "It was fantastic."

Herrera, an Oxford University geology graduate student at the time, was a member of BP's North Slope field party in the summer of 1960.

"We had a little Bell G2 helicopter, and we also had a Piper Cub on floats, because the lakes were sufficiently melted around the edges to land on the water. We had four geologists, three geological assistants, and the cook in the camp. The idea was that the geologist and assistant would work as a pair.

"We would set up base camp on the edge of a lake, and operate in a thirty-mile radius, which was a half-hour flight for the G2 Bell. The helicopter would take us thirty miles out and drop us off. We would walk all day, mapping and looking at rocks. Then we would be picked up in the evening, if we were lucky.

"They were long days. The first party would be dropped on the ground at seven in the morning and would be picked up at seven at night. That's how it went, seven days a week, week in and week out. The only respite would be if the fog came in and the helicopter couldn't fly."

Did BP's 1960 field party know that it was looking at a world-class petroleum province on the North Slope?

Yes and no, Herrera says. "We started off in the Brooks Range because we assumed the foothills were full of oil. It wasn't until wells were drilled in 1963 and '64 that that mistake was realized."

Herrera says that when he joined BP in 1960, the company's concept of exploration "was radically different than, say, for example, a company like Texaco. Until a Texaco geologist or geophysicist in the United States had been in the country for five years, he simply wasn't earning his salary. They thought it took him that time to amass the detailed knowledge which they thought was essential to find oil."

BP's attitude by contrast, says Herrera, was that "after someone had been in a place two years you had to get rid of him. Get him out of there, because he ceased to look at the big picture. And, at that time, BP was interested only in the big picture."

Herrera, who now heads the oil industry's effort to open a portion of the Arctic National Wildlife Refuge to drilling, recalls experiences that led him to believe development need not mean destruction of the environment.

As a child in Wales, Herrera would visit his grandfather's house in the southern coal fields. "The river that ran near his house was black," he says. "There wasn't a living thing in it, because of the coal dust. I remember playing cricket on the side of the river, and the ball kept going into the water. You couldn't see it because the river was so black. . . .

"Those rivers are running sparkling clean now. Vegetation has grown back where it was obviously incapable of growing. It is amazing how they have transformed the whole area." He believes that the coastal plain of Alaska's North Slope can likewise be eventually restored to its original condition after oil drilling.

ROGER HERRERA

In 1963, geologist Roger Herrera was in on the exciting early days of BP's North Slope exploration, where a series of teams was at work 20 hours a day, every day.

Chapter 10

Unwrapping the Arctic

Bryan Cooper, in *Alaska—The Last Frontier,* describes the North Slope as "a desolate region, far north of the tree line, the rocks on the hillsides broken down by the perennial frost into dismal grey acres." Joe McGinniss in *Going to Extremes* calls it "that part of North America which could make you believe that the earth was indeed flat and that, at last, you had come to its edge."

Into this other-worldly landscape the oil companies began pouring their energies. Field work in the Arctic foothills of the Brooks Range revealed large geologic structures readily obvious even without seismic surveys. Equipment to drill the first wells on federal leases there was mobilized in the spring of 1963. Governor Egan had not yet decided on selecting land for the new state, so the entire North Slope was still owned by the U.S. government.

In mid-July, British Petroleum and Sinclair Oil were the prime movers in developing the Gubik Unit No. 1 well near Umiat in the central North Slope. They made use of a Navy drilling rig left over from the days of federal exploration of Naval Petroleum Reserve No. 4 (Pet-4).

"All they did was put a few new batteries in it and fire it up," says retired BP geologist Roger Herrera. The natural gas well was completed in November 1963, and the dream of furnishing Gubik gas to Fairbanks through a pipeline from the Slope was momentarily resurrected.

In late 1963, BP and Sinclair brought a Canadian drill rig down the Mackenzie River 2,000 miles to the Arctic Ocean, and early that winter floated it to the mouth of the Colville River on the upper North Slope. The rig was loaded onto trucks and hauled sixty miles to Umiat, there to begin drilling at East Umiat and Little Twist.

At the same time, BP and Sinclair conducted a seismic grid survey of the Arctic coastal plain between the Colville River and the Canning River to the east. They uncovered a huge subsurface structure lying beneath the Colville River delta and a smaller structure near Prudhoe Bay.

THE STORY OF RICHFIELD OIL COMPANY'S SEARCH for North Slope oil reflects the heady excitement of closing in on one of the world's great oil fields. Discoverer of Alaska's first substantial oil deposits—at Swanson River on the Kenai Peninsula—Richfield was now poised on the edge of something much bigger.

Most of Richfield's geologic work on the Slope during the 1961 and '62 seasons had been in the foothills area, but in the summer of 1963 its crew had

Richfield geologists Gil Mull (left) and Gar Pessel were in on some of the exciting North Slope explorations of the early 1960s that pointed the way to the Prudhoe discovery.

worked toward the upper Slope, south of Prudhoe Bay.

Richfield geologist Charles G. "Gil" Mull recalls how he and the rest of the crew moved closer and closer to the Slope's oil riches.

"We started in the Umiat area in

GIL MULL

Richfield Geologic Camp on North Slope in the summer of 1963.

early June, mapping the foothills anticlines in that area," he said.

"Very early in the project we could see that the foothills anticlines were all detachment 'rumpled-rug' type structures . . . overlying a thick shale section, so it seemed to us that it was very unlikely that there would be any structure at depth beneath the foothills. Indeed, the Umiat foothills structure had oil in a shallow horizon, but a field that size was clearly not going to be economic on the Slope."

Mull says the Richfield geologists "were not specifically dispatched to go north. We started looking at the regional stratigraphy and quickly realized that we were going to have to map the area in more detail than had been done before—and Harry Jamison [in Richfield's Los Angeles office] gave us the leeway to do what we thought needed to be done. In contrast, some of the other companies concentrated mostly on stratigraphic reconnaissance, and had only very generalized geologic maps."

Mull and fellow Richfield geologist Garnett "Gar" Pessel turned their eyes north and east. After starting in the Umiat area, Mull says they moved to Schrader Lake in the Alaska National Wildlife Refuge in late June and then back west to small Cache One Lake near the Echooka River in late July. (Although the Interior Department had turned down BP's request to do geophysical work within the refuge, all companies were permitted to send in field parties for more limited studies.)

In their searching of the region south and east of Prudhoe Bay, Mull and Pessel located a sandstone outcrop saturated with oil on the banks of the Sagavanirktok River, part of a belt of porous Cretaceous to lower Tertiary sand they mapped between the Toolik and Kavik rivers.

EARLY IN AUGUST 1963, Richfield's Harry Jamison received a memo at his Los Angeles office from Ben Ryan, who was Mull's and Pessel's boss. Attached was a handwritten note from Pessel.

"The most outstanding feature to date has been the nature of the Tertiary formation between the Toolik and Kavik rivers," Pessel wrote. "Those sands are not good, but are more correctly called fantastic."

The story of Richfield Oil Company's search for North Slope oil reflects the heady excitement of closing in on one of the world's great oil fields.

Jamison knew Pessel to be a soft-spoken, conservative geologist, not given to hyperbole. So Jamison sat up and took notice.

Pessel's note described the thickness of the outcrop, plus its porosity and permeability—two characteristics critical to oil being released from rock.

"The sand had a strong odor (sweet), brown stain, and gives a definite oil slick on the water," Pessel wrote.

"Such is the nature of these sands that I feel inclined to offer my feelings at this point. We have a good section of excellent reservoir possibilities, and positive proof of the petroliferous nature of these sands. If one cannot get an oil field out of these conditions, I give up!"

Agreeing with Pessel's evaluation that the only way to confirm the oil potential of the area was to carry out seismic testing, Ryan had simply added "I concur" at the bottom of Pessel's note.

NOW JAMISON AND HIS EXPLORERS had to persuade Richfield to spend a fortune to expand their work on the North Slope. Jamison also realized Richfield should try to acquire "protection acreage" if and when the area was offered for lease, to solidify their position in the region. Jamison had heard rumors that the state might select federal land on the North Slope for state ownership and then offer it for competitive leasing.

In urging his boss, chief geologist Mason Hill, to give a quick OK to a five-month geophysical reconnaissance program expected to cost a million dollars, Jamison wrote: "It is imperative to be in the forefront of exploration in this area in order to guarantee Richfield's participation regardless of the type of leasing that evolves."

"The state might use some type of development contract approach with work requirements," he wrote to Hill. "If we don't have seismic reconnaissance, we won't know where to get leases, and leasing is about to begin."

Mason Hill was said not to favor exploration on the North Slope. Some say Jamison waited until Hill was out of the country before recommending that Richfield do the Arctic coastal plain geophysical work. In any case, the most important person Jamison had to convince was Richfield's vice president for exploration, William Travers. Only Travers had authority to approve expenditures of the magnitude Jamison was proposing.

Jamison, along with Richfield land manager Frank McPhillips, went to Travers' office for the all-important meeting to seek Travers' approval. Jamison says he softened Travers up with a good joke, laid out the situation, and came away with a go-ahead for the North Slope seismic work.

> *"It is imperative to be in the forefront of exploration in this area in order to guarantee Richfield's participation regardless of the type of leasing that evolves."*
>
> *—Harry Jamison*

EXPANDED EXPLORATION COST MORE than Richfield had anticipated. Richfield hired United Geophysical Corporation crews to run three long north-south seismic shot lines on the North Slope, at a cost of about $150,000 a month. By early 1964, Richfield's total geophysical survey cost on the Slope had grown to nearly $3 million.

Richfield began looking for a partner to share expenses.

"Richfield's [chairman] Charlie Jones first went to Chevron," says oil industry veteran Robert O. Anderson, "because Richfield had a big-brother relationship with those guys based on Swanson River. But it didn't take."

Howard Vesper, Chevron's president of western operations at the time, says everyone in Chevron knew about Richfield's offer of the North Slope deal.

"Somewhere the offer got lost or was turned down," says John Carson, later Chevron's chief geologist.

Then Mason Hill sent Jamison across the street to talk to Humble Oil and Refining Company (now Exxon). Richfield had been successful in exploring several of California's oil basins with the company from Houston. Hill now thought that Humble, the giant of the oil industry, might be interested in Alaska's North Slope.

Jamison put on a show-and-tell for J.R. "Jack" Jackson, Humble's California exploration manager. Jamison displayed the oil-saturated Sag River sand that Gar Pessel exclaimed about in his memo, plus a map with locations of the two dozen or more North Slope leaseholds Richfield had acquired.

Jamison also showed a remarkable north-south seismic line developed in Richfield's surveys. The line across the east side of an anticline revealed opposing geometric attitudes on a folded formation—one of the prime ingredients of a subsurface "oil trap."

Jamison says that with this information, Jackson persuaded Exxon's board of directors to buy a half interest in Richfield's North Slope lease play for $1.5 million in cash and to commit $3 million for more seismic data work. For its investment in early 1964, Exxon would reap billions.

WHILE RICHFIELD AND BP and other operators began exploring the North Slope, companies had been given the first chance to drill offshore in Cook Inlet on leases acquired during state sales of submerged lands in December 1959 and December 1961. At the sale on December 19, 1961, Amoco's Chakachatna group paid out more than $7 million, Shell's SRS group added $5 million more, and other bidders came in with $3 million. In the spring and summer of 1962, numerous Cook Inlet drilling projects got under way.

These two groups of majors raced for the "discovery royalty" on Middle Ground Shoal offshore from the Kenai Peninsula's East Foreland. The group to make initial discovery on the giant geologic structure would pay the state only a 5 percent royalty—instead of the usual 12-1/2 percent—on the first ten years' production. The winner would benefit to the tune of tens of millions of dollars.

Amoco's Chakachatna group was made up of Sinclair, Phillips, Skelly, and Amoco. On May 15, 1962, it began drilling the first well on Middle Ground Shoal. Five days later, Shell—operating for the SRS group of Standard Oil of California (Chevron), Richfield, and Shell—began its well.

Mother Nature had a lot of fun in 1962. In early June, mud from Amoco's Middle Ground Shoal well, used to lubricate the hole and to keep gas and water pressure from escaping, suddenly lost circulation. The mud-encrusted coal-bed formation had cracked, allowing fluids to escape from far below up to the seafloor. About 1,500 yards north of the drilling platform, the water churned, exploding gas, water, and mud violently into the twilight sky. From a thousand feet down, the methane gas that had fractured the hole was forcing the fluids up to the seafloor.

Into the other-worldly landscape of the North Slope, the oil companies began pouring their energies.

After a few hectic days, the blowout was brought under control, but just as suddenly a second one began. From a mile down this time, the mud blew higher as the Amoco drilling crew watched helplessly. A huge crater formed at the base of the platform, and though the rig never was in critical danger, the well blew three more times before in late July it "bridged over." The following month, Amoco began drilling a well slightly to the north and completed a producing oil well later that year.

Shell encountered no blowouts while drilling Middle Ground Shoal. It suspended operations that September to avoid Cook Inlet's winter ice. A year later, after making its first open-hole test, Shell announced it had made a discovery on Middle Ground Shoal. However, Amoco was now claiming that its June 1962 blowout had been a discovery.

The Alaska Oil and Gas Conservation Commission would later decide the Amoco blowout had indeed been the first discovery on Middle Ground Shoal and the Chakachatna group was entitled to the discovery royalty.

Amoco had another run-in with Cook Inlet during 1962, in an area about twenty-five miles north of the Middle Ground Shoal blowouts. Amoco was drilling another offshore well on the North Cook Inlet structure when suddenly it, too, went out of control, discharging a light oil condensate onto the water. The strong upper-inlet tidal currents carried an oily sheen toward Kenai, prompting a public outcry led by area fishermen.

Resources commissioner Phil Holdsworth flew in to assess the potential damage. After meeting with the fishermen, he agreed there wasn't time to move the drilling rig and cap off the well before winter ice began forming. To minimize potential harm to sea life (and placate the fishermen), Holdsworth decided to torch the condensate coming from the runaway well.

Thus all winter long, a huge flame spitting out of the inlet and into the dark northern sky could be seen from as far away as Anchorage. When the ice moved out in late March, Amoco moved back in, redrilled—very carefully—and completed a commercial gas well in November 1963.

Union Oil drilled for gas onshore in upper Cook Inlet during 1962 but came up with a dry hole. Later, former Union geologist Lum Lovely, too, spent almost all the $500,000 cash he had received from selling North Slope royalty to drill in the same area. Lovely drilled his well "straight-up"—that is, he paid for it all by himself. The oil majors had offered to pay for information from the well with so-called "dry hole money" but he turned them down. He ended up owning his own dry hole.

> *"Those sands are not good, but are more correctly called fantastic. . . . If one cannot get an oil field out of these conditions, I give up!"*
>
> —*Richfield geologist Gar Pessel*

THE STATE WAS READY to take in millions of more dollars with its July 1962 competitive sale of Cook Inlet leases. Parcels offshore of Kalgin Island had been withdrawn from the sale because state and Interior Department officials couldn't agree on the boundary line between state and federal waters. Despite this, nearly the entire upper Cook Inlet was bid on by the major oil companies, who paid the state nearly $16 million.

Charlie Barnes and I bid, too. We had formed limited partnerships to bid for state offshore leases, and at the July 1962 sale we bid as Alaska Offshore Associates.

We bid on tracts in Knik Arm north of Anchorage and several in Wide Bay. Although no minimum bid amount was set by Holdsworth, a "gentlemen's agreement" developed between the state and the industry that the state would not accept bids of less than $1 an acre. There was nothing in writing,

Pan Am's (AMOCO) North Cook Inlet blowout in 1962. The state ordered the torching of the oil to minimize potential harm to sea life.

but everyone pretty much understood what the rules were. Holdsworth and lands director Roscoe Bell reasoned that if they actually set a formal minimum bid— say, $1 an acre— a court might require them to accept any bid higher than $1 an acre. Instead, they wanted to maintain their ability to reject any bid, no matter how high.

Despite the unwritten agreement, we decided to bid 55 and 75 cents an acre on the Knik Arm parcels. And, jointly, Richfield, Sinclair, and Phillips bid 21 and 46 cents an acre for two small Wide Bay tracts adjacent to several acquired at the December 1959 state sale.

We outbid Shell on one Wide Bay parcel, but our euphoria evaporated when Phillips outbid us for the same parcel. Holdsworth summarily rejected all bids of less than $1 an acre. Although we and the companies appealed, the minimum unwritten bidding rule prevailed.

Then came a personal tragedy. In October 1962 Charlie Barnes died following intestinal surgery. By then, he and I had an interest in nearly four hundred oil and gas leases throughout the state, including the North Slope, and had started Alaska Title Guaranty Company and several other service-oriented businesses.

I had begun the practice of law with former Department of Interior solicitor Ted Stevens in Anchorage. Now, with Charlie's death, I had to decide whether to continue practicing law while running the businesses or to give one of them up.

I left the law and continued bidding for leases. At one time, the limited partnerships formed by me and Charlie held more leases offshore in Cook Inlet than anyone except the majors. I was able to sell our leases to the majors for a nice profit for me and Charlie's estate, always keeping an overriding royalty.

WINTER DRILLING IN
COOK INLET

JOE RYCHETNIK

STEVE McCUTCHEON/
ANCHORAGE MUSEUM OF HISTORY AND ART

ANCHORAGE DAILY TIMES/ ANCHORAGE DAILY NEWS

Offshore Cook Inlet platform in 1971.

Flaring gas from Cook Inlet platform in 1996.

Union Oil's Monopod still operates at Trading Bay. (1966 photo)

INSIDE STORY

I NEARLY GET RICH

In the mid-sixties, Alaska was aglow with the excitement of oil development. Offshore platforms that sprouted in Cook Inlet had begun producing oil. And eyes were turning far to the north as some people began predicting Mideast-scale oil fields for Alaska's North Slope.

Other spectacular things were happening, including a nearby event that hinted at wealth for me and my new business partner, Jerry Ganopole (the former Texaco geologist and I had formed Alaska Exploration Corporation in 1963). Placid Oil Company, owned by none other than H. L. Hunt of Dallas, had floated its drill rig No. 46 all the way from Belgium to a site just off southern Kalgin Island in Cook Inlet.

Earl Grammer and I had already made a nice piece of change from optioning our Kalgin Island leases of 1957 to two major oil companies; first to Shell and then to British Petroleum. Both companies had carried out geophysical surveys around the island, but neither exercised their option. That fine old Alaska oil pioneer Earl Grammer died in late 1965.

Now, H. L. Hunt had bid tracts offshore from the island. He was eager to drill two wells offshore, just adjacent to our upland holdings, so we and Hunt agreed to swap royalties. If he discovered oil offshore, a piece of the action would go to me, Grammer's heirs, and my partner Ganopole.

In the spring of 1966, Hunt's crew scooped gravel off the southwest shore of Kalgin Island at Oldman's Bay, creating a huge pit on the sea floor, visible at low tide. At high tide a tug gingerly maneuvered the mammoth drill rig up on the beach, and as the tide receded, the towering concrete and steel monster became anchored to the island's rocky shore by its own immense weight. On June 3, 1966, the Placid crew began drilling the first Kalgin well.

That summer, Ganopole and I went by crew boat to observe "our" rig. I recall passing a half dozen offshore drilling platforms standing like so many tethered elephants in the swirling, slate-gray Inlet waters against a backdrop to the west of the Alaska Range's skyscraping mountains. Moving through extremely choppy water, we passed bleak swatches of stunted spruce trees on the island's northern edge.

Suddenly, as we came around the northwest reach of the island, our eyes encountered a blazing light that illuminated the horizon like some space rocket launch at midnight. There, outlined against the surreal sky, was the drill rig—a four-story, rock-eating behemoth, looking in this forlorn setting like some alien beast.

As part of our agreement with Hunt, we were entitled to all data from the well. Ganopole had the expertise to examine the drill-stem cuttings, electric logs (E-logs), and cores from the well. After Ganopole and the Hunt geologists found little evidence of hydrocarbons from the initial well, the ponderous rig was floated off the beach at high tide and moved to the north end of the island. Drilling of a second well began in late August.

After several weeks of drilling, a core taken from nearly three miles down emerged dripping with rich, black oil. It had come from the same horizon where the E-log showed several hundred feet of possible "pay." Apparently the drill bit had pierced oil-soaked sand, and all that remained was to find out how much oil we had discovered.

For the next few weeks, Jerry and I kept reminding each other not to panic. We didn't want anyone to know the secret of what had come out of the hole, and we did our best to keep from thinking about how we were going to spend our riches.

Oddly, though I savored for about a week the euphoria that came with the possibility we had struck it rich, all I can recall of that intense experience was a sense of the strange, awesome responsibility I would be saddled with if I became a millionaire. I was puzzled about how wealth might change my life. Instead of happiness or excitement, I was left with a kind of nagging unpleasantness.

But it was all a gilded dream, anyway, and I wasn't too disappointed at its puncturing. There was oil at Kalgin all right, but it was worthless "dead" oil, lacking what people in the business call "drive," a natural pressure that almost always accompanies genuine discovery.

Undoubtedly back in early geologic times, a sizeable reservoir of oil existed beneath the surface of Kalgin Island, and at that time it was probably accompanied by pressure of "gusher" intensity. Somehow, Mother Nature allowed that pressure to dissipate and rob the oil accumulation of its value.

As expectations for a find dwindled, Placid's crew continued for a time to "perforate, acidize, and shoot" the hole, but when the drill bit reached 14,000 feet with no significant change, they threw in the towel. Talk of drilling a third well on the east side of the island never materialized.

Sadly, Kalgin Island was the last chance for Earl Grammer's name to be associated with an oil gusher in Alaska. Even so, by the time he died in late

1965, he was a millionaire, with most of his fortune amassed from leasing oil and gas lands.

To his sister, Elsie, he left a substantial estate, and he also bequeathed large sums to organizations that help disabled and ill children: Rose Polytechnic Institute in Terre Haute, Indiana, the Shriners Crippled Children's Association, and the Alaska Crippled Children's Association. Grammer's real legacy became one of heartfelt charity and kindness toward America's sick and crippled youngsters.

Many wildcatters and oil explorers would follow in Grammer's footsteps, but none would be more persistent and determined in their quest and few would contribute so much to so many even after their death. For me, it was a pleasure to know this determined little man and to derive inspiration from the way he did business and the way he treated others.

Chapter 11

The Selection: Indecision

The most important decision in Alaska's transformation into an oil state was made in such a convoluted manner that it seems to have occurred almost by chance. Involved were a governor with very little savvy in the oil business, state bureaucrats who were angling to get North Slope land for Alaska so the state could reap millions—perhaps billions—in oil royalties, high-rolling oil companies with competing interests, and little guys who didn't want to be shut out of the action.

ROSCOE BELL thought part of his job as lands director was being a salesman for the state's minerals. From the beginning, he wanted the state to select federal land on the North Slope for state ownership and then lease it to the major oil companies. In the spring of 1961, representatives of BP, Sinclair, Shell, Richfield, and Exxon were urging the same thing. Particularly BP.

But final approval on which land to select for the new state had to come from a governor with serious concerns about turning land over to the oil companies. The cost of organizing the new government had forced Governor Egan to offer state land for oil and gas leasing, but he often expressed his concern that he might be "giving away more once-in-a-lifetime assets" than he should. In 1961, he tried to gain revenue by increasing the state income tax, but the legislature opposed him. Oil money remained the quickest way to raise cash, so he reluctantly directed Roscoe Bell and Phil Holdsworth to continue offering state lands for leasing.

Pressured to select land on the North Slope, Egan instead put pressure on Interior Secretary Stewart Udall to hold more federal lease drawings and award more federal development contracts in that region. Egan's reasoning was simple: the state was already receiving as its share of land reclamation funds 90 percent of federal oil revenues from the Slope. He saw no reason to select North Slope land for state ownership just to turn around and lease it out when the state was already making money from the federal lease program.

Meanwhile, the state was proceeding with lease sales of its own. The sale on December 19, 1961, for offshore tracts in upper Cook Inlet, had especially caught the attention of Alaskans. The state took in more than $15 million. Egan took great pride in telling his constituents that because of the large amount of money received, "no tax increase would be needed or sought in the foreseeable future." Egan also said that millions of dollars in bonds authorized by the voters for road work and University of Alaska construction now would not have to be sold. It was a great day for the state and for Egan.

Alaska's budget had grown to nearly $60 million, with cash from oil leases providing a quarter of that amount. Egan began feeling that the state needed an annual infusion of oil money to keep the budget pumped up. Oil-lease money, which until then had been problematical, now seemed a necessity.

———————

SHORTLY AFTER STATEHOOD, major oil companies began urging Holdsworth and Bell to get moving on state selection of land on the North Slope. Bell later recalled thinking, "Someone should be doing something up there [on the North Slope], and it was a long jump, so it would take some special concessions to get companies to make the investment up there."

The major companies knew Bell's land planning background would make him receptive to dealing directly with them. It was more orderly, more controllable, for state officials to deal directly with the oil companies. Bell believed that exploration permits and other "frontier" financial incentives had worked well in Canada, so why not in Alaska? The government would have more control over exploration activity.

In order to offer large blocks of acreage—say, half a million acres each—the lease term should be long enough for companies to carry out exploration on a grand scale. Bell believed the length of a state lease on the North Slope should run for at least ten years, with rentals as low as 10 cents an acre.

Bell's proposed "concession permits" would require an operator to meet his drilling obligations or pay a cash penalty. A discovery royalty—that is, a royalty lower than normal—could be used as an incentive. His exploration concessions would cause "exploration to be accelerated," and drilling could be expected "within a couple of years."

He envisioned a Canadian "checkerboard" system like that used in the province of Alberta, where the government reserves the right to reclaim at least half the leases following a discovery. Then offering the reclaimed land competitively, the government is more than justly compensated with cash bonuses and royalties for giving the original incentives.

Bell argued against a system of small leaseholds or noncompetitive leasing because it placed hurdles in the way of oil operators trying to acquire blocks of land large enough for effective exploration. The three to five years it would take a company to assemble enough small lease blocks on the North Slope would be "wasteful," and at least $1 million would have to be paid to the "little guys" rather than to the state.

> *The cost of organizing the new government had forced Governor Egan to offer state land for oil and gas leasing, but he often worried he might be "giving away more once-in-a-lifetime assets" than he should.*

Bell said he was not totally unsympathetic to the "middleman," but he believed his function was to provide as much money to the state as possible from its land and minerals. Thus he refused to give to "speculators" what rightfully was the government's.

Bell's philosophy meshed nicely with oil-company thinking. In a July 5, 1961, memo, state petroleum geologist Don D. Bruce told about a recent meeting he had with John Zehnder of British Petroleum.

"They [BP] would like to obtain a special concession for development of petroleum resources in the Arctic Slope which would range between two and three million acres, because like most major companies British Petroleum has reached its maximum acreage limitation," Bruce said in the memo to his boss, Mines and Minerals Director Jim Williams.

"I discussed the matter with Roscoe (Bell)," Bruce said, "and he seemed quite interested" in asking the major oil companies to submit proposals for special concessions on the Slope.

DON BRUCE WAS A RECURRING FIGURE in the state bureaucracy's dealings with the industry. Ever since he was first hired in October 1959, Bruce had urged Williams, Holdsworth, and Bell to see that the state selected federal land on the North Slope and leased it to the major oil companies.

Bruce and Bell met on July 7, 1961, with representatives of BP, including its chief geologist from London, M. L. Falcon. After the meeting, Bruce again wrote to Williams: "They are considering a concession consisting of between 500,000 and 1,000,000 acres."

Three days later, Williams replied to Bruce in a memo that included a realistic political assessment of the political fallout from turning huge blocks of land over to the oil companies: "Public relations will be a problem. Public resentment toward concessions is quite general, I believe."

As state lands director, Roscoe Bell campaigned to have Alaska select federal land on the North Slope for state ownership and then lease it to the major oil companies. His hardest sell was Governor Bill Egan. (1970 photo)

Bruce was back to Williams on July 21 with more industry feedback. "Roger Gehring of Sinclair telephoned regarding rumor that his Tulsa office had picked up that the state was considering issuing special concessions in the near future," he wrote. "Sinclair wants one," said Bruce. Bruce then arranged a meeting of state and Sinclair representatives.

The upshot of the meeting was general agreement to keep the concession idea on a back burner. "It was decided that it would be in the best interest of the State not to bring the subject up until after the selection of the land," Bruce wrote Williams.

This early back-and-forth between the bureaucracy and the industry led to an August 1, 1961, message from resources commissioner Holdsworth to Governor Egan. "Members of the industry have approached us about a land selection on the North Slope," Holdsworth told Egan. He attached a copy of a memo from Bell in support of a North Slope selection, and Holdsworth pointed out to Egan that under Alaska law, the governor had the authority to issue "exploration permits to spur oil and gas exploration north of the Brooks Range."

Egan sent back a one word reply: "No."

———————

DON BRUCE WAS BACK during 1962 with more bulletins for his boss about the eagerness of the majors to develop the North Slope. And Bruce had a new angle that he felt might help move the governor from "no" to "yes."

On May 11, 1962, Bruce wrote to mines director Williams, telling him that during the past week he had been approached by people from Sinclair, Shell, and BP, again pushing the state to select land on the Arctic Slope and issue exploration permits. He said Texaco, Amoco, and Union also were showing interest.

"A new approach to obtaining approval by the Administration," Bruce wrote, "might be to signify the potential economic impact such a program should have on both Fairbanks and Valdez. . . .

"Almost all studies of pipeline facilities indicate the most feasible route, economically, to be through Anaktuvuk Pass to Fairbanks, then down the Richardson Highway to the deep-water port in Valdez. A discovery on the Arctic Slope would not only result in revenues from the production of oil and gas, but would provide for millions of dollars in the construction of the pipeline, storage tanks, and terminal facilities, especially in Valdez."

Valdez, of course, was Egan's hometown, the little community where he had sold groceries and where he had seen his family and fellow citizens suffer through hard times.

The Valdez connection didn't get far with Williams, who wrote to Bruce a few days later, pointing out that Holdsworth had been careful not to mention Valdez in his discussions with the governor. Egan was highly sensitive on the issue of public perceptions of his actions. He would be offended at the thought that anyone would think he was showing favoritism—to the oil industry or to his hometown.

HOLDSWORTH BELIEVED that Egan was beginning to show interest in North Slope land, but only if rental income from leases there was no less than what the state was pulling in from its 90-percent share of federal lease rentals or from offshore tracts in Cook Inlet. Egan's attitude toward the Slope "appears more favorable than it was a year ago," he said.

The situation was coming to a head as oil company enthusiasm grew and as the Bureau of Land Management prepared for noncompetitive lease drawings on the Slope. BP, Amoco, Union, and Atlantic Refining let the state know it wanted to work out lease deals. But with the BLM preparing its tract sheets in preparation for the drawings, a big chunk of North Slope land would soon be out of state reach. The state needed to make a decision soon.

In late June 1962 came what seemed to be a breakthrough decision from Egan. The governor told Holdsworth to instruct lands director Bell to "review the recommendations made by the industry and come up with a firm proposal as to areas, sizes of concessions, fixed rental terms, competitive bonus bid features and method of checkerboarding after discovery."

The state lease sale on December 19, 1961, had especially caught the attention of Alaskans. The state took in more than $15 million.

Bell's mineral leasing staff immediately prepared a twelve-page memo detailing a "permit-concession program." It recommended that the state select for its ownership 5 million acres in the central part of the Arctic coastal plain between Naval Petroleum Reserve No. 4 and the Arctic National Wildlife Refuge.

"This area has been suggested by one or more industrial interests," Bell told Holdsworth. "We have been assured by industry representatives that the area would all be taken up if the State made it available. Furthermore, the WOGA has expressed keen interest in the concession approach to North Slope development."

Bell met with Egan in mid-July and got the governor's blessings for the plan. Bell then prepared a press release announcing that the state would file for several million acres not then available for federal leasing. The release said the state "has been assured by a number of major oil companies that if the land were opened to concessions," they would bid for it on the basis of development and drilling commitments (though not cash bonuses) for the next five years.

In the press release, Bell said the concession arrangement had been conceived by the legislature and paralleled the Canadian leasing system. He intended to issue the release once he had filed the selection applications in the Fairbanks land office.

Bell flew to Fairbanks in late July, his selection applications for 4.9 million acres in hand. Bell was told before he left Anchorage not to file the applications until he was met in Fairbanks by Egan's campaign manager, young Anchorage Democrat and attorney Gene Guess. The state primary was coming up the following month, with the general election in November.

"We didn't connect [meet]," Bell said later, "but I talked to Gene by phone, and he had talked with Egan." The result was that Bell returned to Anchorage, his briefcase unopened.

Bell said later he decided not to file the applications because "there'd be a lot of static if I filed, because of the campaign."

Translation: Gene Guess told him not to file.

FEARING ALIENATION OF VOTERS by appearing to favor "big oil," Egan had decided not to select North Slope land for the state. In the Democratic primary Egan was pitted against a popular Anchorage mayor, former mail carrier George Byers. Earlier he had been jolted by the surprise decision of his own attorney general, John Rader, to run against him, though Rader later changed his mind.

Egan's political advisers decided that selecting a huge amount of land on the North Slope and offering it to the majors could make Egan appear guilty of a land giveaway. The little guys—his voting constituents—might see it like that. They'd see it as just another way of keeping them from competing.

The "little guys" of Fairbanks had always been in the thick of the action. Among the most politically vocal of all the oil "speculators," they held more North Slope federal oil and gas leases than any "outsiders." It seemed to Egan in his campaigning that nearly everyone in Alaska, particularly the people in

Fairbanks, opposed a land selection on the North Slope. A leasing scheme giving concessions to "big oil" could cost dearly at the ballot box.

"Whether the land is selected and put up for exploration or just selected," Guess said in a note to an Egan aide, "it is going to raise a fuss among oil and gas lease brokers, i.e. Jack Roderick, Charlie Barnes, Tex Noey, Locke Jacobs, etc. Naturally, they, as middlemen, would be excluded, again. I see no reason to raise this point before Nov. 6th [date of the general election]."

In the fall, before the 1962 general election, I wrote to Egan, encouraging him to stay away from the concession idea.

"I do not believe that it would be in the best interest of the state to offer certain lands on the North Slope on a concession basis," I wrote. "The middleman, promoter, independent, speculator, if you will, has a place in Alaska, and unless this state encourages people to risk their money here, you will see an ever-lessening interest on the part of the independent oil operators and others in oil development in Alaska."

When Egan got around to replying after the election, it was with some hearty rhetoric that left his hand concealed. "Let me assure you, Jack," he wrote, "nothing will please me more than that day when independent Jack Roderick brings in his first producer. Those Horatio Alger overtones are certainly heartening. Such tenacious pursuit of that which is said to be at the end of the rainbow is bound to pay off—not only for you, but for the future of our great State."

———

SOON AFTER EGAN WON the August Democratic primary, he received a letter from Colorado independent oilman John J. King, who said he had been told by several sources that Egan delayed land selection on the North Slope in July because of "political considerations." Rumor had it, said King, that Egan would support the selection only if the oil pipeline terminated in Egan's hometown of Valdez. King asked Egan to select land on the North Slope, because he didn't like dealing with the federal government.

King, as one of the most colorful independents on the Alaska scene, was just the kind of guy to face up to the governor in this pugnacious manner. King began each morning in his downtown office high above the city of Denver by serving the ubiquitous martini to visitors. The irrepressible oilman regaled assembled landmen, lease brokers, and independents with tales of the giant oil field to be found someday on the North Slope, hopefully on his leases.

Sometimes a series of oil and gas lease maps, controlled electronically, would descend from the ceiling, showing King's federal leases on the Slope, colored in yellow. Few of the hangers-on thought his "moose pasture" was anything but worthless tundra. None believed an area so far from the market could produce commercial oil.

King's letter accusing Egan of making public policy based on "political considerations" was anathema to the governor. Egan replied to King (but not until after he won the general election) that while he might change his mind in the future, now was not the time to select land on the North Slope.

King's complaint about "political considerations," Egan wrote, "raised my eyebrows, and gave cause for me to wonder." Egan assured his critic that, "Politics to me is the science of good government—in behalf of *all* the people."

> *Colorado independent oilman John J. King said he had been told by several sources that Egan delayed land selection on the North Slope in July because of "political considerations."*

Egan was hot about being accused of political manipulation, and he wondered who might be passing on rumors to John King. Later he wrote to Holdsworth: "This incident strongly indicates to me that some of our people seem to have a mistaken impression about where their chief interest should lie."

Holdsworth had a theory. "To the best of my knowledge," he told Bell, "there is only one employee in the department who has had occasion to have direct contact with Cortez Oil Company [King's company]." Don Bruce, who BP later appointed as its agent to sell some original Prudhoe Bay seismic data, "was an odd person who really did some harm," Holdsworth told me later.

Bypassing Holdsworth, Bell wrote Egan that the rumors probably were started by "private oil scouts, representatives of companies, and representatives of the petroleum publications, as well as the petroleum reporters of the newspapers who are frequently very free in expressing opinions that they have been able to form from many sources. I believe that the individuals consulted by Mr. King were either persons outside the division of lands or were possibly former employees of the department of natural resources."

ALTHOUGH EGAN BACKED OFF on choosing North Slope land, he still wanted to continue weighing the pros and cons. As he campaigned during the fall of 1962 for election to his second term, he authorized Bell to solicit comments from oil companies on why the state should select land on the Slope.

Bell mailed requests for comments to the major oil companies likely to respond, most of whom quickly replied. They said that if the state would select a large amount of acreage in the central portion of the North Slope's coastal plain, they would lease the land and carry out a lot of exploration work. Most oil companies preferred that the land be offered on a competitive or concession basis.

Interestingly, their nominations for land did not include acreage along the northern coastal plain near Colville or Prudhoe Bay. At this point, the smart money was still in the northern foothills of the Brooks Range.

British Petroleum couldn't understand why Governor Egan was reluctant to deal directly with the oil companies. Why didn't Alaskan officials act more like foreign country ministers?

Independents said they preferred noncompetitive leasing. They feared that the concession idea and competitive leasing would exclude them from successful bidding.

AFTER WINNING REELECTION, Egan continued to ponder a decision. In a February 1963 letter to Interior Secretary Udall, he confessed that "the matter of the wisdom of State selection of a large block of land on the North Slope has been a vexing one for me." But because the state was still receiving lease revenues from federal land on the Slope, Egan continued to believe Alaska's best course was to let the U.S. government keep on with its noncompetitive oil and gas lease drawings.

In May 1963, Egan reached a decision on the matter. North Slope land would not be among the tens of millions of acres of federal property that the new state of Alaska would choose for its own.

Egan wrote to Alaska's Congressional delegation and to Secretary Udall, urging them instead to accelerate the federal leasing program on the Slope. He told Holdsworth to keep the pressure on Bureau of Land Management administrators to do likewise.

One of the first people Egan told of his decision was his political critic John J. King. Egan told the oilman in a letter that his decision was subject to change, but he reminded King that the state already was receiving 90 percent of federal oil and gas revenues on the Slope. So there seemed to be no compelling reason to make a selection at this time. And in Egan's judgment, state ownership wouldn't speed up exploration.

"Like Egan, I wasn't for the selection either," Holdsworth told me. "After all, we got 90 percent of it anyway, and we couldn't do any better managing it ourselves. So, why not put the bee under the butts of the federal people and get them to lease more land."

GOVERNOR EGAN'S LATEST 'NO' didn't deter British Petroleum from pressing its case. BP reminded Roscoe Bell and his staff that BP faced the same government budgetary cycles as they did—with the same requirement to spend appropriated funds before a fiscal year ends. Local BP personnel said that if the state didn't select and offer land on the Slope, they would be forced to return exploration money to the Crown. This close communication and symbiotic outlook between BP personnel and Alaska's public officials eventually paid off for the British.

Vitally interested in changing noncompetitive leasing to bonus bidding or some kind of a large acreage concession idea, Harry R. Warman, president of BP Exploration Company of Alaska, Inc., wrote directly to Governor Egan on June 13, 1963:

"The present method of noncompetitive leasing has now been in operation for some time and has, in our opinion, proved totally unsatisfactory. We can only hope that immediate and realistic action by the Alaska Division of Lands will preclude the possibility of this method being perpetrated elsewhere in Alaska on State land selections."

Warman faulted the system because it required companies to buy up individual noncompetitive leases in order to get enough land for serious exploration. Competition from West Coast oil companies had been too unruly, he said. Those companies successfully assembled such lease blocks, but BP could not.

"The attraction of this noncompetitive method to numerous speculators is self-evident," wrote Warman, "and for this reason alone imposes an unnecessary expense and hardship upon the companies seriously exploring for oil."

Warman's complaint that BP was being shut out ignored the fact that BP had successfully acquired noncompetitive leases in blocks in Cook Inlet and elsewhere, assembled mostly by consulting geologists and local lease brokers. BP's most legitimate grounds for complaint would have been its failure to find oil on its noncompetitive leaseholds.

Egan rejected Warman's arguments, telling him that only "minor problems" had cropped up where the state had offered land under noncompetitive leasing. "I can see no reason at this time for considering any change in our present policy," Egan wrote.

Outmaneuvered by West Coast American oil companies whose personnel were trained to acquire individual leases, BP preferred dealing directly with the government. Skilled in negotiating with government managers who controlled land in foreign countries, BP personnel didn't like the various methods of dealing with individual leaseholders. BP couldn't understand why Egan, in control of much of Alaska's land and resources, was reluctant to deal directly with the oil companies. Why didn't Alaskan officials act more like foreign country ministers?

> *"The present method of noncompetitive leasing has . . . proved totally unsatisfactory. . . . The attraction of this noncompetitive method to numerous speculators is self-evident."*
>
> *—BP's Harry Warman, to Governor Egan*

ROSCOE BELL also continued to push for state selection on the Slope. He asked Holdsworth to discuss it again with Egan. In a "confidential" July 31, 1963, memo to the governor, Holdsworth laid out several reasons that pointed to the value of state ownership.

"At the present time," he wrote, "half of the exploration activity within Alaska is conducted north of the Brooks Range." It was here, on the North Slope, that major new oil discoveries were likely to come.

If the federal government continued to offer noncompetitive leases on the Slope, Holdsworth reckoned that the state's 90 percent share of rental income would amount to less than a million dollars a year. He now suggested that the state could do far better.

Despite Holdsworth's advice, Egan asked Interior Secretary Udall to offer noncompetitive lease drawings for all federal land on the Slope that the oil companies had said they would bid for if the state selected it. Egan still wanted to maintain the status quo.

Udall had already decided to open almost all the eastern half of the Slope to noncompetitive leasing. His staff at the Bureau of Land Management was already preparing tract maps covering nearly 16 million acres between Naval Petroleum Reserve No. 4 (Pet-4) and the Alaska National Wildlife Refuge. Four separate federal drawings of 4 million acres each were already scheduled at three-month intervals; they would begin as soon as possible.

This was just what Egan wanted. Oil exploration would continue, and the state would get its share of federal lease money. Egan wrote proudly to Alaska U.S. Senator Bob Bartlett that, "Many in the oil industry feel that the Arctic areas of Alaska could well turn out to be one of the truly strong oil reservoirs of the United States, if not the world."

At the Alaska Chamber of Commerce "Salute to Alaska Oil Industry" dinner in October 1963, Egan continued his upbeat as-sessment: "Some petroleum men dare hope that Alaska's North Slope may rival vast reserves of the Middle East. It is probably true that an oilman is welcome wherever he goes in this world. Have no doubt about it, you are welcome here. It is correct to say that the Alaska petroleum industry and the State of Alaska were born almost simultaneously. There is no reason why we shouldn't remain members of a close and happy family."

Egan's remarks were made shortly after Shell discovered oil at Middle Ground Shoal in Cook Inlet, and his words reflected his excitement at the find. They showed his optimism about the prospect of an ever-increasing stream of oil revenue to the state.

Pan Am's (Amoco's) Romig Park Well in Anchorage in 1964.

ANCHORAGE DAILY TIMES/ANCHORAGE DAILY NEWS

THE J. BERRINGTON ENTWHISLE STORY

Colorado oilman and Egan critic John J. King, an inveterate prankster, is best remembered by his friends for the J. Berrington Entwhisle caper.

J. B. Entwhisle was listed in the Washington, D.C., social directory. His name appeared opposite Dwight D. Eisenhower's in the London Blue Book. The Denver telephone book listed J. B. Entwhisle, and there was a Denver bank account in his name. He was even mentioned in *Who's Who In America.* J. B. would periodically wire large amounts of money to accounts around the world for oil transactions, and his agents were instructed to carry out orders of considerable financial magnitude. He seemed to be an oilman of some substance.

One day in the late 1960s, a one-eighth page, black-bordered ad appeared in the *Denver Post* with this announcement:

"The following offices will be closed to honor our good friend and associate, J. B. Entwhisle." John King's office stayed closed. But the offices of those who knew better remained open.

J. B. Entwhisle hadn't died. He had never existed. With proper social convention and public recognition, he had been allowed to slip away simply and quietly. John King's lawyer had convinced him that some people, particularly those who took social registers seriously, would not take kindly to the fact that not only was J. B. Entwhisle no longer alive, he had in fact never existed. So King retired him, and the socially conscious never knew.

Colorado oilman John J. King had a humorous side. Just ask J. Berrington Entwhisle. (1967 photo)

CONNIE COWETT AND JOHN J. KING, JR.

165

Chapter 12

The Selection: Egan Says Yes

The state of Alaska eventually decided to claim a big chunk of federal land on the North Slope. But it took a whole new line of reasoning to win Governor Egan's OK.

Lands director Roscoe Bell had long been pressing for state selection of North Slope land. Egan seemed to have scotched the idea once and for all, however, when he told the U.S. Interior Department to push on with its own land-leasing program.

Bell found his answer in late 1963 when federal officials raised the problem of determining the mean high tide along the Arctic coast. At statehood, Alaska had been granted title to all shore and tidelands. The federal government owned all the land above mean high tide; the state owned the land from mean high tide seaward three miles. The Bureau of Land Management now had to determine the location of the mean high tide line. It also had to figure out which rivers and streams on the North Slope were navigable, since minerals underlying navigable waters would belong to the state, while those beneath non-navigable waters would belong to the federal government.

Who owned what along the Arctic coastline turned out to be a very complicated question. Trying to survey the shorelands and streams was problematical because of the meandering watercourses and gently sloping plain. The federal people were ready to throw their hands up at the task of preparing timely and accurate tract descriptions for their noncompetitive lease drawings.

"We were talking with the BLM officials about their surveying the Arctic coastline," Bell later recalled "and they said such a survey would be almost impossible to do."

Resources commissioner Phil Holdsworth remembers the same thing. "They said it would take a hundred years to survey the land up there."

Bell's solution to the problem was to eliminate the need for a federal survey. The state would simply make a land selection along the coastline far enough inland so that the tidal boundary and much more would be included. The federal government would no longer be obligated to carry out an "impossible" survey.

In mid-November, Bell had some encouraging words for oil companies that wanted the state to select North Slope land and lease it to them. He told a group of WOGA representatives in Anchorage that while he wasn't looking toward any "general, large land selection on the North Slope," he was considering selecting a "narrow strip surrounding the area of the river mouth or mouths."

One day later, he passed on similar information—but couched in different terms—to a group that opposed state selection on the Slope. He told the newly formed Alaska Independent Petroleum Association (of which I was a member) that he saw no reason for the state to select land on the Slope. "However," he added, "there might be a tidal problem at the mouth of the Colville River, which could change my decision."

BELL WROTE TO HOLDSWORTH in early December, asking him to seek Governor Egan's authorization to select acreage along the Arctic coastline. The land lay north of where Bell, back in mid-1962, had tried unsuccessfully to select some 5 million acres for the state. Bell told Holdsworth the present selection was needed to cure "the unsolvable Arctic coastal plain boundary problem."

Holdsworth followed up with a memo to Egan explaining the tidal and title problems. He pointed out that a state selection of land along the northern Arctic coastline would not conflict with the BLM's plan to continue holding noncompetitive lease drawings to the south.

Egan agreed with the plan. On January 3, 1964, he wrote to Interior Secretary Stewart Udall. In order "to eliminate the need for defining the limits of the tidal waters along the Arctic Ocean coastline," Egan said, he had decided to select land for the state in that area. Shortly afterward, Bell filed formal selections totaling 1,595,170 acres.

The selection had some geologic support, although it was never sold to Egan in that way. The land selected by Egan had only recently been subjected to geophysical surveys. Major oil companies indicated they were now prepared to offer large lease bids for the land if owned by the state.

Bell's hope was to offer the land up for competitive bidding. "Present law allows us to classify land competitive, so long as water is included," Bell reminded Holdsworth.

———

THE PACE OF NORTH SLOPE oil exploration seemed to be fine with Governor Egan in early 1964. The state had now laid claim to a million and

STEVE McCUTCHEON/ANCHORAGE MUSEUM OF HISTORY AND ART

The great Alaska earthquake of March 27, 1964, altered Governor Egan's slow and cautious approach to leasing the state's North Slope land to the oil companies.

a half acres and could offer it for lease at some point in the future. Meanwhile, Alaska continued to receive its 90 percent share of ever-increasing revenues from federal leases.

On January 3, 1964, Egan wrote to Interior Secretary Udall, saying he had decided to select federal land along the Arctic Ocean coastline for state ownership. It included Prudhoe Bay.

On March 27, 1964, the picture changed with a jolt. Southcentral Alaska was shaken, for almost five incredibly long minutes, by one of the world's great earthquakes. Clay strata underlying parts of Anchorage opened beneath downtown buildings. The coastal bluff south of downtown and a large portion of a housing subdivision slid into Cook Inlet's icy waters. Harbors at the small coastal towns of Kodiak, Valdez, and Seward were destroyed by huge tsunami waves. More than 100 Alaskans died, mostly in small villages along the coast— including thirty-one people in the governor's hometown of Valdez. The earthquake, measuring about 8.5 on the Richter scale, devastated transportation systems and other infrastructure serving nearly half the state's population.

New money had to be found to help solve the problems created by the earthquake as almost the entire state's economy came momentarily to a standstill. Even if oil production from Cook Inlet could be increased, not enough new revenue could be expected to fill the financial fissure created by the earthquake. Swanson River royalty income remained steady, but small. Egan began looking more closely at possible North Slope oil lease monies as a partial answer to the state's financial dilemma.

A FEW DAYS AFTER THE EARTHQUAKE, Phil Holdsworth commented in a letter to Assistant Interior Secretary John Carver that, "It will be interesting to see just how desirable this (Arctic Slope) land is to the oil and gas industry now that it is available."

Very desirable, it would appear. New geophysical work pointed more and more favorably toward the land selected by the state.

In the winter of 1963-64, BP and Sinclair drilled six dry holes in the northern foothills of the Brooks Range. But now, BP's interest shifted farther north, toward the coastal plain, based on geophysical work during the summer of 1963 and a comprehensive geological picture it had compiled on 10,000 square miles of the North Slope. And Gar Pessel's fall memo to Harry Jamison, followed by Richfield's seismic work, had triggered Richfield and Exxon to likewise look toward the coast.

BP and Sinclair geophysicists had located three large geological structures below the Arctic coastal plain—two of them beneath land the state had selected. BP now wanted the state to offer the land up for competitive lease bidding.

BP renewed its pressure on the state, again complaining about being muscled out of lease blocks by more aggressive U.S. companies and threatening to pack up and go home. After a June 1964 meeting with BP, Bell told Holdsworth that BP is "apparently being outbid by West Coast U.S. companies in acquiring blocks. They [BP] have on hand under lease an exploration program that extends into the next year, but if they cannot get more land they will probably figure on pulling out unless they have a discovery before that time."

"We should move ahead as rapidly as we can," Bell said, to get all the planning out of the way for a competitive lease sale in December.

Apparently sympathetic to BP's plight as well, Holdsworth wrote in July to Senator Bartlett in Washington that BP "may withdraw from Alaska if there is no opportunity to increase its Arctic holdings in the near future."

BP seemed to receive every courtesy as the state moved toward its first North Slope sale. Near the end of September, deputy resources commissioner Chuck Herbert sent Holdsworth

On March 27, 1964, the situation changed with a jolt. Southcentral Alaska was shaken, for almost five incredibly long minutes, by one of the world's great earthquakes.

a list of the tracts to be offered at the December sale. The list had been prepared by Bell and his staff. Attached was a handwritten memo from Herbert:

"Roscoe (Bell) says that the attached is the recommendation of acreage for the December 9 sale. Suggest that announcement be made as soon as possible and that Thomas of BP be invited to Juneau to present his arguments in confidence, if BP would be hurt." At the bottom of the memo, Herbert had written Alwyne Thomas's Los Angeles phone number.

BP's Thomas was indeed invited to Juneau to present his case in confidence. Whether any change in the lease offering was made as a result of Thomas's plea is not known.

LOOKING BACK ON THE convoluted history of the state's decision to select land on the North Slope, an intriguing question arises: What if Egan had *not* chosen this land for the state? Would the federal government then have offered it for noncompetitive leasing? Probably so: the Bureau of Land Management had held lease drawings on acreage immediately to the south, and many Alaskans had filed successfully. If the lands at Prudhoe Bay had been offered the same way, individuals, including many Alaskans, would have become billionaires.

As it was, Egan's decision to select North Slope land in early 1964 made Alaska the "owner state," and royalty owner of one-eighth of Prudhoe Bay's oil. Made solely to solve an immediate bureaucratic land-title problem, Egan's decision would be the most important ever reached by a public official in the history of Alaska. Soon Alaska would become the No. 1 oil state in the nation. Under the state's selected acreage lay the Prudhoe Bay, Kuparuk, West Sak, and Ugnu oil fields—enough oil to furnish a quarter of America's domestic needs for decades, and enough to fuel Alaska's economy well into the 21st century.

INSIDE STORY

THE LITTLE GUYS LOSE

Independent leaseholders in the Alaska oil game were on the run in the '60s, But these little guys, myself included, didn't go down without a fight.

In late 1963, the state had offered for noncompetitive leasing a quarter of a million acres on the west side of Cook Inlet in the former Cook Inlet Bombing Range. At the same time, nearly 50,000 acres were offered for competitive bidding.

Phil Holdsworth and Roscoe Bell came up with the decision to offer those 50,000 acres competitively. Their rationale was that acreage within twenty-five miles of an Amoco gas well on West Foreland was especially valuable and capable of producing commercial gas. Thus it should be offered only to the highest bidder—and Holdsworth said he had authority under state law to classify territory surrounding the gas well as competitive.

A group of "little guys," most of whom wanted to secure leases in order to sell them to the actual oil operators, thought Holdsworth had no such authority. Organized as the Alaska Independent Petroleum Association, we sued. We claimed Holdsworth couldn't possibly have the necessary geologic information needed to make such a technical decision. Acreage twenty-five miles from the well couldn't be categorized as provably valuable for oil and gas. Our lawsuit sought to enjoin Holdsworth's classification order.

Our real fear, of course, was that if Holdsworth and Bell succeeded in classifying land on West Foreland as competitive, they would have an opening to classify all state land the same. If that happened, I and the other little guys couldn't lease for oil and gas anywhere; we would be priced out of the market.

I filed suit on behalf of the association. My first witness during the hearing before Superior Court Judge James Fitzgerald was association president Waring Bradley. Bradley had been instrumental in getting several wells drilled by outside independent operators. "Elimination of noncompetitive procedures will give major oil companies a virtual monopoly on state lands," he said.

The association's secretary, geologist Jerry Ganopole, who would become a business partner of mine, testified that Holdsworth's "maneuver amounts to ignoring the state's best long-range interests for the sake of getting immediate cash into the state treasury to cover next year's expenditures."

Former Union Oil geologist Lum Lovely called it "selling out the citizens and taxpayers of the state." And local lease broker Charles Ledbetter testified: "If this move were to go unchallenged, it would practically shut out the independent oil operators in Alaska."

Minutes before the Cook Inlet sale and drawing was to begin in the Loussac Library basement in Anchorage, a smiling Holdsworth appeared with the judge's order. The judge ruled that Holdsworth had the authority to classify the land and ordered the sale to proceed.

This seemed to be what Roscoe Bell was waiting for. The lands director asked the 1964 legislature for its approval for increasing the size of competitive leases and classifying *all* state oil and gas land as competitive. The 1964 legislature passed an amendment to the Land Act that gave the state commissioner of natural resources authority to classify land for competitive leasing if such a classification would be in the "best interests of the State"—a liberal requirement that would give the commissioner a much freer hand. No longer would the commissioner need to determine that the leasehold was near an existing discovery or was prospectively valuable for oil and gas.

Governor Egan signed the classification amendment and resources commissioner Holdsworth immediately classified all North Slope land competitive. Leaseholds would be offered up to the highest bidder. It would eventually mean the end of us "little guys."

Chapter 13

One for the Little Guys

Secretary of Interior Udall had promised Governor Egan he would hold four 4-million-acre noncompetitive oil and gas lease drawings on federal land on the North Slope. Egan now directed his commissioner of natural resources, Phil Holdsworth, to put together a competitive lease sale on state land on the Slope. This way, the state would continue to collect its 90 percent share of federal oil and gas revenues, plus receive cash from bids on its own Slope land.

The first 4-million-acre federal drawing was held June 11, 1964, for land lying east of Umiat between the Kuparuk and Sagavanirktok rivers. More than two dozen major oil companies and independents filed, along with a batch of "little guys" that included some well-known names: former Territorial governor Mike Stepovich, not-yet-governor Bill Sheffield, not-yet-Alaska Supreme Court Justice Jay Rabinowitz, future attorneys general Grace Schaible and Charlie Cole, state senator and lieutenant governor-to-be Lowell Thomas, Jr., and future Senate president Chancy Croft.

Fairbanksians Tom Miklautsch and partner Cliff Burglin filed. So did Locke Jacobs' group, already committed to Richfield. Earl Grammer, Jack Walker, Lum Lovely, Charles Ledbetter, and my new company, Alaska Exploration Corporation, also took part.

This drawing turned out to be the most profitable ever for these "little guys." For Richfield, these were some of its finest leasing hours as it acquired numerous tracts. Unprepared as usual and thus, again, unsuccessful in acquiring winning leases, BP and Sinclair, filing separately, won only one tract each. In contrast, Shell, leasing by itself, won eight tracts.

Most major West Coast oil companies acquired some leases, but Richfield used a clever leasing-team strategy that won it much more than its "share." Before the drawing, Richfield let it be known that it would pay winners $2.50 an acre plus a 2 percent overriding royalty for their leases. Richfield stationed people in key oil and gas cities throughout the U.S., ready to put their offer in front of successful drawees the minute their names were known.

Winning names and addresses from Dallas, Houston, Denver, Los Angeles, Anchorage, Juneau, and Fairbanks were read by the Fairbanks land office manager—and the landmen and lawyers of Richfield were most often first to contact them. With this aggressive team approach, Richfield acquired more leases from the mid-1964 drawing than any other company.

Noncompetitive lease drawings had been good to Richfield in Alaska. Richfield's Harry Jamison later offered his assessment of the system, taking a broad view. He said that this "lottery system" created "a middleman situation that was essentially nonproductive. This tended to skim some of the cream off of the good things that happened, whether it be dollars or overrides on production or whatever. The perception today is that all it does is create another layer of nonproductive interference in skimming some of the benefits off what is rightfully the province of the government.

"The other side of the coin, however, is that the competitive system, just by its nature, tends to eliminate the small individual who does not have the money to get into the game with the bigger boys."

THAT FEDERAL DRAWING was held inside Fairbanks' only movie theater. Doors to the dimly lit cavern on Fairbanks' main street opened promptly at 9 a.m. on June 11. Lying on the table at the front of the brightly lit stage were the BLM drawing documents. Lolling in darkened seats, the audience watched as the papers, prominently displayed in eight wicker baskets, were arranged by land office personnel.

At center stage stood a large plastic, transparent globe. Inside could be seen card stubs, torn from lease application forms, each stub giving the description of the land being applied for, the name of the applicant, and his or her

Ed "Pappy" Devine raised money from Copper River Valley residents to lease more than one-half million acres in Alaska. Pointing to a "mud volcano" near Glennallen.

address. Precisely at 10 the land office manager began explaining procedures to be used at the drawing. Lease maps and tract lists perched precariously on their laps, the oilmen in the audience were at attention.

As the land office manager spoke, BLM employees started writing numbers on maps pinned on side walls. Slowly it became apparent that these were "density maps"—with each number being the number of applications filed on individual drawing tracts. Adjusting to the dark, it also quickly became apparent that on one of these maps, the numbers 1 or 2 had begun to appear. These 1's and 2's were on a cluster of tracts in a particular area, off by itself, where only one or two people had filed. In fact, this chart showed only the number "1" on most tracts.

It became painfully obvious that these remote filings could not have held any interest for the major oil companies. Three Fairbanks businessmen had paid rental and filing fees of almost $80,000 for nearly three dozen lease applications in this area—with the intention of selling any leases they won to oil companies. Looking at the density map, one of the three businessmen suddenly became aware of the mistake of filing where no oil companies were interested.

He immediately began handwriting a notice of application withdrawal. He rushed this to the land office and stated that he and his partners'

177

applications, which had not yet been drawn, were herewith being withdrawn. He knew if their stubs were drawn by the land office manager, the leases would issue and he and his partners would be stuck.

I sat in that dark theater as part of the audience. And I noticed with some nervousness the density map that showed the parcels Jerry Ganopole and I had filed on in the Toolik area. What I saw was the numbers 1 and 2. One or possibly two applications. Who the other applicant was on our tracts I couldn't know, but most likely it wasn't a major oil company. Why did we, and not the oil companies, find this area attractive? We had relied on Jerry's regional geology cobbled together from published government reports.

> **This drawing turned out to be the most profitable ever for these "little guys."**

For the first and only time, Jerry and I had borrowed money from a bank to pay for leases for ourselves personally. We were no company's nominee, and we had no buyer lined up. We had put up $25,000. For two Alaska "little guys" in the mid-1960s, that was a big gamble.

As the names of the winners in our area were read, we discovered that our sole competitor was a Catholic bishop. I couldn't believe that Francis D. Gleason, the bishop of Northern Alaska, knew any more about leasing oil and gas land than Jerry and I did. Was he a nominee for a major oil company? Unlikely. A major oil company wouldn't use a Catholic bishop for a nominee. Had some renegade geologist or a Fairbanks promoter teamed up with the church? Were the three Fairbanks businessmen in with the bishop even as they desperately tried to withdraw their applications?

Jerry and I hadn't been sure about filing in this area; we knew we were taking a chance. It now seemed certain our filings made no sense from the beginning. I sat stunned, contemplating my dilemma. Suddenly a figure approached me along the row of dark theater seats. A voice calm but foreboding as doomsday said: "Jack, we shot that area, there's nothing there." Turning quickly toward the voice, I recognized the kindly face of the chief geophysicist for Shell, a man I got to know well in the mid-1950s while reporting for the Alaska Scouting Service. He was attempting to help me avert disaster!

I thanked him for his advice, then sat numbly staring at my lists and at the density map. An awful chasm began to open at my feet and began drawing me in. On stage, the land office manager called out the name of another winner: "Alaska Exploration Corporation." And another. Panic!

For one straw-clutching moment, I pondered: if Fairbanks businessmen could withdraw their applications, so could I. I could race to the land office like they had—or stand up, right then, and shout "I want out!" But it was too late. The land office manager at this point was continuing to drone out the name of our corporation.

I began to think, "Roderick, you're supposed to be an oilman, so act like one. You wanted to play the game, so play it. You got your Toolik leases, so try to act like you wanted them." I settled back until the drawing ended.

Back in the hotel room, I phoned Jerry and described the situation. I could hear both disappointment and panic in his voice. But there was absolutely nothing we could do. If Shell said our leases were worth zero, they were worth zero. Still, we owned them.

As I was packing to leave, I heard a knock on the door. It was Mobil landman Bill Cook. "Jack," he said, "do you have any of your Toolik leases left? We'll pay you $3 an acre plus a 2 percent overriding royalty for three of your Toolik leases." Would we be interested? I allowed as how we might.

An hour after the drawing, Jerry and I had recouped most of our loan. We had sold leases that Shell said were worthless for $3 an acre. Shell's discards were now colored yellow on Mobil's lease map. It didn't seem to matter what was underneath the land, so long as Mobil could show yellow on its North Slope map. It didn't make sense—but in the early stages in any newly explored geologic province, companies had to make sure they had some stake in leases or they would lose out entirely.

Richfield used a clever leasing-team strategy. The company stationed people in key oil and gas cities throughout the U.S., ready to put their offer in front of successful drawees the minute their names were known.

Our near-loss had turned into a handsome profit. We sold our remaining leases to other companies and after repaying the loan and our other expenses, we netted over $50,000—more than we ever made in any other lease drawing.

A week after the drawing, also having sold his Toolik leases, Bishop Gleason filed for two more leases in the same area, acting perhaps on the advice of his guardian angel.

Following a protracted appeal, the Fairbanks businessmen were permitted to withdraw their applications and be reimbursed for their lease rentals. Subsequent federal oil and gas lease drawings, needless to say, no longer posted density maps. Once you filed, you stayed, win or die.

THE FILING PERIOD for the second 4-million-acre federal North Slope drawing opened in January 1965. By the time the April 13 drawing was held, more than 30,000 lease applications flooded the federal land office in Fairbanks. The major oil companies had completed geophysical surveys of the area and knew which parcels looked good, so of a total of 1,500 parcels offered, only 268 received applications. On one parcel in the middle of the best leasing area, more than 300 applications were filed.

The third federal drawing, on November 15, drew 1,700 applications for 160 parcels in the Brooks Range foothills area south and west of the area in which the first filings had been made. This drawing attracted only two majors, Amoco and Union, plus a number of independents, including Empire State and Allardyce Petroleum.

By the time the fourth drawing was to be held, Interior Secretary Udall had put a freeze on all federal land in Alaska because of Native land protests and claims, and the drawing was never held.

SPOTLIGHT ▮▮▮▮

COOK INLET ACTION

Shortly after the 1964 earthquake, and as the state prepared for its first North Slope sale, Amoco President Randolph Yost announced that his company had brought in "Alaska's biggest oil producer, with pay thickness comparable to those found in the prolific Middle East."

The Chakachatna group's Middle Ground Shoal well No. 4 had tested an average of 650 barrels per day at each of eight different geologic horizons, Yost said. Not only that, there was 1,500 feet of net oil pay in the well at depths between 5,400 and 9,800 feet. Already, Yost said, a 32-well field platform was being fabricated on the West Coast for the area.

By the end of 1965, new oil and gas fields had been discovered in Cook Inlet by Union, Marathon, Texaco, Superior, and Mobil. New pressure was put on the state to hold another Cook Inlet lease sale. On September 28, 1965 the state staged its fifteenth sale.

"It was one of the most interesting we ever held," resources commissioner Phil Holdsworth exclaimed enthusiastically. "We had as high as twelve bidders on a single tract and a lot of new company names . . . an increase in independents."

Independents bid on a variety of small offshore tracts. Major Continental Oil, along with Apache, Petroleum International, and Anadarko Production bid, as did locals Frank J. Novosel, Cliff Burglin, Lum Lovely, Waring Bradley, William G. Zaegel, and my Alaska Exploration Corporation. Independents bid as high as $6 an acre, in some cases offering more than the majors.

"This is a healthy situation," Holdsworth stated. "Nationwide it has been proven that independents produce more oil than majors in the domestic industry." The 226 parcels sold at the sale brought the state $4.6 million, an average bid of $15 an acre.

Middle Ground Shoal was now producing oil, and production of gas from North Cook Inlet and oil from Granite Point was about to begin. Construction of six more offshore platforms was in the planning stage. To begin oil moving to West Coast refineries, a 42-mile Cook Inlet oil pipeline was being built along the west side of the Inlet from Granite Point to a marine terminal at Drift River. Six of Alaska's fourteen gas fields—Kenai, Swanson River, Sterling, MGS, Birch Hill, and South Barrow—were producing.

Despite the fact that new independents had arrived to acquire Cook Inlet leases, those who had poured in following the Swanson River discovery by now had quietly begun to disappear. With little hope of getting in on the activity on the high-cost North Slope and with only the majors seeming to have success in Cook Inlet, all but a few of the more than 100 independents that were active in the late 1950s and early 1960s had left the state. "Little guys" like Locke Jacobs and Jack Walker, no longer able to participate by resorting to the free-wheeling leasing methods of earlier days, began to fade. Most significantly, in late 1965, oil pioneer Earl Grammer had died.

Thus in some undefinable way, 1965, still several years before the immense Prudhoe Bay discovery, seemed to signal the end of an era in Alaska oil development. Alaska was on the cusp of becoming a major oil state, but it would still be years before we knew it for sure.

Pan Am's (Amoco) self-contained platform on Middle Ground Shoal in 1962.

Chapter 14

Prudhoe Bay Leased

As the state geared up for its first competitive lease sale on the Slope, Governor Egan was coming under pressure from the "little guys" successful at the June federal drawing and from oil companies with little or no geophysical information on the million-plus acres selected by the state. They didn't want Egan to hold any state sale at all. The oil companies, on the other hand, notably BP and Sinclair, were quietly lobbying state officials to select even more Slope land for the state and to offer it for competitive lease.

The state went ahead with its plans for the first sale: leases in the Colville area would go on the block December 9. And even before the first sale, lands director Roscoe Bell announced that a second sale would be held the following July for lands to the east of Colville, near Prudhoe Bay. The majors were about to get what they wanted: a chance to bid directly for oil leases that their geophysical surveys increasingly said were hot prospects.

At the sale on December 9, 1964, BP and Sinclair bought leases on most of the 600,000 acres offered. Bids on the 128 parcels lying west of Prudhoe Bay in the Colville area averaged about $32 an acre. The joint bids by BP and Sinclair came to nearly $4 million of the sale's $6,145,000 total. BP and Sinclair's bids outlined a broad, domelike structure lying in a southeast-northwest direction.

Geophysicist Arthur Bowsher said the Sinclair staff in Anchorage actually didn't want the company to bid in the December state sale. "They requested that bids be planned only for the Prudhoe Bay structure," he recalls.

Instead, Sinclair official Loren Ware "instructed them to prepare for strong bidding on the Colville structure," Bowsher said. "His reasoning was that no one truly knew the stratigraphy or the reservoir properties of either structure. Even though he too believed Prudhoe to be the most attractive, the fact was that the Colville acreage had come up for bid first."

The "little guys" at this time were down, but not out. At the bidding on Colville, several of us made a try at competing with the high rollers and came out of it with some success. Several "little guys" won eleven tracts by spending $32,000 at $1.25 an acre. My Alaska Exploration Corporation bid between 51 cents and $2 an acre on eighteen tracts, winning one, near the Kuparuk River, with a bid of $1.08 an acre. On one side of our parcel was Richfield's and Humble's bid of $1.57 an acre and on the other was BP's $2.56. Subsequently we assigned our lease to Apache Corporation of Minneapolis for about $10 an acre.

THE PERIOD BEFORE the state's Prudhoe Bay sale of July 1965 brought the surprise withdrawal of one of the major North Slope players. During the winter of 1963-64, as one well after another in the Brooks Range foothills was plugged and abandoned, Sinclair Oil lost more and more of its nerve. Sinclair's domestic exploration manager, Loren Ware, pleaded for more support for Alaska, but his words in Tulsa and New York fell on increasingly deaf ears.

Zed Grissom, who was Sinclair's Alaska district manager at the time, and is now an Alberta, Canada oil independent, says the "decision to withdraw was made by gutless management at the top. That's why we pulled out."

No matter whose blunder it was, it was one Sinclair would live to regret. At the state's 1965 sale of Prudhoe Bay leases, BP would bid without Sinclair.

(Some time after the Prudhoe Bay sale, BP offered to sell a share of its leases to its former partner. Sinclair, by then trying to shut down its Alaska operations, declined. Following the Prudhoe Bay oil discovery, Sinclair realized its grievous error and sent representatives to London for a shot-in-the-dark buyback attempt. Sinclair's people were received cordially at Britannic House, and their offer was politely turned down.)

BRITISH PETROLEUM was getting its hopes up about Prudhoe Bay even as Sinclair was beginning to think about backing out. Retired BP geologist Roger Herrera tells about BP geophysicists coming into the company's Palos Verdes, California, offices one day in early 1964 and unrolling a huge contour map of the Slope.

"They were grinning like Cheshire cats," Herrera says. "'What do you think of this?' they said.

"Everybody looked at the maps and said, 'Aw, come on.'

"'Oh no, this is true,' the geophysicists insisted, 'this is absolutely genuine.'"

What had excited the geophysicists was data outlining the fabulous Prudhoe Bay structure.

"It was so big," Herrera said. "In those days, it was rather uniform and perfect. It had none of the irregularities we now know actually exist."

Even so, BP's Palos Verdes geologists said to forget it. They were very suspicious of the data. "In those days we literally didn't know how deep the permafrost was," Herrera said. "We guessed that it affected the seismic interpretation radically.

In the mid-1960s, a cautious Sinclair Oil made an immense miscalculation in deciding to withdraw from the North Slope, despite pleas from Sinclair executives Zed Grissom (left) and Loren Ware. Grissom blames the decision on "gutless management at the top."

"At first the reflections off the permanently frozen ground became difficult to interpret. Later, we used a new sound-velocity technique that beamed through the permafrost. When we put this data into the computers, the whole structure was eliminated on the screen. It sort of disappeared.

"I heard somebody say, `There, I told you so. It's too good to be true. There's nothing there.'"

Despite the geologists' misgivings, BP's London managers believed the geophysicists had plotted a massive structure near Prudhoe Bay. Better still, BP thought it was the only company that had mapped it.

Before the July 1965 Prudhoe Bay sale, a rumor circulated that Alaska BP personnel had been told by London headquarters to limit their bids.

"Nonsense," says Geoff Larminie, a former BP manager for Alaska. "We knew exactly what we were doing in 1965, and we weren't short of money." Larminie says BP carried out a strategy of bidding on the entire Prudhoe Bay structure, with a concentration on the section BP thought the most promising, the flanks.

THE PARTNERSHIP OF RICHFIELD AND EXXON jumped into the Prudhoe Bay lease sale with a determination to outbid BP. Richfield and Exxon had lost out at the 1964 Colville sale when BP and Sinclair bid around $32 an acre.

"We decided we had to bid at least three times what BP bid in 1964 to get the tracts," recalls Charlie Selman, a Richfield geophysicist at the time.

So on July 14, 1965, Richfield and Exxon bid as high as $94 an acre for Prudhoe Bay's crestal tracts, outbidding BP, Atlantic Refining, Chevron, Shell, Mobil, and Phillips. The state took in almost $4 million for leases on forty square miles of land on the crest of the Prudhoe Bay structure, with proceeds from the entire sale totaling just over $6 million.

BP's bids for the same crestal tracts averaged about $47 an acre. Bids by Chevron and Shell were much lower. BP's overall average bid, including acreage off to the east, was just over $16 an acre. The difference was that BP put nearly a quarter of its money on 32 "flank" leases, with bids as low as $11 to as high as $32 an acre.

Mobil and Phillips jointly bid $12 an acre and Atlantic Refining no more than $6 an acre. Our Alaska Exploration Corporation and Fairbanks attorney

Richard Cole won one lease for $1.10 an acre and later assigned it to Texaco for a nice profit.

By spreading its bids across the entire structure, BP captured more than half the oil in Prudhoe Bay.

Richfield's Harry Jamison recalls: "We bid higher on the crest and then lower on the flanks. . . . That's exactly why we got the crest—the gas cap—and a portion of the oil. BP got the oil rim."

RICHFIELD AND EXXON'S COUP in picking up most of the Prudhoe Bay crest raised some suspicions at BP.

"We were sure some of our seismic had been stolen, probably from a contractor, because of the way the bids came in," says BP's Geoff Larminie. "We were bloody sure that this had a significant impact on the bidding at the sale."

Suspicions turned toward Richfield, as the active exploration member of the Richfield/Exxon partnership. Richfield's bid pattern indicated that it possessed an interpretation similar to that indicated by BP's original Prudhoe Bay seismic data. That original seismic picture, before BP had it digitized and computerized and adjusted for the effects of the permafrost, had shown that most of the oil in the Prudhoe structure would be trapped on the crest.

"It was a total shock," says Roger Herrera of BP, when Richfield bid on the crest. "We were absolutely convinced we were the only company having seismic over the structure. After the sale it became clear as crystal that ARCO [Richfield] had the same seismic information that we did."

Larminie says independent oilman John J. King shed some light on the history of that time when he visited Larminie in his office one day in 1970.

> *"We were sure some of our seismic had been stolen, probably from a contractor, because of the way the bids came in."*
>
> —BP's Geoff Larminie.

"After we had been sitting there for about an hour, he says 'God, doesn't anybody have a drink around here?'

"I said "no, we don't have any booze in the office.'

"He says, 'You guys must know that you lost some seismic at some stage,' and he handed me back a roll of our North Slope seismic maps.

"There's no way J. J. could have done it unless he got it from somebody who got them from somebody.

"It was old seismic. That's the interesting point. . . .very early stuff, only a contractor's interpretation. The real thing was what our interpretation boys in the playback division did with it after they got the tapes."

Sinclair Oil lost more and more of its nerve, finally making a surprise decision to withdraw from the North Slope. The company's district manager at the time says the decision "was made by gutless management at the top."

BP had carefully massaged its original seismic data with computers, adjusting the seismic velocities for the effect of the frozen Arctic coastal permafrost. This frozen mantle, some of it 2,000-feet thick, skewed seismic waves before they returned to the earth's surface.

Larminie says that by the spring of 1965, BP knew the Prudhoe Bay structure was much larger than originally thought. The company then believed that oil would most likely be found on the flanks of the structure. BP's decision was to bid across the entire structure, with higher-than-normal bids on the flanks.

BP'S SUSPICIONS WERE UNFOUNDED, people at Richfield say. "The structure at Prudhoe Bay was obvious on the seismic data that all the companies had," Gil Mull says. "BP certainly should not have been surprised that other companies also saw it in their data. After all, several companies bid on the Prudhoe tracts and obviously had somewhat similar interpretations."

Geophysicist Charlie Selman says his company, Richfield, knew BP was spending a lot of time and money on detailed permafrost analysis. But Richfield, then being absorbed by Atlantic Refining, decided not to do any of its own.

Selman says Richfield had hired a man named Rudy Berlin—a former employee of BP's geophysical contractor, Western Geophysical—prior to the Prudhoe Bay sale. "Rudy Berlin told me that BP had done extensive velocity work from their seismic data that broadened the Prudhoe Bay structure," Selman says.

Richfield bid with its own information, however, Selman says. "Berlin's biggest contribution to our Prudhoe Bay data was the refinement of the data showing the truncation lines of the various formations."

BP wasn't as clever as it seemed to believe it was, says Gil Mull of Richfield. "Don't get me wrong, BP was, and is, a sharp company. But I don't think their exploration strategy and knowledge of the area at the time was any sharper than anyone else's."

Selman remembers that "Paul Bollheimer was the Richfield geophysicist who first recognized the Prudhoe Bay structure. We had programmed a line about three or four miles south of the coastline that showed a rollover, and Bollheimer sketched in a structure to the north that turned out to be Prudhoe Bay. Subsequent work and seismic maps drawn by Pete Clara were used for bidding purposes.

"If memory serves correctly, the five people who selected the tracts for bid were Harry Jamison, Armand Spielman, Ben Ryan, George Shepphird, and myself. Our bidding strategy was formulated by looking at BP-Sinclair bids in the Colville area and in essence going triple their bids there. Actual bids were worked up by the Los Angeles land group under Frank McPhillips."

After the Prudhoe Bay sale, relations between BP and Richfield "were at an absolute all-time zero," says BP's Herrera. By that time, Atlantic Refining and Richfield had merged, forming the Atlantic Richfield Company (ARCO). Herrera says a member of BP's board of directors began traveling the world advising BP employees to have nothing to do with ARCO.

"ARCO stole BP's Prudhoe seismic data," this director told BP employees, according to Herrera, and they should have no dealings with the company.

INSIDE STORY

IRON MEN

Amoco seemed on a roll. In mid-1964, company president Randolph Yost had announced its big find at Middle Ground Shoal. And in September, the company upstaged even itself with a dramatic mineral discovery. At an Anchorage press conference, Yost announced that Amoco had completed staking some 10,000 acres of claims on "roughly a billion tons of recoverable iron." It was a reserve, he said, "larger than any yet found in the United States with the exception of those in Minnesota."

Now the public knew what Amoco had been up to. The previous June, Amoco had hired all the helicopters in Cook Inlet, at tremendous cost—and grounded them. Rumors raced through Anchorage that the catastrophic earthquake that spring had shifted huge slabs of iron ore to the surface, and that Amoco had found them. As rumors multiplied and ricocheted, the grounded helicopters stayed put, effectively keeping any potential airborne snoopers on foot.

But the September announcement came as no surprise to me and my partner in Alaska Exploration Corporation, Jerry Ganopole. Along with everyone else, we had been trying to uncover Amoco's secret. Why had they grounded the helicopters? And was there any truth to the rumor that an Amoco crew was out on the Alaska Peninsula, near Kamishak Bay, about two hundred miles southwest of Anchorage?

We hired a floatplane, and I set off to find out. Kamishak Bay was brown bear country—an area where the huge animals were known to rear up on their hind feet and take swipes at low-flying planes—so I also hired a young man with a rifle to accompany me for protection. We landed on the shore of a small lake near McNeil River. After a half-day hike to a place shown on the map as Chenik Mountain, the vigilant rifleman and I stood in the darkness atop a high, rocky ridge, where we unrolled our sleeping bags.

The next morning, we awoke to see far below us a large group of men in bright orange vests, busily painting red lines on the valley floor. They were plodding head down, laying out what appeared to be straight survey lines. The large size of the group and their brightly colored outfits told us we were looking at the Amoco crew. We climbed down the steep slope toward the valley, avoiding the crew, and soon located one of Amoco's corner stakes.

With the crew far off, we began staking alongside Amoco's red line. Starting from the corner stake, we plotted as we went along, walking off parallel to

Amoco's line, pounding in our stakes as fast as we could. At the end of a very long day, we had staked five claims. Four days later, Jerry and the rifleman returned and staked three more.

The story ends badly both for us and for Amoco. Despite Amoco's dramatic September announcement, the ore was only 15 percent iron. After two test drilling seasons, Amoco ceased assessment work. It let its claims die, and so did we.

Chapter 15

The Birth of ARCO

n the summer of 1965, Atlantic Refining board chairman Robert O. Anderson and Richfield chairman Charles S. Jones began discussions on a possible merger. Despite the fact that Richfield had discovered Swanson River oil, held most of Prudhoe Bay's crestal acreage jointly with Exxon, and had explored most of Alaska's sedimentary basins, this aggressive, imaginative company was in serious trouble. Although it had at times seemed the best, if not the luckiest, exploration company in Alaska, its very success seemed part of its problem. Success in Alaska had again brought its corporate problems to the attention of federal regulators.

"Richfield was a strong Republican organization," says Atlantic's Anderson. "The Kennedys never forgot a slight. Bobby [Attorney General Robert Kennedy] told his Justice Department to look at the Richfield situation." Now, despite its achievements in high-risk Alaska ventures, Richfield could no longer ward off the power of the Justice Department.

Bob Anderson first visited Alaska in May 1965 to review his company's activities. To his dismay he found that Atlantic had participated in only one Alaska well, had drilled none of its own, and had gathered very little North Slope geological or geophysical information. It was obvious to Anderson that Atlantic was far behind its competitors.

An anecdote about the reputed company attitude toward Alaska at the time has one Atlantic Refining executive, who accompanied Anderson on his

1965 visit, remarking: "I'll drink all the oil anybody finds on the North Slope." This supposed utterance missed the mark so badly that it became an inextricable part of Alaska's oil exploration folklore.

Anderson had been elected chairman of Atlantic's board just a short time before his Alaska visit. Three years earlier, Anderson, then forty-four, had become a member of the board when he and his brother merged their independent Hondo Oil Corporation into Philadelphia-based Atlantic Refining. The brothers became Atlantic's single largest shareholders.

As chairman, Anderson soon found crude-short Atlantic to be an almost passive exploration company. His first task was to breathe life into its exploration arm. He had to find new crude reserves in order to rebuild a once-proud organization. But how?

RICHFIELD WAS TARGETED in the 1960s by the Justice Department's antitrust division, which filed a lawsuit alleging control of the company by Sinclair Oil and Cities Service. These two companies, the lawsuit said, had to divest themselves of their interest in Richfield within seven years. During the 1930s, Sinclair and Cities Service had helped pull Richfield out of bankruptcy and in the process ended up with, respectively, 28.4 percent and 29.6 percent of Richfield's common shares. As a result, they had effective control of Richfield operations.

Richfield's then-chairman Charlie Jones says Richfield's exploration plans were always insulated from Sinclair board members. But Harry Jamison, a Richfield geologist in Los Angeles during the early 1960s, says he provided Sinclair's

Several executives of the newly formed Atlantic Richfield Company pose during a visit to the North Slope in the fall of 1966. From left to right: Louis Davis, John Sweet, pilot, "Mo" Benson, Thornton Bradshaw, Harry Jamison. Atlantic Refining stepped into a top spot on the Slope thanks to its merger with Richfield.

HARRY JAMISON

one-man Los Angeles office with Richfield's current drilling information on a regular basis. Even Jones says Richfield invited Sinclair to participate with it and Cities Service in foreign ventures and that Sinclair accepted twice, both times in

Hugo Anderson, (right), Chicago banker who financed Havenstrite dedicated ARCO Anchorage Tanker in 1973 with Anchorage Mayor Jack Roderick and his wife, Martha Roderick.

Canada. In Alaska during 1961, Sinclair, Richfield, and BP jointly drilled a well alongside the Bering River on the eastern shore of the Gulf of Alaska.

Under pressure from the Justice Department, Charlie Jones went out to find a buyer for Richfield Oil Corporation. This would satisfy the department's demand that Sinclair and Cities Service divest. It would also mean the end of Richfield as a separate company.

Phillips, Exxon, Tenneco, and Sunray had shown interest in acquiring Richfield, but Jones felt BP would be the most ardent suitor. Jones visited London, but his $80 per share asking price was too high for the Brits. For a while, it looked like Cities Service might actually be the bridegroom, but each time offers fell through.

Atlantic's Bob Anderson was very interested, but he also found the $80 per share asking price too high. Instead of walking away as others had, he made a counter-offer. Atlantic would trade one share of its new convertible preferred stock for one share of Richfield's common. Each share of Atlantic's preferred could later be converted into 85/100ths of a common share of Atlantic. Charlie Jones pondered the offer. After consulting his financial advisers, he agreed.

Thus on September 16, 1965, after having almost no Alaska presence, Anderson suddenly found himself leading one of only three major oil companies seriously exploring the North Slope. Later asked whether he knew what he had acquired on the North Slope in the merger, Anderson replied: "Just plain luck."

195

The Atlantic/Richfield merger agreement was signed only two months after Richfield had come away with major holdings from the state's Prudhoe Bay lease sale.

RICHFIELD, THE LEADING EXPLORER for Alaska oil and a principal West Coast marketer, had expired. Its relatively small size and its aggressive exploration style made most Alaskans feel it was particularly sympathetic to the political aspirations of the Territory and new state. Not only those Alaskans of an especially independent bent, like Locke Jacobs, but the entire Alaska community mourned its passing.

Ratified by shareholders of both companies on January 3, 1966, the merger of Atlantic and Richfield catapulted the new organization into seventh in size of all oil companies in the United States. Crude oil from Richfield's 1965 Prudhoe Bay leases would make the new company immensely profitable.

Shortly after shareholders approved the merger, Bob Anderson and Richfield executive "Mo" Benson flew to the North Slope. It was then that Anderson decided the name of the merged organization would be Atlantic Richfield Company.

(The merged Richfield later played a part in the demise of one of the oil companies that had helped pull Richfield out of bankruptcy in the 1930s. On March 7, 1969, most of the assets of Sinclair Oil Company were acquired by Atlantic Richfield, including lease interests at Kuparuk on the North Slope that turned out to be very profitable.)

Atlantic Richfield (ARCO) named Richfield's Harry Jamison as its first Alaska district manager. Geologist Jamison was a UCLA graduate when he was first hired in 1950 by Richfield's then chief geologist, Mason Hill. Starting out "sitting" wells in California's Cuyama and San Joaquin valleys, Jamison then spent time with Richfield in Oregon and Washington before being assigned the responsibility of Alaska in 1960.

Jamison got the nod from ARCO after he made a presentation to Atlantic Refining's North American production head, Louis Davis. Jamison felt confident that afternoon in Los Angeles as he explained Alaska's petroleum potential to Davis, and for good reason. Jamison had supervised Richfield's work for five years in most of Alaska's geologic basins. And of course Jamison had the blessing of his boss, Mason Hill.

Atlantic geologist John M. Sweet was chosen as Alaska district geologist for Atlantic Richfield. Like Jamison, Sweet was a "people person" and later became one of the few major oil company employees to win election to the Alaska legislature.

SPOTLIGHT

THE MEN BEHIND ARCO

When Bob Anderson took over at Atlantic Refining in the mid-1960s, a primary asset of the company was its newly hired president, Thornton F. Bradshaw. Anderson says Bradshaw "was really not an oilman. Brad automatically deferred to me on oil matters. He never tried to second-guess me. He respected my judgment on oil and the business side, so we worked side by side. Brad had a great sense of issues and people. We both had a strong commitment to the 'public interest.'"

Robert O. Anderson

As a young man, Anderson studied under the enfant-terrible of U.S. education, Robert Hutchins. Students at the two-year University of Chicago in the 1930s, under Hutchins, had little choice in course selection. They were force-fed Aristotle, Marx, Freud, and other world thinkers before narrowing in on a profession.

"Anderson and Bradshaw operated more like sociologists than businessmen" says Francis X. McCormack, former general counsel of Atlantic's successor company, Atlantic Richfield (ARCO). "Their personnel policies encouraged the hiring of minorities and women."

In the early 1980s, ARCO's threat to withdraw from the Anchorage Petroleum Club forced it to open its membership to women, and ARCO was the first major U.S. oil company to select women for its board of directors. Under the leadership of Anderson and Bradshaw, ARCO also became the first U.S. oil company to publish an annual "Social Performance Report," which singled out what the company was or was not doing to help the communities in which it did business.

Chapter 16

Tough Days On The Slope

he excitement of the state's lease sales at Colville and Prudhoe Bay in 1964 and 1965 soon developed into the toil of trying to turn the promise of oil into reality. A frustrating series of stops and starts would be the prelude to the eventual Prudhoe Bay discovery.

The state had taken in more than $12 million from its two North Slope lease sales. Rentals on this leased land were bringing in almost $1 million a year, while another $2 million a year poured in from the state's 90 percent rental revenue-sharing formula on about 5 million North Slope federal acres. However, by the end of 1965, most of Prudhoe Bay had been leased, so there was no immediate prospect of another bonanza to the state from sale of leases. And prospects of actually finding oil were uncertain.

———————

THE FIRST ATTEMPT to discover commercial quantities of oil on the state's Arctic coast land got under way in mid-November 1965 on a lease acquired by BP and Sinclair at the Colville sale. By this time, Sinclair had closed its Anchorage office and had backed out of any further North Slope deals. But Sinclair remained in charge of drilling the Colville well.

The incredible size of the Colville oil structure meant a great wave of excitement in the oil community as everyone waited to find out what the first find on the coastal plain would be like. A discovery on this largest of all coastal plain structures would undoubtedly signal expanded exploration of the entire Slope. Oil and state officials watched closely as the well proceeded.

Early drill-stem tests showed potential production of as much as several hundred barrels of oil per day. Then came the letdown: the productive sandstone section was found to be too thin to provide commercial oil. Early in 1966, Sinclair and BP abandoned the well.

THE NEXT OPERATION that generated some hope was a well called Susie, on federal land about sixty miles south of Prudhoe Bay. Before the Atlantic Richfield merger, Richfield and Exxon had formed a drilling unit to drill the well near a U.S. Survey bench mark. Several of these geographical reference points in the Sagavanirktok River area had been given women's names: Clara, Betty, Susie. The well would be drilled near Susie.

Richfield had picked up the acreage at the first 1964 federal lease drawing. Geophysical reflections on the land showed an east-west trending anticline, a reversal in dip of the strata, which could form a possible oil trap.

The newly formed ARCO planned to go ahead with the Susie well before work got under way on its first well at Prudhoe Bay. "The Susie well . . . was drilled because of an obligation to the USGS on a development contract," says ARCO's "Mo" Benson in "Prudhoe Bay. . .Discovery," Gene Rutledge's 1987 publication. "The Prudhoe Bay State No. 1 was to be drilled second since leasing provisions did not require the immediate drilling to hold that tract."

Geologist Gil Mull recalls, "The Susie looked like a reasonable prospect because it was the first subsurface structure north of the oil-saturated sandstone outcrop that Gar Pessell memo reported—only about fifteen miles away."

Old-timers like to tell of the excitement generated by the first oil-rig airlift to the North Slope. The rig would be used to dig the Susie. Transporting an entire drill rig to the Slope in early 1966 would be a humongous operation requiring permission from the U.S. Air Force, because the military had exclusive right to the type of plane that could do the job, the Hercules C-130.

Richfield's Charlie Jones phoned the president of Lockheed Aircraft, who called the Secretary of the Air Force, who gave his OK. Only then could the Loffland Brothers rig, located at Exxon's Bear Creek No. 1 drill site at Cold Bay, be airlifted by C-130 to the Slope.

Moving was accomplished by people like Richfield's Benny Loudermilk, says Harry Jamison. "He was an old Richfield roughneck, driller and tool-pusher. He was just as rough as a cob with a heart of gold."

Jamison says Lee Wilson, ARCO's drilling and production superintendent, "was intelligent enough to let practical men like Loudermilk, Bill Congdon, Joe Mann, and Ernie Arp get up there and get the job done."

Drilling the Susie began in late February 1966. By late June, drilling below 10,000 feet, the well was suspended for the summer. In those days on the Slope, the state prohibited drill rigs from operating from mid to late summer—from "breakup to freeze-up"—because of concerns that drilling equipment would scar the tundra during the annual surface melting.

> *"A lot of people were saying just forget it. Just let it go. It was nip and tuck whether we would just walk away and relinquish all our leases on the Slope."*
>
> —BP's Roger Herrera

As the Susie was on summer standby, ARCO chairman Bob Anderson was telling the Alaska State Chamber of Commerce his company planned to spend $33 million on capital expenditures in Alaska during 1967. Most of it would be in Cook Inlet, but a substantial portion would be on the Slope. Anderson said the planned investment by ARCO "is one of the largest of any oil company, and was due to recent exploration successes in high-cost exploration areas, most notably Cook Inlet."

A few weeks earlier, Union Oil President Fred L. Hartley said his company would spend $25 million in Alaska during 1967.

Drilling on the Susie well started again in late October 1966. Some minor oil shows were found between 1,800 and 3,500 feet—but that was it. The well was drilled to 13,500 feet, but was finally plugged and abandoned in January 1967. The Susie rig was later moved to Prudhoe Bay to dig ARCO's historic State No. 1 well.

BRITISH PETROLEUM was going through a period of major reassessment of its position in the North Slope. Its attempts to drill successfully for oil and its requests for further state lease sales were being frustrated. Was the Slope worth all the investment BP was making there, company officials began asking.

Following the 1965 Prudhoe Bay sale, BP immediately requested that more offshore land be offered for lease in both the Colville River delta and the Prudhoe Bay area. Alwyne Thomas asked the state to hold another North Slope sale before the end of the year, requesting as usual that BP's "nominations"—the land the company wants—remain confidential. Unless the sale was held, Thomas pointed out, BP's Alaska operation wouldn't be able to spend its appropriated budget for that year.

Resources commissioner Holdsworth rejected BP's plea for more land, cancelling a planned November North Slope lease sale. Holdsworth cited a lack of sufficient interest. In his view, BP was the only company showing a real interest in the area, so there would be no effective competition in the bidding at a sale.

BP was also getting bad news from the field, as the well it had been digging at Colville with Sinclair Oil turned up dry.

"We have done our part," British Petroleum's L. O. Gay said at the time. "We'll hang on and let someone else carry the load for a while."

BP resigned itself to waiting for results of the first well to be drilled at Prudhoe Bay by ARCO. Retrenching severely, BP concentrated its Arctic personnel in one office in Palos Verdes, California, to await ARCO's Prudhoe Bay results.

BP's Roger Herrera says his company withdrew to Palos Verdes not only because of the Colville dry hole and its failure to get more land on the Slope, but also because for the first time, the British government placed a budgetary crimp on exploration. Herrera says this financial restraint also prompted a BP decision to pull out of the Canadian Arctic islands.

The Arctic Slope Native Association filed a lawsuit claiming the Inupiat Eskimos had "aboriginal title to the land . . . from time immemorial."

Geologist Herrera recalls a visit to his Canadian Arctic island geologic field camp in August 1965 by BP's chief geologist, Norman Falcon.

"The weather had been nice and the geology up there had been spectacular," Herrera said. "We mapped huge areas and felt we had done an outstanding job. We were beginning to get highly enthusiastic about the theoretical prospects up there—the oil potential. Despite this, Falcon said BP was closing down the Arctic islands of Canada. All of us were absolutely crushed, totally devastated. We couldn't understand what was going on."

A great discussion followed within BP, says Herrera, on whether to drop everything in the Arctic, including Alaska. "A lot of people were saying just forget it. Just let it go. It was nip and tuck whether we would just walk away and relinquish all our leases on the Slope.

"The faction that finally prevailed was the one that believed we should just sit on the leases and pay the rents, keeping a warm shutdown position."

As a British Petroleum official, Welshman Alwyne Thomas worked to persuade the state of Alaska to open up more oil lands on the North Slope. (1967 photo)

Following the Colville well abandonment, ARCO's Susie drill rig was the only one operating on the Slope. Prospects for an early North Slope find looked dim. Major oil companies began divesting themselves of huge chunks of acreage by failing to pay rentals. ARCO alone summarily dropped more than 100,000 acres.

These relinquishments were a particularly bad omen because the Bureau of Land Management was no longer issuing leases on federal land where there was a conflict with Native claims. By early 1966, the Arctic Slope Native Association had claimed the entire North Slope. Later that year, Interior Secretary Udall imposed a freeze on all action involving federal land in Alaska.

ARCO'S SUSIE AND SINCLAIR'S COLVILLE were dry. A later attempt— Union's Kookpuk well seven miles southwest of Sinclair's Colville dry hole— also was abandoned. During this period, all eyes were turning toward Prudhoe Bay, where no well had yet been drilled. But first, the oil companies wanted the state to offer up the rest of its Prudhoe acreage.

Harry Jamison was telling the state's Phil Holdsworth and Roscoe Bell that ARCO wouldn't drill at Prudhoe as long as offshore acreage there remained unleased. No company would consider drilling a wildcat well unless the entire geologic structure was under lease, he contended.

Exxon, which held a partnership interest with ARCO in the Prudhoe leases, also was on the offensive. In a letter to Governor Bill Egan, Exxon's Los Angeles exploration manager pointed out that some unleased offshore acreage existed to the north of the proposed crestal drill site. ARCO and Exxon, Fred Sollars said, "cannot afford to drill the Prudhoe Bay structure with unleased lands offsetting our proposed drill site."

BP's Laurie Gay flew to Juneau in early 1966 to tell Egan that although BP did not have much money to bid with, his company still wanted the state to offer the Prudhoe tracts immediately. Egan had heard BP's "poverty" arguments and complaints of its inability to acquire sufficient acreage on the Slope long before. The governor remained unimpressed with BP's contention that it needed to justify the high costs of exploration on the Slope by being offered more competitive leases.

> *"We have done our part. We'll hang on and let someone else carry the load for a while."*
>
> —*BP's L. O. Gay*

The state had set aside November 22, 1966, as the date for a lease sale, but no specific North Slope acreage had been scheduled to go on the block. Bell sought advice from his staff on what land to offer. On October 7, he asked Governor Egan to allow him to offer nearly 38,000 acres offshore in Prudhoe Bay. The land lay atop the Prudhoe Bay structure.

Governor Egan said no. Only three days earlier, on October 4, the Arctic Slope Native Association, representing Inupiat Eskimos on the Slope, filed a lawsuit seeking to enjoin the state from selecting or leasing North Slope land. The suit claimed the Inupiats had "aboriginal title to the land by reason of use and original occupancy from time immemorial" and that "title has never been terminated by law, treaty, or sale." Because of the lawsuit and other Native land protests, Egan decided to not offer the Prudhoe Bay tracts. (He also withdrew four offshore Katalla tracts because of Chugach Native protests.)

Egan's decision came just a month before the general election that pitted him against Republican Walter J. Hickel, who had been gaining Native support for what was viewed as sympathy for their cause.

Chuck Herbert, then deputy resources commissioner, says Egan withdrew the Prudhoe tracts because he thought the companies didn't have enough information to operate safely offshore in the Arctic. "We didn't feel the industry had the technical expertise to meet Arctic conditions, yet," Herbert says. But that factor wasn't even considered by Egan.

Egan perhaps felt the state should wait until more companies showed bidding interest. Bell had advised Egan that only ARCO, Exxon, and BP were likely bidders. But the primary reason for Egan's decision was the Eskimo lawsuit and other Native protests.

So Egan, in effect, denied Laurie Gay's request, ARCO's and Exxon's pleas, and cut the heart out of the scheduled November state lease sale. With only a single well now tentatively planned for the entire North Slope, Egan had withdrawn those tracts which ARCO and, presumably, other companies needed before they would drill at Prudhoe Bay. But a sea change in the politics of Alaska was about to occur, a change that would greatly benefit the oil industry, and most particularly Atlantic Richfield, Exxon, and British Petroleum.

INSIDE STORY

EGAN'S "DEEP THROAT!"

Resources officials under Egan sensed that the governor was talking from time to time with a close contact in the oil industry. When he had a particularly puzzling question concerning oil, he would phone this person. "He was very suspicious of oil people," resources commissioner Phil Holdsworth said, "but there was someone in the industry he would periodically talk with."

Was it an oil lobbyist? Someone from outside? Was it former Chevron landman Charlie Hagens? Or Egan's Anchorage neighbor, Exxon landman Bob Walker?

"I don't think so," says John Havelock, attorney general in a later Egan administration. "I had the impression it was somebody higher up. Egan had a network of people he was very secretive about. . . . I think he had a 'deep throat' in the industry, whom he relied on a lot for estimates of the industry's position."

The connection was Howard Vesper, president of western operations for Chevron. Vesper first got to know Egan while flying with him in Chevron's plane to the dedication of the company's refinery at Nikiski in 1959. "A six-piece band was playing off-key," says Vesper, "and it was the first time I learned how politicians operate. About five hundred people were there and Bill went around the entire circle shaking everyone's hand and putting us way behind schedule."

On a subsequent visit to Alaska, Vesper spoke to the Alaska Chamber of Commerce in Ketchikan, then boarded a floatplane bound for Annette Island Airport so he could catch a jet to Seattle. Strong winds forced the floatplane back to Ketchikan. Governor Egan ran into Vesper in the lobby of Ketchikan's Ingersoll hotel and learned of his predicament. Egan, on his way to Annette Island by Coast Guard ship, offered Vesper a lift.

When the vessel reached the point where the floatplane had been forced back, they hit violent weather. The ship plunged up and down, lurching from side to side, and icy water poured into the hold. The ship seemed to be going down.

Vesper recalls: "Egan and I got into adjoining bunks in the forward part of the ship. I prayed. We braced ourselves against the bulkhead, hanging on for dear life, and rode out the storm. After that, it was no longer 'the governor and Mr. Vesper'; it was 'Bill and Howard.'"

Vesper and his wife periodically visited Juneau to refresh their friendship with the Egans. During his last two years with Chevron before retiring in 1967, Vesper continued to receive phone calls from Egan, seeking his advice—and Egan's lieutenants continued to ponder the identity of the governor's mysterious counselor.

Chapter 17

Oilman Wally Hickel

I n the early years of statehood, Republicans had rough political sledding. The bulk of the political power in Alaska rested in the hands of Democrats. Bill Egan was a Democrat. So was the entire Congressional delegation.

In 1966, Egan was running for his third term. The state constitution prohibits a governor from serving more than two successive terms. But illness had prevented Egan from assuming his duties until several months after his first term began in 1959. Thus he felt he could run a third time in November 1966. A majority of Alaskan voters felt otherwise. As the British might say, they "sent him packing."

Voters returned Democrats Bob Bartlett and Ernest Gruening to the U.S. Senate but a Republican was elected to Alaska's lone seat in the House of Representatives. Anchorage attorney Howard Pollock beat a longtime Democrat, Congressman Ralph Rivers. More significantly, Republican Walter J. Hickel, an Anchorage hotel owner, became the 49th State's second governor.

Native leaders had grown disgruntled with what they perceived to be Governor Egan's lukewarm support for their land claims. During the election campaign they viewed Hickel as being more sympathetic to their cause. Hickel would now be the one who would have to deal with the North Slope oil and gas leasing that had become a bone of contention between Natives and the oil companies. Eskimos were claiming all of the Slope, while the oil companies wanted to lease more of it.

As Hickel prepared to take office, federal leases were no longer being offered because Interior Secretary Udall's land freeze had been imposed in response to Native land claims. And Egan, near the end of his term, had decided against offering more of the state's Prudhoe Bay land, under pressure of the pending North Slope lawsuit and other Native land protests.

———————

THE NEW GOVERNOR brought with him to Juneau a vigorous developer's attitude and business manager's style. To this man who arrived in Alaska with 37 cents, leadership meant getting things done.

"If a leader does nothing, the bureaucracy does nothing," Hickel once stated. "Making people believe is more influential than any one act."

His predecessor's style had been highly personal. Egan talked to everyone and anyone even remotely involved with the issue at hand. He even had access to a highly placed oil company executive outside Alaska, his "deep throat," with whom he occasionally conferred on oil and gas matters.

Egan liked to wait until the last moment before making a decision. He never disclosed to anyone, including his wife, Neva, what that decision was prior to making it public.

Hickel's style was more instinctive, more spontaneous. Without much deliberation or reflection, he would say, "I'm making it work my way."

Hickel regularly phoned his commissioners to make sure they were carrying out his directions. He had named Fairbanks banker Frank Murkowski as commissioner of economic development, former Anchorage mayor George Sharrock as commissioner of commerce, and a development-oriented Southeasterner, Bob Ward, as commissioner of administration.

Hickel's personal attorney in Anchorage, Don Burr, became, for a short time, state attorney general. He appointed former Amoco supervisor of budgets and personnel J. Scott McDonald as his administrative assistant. Holdovers from the Egan administration (at least for the moment) were Phil Holdsworth, Chuck Herbert, and Roscoe Bell.

———————

HICKEL IMMEDIATELY began speaking and acting like an oil industry partner. With Hickel as governor, the state climate toward oil leasing changed overnight from caution to action. He countermanded Egan's Prudhoe Bay

HARRY JAMISON

The drill tower at ARCO's historic Prudhoe Bay State No. 1 well stands alone at Prudhoe in May 1967.

offshore lease withdrawal. Less than two months after Hickel's inauguration, the state offered the withdrawn parcels at a special oil and gas lease sale.

Hickel said he and his staff "put the pieces together at Prudhoe Bay in three weeks time. There were 50,000 attractive acres up there, and Alaska's destiny was in those resources."

The new governor knew that Native groups opposed such a sale. But he believed that besides helping oil companies, the sale might force Congress or the courts to move more quickly on Native land claims. And he felt that Native groups, not the state, had the burden to stop the sale.

Hickel, like Egan before him, came under pressure from the oil industry and some of his own officials. Everyone was pushing the governor to "go with the sale," recalls Roscoe Bell. He and Chuck Herbert believed that no company would drill at Prudhoe Bay unless it had under lease the offshore tracts.

Bell wrote to Hickel on the very day of his inauguration, December 5, 1966, urging "early scheduling of a special lease sale." Herbert recommended the same thing.

ARCO's Harry Jamison had met Hickel at business gatherings in Anchorage. He now went directly to talk with the governor and pleaded the industry's case for a Prudhoe Bay offshore sale.

Geologist Gil Mull says there is a simple geological reason why a company would want to have offshore acreage also under lease. "The Prudhoe Bay structure is composed of sediments deposited both in shallow marine seas and by streams on land," he explained. "Over millions of years these sediments were folded, broken by faults, and truncated by younger strata. The combination

211

of these geologic events resulted in a structure that mostly lay onshore. But part of the crest of the structure seen on the seismic data lay offshore, beneath the shallow waters of Prudhoe Bay, and no company would want to drill a well with adjacent unleased tracts overlying some of the higher parts of the structure."

Less than a month after taking office, Hickel approved a special sale of the tracts and, in his words, "put all the Prudhoe Bay pieces together."

WHEN NOTICE OF THE SALE was announced in late December, Hickel began to receive strongly worded Native messages of protest. There was no question that Natives unanimously opposed the sale. Native Anna Barnes telegraphed Hickel: "You never even bothered to investigate the situation as Egan promised to do."

One week before the sale, Hickel met with Native leaders. He got them to agree not to file protests against the sale in exchange for the state joining them in their claims against the federal government. They were promised

HARRY JAMISON

Alaska Governor Wally Hickel (right) pays a visit to the first oil well at Prudhoe, in the spring of 1967. Hickel and state lands director Roscoe Bell (left) talk with ARCO's Bill Congdon (second from left) and Bill Langdon at the Prudhoe Bay State No. 1 well.

212

that oil-lease money would not be locked in escrow; circulating cash, the Natives agreed, would be better for Alaska than banked cash.

At the Prudhoe Bay sale of January 24, 1967, all but 10,000 of the 47,000 acres offered lay offshore in the Beaufort Sea. ARCO and Exxon bid together, spending more than $1 million for seven leases, with bids averaging $35 an acre. Some of their bids were less than $10 an acre, but for two offshore tracts, they bid $121 and $233 per acre. BP, bidding alone, acquired six parcels with bids totaling $260,000, averaging about $17 an acre.

BP bid over the entire top of the structure, acquiring leases on the eastern edge only. ARCO and Exxon won "top" leases—leases on the tracts closest to the crestal acreage they had won in July 1965. Spreading its bets across the entire lease area, BP had reduced its chances of winning the "best" tracts, but increased the likelihood of winning "marginal" flank acreage. Again, as in the July 1965 Prudhoe Bay sale, its strategy turned out to be a stroke of luck, because most of the oil lay on the flanks (in the Endicott field).

On the day of the sale, Hickel wrote to the presidents of the successful oil companies. To Charles F. Jones, president of Exxon (no relation to Richfield's Charlie Jones), and Thornton Bradshaw, president of ARCO, he wrote: "Your bids are a satisfying indication of your desire to develop Alaska and of your faith in our administration's ability to resolve the Native land claims issue without jeopardizing your investment.

"I want to assure you personally that we are determined to solve the land claims matter fairly and equitably, while allowing Alaska's economic development to continue unimpeded."

ARCO WAS NOW getting ready to drill. Just three weeks after the January 24 Prudhoe sale, Harry Jamison wired Governor Hickel that ARCO would soon be starting a well.

ARCO's Susie drill rig was being moved to Prudhoe Bay for the job. But the move wasn't made without a little soul-searching within ARCO about the wisdom of going ahead with drilling at Prudhoe.

ARCO chairman Bob Anderson says it was a "consensus" decision to move the rig to Prudhoe and go ahead with another well after the Susie well came up dry. But, Anderson said, "If the Prudhoe well had been dry, we were going home. It was our last shot."

213

Jamison says the momentum that had built up during the preceding several years kept the Prudhoe project moving, even when it seemed iffy.

"The acreage was put up by the state, we acquired it, and it would have been a very, very awkward situation to have backed out of that sort of virtual commitment."

ARCO MOVED AHEAD. The Susie rig was put in place at Prudhoe, and in April drilling began. Jamison believed that startup of the well might give Hickel leverage in his dealings with Native groups. He felt personally grateful to Hickel for making the offshore leases available and wanted to show his own and his company's appreciation.

So Jamison had ARCO charter a DC-3—jets could not yet land on the North Slope during the spring and summer when the permafrost was soft—and on May 2 flew Hickel, Holdsworth, Bell, and a number of ARCO and Exxon employees to the Prudhoe Bay drill site. Jamison wanted not only to impress on Hickel and his staff how important the Prudhoe leases had been to ARCO, but also to let them observe how carefully ARCO's crews were treating the surrounding tundra.

As they stepped off the plane into water about ankle deep from spring ice breakup and melting permafrost, ARCO drilling supervisor Bill Congdon suddenly shouted at Jamison, "Goddamit, Harry, we gotta suspend this s.o.b. right now!"

Taken aback, especially since he had the governor in tow, Jamison nonetheless knew that if Congdon believed the well should be shut down, it should be. After an awkward moment of embarrassment in which he tried to explain Congdon's outburst to the visitors, Jamison barked the order: "Shut her down."

Bell remembers well the spectacle that greeted them when they arrived at the drill site: "It looked like a Midwest barnyard with muck knee-deep." While Hickel and other visitors were there, the well coughed up an eight-inch piece of wood, perhaps trapped in permafrost for thousands of years.

A day later, less than two weeks after the onset of drilling, Prudhoe Bay State No. 1 was suspended for the season at a depth of about 2,000 feet because of the state's ban on drilling after spring breakup. Drilling wouldn't begin again until late November.

On the flight back to Anchorage, Hickel made one of his typical off-the-cuff comments, declaring there were 40 billion barrels of oil on the Slope.

"I was sure then he was wrong," Jamison recalls, "but now I have to give him credit. He was a lot more right than I was."

SPOTLIGHT ▐████████

PRUDHOE'S VIRTUES

ARCO and Exxon had specific geological reasons for believing Prudhoe would be a winner.

"Certainly, we all realized it was extremely risky," says ARCO's Harry Jamison, "but it was really the culmination of exploration work. Not only in time, but also geographically . . . moving from the foothills up to the north, into a totally tundra-covered area.

"We knew from the regional structural grain that we were on an almost east-west trending megastructure on the North Slope," he says. Under the Arctic coastal plain lay a large sedimentary basin flanking the north side of the Brooks Range. The northern side of the basin formed the Barrow Arch megastructure, including Prudhoe Bay, where all the major North Slope oil fields are located.

"The difference at Prudhoe," Jamison says, "was that we could also see, technically speaking, the unconformity that formed a portion of the trap." This "unconformity" was an erosional surface that might help in trapping oil.

"We didn't know precisely what it was, but it had a different series of elements than either the Colville High or the Barrow High." The rocks in the sedimentary basin "pinched-out" at Prudhoe differently than elsewhere in the region, making it a more promising target than the area northwest at Colville River or along the ancient arch toward Barrow. Jamison was about to be proven correct in a big way.

Chapter 18

Discovery!

After freeze-up of the land in late November 1967, ARCO reentered the Prudhoe Bay State No. 1 well. One month later the first significant hydrocarbons were encountered.

"The first evidence we had was primarily gas," Harry Jamison says, "but we did encounter oil shows. We were overwhelmed by the thickness of the section. The two prime zones were the Sadlerochit and the Lisburne [geological formations], and the magnitude of the shows and the test results were astounding."

Jamison and ARCO's geologists knew they had something spectacular on their hands, but they had to wait for a second confirmation well to be sure.

Geologist Gil Mull, representing Exxon, was on the rig at the time of the discovery. "The gas readings on the mudlogger had gone off the scale," he recalls. "It was pretty obvious that we probably had a gas well.

"We were cutting cores on Christmas Day and on December 26 went back in with test tools, which were opened on the morning of December 27. There was an immediate strong blow of gas to the surface, which was ignited and blew strongly for hours from the end of a flow pipe. It sounded like the roar of a nearby jet plane."

Mull says the "flare was still burning the following morning, and it wasn't until midmorning on the 28th that we were able to start coming out of the hole [removing the test tools]. But by that point the drill string, which had

217

been on the bottom for over twenty-four hours without rotating, was stuck on the bottom and we had a fishing job."

Security on the discovery well was not particularly tight. "We were flying to Fairbanks to send phone messages," Mull says, "but activities on the drill floor were pretty much as normal. None of the crew was excluded from the drill floor. However, even though we were damned remote, some rumors did get out.

"For example, after it was obvious we were stuck in the hole and that it would be days before we could get the fish out, run a string of casing, and be back to drilling, I went to Anchorage for the interim. At dinner at the Alyeska lodge on either New Year's Eve or New Year's Day, I ran into a group that included [publisher] Bob Atwood.

"I remember him saying in effect, 'Hey, I hear that you all got gas up there.' Which came as a shock, because even though the well was not super-tight, we weren't talking about it. It illustrates how difficult it is to keep things tight. After all, burning a big flare for twenty-four hours is hard to hide from the drill crews, who were rotating in and out."

ARCO went public in mid-January 1968 with an announcement from exploration manager Julius Babisak that the company had made a discovery at Prudhoe Bay. He stressed that it was natural gas, not oil, that had been found.

GIL MULL

First Prudhoe oil discovery! Natural gas burns as it erupts from ARCO's Prudhoe Bay State No. 1 oil well on December 27, 1967.

"Rumors have circulated recently," said Babisak, "that oil has been discovered . . . but only natural gas at about 8,500 feet was found."

But by February, the report was of increasing signs of oil. A press release from Harry Jamison said the well had "sealed off a 470-foot sand section of which the top 400 feet is gas-producing and the lower 70 feet is oil-saturated."

In March, after a four-and-a-half-hour "inconclusive" test, ARCO said the well had been tested, and produced 1,152 barrels of oil per day. ARCO's cautious press release said that although "the test is encourag-

ARCO's Sag River No. 1 well in June 1968 confirmed the earlier spectacular find at the Prudhoe Bay State No. 1 well.

ing, additional information such as production rate and areal extent of the horizons tested will be required to determine if the well is a commercial find."

Kiplinger's *Changing Times* advised its March readers that "petroleum has become Alaska's biggest new industry. . . . Explorations in Bristol Bay, Gulf of Alaska and the Arctic Slope indicate that Alaska may become the richest oil state."

"AFTER THE DISCOVERY," Jamison says, "we had a security problem. We wanted to maintain tight security on the well, so no information could be divulged without R. O. Anderson's approval." ARCO chairman Anderson didn't want his company accused of manipulating its stock by means of leaked information.

"Every time a press release would come out, I was deluged there in Anchorage with inquiries," Jamison says. He couldn't say anything until he checked with Anderson.

During the period of what Jamison describes as the "goldfish bowl atmosphere," ARCO geologist Marvin Mangus briefed planeloads of executives, politicians, United Nations representatives, reporters, and others as they toured Prudhoe Bay.

In addition to being one of Alaska's foremost arctic geologists, Mangus is also a nationally recognized Alaskan artist. He painted throughout his Arctic oil career. "Sometimes, sitting on a well, when you're only running two or three ten-foot samples an hour, you've got a lot of time on your hands," he said. "I'd go off looking around the rig, get a piece of plywood, and cut it to easel size and nail it to the wall.

"We usually had a workbench to set my paint box and palette on . . . and I would paint scenes for these guys who contributed so much to the state. My goal was to try to establish their place in Alaska history."

WITH GROWING EXCITEMENT, ARCO went to work on its second Prudhoe well. The Canadian rig that had drilled the Colville and Kookpuk dry holes, stacked on Pingo Beach at the mouth of the Colville River during the winter of 1967-68, was now loaded on trucks and driven across the sea ice behind the Beaufort Sea barrier islands. With superhuman effort plus a little luck, ARCO was able to bring the rig to the new well location at the mouth of the Sagavanirktok River before spring breakup.

In May 1968, drilling began at the Sag River No. 1 well at a spot seven miles southeast of the first well. Security was tight. "It was a super-tight hole," Mangus says. "The cores pulled were completely covered on the drill table. Only company personnel could look at them. Bill Walters, ARCO engineer, ran the blocks and no mud loggers were allowed on the floor."

ARCO's geologists knew they had something spectacular on their hands.

Geologist Gil Mull says that when cores were brought out, "the rig driller was behind a big sheet so he couldn't see. Only the geologists were on the rig floor opening up the core barrels and extracting the cores.

"At times even *that* couldn't hide what was being found. When we unscrewed the core head from the drill string, what came out on one of the cores instead of solid rock was just a pile of disaggregated sand, gravel, and oil that ran through the rig floor and into the rig cellar. All the roughnecks could immediately tell what was being found."

In late June, ARCO announced the Sag River well could produce 3,567 barrels of oil a day. Continuous cores of a full section of about 400 feet of sand from the same formation in which mostly gas had been found at Prudhoe Bay No. 1 was saturated with oil in Sag River No. 1. It was a remarkable confirmation of the richness of the first find.

"If you're a geologist and you know the vagaries of sand deposition, and know that you've mapped the whole structure, and all other factors, even with the magnitude of a Prudhoe Bay, it's still amazing to me that we could have moved out that far and done these

The February 16, March 13, and May18, 1968 Anchorage Daily Times *herald the ARCO discovery on the North Slope.*

things correctly and verified our conclusions with that well," says Harry Jamison.

Why a seven-mile step-out, and in that particular direction? "Seismic and subsurface knowledge told us we needed to move in that direction," says Jamison. "The unconformity also tended to lead us there. We also wanted to get down through the Sadlerochit once again into the Lisburne, and that appeared to be a good Lisburne location.

"We wanted to get off the crest, because we'd pretty well established the fact that we had a gas-over-oil column 400 feet thick. We needed to get structurally lower, far enough down on the flank of the structure so that we could reasonably expect to encounter primarily an oil column and not a gas column."

There was also another reason for the site of the second well. "We wanted to get to an area where we could operate in the summer months with an airstrip," Jamison said. "You have to get fairly close to a river with a gravel source . . . so we're now on the banks of the Sag River."

GIL MULL

ARCO executive Harry Jamison says the Prudhoe Bay discovery created a "gold-fish bowl atmosphere" as plane loads of oil people, politicians, and reporters rushed to the site in 1967.

MEANWHILE, THE PRUDHOE DISCOVERY WELL had been tested and now was producing 2,415 barrels per day from a fifteen-foot section of sand below 8,656 feet. The two wells, seven miles apart, were expected to produce at Middle East volumes and rates! Subsequent wells would test at phenomenal flow rates of 20,000 to 30,000 barrels of oil per day. The Sag River well had confirmed that a giant world-class "elephant" oil field had been discovered on the North Slope of Alaska.

Once the Sag River well data was released, Jamison says, "it was just a madhouse. Once that bridge was crossed, from then on it was Katy-bar-the-door."

In late July 1968, the international geological consulting firm of DeGolyer & McNaughton described the discovery at Prudhoe Bay as "one of the largest petroleum accumulations known to the world today."

The report said the Prudhoe Bay field contained 21 billion barrels of oil in place and nearly 38 trillion cubic feet of natural gas. The Sadlerochit reservoir sandstone, the primary rock source lying at a depth of approximately 8,800 feet, was expected to contain 9.6 billion barrels of recoverable oil and more than 21 trillion cubic feet of recoverable gas, plus 16 trillion cubic feet in solution with the oil. "Prudhoe's oil is good-quality medium gravity crude," the report said, "with less than 1 percent by weight sulphur content."

The oil sands at Prudhoe stretched over an area approximately 45 miles long and 18 miles wide, making the area North America's largest oil field. Compared with Prudhoe's expected 9.6 billion barrels of production, the next largest, in East Texas, contained 6 billion barrels of recoverable oil.

I CAME WITHIN JUST A FEW MILES of being a highly paid player in the drama of the North Slope discovery. ARCO decided to drill its Toolik No. 1 well on land next to a leasehold Jerry Ganopole and I had acquired at the 1964 federal drawing. We had assigned our leases to Mobil and ARCO, but we kept an overriding royalty interest. ARCO planned to drill at Toolik, only twelve miles south of its Prudhoe Bay discovery well, to see if the oil field extended that far.

I got the news in a roundabout way. In mid-1968, I was serving in Bombay, India, as regional director of the Peace Corps. That July, at a lunch at the American consulate in Bombay, I was seated next to the Chief Justice of the State of Maharashtra. He turned to me and remarked that he had just read in the *International Herald Tribune* that a large discovery of oil had been made in Alaska, at someplace called "Prudo."

Excitedly I phoned Anchorage for the latest news. I got information on the Sag River find, and learned that the next ARCO well would be drilled on the lease next to mine.

So for the second time—the first being the Kalgin Island wells in 1966—I was certain I was going to become very rich. When drilling got under way at Toolik No. 1, I waited patiently for confirmation of a discovery. But the well turned up dry; the Prudhoe Bay field and its fabulous riches stopped several miles short of our lease.

BP GOT INTO THE ACTION after a curious detour when ARCO tried to buy into BP's Prudhoe land. BP people love to tell about how much of Prudhoe Bay might have slipped out of their hands were it not for a naive ARCO blunder.

"In the late spring of 1968 ARCO was making approaches to London, offering to drill a well on our acreage for a significant interest in Prudhoe," says BP's Geoff Larminie. "The sum being spoken of was, I believe, a well and $20 million.

"Immediately we were dead suspicious. London certainly dithered. We do know there was a temptation to accept ARCO's offer, but [BP officials] Warman, Kent, and Thomas somehow or other eventually decided to hold out against this and decide that BP would drill another well."

Roger Herrera recalls his company's officials in London being very interested in ARCO's offer, wanting to know what ARCO had found at Prudhoe. No one could authenticate any information about the discovery.

"There was lots of speculation in London about what ARCO had found," says Herrera. "Soon after ARCO reached total depth, BP received a call from Los Angeles, saying ARCO was interested in talking to BP about a potential farmout," a deal in which ARCO would dig wells on BP's leaseholds and get a big share of any profits.

"No one in BP was wildly for or wildly against such an idea," Herrera says. "We had been sleeping on the leases for several years, so enthusiasm wasn't built up.

"To negotiate the farmout, ARCO sent a team across headed by one of their big wheels," he said. "As soon as he walked into the room, everyone knew that this was big time. Some said afterwards that if ARCO instead had sent over a young geologist, there might have been meaningful discussions."

"ARCO blew it," Herrera commented. "They were sent packing." Once London realized there had been a major oil discovery on the North Slope, said Herrera, "they were hell bent for leather."

> *"In the late spring of 1968 ARCO was making approaches [to BP], offering to drill a well on our acreage for a significant interest in Prudhoe. . . . Immediately we were dead suspicious."*
> —BP's Geoff Larminie

BP'S FIRST TASK was to get a drill rig to its Prudhoe acreage. "We got in touch with Puget Sound Tug and Barge, who had experience in supplying the DEW line [early warning system], coming from Seattle via Dutch Harbor around Barrow," recalls Geoff Larminie. "I told Puget Sound I wanted to see Leo Collar. It was urgent and we wanted to talk business, and I'm terribly sorry but the only place to do it was in my office on the Fourth of July.

"When Leo Collar and his entourage walked into my office he had a big grin on his face, and I thought, you know, it's almost like asking someone to come on Christmas day. So, as he walked through the door, I said, 'Long live General Burgoyne,' and he burst out laughing. Before we got down to negotiations, I said, 'This is our revenge.'"

Collar's company barged a drill rig on the demanding route from the Kenai Peninsula and through the Bering and Chukchi seas, around Point Barrow, to the drill site at the Putuligayuk River—the Put River—six miles south of ARCO's first discovery well.

"We had to get the rig moving to catch the ice and get it round," Larminie says. "We had six weeks from July Fourth to do it. It was while that was en route that word finally came of what had been found [by ARCO] in Prudhoe."

The 1968 sea-haul was later augmented by a great air flotilla that carried thousands of tons of oil-field material on nonstop flights from Fairbanks to the Slope. The airlift of the Susie drill rig had been big, but this was gigantic. The BP airlift comprised five chartered Hercules C-130s, costing $250,000 per month each, plus three Super Constellation aircraft.

More than 25,000 tons of equipment and supplies were flown to a new airstrip at BP's Put River location. Two complete drill rigs were airfreighted to the Slope, and another lighter rig was flown in later. The effort continued throughout the 1968-69 winter, with the Hercs transporting drill rigs, equipment, pipe, and all the supplies needed for drilling lots of oil wells.

At the time ARCO announced its Sag River discovery in July 1968, only four drill rigs were on the Slope. By the end of 1968 there were more than a dozen. Industry interest in the Slope grew to where at least a dozen oil companies put seismic crews to work on the Slope, including Amerada Hess, Marathon, Getty, Louisiana Land and Exploration, and H. L. Hunt.

BP'S PUT RIVER WELL NO. 1 began drilling on November 20, 1968. The well was designed to be located "outside the edge of the gas and in the oil leg of the Prudhoe structure," and it was, says Larminie. BP wanted to determine the thickness of the Prudhoe oil column at Put River and to then use this information to reevaluate its original seismic data.

Communications security was a problem. The people at the well had to communicate with company officials, but without others listening in.

"Everyone was sharing these terrible radio frequencies," says Larminie. "We had a very good radio man in London who knew the international system . . . frequencies, the VHF and rural problems . . . but we didn't have FCC authority to use the frequencies. So, as we were getting closer to the target at Put River No. 1, we were sending information out in sealed bags—airlifted, hand-carried stuff.

"Inevitably, of course, we went into the reservoir, so we got the first real information [about a BP oil find]. The weather was terrible. We needed to tell London and couldn't operate in the clear on the radio.

"By great good fortune we had two Welsh-speaking geologists, one on the rig and one in Anchorage. So we organized a report that would be carried in the clear on the frequency everybody listened to all over the Arctic. Welshmen Harvey Jones and Ron Walters conducted a conversation in their native language transferring all the Put River information from the rig to Anchorage. Although used only once, this secure link worked.

"To give you some idea of how closely everybody was watching everybody else, within less than a couple of weeks, SoCal (Chevron) transferred a Welsh geologist to the Slope . . . so Welsh was out thereafter."

On March 13, 1969, BP announced the big news. Its first well had come up with oil in porous sandstone below 8,000 feet, with an oil column thickness greater than that at Prudhoe Bay. It was a major extension of the Prudhoe Bay discovery, like the Sag River State No. 1 well. BP immediately drilled more wells.

BP confirmed the magnitude of its find with a September 28 announcement based on an "independent review" of eight of its wells in the Prudhoe Bay area. Under the BP leases lay an estimated 4.8 billion barrels of recoverable oil. BP possessed a vast ocean of oil.

PART III: AN OIL STATE

"More than anything else about the oil boom, it is the threat of becoming bourgeois that rankles. The Alaskan has been called an exploiter and a primitive hedonist . . . but he has never been called ordinary."

— Robert Zelnick
New York Times Magazine

Chapter 19

Independent Tom Kelly

From the moment Wally Hickel took office as governor in late 1966, he wanted Tom Kelly of Houston on his staff. Kelly knew the oil business from the inside out and was a longtime business colleague and personal friend of Hickel.

The stepson of oil independent Michel T. Halbouty, Kelly earned a masters degree in petroleum geology from Texas A & M. He went to work for Continental Oil Company, then joined his stepfather as executive vice president of Halbouty Oil. When Kelly stepped off the plane at the Anchorage airport for the first time, ready to operate Halbouty's leases near the new Kenai oil field in 1958, it was Wally Hickel who met him at the airport.

"Our relationship for several years was that of very close personal friends and confidants," says Kelly of Hickel, who became godfather to one of Kelly's children.

During the late 1950s and early '60s, Kelly not only ran Halbouty's Alaska oil exploration activities but also managed several Halbouty/Hickel joint ventures: small transportation, communications, and telephone businesses; shopping centers; and a proposed hotel complex. As a wildcatter and small-business manager, Kelly became thoroughly familiar with Alaska's oil and gas laws and its politics.

After his election, Hickel immediately began looking for a spot in his administration for the 36-year-old Kelly. Though Kelly didn't want to be Hickel's assistant, he was interested in the position of resources

229

commissioner, the job Phil Holdsworth held. Hickel had asked Holdsworth to stay on in his new administration.

HOLDSWORTH SERVED FOR NINE MONTHS in the Hickel administration before being fired.

"Hickel had no idea of replacing me," says Holdsworth. "But Mike Halbouty had contributed $1 million to Wally's campaign for governor."

"Wally waited until he went over to Tokyo on a trip, and then his hatchet man, Pat Ryan, asked for my resignation. (This Pat Ryan is not related to Irene's husband.) The hatchet man kept telling me I was the last commissioner to stay on, all the rest of them were gone long before. So I told him, 'I'll write the letter of resignation and give it to Wally first thing when he gets back.'"

Holdsworth says he closed his resignation letter to Hickel sarcastically, stating he hoped Hickel's asking for his resignation didn't get the governor "into more trouble than you're already in."

Phil Holdsworth's long and distinguished public career had come to a close. As territorial commissioner of mines beginning in 1952, and for nearly a decade as the state's first resources commissioner, he played a key role in taking Alaska from an unsophisticated "colony" to a powerful oil state. Throughout, Holdsworth retained his credibility both with public and oil company officials.

Kelly remembers Holdsworth's firing and his own hiring somewhat differently. "Halbouty didn't contribute $1 million to Hickel's 1966 campaign," Kelly insists. "It might have been $5,000." Kelly says that since he was Hickel's campaign fund-raiser outside Alaska in 1966, "I ought to know."

Kelly says Hickel kept courting him to join his administration as resources commissioner. "Hickel is one of those people who won't take no for an answer," he says. "He kept coming back all the time and wanting me to take the job."

Hickel and Kelly began talking in earnest about the job during the general election recount in November 1966 when Hickel beat Bill Egan by fewer than 1,000 of the 65,000 votes cast. But it was not until June of the following year that Kelly decided he would join Hickel, and it was October before he actually took office.

Before he accepted the position, Kelly says, he and Hickel discussed the problems both foresaw in the oil and gas area. They agreed that during the

Egan years, state officials had become too cozy with the oil industry, appearing to acquiesce in whatever the major oil companies wanted.

"To a large degree, Wally campaigned on that, stating that the only administration the state had since statehood was passive in its oil and gas regulations," Kelly said. "Hickel's frame of mind was that we ought to do better than that."

According to Kelly, part of the problem he and Hickel perceived was that no one in the resources department had ever experienced "the dog-eat-dog competitive arena the oil industry is noted for. My charge was to have a free hand to run the department in a manner I thought appropriate and in the best interest of the state, and not to have to deal with the hatchet man, Pat Ryan."

Kelly says Holdsworth left "on less than pleasant terms." He says the two never met during the transition period because by that time Holdsworth had cleared out. "He left no memoranda addressed to me or information of any sort." Kelly's only contact was with Holdsworth's deputy, Dale Wallington, who briefed him on issues facing the department.

KELLY SAYS HE FELT no animosity toward Holdsworth—but he felt differently about Roscoe Bell, the state lands director.

"I fired Roscoe Bell almost immediately after taking office," Kelly said with relish.

Tom Kelly found that being state resources commissioner was a tough job in the late 1960s as he faced conflicts with fishermen, independent leaseholders, and the major oil companies.

"I guess I should put it this way: I let it be known that I was going to fire him so I guess he didn't stay around long enough to let me have that pleasure."

Kelly thought Bell autocratic. Kelly felt that both he and Halbouty, as independents, had been treated arbitrarily by Bell. Kelly viewed Bell's dealings with the oil industry, particularly the majors, as "too passive." Whatever the majors wanted, Kelly believed, Bell was ready to rubber-stamp for them.

> *"Wally [Hickel] waited until he went over to Tokyo on a trip, and then his hatchet man, Pat Ryan, asked for my resignation."*
>
> —*Phil Holdsworth*

Despite personal and philosophical differences, Bell and Kelly were much alike in that both took great pride in protecting the "public interest."

A consummate bureaucrat and planner, Bell spent his entire professional life in academia or government. He says he accepted the job of director of the division of lands shortly after statehood "because of its breadth of opportunities and so that Alaska's land would be put to work expeditiously for the people of Alaska." He had left his long career with the federal Bureau of Land Management "because its procedures were so cumbersome that nothing was ever done." By contrast, the new state, he thought, "provided good tools—a new constitution and laws—and I wanted to live up to the challenge."

Tom Kelly had spent his professional life as an entrepreneur in the private sector. He brought to public service what Bell lacked, experience in the oil exploration business. He knew how companies acted and reacted. Having dealt with major oil companies in his work with Halbouty, he thought he could anticipate their reactions to changes in public policy even before such decisions were made. He also thought he knew the companies' soft spots.

Kelly viewed public service as a challenge. After being appointed by Hickel, he said that "When you're dealing with a public resource, the highest price is the fairest price. That's because a state official has a fiduciary responsibility to maximize the state's value of its resources." As an assertive independent Texan and as the first "real" oilman in Alaska to be placed at the public policy level, Kelly's impulse was to lease more oil and gas land.

ONE OF TOM KELLY'S FIRST ACTS as resources commissioner was to call for nominations from oil companies for offshore lands in Bristol Bay that the state should offer for lease.

Bristol Bay fishermen, led by Independent state representative Jay Hammond, of Naknek, protested vehemently, fearing damage to the world's richest salmon beds. Earlier, these fishermen had prevented the Egan administration from offering oil and gas tracts in the bay.

Hickel and Kelly, however, believed certain areas on the eastern shore of Bristol Bay could be explored without injury to the environment. Thus at the state lease sale in March 1968, Kelly offered lands lying inside Port Moller and neighboring Herendeen Bay.

"There were no five-year leasing plans then, as there are today," Kelly says. "In those days, we were hip-shooters. If we decided somebody was interested in an area, we would offer it for lease. Those were the days when government was flavorful."

During the 1968 legislative session, Representative Hammond sought to make Bristol Bay a sanctuary. Hammond's bill would have required legislative approval before any Bristol Bay offshore oil leasing took place. The bill, prohibiting oil platforms in the bay's drift gill net areas, passed both houses of the 1968 legislature but was vetoed by Hickel.

(Four years later, Senate President Jay Hammond would shepherd a similar sanctuary bill through the legislature, prohibiting oil exploration offshore in Bristol Bay. Future legislatures—and future governors, Hammond included—would confirm the drilling ban, thereby protecting the bay's salmon spawning and fishing grounds.)

Despite fishermen's protests, twenty-one oil companies bid for Port Moller and Herendeen Bay leases in March 1968, paying nearly $3 million in cash bonuses. Unaware in 1968 of the importance of the opening salvo in the fish-versus-oil debate over offshore drilling in Bristol Bay, the major oil companies—their attention focused on the North Slope—made little effort to address the fishermen's environmental concerns.

"Oil spillage" and "detention of tankers" had become legislative catch-phrases in 1968, and the potential of tanker spills was a hot issue. Interior Secretary Stewart Udall had advised oil companies to cooperate in an emergency program to reduce Cook Inlet pollution. And he said they should not conduct exploration or development work in Bristol Bay unless they could offer assurance that "their operations will not pollute the environment."

An oil industry spokesman, grossly underestimating and misinterpreting the problem, replied in April 1968: "This is a state matter, and the Department of Interior has no legal power to enforce any delays in Bristol Bay."

NEAR THE END OF 1968, Tom Kelly faced an especially delicate task. He was responsible for selecting a large chunk of federal land on the North Slope for state ownership—a selection that would negate the federal lease applications of many independents and other small guys in the oil and gas game.

Governor Hickel had been chosen by President-elect Richard Nixon as his Secretary of Interior. Before leaving for Washington in late 1968, Hickel told Kelly to select 6 million federal acres for oil and gas purposes, nearly 2 million of which were to be on the North Slope.

In the aftermath of the Prudhoe Bay discovery, federal oil and gas applications already filed on the North Slope had become extremely valuable. Dozens of Canadian and U.S. independents had filed federal noncompetitive lease applications on the Slope, and major oil companies were ready to pay large sums for options on these unissued applications. Canadian independents, particularly, sold options on their North Slope applications to the majors.

Federal leases weren't being issued at this time because of the land freeze prompted by Native land claims. But the value of the applicants' mineral rights on the Slope continued to soar during the freeze.

Kelly knew that if he selected the land for the state, the Bureau of Land Management would reject all existing federal lease applications filed on the same acreage, wiping out the little guys. A year earlier Kelly had been one of them; now he was about to force them out of the North Slope leasing game.

To add insult to injury, Kelly would have to classify the land for competitive bidding, and most of the lease applicants couldn't afford to compete with the major oil companies. "The primary purpose in selecting this acreage," Kelly said later, "is to acquire the maximum bonus, rental, and royalty revenue from oil and gas production to benefit all the people of Alaska. If we do not lease competitively, we lose the initial benefits of bonus and the higher rental."

Kelly believed the pending lease applications that would be affected by his North Slope selection numbered no more than fifty. In fact, as of the end of July 1968 more than 1,200 noncompetitive lease applications had been filed, covering half a million acres. The *Fairbanks News-Miner* reported that if Kelly selected the 2 million North Slope acres and classified them competitive, 150 Fairbanks residents would lose out.

A memo from state minerals officer Pedro Denton to lands director Joe Keenan, on December 12, outlined the expected fallout from Kelly's selection:

"1. Possible creation of a public image of grabbing without regard to the little guy and pending rights;

"2. Political pressures are probably the most important consideration;

> *"When you're dealing with a public resource, the highest price is the fairest price."*
>
> —*Tom Kelly*

"3. Will create mistrust of the state and make it risky to file in new areas as long as the state has the right to select."

Kelly went ahead anyway and selected the 2 million acres for state ownership. He immediately classified the acreage as land to be offered for lease by competitive bid. With this action, pending federal oil and gas applications filed by Canadian, Alaskan, and Lower-48 "independents" were effectively wiped out.

With Walter Hickel now in Washington, D.C., as Secretary of Interior, most of the little guys directed their anger at his successor, former lieutenant governor Keith Miller, and at Kelly—mostly Kelly. His decision to select and classify the land had cost them a chance at big money and put them out of business on the Slope. Himself a longtime independent oilman, Kelly now was pitted against his own kind.

SPOTLIGHT ■■■■

THE FLOOD TAX

Governor Hickel learned how handy oil riches can be when he needed money to help rebuild a flood-ravaged Fairbanks. Hickel promoted legislation to raise the oil severance tax—the tax that is levied against producers for "severing" the supply of oil from the earth. The impetus for the move was the disastrous Chena River flood at Fairbanks in mid-August 1967. Rampaging water inundated downtown streets and homes, and it was crucial to begin reconstruction before October's freeze.

Hickel promptly called a special session of the legislature. "In four days," he liked to say, "we raised taxes to rebuild Fairbanks." The money was to come from a 100 percent increase in the oil severance tax, Alaska's only readily available quick-fix revenue source.

The "flood disaster tax" was levied on all existing oil production in the state, which at that time meant only Cook Inlet. The existing 1 percent severance tax was increased to 2 percent and would remain in effect until $7.5 million had been raised or for two years, whichever came first. Thus only a short time before the discovery of oil at Prudhoe Bay, Alaska's oil severance tax had doubled.

State Senator John Butrovich, a Fairbanks Republican, promoted another severance-tax increase in the 1968 legislature. Most Democrats supported the measure, so an additional tax of 2 percent was enacted. The new levy, added to the basic 1 percent tax and the 1 percent time-dated Fairbanks flood disaster tax, placed the severance tax at 4 percent.

Although the Prudhoe Bay oil find was known by this time, the 1968 tax increase really had nothing to do with the North Slope. Lawmakers were simply trying to play catch-up in Cook Inlet. Not until later did lawmakers, and the Alaska public, realize the true significance of the Prudhoe Bay discovery.

Chapter 20

What Price Is Right?

om Kelly inherited an especially thorny oil problem as he took over as resources commissioner in late 1967. Left simmering from the Egan administration was the matter of how much royalty money the state should get for Cook Inlet oil. The main question was, how much could the oil producers deduct in expenses before paying the state its one-eighth royalty share? Only months before the spectacular Prudhoe Bay discovery, what question could be more important to the financial future of Alaska?

Ever since Chevron began shipping Swanson River oil to its Richmond, California, refinery in 1958, it had posted a price for its crude. To arrive at this price, Chevron took the posted price at the oil field at Signal Hill in Los Angeles and deducted pipeline and tanker costs from Swanson River to the California refinery. The Swanson River wellhead value thus became the Signal Hill price less the expenses of transporting the oil to California.

When Governor Egan christened Shell Oil's first drilling platform in Cook Inlet, on December 14, 1965, Chevron was posting its Swanson River wellhead value at about $3 a barrel. The Swanson River field was on leased federal land, and the state got 90 percent of the royalty collected by the federal government—a royalty that was based on Chevron's wellhead value. The state questioned the value as being too low, but federal officials considered it fair to all concerned.

Once offshore production began on state leases in Cook Inlet, each producer determined its own value for the oil. These values were used to buy, sell, and trade Cook Inlet oil—and, most importantly to the people of Alaska, it was on the basis of these values that producers calculated the royalty money they owed the state.

On the last day of January 1966, at a historic formal ceremony in the Anchorage office of state lands director Roscoe Bell, dutifully covered by the local press, Shell Oil's West Coast land manager, Durland Clark, handed Bell a check for $9,697.76.

This money was the first payment directly from an oil company to the state for royalty oil produced on leased state land. It represented the royalty amount due, based on Shell's calculated value for 26,000 barrels of oil produced from its platform "A" on Middle Ground Shoal in Cook Inlet during the last eighteen days of December 1965. Extremely pleased, Bell turned the check over to a staff member.

This amiable encounter between a major oil company and the state of Alaska masked a ferocious state vs. industry debate over royalty payments that was to last for many years.

———————————

A FITFUL SERIES of stops and starts marked the history of Alaska's attempts to control royalty pricing. In 1959, just a few short months after statehood, resources commissioner Phil Holdsworth had sought assistance from the WOGA in drawing up Alaska's first leasing regulations. The oil lobbying group then helped to make attorney Jim Wanvig available to draft the regulations.

With only a small amount of Swanson River crude expected to be refined in Alaska, Holdsworth reasoned that the valuing of Cook Inlet oil should take place outside the state. The royalty to be paid would be based on the refinery price minus transportation costs for the oil to get there.

Thus, Alaska's royalty would be "netted back" from prices paid by refineries in California, Puget Sound, the Gulf of Mexico, the East Coast, or even foreign countries. This was the same net-backing system used by Chevron at Swanson River. In the spring of 1959, Wanvig had seen to it that net-back language was placed in royalty provisions of the state's competitive oil and gas lease form.

Holdsworth also decided the state should pay some of the costs of transporting Cook Inlet crude oil from offshore platforms to the shore at Nikiski. He said these platform-to-shore charges could be deducted by producers in making their royalty calculations.

Soon after Shell Oil's Durland Clark handed Roscoe Bell his first royalty check in January 1966, what few royalty valuation procedures existed within the Egan administration began to unravel.

Shell's first check included deductions for pipeline transportation charges from platform "A" to the shoreline. When, in April, production began from Amoco's platform "Baker" at the north end of Middle Ground Shoal, monthly oil production reports and quarterly severance-tax returns filed by Amoco and Shell showed deductions of different amounts on oil taken from the same field.

Texas entrepreneur Frank Cahoon (standing, right) headed an outfit that made a deal with Alaska in 1969 to build a refinery and buy the state's royalty oil. Seated are Tom Kelly (left) and Commissioner of Administration Thomas Downes (right) signing the agreements while attorney Risher Thornton (left) and Attorney General G. Kent Edwards (center) look on.

During the first half of 1966, royalty payments rolled in to the state treasury. Amounts were never questioned, production volumes were never checked; producers' computations were simply accepted.

THE SURPRISING FACT that Amoco and Shell were reporting different royalty values for crude from the same field came to light later that year during a routine state examination of producers' royalty and tax reports. For the first time, the state began questioning the deductions that producers were taking. Some state officials thought the deductions were proper; others felt they were way out of line.

Bell and his staff met with representatives of oil producers. Each company said it had a different set of economic variables. Each, therefore, reported different wellhead values. State petroleum engineer O. K. "Easy" Gilbreth, when asked what the state's oil pricing policy was, said he thought deductions for transportation and cleaning costs had been "agreed upon." Unfortunately, they had not.

In September, Amoco offered Bell a royalty valuation agreement. Bell and his staff rejected it on grounds that it contained language that was overbroad. There the matter stood. Bell made no counteroffer. The matter floundered.

ON DECEMBER 15, 1966, ten days after Wally Hickel was inaugurated as governor, Amoco production superintendent Art Piper and deputy resources commissioner Chuck Herbert spent the afternoon in Herbert's Juneau office. There the two men incorporated Amoco's "Baker" platform accounting methods into a joint royalty pricing agreement.

Herbert wrote to the file: "About 7 or 7:15 A.M. [the next morning] I sat down at my typewriter and typed out a draft agreement of principles for calculating platform-to-shore transportation charges against the state's royalty. I handed it to Art (Piper) and asked him if it didn't say what we had been talking about the afternoon before. He thought it pretty much did, and so we soon had a nice, clean draft, which my secretary typed."

Herbert agreed with Piper that the state should pay its share of platform-to-shore charges. They also agreed that cleaning and dehydration costs should be borne solely by the producing companies.

Bell was upset that Herbert tried to take charge of royalty pricing. He contended that the proposed Herbert/Piper agreement was inadequate. Instead,

Bell believed, the state should establish a single wellhead value for all Cook Inlet crude.

Bell, however, later issued a notice of "Allowable Deductions against State Royalty Oil" that was nearly identical to the Herbert/Piper draft, and which abandoned his idea of a single Cook Inlet wellhead value. Bell agreed that the companies would not be allowed to make deductions for cleaning and dehydration costs. (Crude oil is usually run through facilities called "heater treaters" to remove water, gas, sand, and other impurities before it arrives at a point where its wellhead value is determined. These cleaning and dehydration costs are sometimes deducted from the value of royalty oil.)

During the first half of 1966, royalty payments rolled in to the state treasury. Amounts were never questioned, production volumes were never checked; producers' computations were simply accepted.

One week after Bell issued his notice, lawyers for Mobil and Union said their clients would continue to deduct platform-to-shore *and* cleaning and dehydration charges. Ignoring Bell, Amoco and Shell also began taking cleaning and dehydration deductions. In addition, Amoco deducted interest expense on its platform-to-shore pipeline investment. To top if off, company lawyers made clear to Bell that they reserved the right to challenge any final state royalty policy, if one ever emerged.

When production began from the Granite Point platform in Cook Inlet, Mobil adopted what it called a "theoretical crude price" based on Chevron's Swanson River posted price. From this price, Mobil began taking all deductions it felt proper to arrive at its wellhead value on the west side of Cook Inlet. Mobil's partner at Granite Point, Union Oil, began reporting a different royalty value for the same oil from the same field.

By this time Bell was totally confused. Three other Cook Inlet producers were submitting checks for royalty oil in amounts based on three different wellhead values. Nobody in state government seemed to know what was going on.

Amid all the confusion, Bell issued a notice of "Amended Clarification of Standards" for royalty pricing. By early 1967, Bell had issued "Amended Standards," "Clarification of Standards," and now "Amended Clarification of Standards."

WHEN TOM KELLY TOOK OVER as Wally Hickel's resources commissioner in October 1967, the royalty valuation scene was in chaos. Kelly's staff members recommended that he make "a firm decision as to what we believe the pricing structure should be . . . and require payments accordingly." Kelly, they said, should insist on a single Cook Inlet posted price.

Kelly agreed. Setting different values for oil from the same well made no sense to him and, from the state's standpoint, was unconscionable. He planned to halt the various companies' pricing practices—and he didn't plan to stop there. He wanted to recoup what the companies had allegedly shortchanged the state. This meant trying to collect millions of dollars from the producers.

> *Tom Kelly wanted to recoup what the oil companies had allegedly shortchanged the state. This meant trying to collect millions of dollars from the producers.*

With major developments looming on the North Slope in the spring of 1968, Kelly sought outside oil pricing advice. He hired the national consulting firm of DeGolyer and MacNaughton, which advised him to take the initiative. The firm said Kelly should accept Chevron's Swanson River posted price as a reference point and allow deductions to be taken for Kenai pipeline tariffs and platform-to-shore charges on both sides of Cook Inlet. This, the firm pointed out, would allow Kelly to arrive at one royalty price for all of Cook Inlet.

It appeared so simple.

In June 1968, Kelly sent a letter to all Cook Inlet oil producers, noting that the disparity in royalty payments was occurring because no oil field except Swanson River had a posted price. "In the absence of a field posted price at the point of sale," he said, "all producing Cook Inlet fields must begin with [the Swanson River] price."

Chevron's posted Swanson River price would prevail regardless of whether oil was loaded at Nikiski or at Drift River on the lower west side, Kelly said. Operators would no longer be permitted to make different royalty payments for oil from the same well or from the same oil field.

But the Cook Inlet oil producers continued to determine their own wellhead values. To arm himself to conduct the major fight with the producers he now realized he was waging, Kelly hired Houston lawyer and friend Jim Smullen as his independent counsel. At last the state would have an experienced oil-royalty adviser.

Kelly hoped to get the royalty question settled before the oil situation in Alaska became even more volatile. Cook Inlet production was soaring, and Alaska had become the eighth largest oil producing state in the U.S. The 1967 Arab-Israeli "six-day war" and closure of the Suez Canal had sent crude prices and transportation costs skyward.

Kelly thought Alaska law required him to accept royalties based on the highest price any producer received for any oil of like grade and quality produced from any field in Cook Inlet. He believed that royalty provisions in the state's competitive lease form obligated oil companies to pay based on the highest price.

With help from lawyer Smullen and Louisiana oil official Charles Gaiennie, Kelly announced at the end of October 1968 that he would only accept royalties based on this top price. But as they had with the directives from Roscoe Bell, Cook Inlet producers basically ignored Kelly.

KELLY TRIED AGAIN. On July 1, 1969, he announced that he had finally resolved the royalty valuation problem.

The terms of his "solution" were:

— For the past period of July 1, 1968, to the end of June 1969, he would allow producers to set wellhead royalty value at the highest posted price in Cook Inlet, adjusted for different transportation costs from the east and west sides.

— Effective July 1, 1969, the value of all Cook Inlet oil would be "the highest price in the Kenai Peninsula Borough at the point of custody transfer to a common carrier." Henceforth, Kelly said, all crude of like grade and quality regardless of the price the company paid itself at its refinery, or any difference between pipeline tariffs, was to be valued at the highest price paid by any producer at any one time anywhere in Cook Inlet.

Kelly said producers could deduct platform-to-shore costs until July 1969, but only if those charges were supported by detailed accounting data. And, almost as an addendum, Kelly said platform-to-shore charges after July 1969 could no longer be deducted.

Nearly two years had passed since Kelly became resources commissioner. He felt he had finally arrived at a rational state royalty valuation policy.

Kelly now turned his attention to getting refunds from the major Cook Inlet oil producers, which he believed had grossly shortchanged the state. He bolstered this effort by hiring an international geological consulting firm, a Texas law firm, and an accounting firm, and by seeking advice from officials of the oil state of Louisiana.

In order to estimate how much each producer allegedly owed the state in back payments, the value of the royalty from the beginning of production had to be computed. But to carry out such calculations, Kelly had to make some less than perfect assumptions based on less than perfect data.

Legal memorandums began to flow between producers and the state. Settlement negotiations got under way with ARCO, but then Kelly said no deal. Instead, he issued notices of past payment deficiencies to all Cook Inlet producers. And Kelly raised the ante by suggesting the possibility the state could cancel oil-producing leases for alleged understating of wellhead values.

TOM KELLY BELIEVED the dispute over the value of the state's royalty oil could be settled if he could begin selling some of it to an in-state refiner. The state took most of its oil royalties in cash, but also could receive its one-eighth share in the form of oil—"in kind," as it was called. It would be instructive to find out if the price the state received for this royalty oil might be higher than the cash price it was receiving from Chevron and the other majors.

Kelly and Governor Hickel wanted someone to build an oil refinery on the Kenai Peninsula. Chevron had a small Kenai refinery but wasn't interested in upgrading the facility to refine more crude oil or to produce high-end products like gasoline. A new Kenai refinery could provide a nearby source of oil products. "We had a great crude," Kelly says. "It's a fantastic high-gravity sweet crude. Why couldn't we produce our own gasoline and other highly refined products? Why did we have to bring them up from California?"

The refinery would be a purchaser of state royalty oil, and the price it paid would indicate whether the state was getting a fair deal from the majors.

Kelly says he and Hickel had already met with ARCO chairman Bob Anderson to see if ARCO might want to build a Kenai refinery. Anderson turned them down.

Thereupon, said Hickel, "I just took the bull by the horns and told Kelly to go out and find a purchaser."

Kelly knew that major oil producers had no incentive to bring another refinery to the Kenai, but ever-increasing oil production from the west side of Cook Inlet was putting the state in a position to attract an independent refiner. The state could take its royalties in the form of oil, which it would sell to the new refinery. The increases in oil production meant there was now enough royalty oil to support a second refinery.

KELLY'S CHANCE to sell Cook Inlet royalty oil appeared in the person of Midland, Texas, entrepreneur Frank Cahoon. With Texans Joseph and Leon Jaworski (the latter of eventual Watergate fame) among the shareholders, Cahoon formed Alaska Oil and Refining Company and purchased twenty-three acres at Nikiski adjoining Chevron's Swanson River pipeline terminal, hoping to build an oil refinery. In April 1968, Cahoon contacted Hickel and Kelly.

"We obligated ourselves to build an 18-million-dollar refinery," Cahoon later related. He promised Hickel and Kelly that Alaska Oil and Refining would build a state-of-the-art facility at Nikiski and process all of the state's Cook Inlet royalty oil there.

While the state was happy to sell to Cahoon's proposed Big Bear Refinery, the Cook Inlet oil producers weren't interested in selling to him.

"The companies had no great desire to welcome Cahoon with open arms and provide him with a source of crude oil," Kelly said. "There was no great enthusiasm to encourage the building of another refinery. Competition and changing prices and values, I think, were all somewhat disquieting to the oil companies."

> *State Senator John Rader said he felt that Tom Kelly's haste in making the refinery deal probably "hadn't properly protected the public interest."*

On January 31, 1969, Kelly executed a contract with Alaska Oil and Refining to sell it 15,000 barrels a day of royalty oil. According to Kelly, Cahoon agreed to pay "the highest price we could get. More money than what we had been getting from the other companies."

Immediately upon execution of the royalty purchase contract with the state, Cahoon sold his Big Bear Refinery—though it had not yet been built—

to Tesoro Petroleum Corporation of San Antonio. Nobody in Alaska had ever heard of Tesoro. Some stories said Cahoon and his investors stood to make $5 million from the sale of the proposed refinery.

"The concept of Big Bear being peddled to somebody else was unbeknownst to me," Kelly said later. "I never knew that would occur. But I couldn't prevent Cahoon from selling his stock, so that's what he did."

IN JUNEAU, RUMORS RAN RAMPANT that Kelly had known Cahoon in Texas and had been "put in for a piece of the action."

"The gentleman, the prime mover, Cahoon, was acquainted with my wife, Jane, from college days," Kelly said. "That fact, obviously, was where the rumors initially started. But I didn't know him at the time."

State Senator John Rader said he felt that Kelly's haste in making the refinery deal probably "hadn't properly protected the public interest."

Cahoon, and Tesoro's president, Robert West, strenuously lobbied the 1969 spring legislative session for approval of the contract signed by Cahoon and Kelly. At a hearing of the Senate Resources Committee, chairman Elton Engstrom grilled Kelly. Who are these people from Texas, he wanted to know. What brought together this group of outsiders to invest in an Alaska refinery?

Kelly said he assumed it was just a bunch of entrepreneurs taking advantage of a good opportunity. But, said Engstrom, they stand to gain a $5 million profit on a $2.5 million investment. Isn't this unconscionable?

"The big thing we are losing sight of," responded Kelly, "are the benefits accruing to the state by having a refining complex here. I don't think we should hold it against somebody that when he makes a deal he makes a profit out of it."

"Hell," retorted Fairbanks Senator Ed Merdes, "I would like to make money like that. It's a wonderful business deal. But the people of Alaska should have got the profit, not a paper corporation."

"Have you ever made a better deal in your whole life?," Engstrom asked Cahoon.

Straight-faced, Cahoon answered: "I am a gambling man. That is what encouraged me to do it."

Despite persistent rumors and sledgehammer grilling, the "paper corporation" contract was approved. As Cahoon had promised, a refinery was built at Nikiski in 1969, and Tesoro began buying all of the state's Cook Inlet royalty oil.

Still bent on discovering the "true value" of the state's royalty, however, Kelly now demanded that the producers make "royalty deficiency payments" to the state. In September 1970, Mobil sued; the state countersued all the producers in March of the following year.

Four years later a partial settlement was reached in which the state agreed to pay some of the platform-to-shore charges for royalty oil sold to Tesoro. Tesoro agreed to pay a "posted price" for all future royalty oil purchases, thereby negating some of the pressure on the state to find the true market value of Cook Inlet oil. The big fight over the value of royalty oil was about to begin—this time on the North Slope.

ANCHORAGE DAILY TIMES/ANCHORAGE DAILY NEWS

S.S. Manhattan looking for the Northwest Passage in 1969.

PROFILE

THE BILL WALLACE STORY

Bill Wallace, a master mechanic and owner of the American Motors franchise in Anchorage, had drilled for oil in Texas. In Alaska, he caught oil fever and itched to become an Alaskan "independent."

In mid-April 1965, Wallace began drilling with a cable-tool rig on land Jerry Ganopole and I had leased from the state with our Alaska Exploration Corporation, in the Matanuska Valley just north of Anchorage. Wallace also acquired some mineral rights from an adjoining homesteader and convinced local investors he could drill at least half a mile down and maybe make them all rich.

By mid-June, the rig had pounded the Wallace No. 1 well down to below 500 feet. Even at that shallow depth the sides of the hole began sloughing off onto the drilling tools, which became stuck.

A practical man, Wallace simply slid the rig over several feet and began drilling again. When he realized he had to drill deeper than originally planned, he converted his cable-tool rig to a more efficient rotary drill. By the end of 1965, he had drilled below 3,500 feet.

With nary an oil show, Wallace's creditors were hollering and his banker was having kittens. The money had run out.

Drilling for oil cost Wallace his automobile dealership, his savings, and what looked like his future in Alaska. However, by the time construction of the trans-Alaska pipeline began in the early 1970s, Wallace had helped design and build an ingenious compressed-air refrigerated rig to drill holes in permanently frozen ground for the pipeline's support stanchions. He figured out how to keep the ground firm beneath the "hot-oil" pipeline and finally made some real money from Alaska's oil.

Chapter 21

Wally Hickel Goes To Washington

n late 1968, with British Petroleum drilling its first Prudhoe well, an event occurred which sent reverberations through Alaska's political structure and beyond. The state's longtime U.S. Senator E. L. "Bob" Bartlett died at the age of sixty-four of internal hemorrhaging after undergoing heart surgery in a Cleveland hospital on December 11, 1968. Bartlett's death came just two hours after President-elect Richard M. Nixon, victor over Hubert Humphrey in the November Presidential election, appointed Alaska Governor Walter J. Hickel as Secretary of Interior.

Prior to 1967, state law required the governor to appoint to a vacancy in the Congressional delegation a person of the same political party as the member being replaced. During the 1967 legislative session, Republican Governor Hickel and state House majority leader Ted Stevens amended the law to authorize the governor to disregard political affiliation and appoint whomever he wanted. Before 1967, a Democrat would have been appointed to Bartlett's vacant seat, but Hickel now had his choice and he selected Stevens.

A former U.S. prosecutor in Fairbanks, Stevens had come to Interior Secretary Doug McKay's attention in the mid-1950s when he solved a thorny McKinley Park concessionaire problem. He was asked to join the Eisenhower administration in the Interior Department. Just before Ike's second term

253

ended, Stevens was named Interior Department Solicitor. During Richard Nixon's first run for the presidency, against John F. Kennedy in 1960, Stevens served as a member of Nixon's "truth squad." After Nixon's defeat, Stevens returned to Alaska, where *Anchorage Daily Times* reporter Bob Kederick introduced the two of us.

I, a recent law school graduate, and Stevens, a seasoned political veteran and lawyer, sensed we would get along, so we opened an Anchorage law office on the second floor of the Alaska State Bank Building at the corner of Fifth Avenue and E Street. In 1962, while I served as chairman of the Democratic southcentral campaign, Republican Stevens ran for the U.S. Senate against Ernest Gruening. Stevens and I always agreed on the need for two strong political parties in Alaska. I made certain I didn't become involved in Gruening's campaign that year, and Stevens and I didn't discuss politics in the office. Though Stevens lost, he almost single-handedly began rejuvenating the nearly moribund state Republican party.

He ran for the Republican Senate nomination in August 1968 but was defeated by Anchorage banker Elmer E. Rasmuson. Then he had to watch

ANCHORAGE DAILY TIMES/ANCHORAGE DAILY NEWS

Wally Hickel (right) takes over as governor of Alaska from Bill Egan in November 1966. Two years later, President Nixon selected Hickel as his Interior Secretary, and Hickel promised Alaska Native leaders that he would extend the existing freeze on leasing of federal lands.

as a political nemesis, former state House Speaker Mike Gravel, beat Gruening in the Democratic primary and Rasmuson in the November general election. With his dream of becoming a U.S. senator now dead, he and his wife, Ann, went to Mexico to unwind and bear the pain of being at the lowest point in his political career.

Just four months later he would emerge from political purgatory with his appointment to the Senate. Gravel's election had preceded Stevens' appointment, making Gravel Alaska's senior senator. This added a final fillip to their acrimonious future relationship.

I was in Stevens' law office the day after his appointment when he got a call from an old friend from his days in the Interior Department, Democratic U.S. Senator Henry "Scoop" Jackson. Scoop wanted to offer his congratulations. Stevens had a question for the senator: Should he leave his name on the law office door as so many Congressmen did?

"You can't be a good fulltime senator and still practice law at home," Jackson replied.

Stevens had a solution, and it turned out that I was a big part of it. I had bowed out of my legal practice with Stevens some years earlier in order to devote time to oil-related businesses. Now Stevens said to me: "You sit here."

Thus, for about a year, I joined Stevens' partner, Russ Holland, in the practice of law.

AS PLANS WERE DEVELOPING for a trans-Alaska pipeline, Governor Hickel had also pursued his own idea for a major oil-development project. He wanted to build a 420-mile "winter road" from Fairbanks through Bettles up through Anaktuvuk Pass to Sagwon on the North Slope, a road that he believed would stimulate oil exploration on the Slope and reduce the cost of such work. His estimated price tag on the road was $350,000. Following the November 1968 general elections, Hickel polled legislators to help build support for the road.

After Hickel departed for Washington to become Nixon's Interior Secretary, one of Keith Miller's first acts as governor was to order construction of the road. After rejecting private competitive bids, the state highway department began construction. Built in haste during the winter, the road actually cost twice what Hickel had estimated, and the main accomplishment of the project was to damage the tundra.

About half of Alaska is underlain by permafrost in various forms. On the North Slope the permafrost is covered by a shallow mat of soil and vegetation known as the active layer. This thaws out in the brief Arctic summer to form the characteristic marshy, lake-studded landscape of polygon-patterned terrain. The topmost eighteen inches or so of the active layer—the tundra—acts as an insulating blanket. If this is scarred or removed, the permafrost below begins to erode rapidly with each summer thaw, injuring the land and causing unsightly scars.

Heavy construction equipment working on Hickel's winter road damaged the permanently frozen ground. The new road became known derisively as the "Hickel Highway."

> At his Congressional confirmation hearings as Interior Secretary, Hickel tried hard not to make the record of the North Slope road a part of his environmental credentials.

At his Congressional confirmation hearings in early 1969, Hickel tried hard not to make the record of the road a part of his environmental credentials. His successor, Miller, gave little help when, at the road's christening, he said: "This impossible road shall be known by the name of the man whose courage, foresight, and faith in the Great Land gave Alaska what surely will become one of its greatest assets."

The state highway department later estimated that during the one month in the winter of 1968-69 when the "highway" was actually open, only seven and a half tons of equipment were transported over the route. Used only minimally by oil companies, the road failed to speed North Slope exploration. Building it, however, signaled the Hickel/Miller administration's willingness—nay, exuberance—to support industry efforts.

NATIVE LAND CLAIMS and their impact on oil development figured prominently in Hickel's bid to win Senate confirmation of his selection as Interior Secretary. Hickel started off on the wrong foot, telling national media shortly before the confirmation hearings that what Interior Secretary Stewart Udall had done in "freezing" Alaska's land by executive order he could just as well undo.

Assisting Hickel in early 1969 was Anchorage attorney Cliff Groh, who had first come to Alaska in 1952. "I was good at working the system and looking for the main chance when I hit Anchorage," Groh recalls. Capable and street-smart, he was soon admitted to practice law, was appointed Anchorage's assistant U.S. attorney, and became the first president of the leading pro-statehood organization at the time, Operation Statehood.

Somewhere along the line, he says, probably back when he was in the Navy, he became a Republican, because Republicans seemed to have better prospects for financial success. "My life began in grinding poverty," he says. His Polish emigrant father could neither read nor write in any language and made only $9 a week working at a New Jersey steel foundry.

In Alaska, beginning in 1955, Groh won a series of elective offices, including state senator. During the mid-1960s, he represented labor unions, most notably Jesse Carr and the Teamsters. And he was later chosen by the newly formed Alaska Federation of Natives as one of the lawyers to lobby Congress in favor of Native land claims. Groh says his first draft of the Native federation's charter was taken from the standard paragraphs of the Teamsters articles of incorporation and bylaws.

Groh says Hickel called him the last day of 1968 and asked him to come to Washington to help prepare for his confirmation hearings. A loyal Republican, Groh jumped at the chance.

At the time, Groh was still serving as counsel for the Alaska Federation of Natives. Groh believes that Hickel beat Democrat Bill Egan in 1966 "because the Democrats gave the impression that they didn't want to deal with the Natives' land rights." When Hickel became governor, he had appointed a Native Land Claims Task Force, which subsequently recommended that Alaska's Natives be given 40 million acres of land plus $1 billion in cash.

As a Republican and as an advocate for Native rights, Cliff Groh suddenly found himself stuck between Wally Hickel and his own Native clients.

Before Hickel's confirmation hearings, Groh phoned Native leaders to try to convince them of the benefits that would accrue if an Alaskan were Secretary of Interior. He says he gradually realized that the Native leaders' strategy was to oppose Hickel unless he promised to extend Udall's land freeze and to agree to a minimum 40-million-acre grant—a grant, Groh says, that would at that time "have tied up all the land in Alaska."

As a Republican and as an advocate for Native rights, Groh suddenly found himself stuck between Hickel and his own Native clients. In Washington, Groh said, "the Natives came to me to see if they can see him to see if they can get their minimum acreage established. When they see Hickel they can't get a commitment out of him."

When Hickel's confirmation hearings began, Groh resigned as counsel for the Alaska Federation of Natives. Native leaders, he said, planned "to oppose Hickel until they got what they wanted. They thought in the meantime Hickel had to screw the rest of Alaska."

"Hickel finally signed off, to the extent that he could, to the 40 million acres," Groh said. "But when we told the Natives, they said: 'Then, why don't you give us 80 million?'"

Hickel got his confirmation. To get it, he had to assure the Natives that he would extend Udall's land freeze, despite opposition from most of Alaska's sportsmen, miners, and conservationists. Later, Hickel would help persuade Nixon that Alaska Natives should be given 40 million acres and half a billion dollars.

Politics of the moment had made Hickel extend the land freeze, which would now force the state and the oil companies to join in an effort to resolve Native land claims. It had become obvious that Congress would have to settle the land-claims issue before release of any more federal land, including the right-of-way permit for a trans-Alaska pipeline. An easement application for the pipeline already lay somewhere inside the Interior Department bureaucracy, and it couldn't surface until the claims were settled.

THE RALPH WHITMORE STORY

A man who once described himself as "a flat-broke New York City investment banker" ran across a full-column ad in the *Oil and Gas Journal* in the fall of 1968, offering 26,000 North Slope royalty acres for sale. Though intrigued by the ad, the almost insolvent broker considered purchase of a chunk of Alaska's oil country so far out of reach that he reluctantly did nothing.

But the possibilities in Alaska oil continued to dazzle Ralph Whitmore. So when the ad appeared again the following week, he dialed the Denver number listed. The phone was answered by leasebroker Willis Burnside.

Burnside offered Whitmore a 2 percent royalty underlying 26,000 acres leased to ARCO and Exxon. The land, Burnside disclosed, was less than twenty-five miles from the Prudhoe Bay discovery site and less than three miles from the proposed trans-Alaska pipeline. The wells, he said, were close to production.

It was a pitch calculated to make any potential investor salivate, and Whitmore was no exception.

Burnside told Whitmore that his asking price for the 2 percent royalty, $300,000, was a "steal," and that he'd better move fast.

"I'll meet you at the Denver airport as soon as I can get reservations," Whitmore told Burnside.

To help give the appearance he was a legitimate oil man, Whitmore wanted to arrive in Denver by stepping off a plane from Texas, so he flew to Denver via Houston. Whitmore offered Burnside $75,000 — with $1,000 down, $25,000 in sixty days, another $25,000 by the end of the year, and the remainder one year later. To Whitmore's surprise, Burnside accepted.

Whitmore promptly began filing corporate papers for what he called the Alaska North Slope Oil Company. Then he took an old broker friend to the Plaza for drinks.

Whitmore says the friend told him: "Just based on Prudhoe Bay alone, I'll give you $10,000."

Thus amply inspired and highly ebullient, Whitmore sought out other Wall Street brokers. He found them receptive and eager "for a piece of the North Slope action"; by the end of 1968, he had raised $350,000.

Whitmore, who had never been to Alaska, decided it was time "to go up and see what was going on." He flew to Anchorage and opened a bank account. After being told by a leading local banker that "there are no opportunities in Alaska," he visited Fairbanks and the North Slope as a guest of an oil field service company.

On his way back to New York, he spent the night in Anchorage. Seated on a stool in the Whale's Tail, a bar in Wally Hickel's Captain Cook Hotel, he overheard two men discussing how they were going to "steal control of a bank from that widow."

Brideen Crawford was president of the Alaska State Bank. On a hunch, Whitmore phoned the bank the next day and got Crawford on the line.

"Is your bank for sale?" he asked.

"Well," she replied hesitantly, "I've had several offers, one even from Texas oilman Mike Halbouty. But at the moment I can't tell you much more because currently I'm in negotiations. If there's any change, I'll let you know."

She indeed let Whitmore know several months later that she was ready to accept an offer for her bank.

Meanwhile, having paid off leasebroker Burnside (for leases that never produced oil), Whitmore had the balance of the $350,000 to plunk down as the down payment on the bank. In August 1969, the bank deal formally closed.

During the next twenty years, Ralph Whitmore ran the Alaska State Bank, part time at least. He was the bank's principal stockholder and chief executive officer until 1986, when the world oil price plunge forced a half dozen local banks, including Whitmore's, to fail. He claims he was the only Alaska banker who foresaw the oil price collapse, but it didn't save him or his bank.

Whitmore later moved to Beverly Hills, where he was spending most of his time fighting off the Federal Deposit Insurance Corporation and keeping his eye out for new golden opportunities.

Chapter 22

Industry Action

While British Petroleum prospered in Alaska, its former partner, Sinclair, was now nearly gone. But before Sinclair disappeared entirely, it would make one last try on the North Slope.

Even as its merger with ARCO was being negotiated during the fall of 1968, Sinclair remained responsible for the well west of Prudhoe Bay at Colville on land leased jointly by Sinclair and BP. Sinclair geologists remained convinced that a well drilled geologically "downdip" from this dry well at Colville might find oil reserves separated by faulting and a "dip reversal."

On land leased by Sinclair and BP at the December 1964 state sale, Sinclair began its Ugnu No. 1 well in February 1969. The drill rig was brought from Oklahoma City to Fairbanks by rail and barge, then flown via Hercules C-130s from Fairbanks to the drill site in 162 round-trip flights. Melting conditions at spring breakup caused the well to be suspended on May 9. By then the Ugnu well had shown potentially productive oil sands below 6,000 feet. The well remained idle until after the state's huge North Slope lease sale in September.

Two months after the sale, Sinclair announced that the Ugnu drill bit had penetrated twenty feet of Cretaceous oil reservoir. It had discovered an immense new oil field. Had the Ugnu discovery been made a year before—rather than a year after—the Prudhoe Bay discovery, Sinclair might have forestalled takeover by ARCO. Despite this huge oil discovery, Sinclair's assets would shortly be absorbed by its former North Slope partner, BP, and its competitor, ARCO.

(In 1971, ARCO drilled its West Sak No. 1 well, confirming the significance of the neighboring Ugnu, West Sak, and Kuparuk areas. This region is estimated to contain almost as much oil as in the Prudhoe field, but recovering it from the earth will be much more difficult. Field development was slow, with production at Kuparuk not commencing until 1981. Large-scale production has not yet begun at Ugnu and West Sak, where reserves are in the form of "heavy oil" that requires mechanical thinning before it can be lifted to the surface. By 1997, the costs of recovering the heavy oil have become favorable.)

SHAKE-UPS IN THE OIL INDUSTRY continued with merger of BP and Standard Oil Company of Ohio (Sohio). BP began merger discussions with Sohio in late 1968, and by August of the following year, the companies had agreed to merge, effective January 1, 1970.

The merger provided for exchange of most of BP's Prudhoe Bay oil for a majority of Sohio's special shares of stock. Ownership of these shares would give BP the right to earn up to 54 per cent of all of Sohio's shares once net production from the Prudhoe Bay leases reached 600,000 barrels per day.

With the merger, Sohio could now hope to have enough North Slope crude to supply its own refineries, and then some. In return, however, it had to give BP control. So, crowning decades of planning, BP had at last gained a major foothold in America through its control of a leading U.S. oil company.

A DARING CONCEPT for moving Prudhoe Bay oil to market was tested in 1969 by Exxon. The company, looking for an alternative to an Alaska pipeline, hoped that a tanker route through the Northwest Passage would be the answer.

Exxon sent the largest U.S. tanker in the merchant fleet, the *SS Manhattan*, on a voyage to test whether a passage through the Canadian Arctic islands to the U.S. Arctic Ocean was economically feasible. Exxon predominated on the East Coast, but if North Slope crude went through an Alaska pipeline to Valdez and then by tanker to the West Coast, ARCO and BP would control

more of the oil's marketing.

The owners of the 150,000-dead-weight-ton *Manhattan* strengthened its sides, put on a newly devised icebreaking bow, and sent her out of the port of Chester, Pennsylvania, in early August 1969. On September 1 she crossed the Arctic Circle at Baffin Bay, proceeded through Melville Sound, then plowed halfway

Exxon sent the tanker SS Manhattan on a grueling voyage in 1969 to test an oil transport route through the Northwest Passage.

up McClure Strait before being turned back by heavy ice. The *Manhattan* then sailed through Prince of Wales Strait into the Beaufort Sea, reaching Prudhoe Bay on September 19.

After a short visit at Point Barrow, and after being freed from the pack ice by escorting Canadian and U.S. icebreakers, the *Manhattan* returned to the Atlantic Ocean by the same general route to resume her previous rather mundane life as a carrier of grain and, occasionally, oil.

The Northwest Passage had been transited successfully in the past—originally by the *Gjoa,* under command of Norwegian Roald Amundsen, between 1903 and 1906. The Royal Canadian Mounted Police schooner *St. Roch* negotiated the route eastward in 1940-1942 and then westward in 1944; the *USS Seadragon,* a nuclear submarine, made an underwater transit in 1960; and the U.S. Coast Guard icebreaker *North Wind* came through from the Pacific in 1969. But the *Manhattan* was the first commercial vessel to complete the passage.

The voyage itself was successful, but it also pointed up problems that would make it impracticable for giant crude-oil carriers to ply the route. For one thing, the bays of the Beaufort Sea were shallow, and a serviceable tanker terminal in such shallow water was virtually impossible.

———————————

JUST A MONTH before the state's September 1969 Prudhoe Bay lease sale, with the big upcoming event on everyone's mind, the 20th annual Science Conference was held on the Fairbanks campus of the University of Alaska. Even before technical discussions began, a heated exchange took place between Sarah Lawrence College professor Robert Engler, author of the book *The Politics of Oil,* and Frank Ikard, president of the American Petroleum Institute.

The exchange was almost guaranteed by some of Engler's writings. For instance, he had written that "Whenever the [oil] industry has functioned, its concentrated economic power . . . has been forged into political power over the community. Law, the public bureaucracies, the political machinery, foreign policy, and public opinion have been harnessed for the private privileges and the immunity from public accountability of the international brotherhood of oil merchants.

"Formidable perimeters of defense manned by public relations specialists, lawyers, lobbyists, and obsequious politicians and editors keep the spotlight away from the penetrating powers of oil. Instead the focus is placed on the mystique of petroleum technology, corporate benevolence, and the possibility for an amenable public to be cut in on 'something for nothing.'"

The Engler-Ikard debate seemed to reignite the conservationist-versus-developer emotions earlier directed against Alaska's gold, fish, copper, and timber companies. It was now Big Oil's turn. The conservationist argument was led by Fairbanks professor Robert Weeden, who called for a moratorium on North Slope oil development and for a plan to restrain private development in the interest of public values. The moratorium idea only fueled the conference's smoldering fires and the concerns of some Alaskans on the eve of the biggest oil-lease sale in the state's history.

PROFILE

THE PETER ZAMARELLO STORY

Peter Zamarello was one of Alaska's most memorable wheeler-dealers, known as much for his big stories as his big deals. He says he was an oil industry "spy" during the 1960s. "Chevron gave me a $5,000 Leica camera to be used for spying," he claims. "I was a spy and I spied on other oil companies."

Born in 1928 on the Mediterranean island of Chefalonia, Zamarello dodged U.S. immigration officials in 1958 to get to Alaska from New York City. He went to work building houses in Anchorage for contractor Joe Agosto, a fellow Greek, and he soon became manager of Anchorage office buildings whose tenants included Chevron, Texaco, and Union.

Zamarello made a special point of getting to know the tenant-companies' draftsmen and landmen. Rumors persisted that he somehow got his hands on copies of geological and geophysical reports. One of his techniques, it was said, was pawing through tenant wastebaskets.

Zamarello admits scavenging discarded papers outside the buildings. "Union was too cheap to go and get their own Dumpster," he says, "so they kept dumping their garbage in mine."

Whenever Zamarello came to our Alaska Exploration Corporation office, I'd ask him not to unroll his maps. He'd laugh and say, "I just took what I could find. Some of them companies deserved to have their stuff stolen."

Following the Prudhoe Bay oil discovery, Zamarello made a bundle on oil and gas leases along the western boundary of the Arctic National Wildlife Range. By the time oil and gas leasing slacked off in the early 1980s, Zamarello was the single largest shopping-mall developer in the state, building more than 2 million square feet of commercial space in Anchorage and selling over $100 million worth of Alaska real estate, most of it to the Arabs.

When the real estate market crashed in 1986 with the world oil price plunge, Zamarello was in the soup, pursued by bankers and contractors for even a shred of the $150 million he owed. He filed for bankruptcy. But despite this monumental failure, by the late 1980s Zamarello was again bidding on leases in the Beaufort Sea, using the name "Petro Pete" and dealing with money extracted "from relatives."

After bankruptcy, Zamarello did settle for a much smaller office. On the walls are photographs of himself with prominent politicians and members of his immediate and extended family. On a large desk and several tables one sees an eclectic collection of artifacts and ivory—Greek vases, Native art, tusks, a wooden cannon, ceramic dragons.

I got the feeling that Peter Zamarello, still with influential friends, three secretaries, and a great will to survive, would continue to be in the thick of things.

Chapter 23
The Poker Game

Tom Kelly had settled on the exact date of the North Slope lease sale: September 10. The resources commissioner said he chose the date because it was Wally Hickel's birthday. On that date in 1969, the world would learn what Prudhoe Bay's "marginal" acreage was really worth. To increase the mounting excitement, Kelly began predicting to the local press how much money the oil companies would bid for the new acreage; he started by throwing out the figure of $5 billion.

The oil operators were gearing up for the sale. Before bidding, the companies needed to determine what lay beneath the acreage that had already been leased and what reserves their competitors might already have discovered. Most importantly, they needed to estimate how much oil might lie beneath the open acreage the state would be offering for bid.

In the summer of 1969, more than two dozen rigs were drilling frantically on the Arctic coastal plain. The companies hoped, of course, to find oil in these holes, but their primary purpose was to gather information that might help them bid at the September sale.

By the time of the sale, BP had completed or was in the process of drilling ten more wells on the Slope, eight of which were in the Put River area. ARCO had drilled four more, Mobil and Phillips four, Socal and Texaco two each, and Amoco, Shell, Hamilton Brothers-General American, and Canadian Home one each. All were "tight holes" because each operator was keen to

Thomas R. Marshall Jr., state petroleum geologist and land selection officer, recommended selection by the state of land on the North Slope. (1964 photo)

keep all information close to his vest to increase the chances of successful bidding in September.

At the same time, delays in plans for a trans-Alaska pipeline had resulted in several exploration and service companies leaving Alaska. Corporate merger-mania was reducing the number of operators even further. A few independents remained in 1969, but the federal land freeze had stopped state land selections and issuance of federal oil and gas leases.

Alaskans were just beginning to realize what a huge impact the North Slope oil discovery could have on their economy and way of life. In order to articulate what that future might hold, public forums were organized throughout the state. What policies should the state adopt with regard to the oil industry? What changes should be made in view of the huge discovery at Prudhoe?

Meanwhile, claiming a "juggernaut" was about to hit them, the Arctic Slope Native Association vociferously protested the upcoming lease sale. They did not file a lawsuit, however, because they knew the value of their land claims would increase dramatically following the sale.

TOM KELLY, like just about everyone else, was aware by now of the tremendous size of the Prudhoe Bay discovery. He had added eight tracts to his original bid list, four near Simpson Lagoon close to where Chevron was drilling and four a few miles north of Sinclair's Ugnu No. 1 well. Several times in the Lower 48, Kelly had been present where a first oil discovery had been made. If there was unleased acreage near the discovery well, he knew what happened: a leasing frenzy. Bids on unleased acreage could go sky-high. Open acreage on the North Slope at the September sale might be saturated with oil, or it might be marginal. In any event, Kelly was sure that extremely high bids would be made.

Partly to give himself time, but also to heighten the growing excitement over the upcoming bidding, Kelly canceled the state's scheduled July sale of leases on the Gulf of Alaska. And of course his prediction of as much as $5 billion in bids added to the drama; he was smart enough to know that companies might increase their bids if they felt competitors were doing so.

Kelly approached the upcoming sale as he would for the biggest hand in a high-stakes poker game, making bluff and bluster do where he found his cards weak. As part of his strategy, he made a point of letting people know that he was gathering geological and geophysical information about Prudhoe Bay. He encouraged rumors that his staff had assembled more data on Prudhoe than any one oil company, and he took pains to talk like a knowledgeable geologist.

In the past, the state of Alaska never had a good idea of the true value of its minerals before leasing, and Kelly hoped to change that. Kelly sent his petroleum supervisor, Thomas R. Marshall, Jr., to the major oil companies' local exploration offices to collect geological information. Marshall reported to Kelly on November 14, 1968, in a memo that, perhaps for the first time, had one state official talking with another in the lingo of petroleum geologists:

"I observed in accordance with your instructions the seismic logs on all the BP-Sinclair wells in the BP offices, to compare the DST [drill stem tests]. . . . I got some sonic log porosity interpretations and also conventional core analysis data to get an overall idea of the porosity of the Cretaceous section that has been penetrated so far on the deep geosynclinal area. British Petroleum was completely cooperative in showing me all requested well data. They offered even more data that pertained to the immediate problem of porosity determination. Potential for oil and gas values compared to other unselected oil and gas provinces is high over the entire Arctic Slope province except the southern foothills section, which is complex structurally and high topographically."

> *The state's Tom Kelly approached the sale as he would for the biggest hand in a high-stakes poker game, making bluff and bluster do where he found his cards weak.*

Marshall had gotten BP's well data, but what the state needed, and didn't have, was detailed analysis of Prudhoe Bay's geologic structure. Kelly started his campaign to gather geologic data after ARCO's summer 1968 announcement of the rich oil find at its Sag River No. 1 well, its second well at Prudhoe. "We didn't have the geological knowledge to confirm that . . . Sag No. 1 had resulted in the discovery of the largest field ever discovered in North America," says Kelly. Until then, Kelly had not seen any actual North Slope well or seismic data, so he initiated public and private meetings with the oil companies to seek access to their geologic interpretations of the Prudhoe oil field.

DESPITE THESE EFFORTS, the state still was left with a paucity of hard data. "We didn't have a lot of information or data, but we had our own set of maps," says Kelly. With no purchased seismic or interpretive data, Kelly's staff prepared tract lease maps on which state petroleum geologists and engineers superimposed their data. "That was basically to assist us in defining reasonable parameters of minimum low acceptable bid and/or bids," says Kelly.

> *"Our principal objective in the 1969 lease sale was to . . . make up for the rather menial sums received in the early days. Those, basically, leased the field away. So we were trying to play catch-up."*
> —Resources commissioner Tom Kelly

Most of the obviously desirable oil acreage had been leased at the state's 1964, 1965, and 1967 sales. "Those sales brought the state very, very modest amounts of money," says Kelly. "Our principal objective in the 1969 lease sale was to maximize bonus revenues and try to make up for the rather menial sums received in the early days. Those, basically, leased the field away. So we were trying to play catch-up."

In setting minimum bids, says Kelly, the dollar amounts were only guessed at. There were too many variables. "We didn't know when the pipeline would come," he says, "and we didn't know what the volumes would be." Also, Kelly hadn't seen a chemical analysis of Prudhoe Bay oil on which to base assumptions concerning its market price. Therefore, the question of the value of the state's royalty oil from the North Slope had not been raised. There was just too much excitement preparing for the September sale to deal with such regulatory matters.

Despite the gaps in his geological information, but needing to estimate the value of each open tract to be offered for bidding, Kelly estimated a "minimum, median, and generous" tract-by-tract bid value. He knew many strategies oil companies used in preparing bids; they were a critical part of the oil exploration business. It took a general knowledge of the area to be leased, technical information to decide how much to bid on each tract, and a guess as to whom the competitors most likely would be. Hunches, and sometimes just plain luck, often prevailed. Whichever way one figured, the upcoming sale would be exciting.

INSIDE STORY

TOM KELLY'S GAME

"Preparing for the sale was all very clandestine," says Tom Kelly of the state's preparations for the big 1969 Prudhoe sale. "Much of what the companies did and everything we did, you might say, was in the nature of a planned charade. The more mystique we could put out, the better . . . chance of deriving maximum bids."

"We even went to the extent of putting out a lot of hocus-pocus in order to make everybody, including the press, think we knew everything when we really didn't," Kelly says. "We put on a pretty good act."

During the pre-sale period, resources commissioner Kelly and his staff held meetings at various offices in Anchorage. They would meet either at the Division of Lands downtown or at the Oil and Gas Conservation Committee offices out in Mountain View. Sometimes they would meet in a downtown hotel in order to be even more conspicuous. Each time, Kelly or one of his staff members—Tom Marshall, "Easy" Gilbreth, or Pedro Denton—would carry a brown leather briefcase, always the same brown leather briefcase.

Word soon circulated that Kelly and the state had lots of geophysical data, well logs, seismic maps, and geophysical interpretations—all toted around in a brown leather briefcase. In fact, Kelly says, the briefcase held only one well log and a miniscule amount of "bootlegged" seismic data. The reputed deep subsurface investigation data on the Prudhoe Bay structure he was rumored to possess amounted to almost nothing.

In his book *Corridors of Time*, Canadian author Aubrey Kerr quotes "Easy" Gilbreth as saying that the state's North Slope well data was brought out each morning from safe-deposit boxes in Anchorage, transported in armored cars to government offices, and returned under lock and key at the end of each day.

"In fact," says Tom Marshall, "the discovery E-log, mud log, drilling log, etc., were kept in a regular file cabinet. Each night I would put them in a safe-deposit box at the Alaska Mutual Bank in the Teamsters Mall and bring them out the next morning. It was an armload I would set on the seat of my car."

Chapter 24

The Biggest Sale

The long-awaited September 10, 1969, oil lease sale was held in Anchorage's Sidney Lawrence Auditorium, nearly two years after the initial discovery at Prudhoe Bay. The bids at this sale would be the first indication of the true value of Prudhoe's reserves.

The first six bids were on tracts located about twenty miles west of Prudhoe Bay in the Colville River delta where BP and Sinclair had bid the heaviest in 1964. They were jointly bid by Gulf Oil and BP, with Gulf furnishing most of the cash and BP providing coastal plain geophysical data and information from the Colville well.

"When Gulf's and BP's bids were opened, it was unbelievable," Tom Kelly recalls. "A silence came over the audience, and everybody else. We were too shocked to cheer or yell or do anything. We were just kind of dumbfounded."

Gulf Oil and BP had bid an amazing $97 million for the right to lease the six parcels—more money than had ever before been bid in total at any state oil and gas lease sale. "Those in the auditorium—which was absolutely packed—were just aghast," Kelly said. "Everybody was going 'Phewwww.' I think I evidenced a smile or two. I was quite happy. Lots of buzzing was going on as we proceeded to the other tracts in the sale."

THE SALE DREW A BIG CROWD of oil people and reporters. BP's home country was well-represented by Phillip Jacobson of the *London Times*, Alan

275

Osborn of the *London Telegraph,* David Palmer of the *London Financial Times,* and Richard Killian of the *London Daily Express.* Larry Davies' *New York Times* front-page story was accompanied by a photo of Kelly opening bid envelopes.

Oil industry big shots included ARCO President Thornton Bradshaw and Texans Herbert and Bunker Hunt. Oil company jets and chartered aircraft outnumbered taxicabs at Anchorage International Airport. Twelve state troopers, three fire marshals, and a half dozen city policemen provided security for the sale.

> *"When Gulf's and BP's bids were opened, it was unbelievable. A silence came over the audience, and everbody else. We were too shocked to cheer or yell or do anything. We were just kind of dumbfounded."*
>
> —*Tom Kelly*

As oil executives and reporters from around the world filed into the auditorium that early September morning, members of the Arctic Slope Native Association picketed outside. Pacing back and forth on the sidewalk, they carried hand-painted signs and posters: "Bad Deal at Tom Kelly's Trading Post"; "$2 Billion Native Land Robbery"; "Oilmen and Bankers: Make Your Checks Payable to Alaska Natives." Onlookers appeared mostly amused.

Charlie "Etok" Edwardsen, Jr., who stood at the head of the picket line of Arctic Eskimo militants, said: "We propose that today's sales of leases allow and require the imposition of a constructive trust of all the receipts on behalf of the real and true owners of the land. This would illustrate well the miserable smallness of the settlement proposed by the Great White Father in Washington."

The president of another Native group undercut Edwardsen's effort. Don Wright of the Alaska Federation of Natives told journalists that his board of directors "voted unanimously against supporting the demonstration and Edwardsen's statement." The federation was at odds with Arctic Eskimos over land-claims strategy and didn't want to rock the oil boat.

THE CANADIAN MYSTERY-TRAIN STORY illustrates the extremes of secrecy and tension surrounding the sale. To prepare for the event, Hamilton Brothers Oil Company put together a bidding group of ten companies.

Hamilton Brothers also negotiated an agreement with General American Oil Company that allowed Hamilton to drill on a tract ten miles north of the Prudhoe Bay discovery well—in advance of the September lease sale.

Marshy conditions prevented movement of drill rigs overland to the well site at Point Storkersen, so Hamilton brought in a rig from Canada that was specially designed to be transported by helicopters. Hamilton thus became the only company able to drill a well to test state acreage north of the land that was up for sale. The Hamilton-led group of ten companies therefore had a major strategic advantage over the competition.

Members of the Arctic Slope Native Association picket the state's huge September 10, 1969, Prudhoe lease sale.

Security at the remote drill site was extremely tight. A barbed wire fence was erected. Guards and guard dogs patrolled the area. Scanners were used to detect radio transmissions. The rig's floor and derrick were shrouded in canvas so that oil scouts outside the compound, sighting with binoculars or hovering in helicopters, couldn't count the number of thirty-foot sections of drill pipe in the hole. This prevented them from estimating drilling depths, testing procedures, or results.

Drilling with an underpowered rig, workers expected the undersized 3-1/2-inch hole to reach its target depth just before the September 10 sale. Three weeks before the sale, members of the crew were offered the choice of a $1,000 bonus for staying and being locked in at the well site until after the sale or of leaving immediately. Only three of the twenty-nine crewmen left.

Bid headquarters for the Hamilton Brothers group was a fourteen-car Canadian National chartered railroad train. For five days prior to the sale, the train shuttled between Calgary and Edmonton, Alberta, its nerve center being the domed "scenoramic" car.

Information from the Hamilton Brothers well was radioed, using secret code, from an airplane circling the Storkersen drill site, then relayed by couriers to oil executives assembled aboard the rail caravan. Railcar occupants, sixty-five in all, were not permitted to disembark or talk to anyone outside the sealed train. Whenever the train halted, guards patrolling outside made sure no one entered or exited. Meals were served at staggered times to separate bidding groups; certain groups had to be isolated from one another because all ten companies were not bidding together on every lease block.

When the drilling information from the Storkersen well started to arrive, the companies had to decide what to bid on each tract, who wanted to bid on which tract, and the percentage each participant would contribute to a bid. To ensure that the bonus bid envelopes would be delivered on time and to guard against mechanical problems, a Hamilton Brothers jet and an Ashland Oil jet each carried duplicate bid checks from Calgary to Anchorage.

The state's September 10, 1969, lease sale brought in more than $900 million. Among those at the head table for the historic sale were Governor Keith Miller (with microphone) and resources commissioner Tom Kelly (far right).

Now, having spent five days shuttling back and forth on bumpy rails and after analyzing rather hasty and inconclusive data from the Storkersen well, the ten-company group decided to bid $100 million for fifteen tracts comprising 37,500 acres. Of this total, $40 million was bid on Tract 73.

When the bids were opened in Anchorage by resources commissioner Tom Kelly, the group of ten won ten tracts at a total cost of $73 million. Included was Tract 73, on which the group had bid $40 million. The group's judgment on this tract turned out to be faulty; no one else had bid on it, and it subsequently proved to be a bust. But the other nine tracts turned out to be productive.

The Hunt/Amerada/Getty consortium plunked down an astounding total of more than $240 million for five tracts.

Home Oil Company of Canada had put up 25 percent of the bid money for Tract 73, and it watched later as its common-share price plummeted from $81 to $10. Hamilton Brothers also took a significant financial hit on the Tract 73 bid. However, Hamilton went on to many successes, including being the first company to find and produce oil in the English sector of the North Sea. Home Oil subsequently went out of business.

THE BIGGEST SPENDER at the state sale was a consortium that included Herbert and Bunker Hunt and their various trusts, along with Amerada Oil, Getty Oil, Louisiana Land and Exploration Company, Marathon Oil, and Placid Oil, a Hunt subsidiary.

The consortium (the Hunt/Amerada/Getty group) won a tight competition for Tract 57 at the opening of the sealed bids. BP and Gulf bid together on Tract 57, but their offer was topped by the joint bid from Phillips, Mobil, and Chevron of $72,113,000. Then the Hunt/Amerada/Getty consortium's bid was opened. It was for $72,277,000, a mere $164,133 higher than the offer from the Phillips group.

I was sitting directly behind the Hunt brothers in the auditorium when their bid was opened and a gasp went up from the crowd. A rumor moved immediately down the aisle that a Phillips geologist, after selling his company's technical data to the Hunt/Amerada/Getty group, had "gone south."

Next it was said that a Phillips executive had defected to South America. Later, an inconclusive investigation was conducted by the losing bidders. Most oilmen still suspect that something fishy went on.

BP's Geoff Larminie thinks the closeness of the bids was probably nothing more than mathematical coincidence. "What sort of information you put in will determine the amount you'll bid. It's surprising, actually, that there's so much difference so often. When they're close, everybody thinks there's something shady about it. If you basically approach the thing on a systematic basis, putting roughly the same figures in at the end of the day, you'll come out about the same."

> *A rumor moved immediately down the aisle that a Phillips geologist, after selling his company's technical data to the Hunt/Amerada/Getty group, had "gone south."*

Bidders had undoubtedly put similar geologic information into their computers, and the Hunt/Amerada/Getty group might have added a little something extra, as is often done, just to be safe. But it's highly unlikely that bids this large, and this close, were the result of just plain happenstance.

The Hunt/Amerada/Getty consortium plunked down an astounding total of more than $240 million for five tracts at the sale, plus nearly $30 million for eleven other parcels. Their acreage included in-filling within the boundary of the Prudhoe Bay structure, with most of it sprawling out on the edges of the Prudhoe field. (The consortium brought in its first well on Tract 57 in April 1971 and by 1995 had produced 72 million barrels of oil from that parcel. This translates to a gross income, before taxes, royalties, and drilling costs, of more than $1 billion.)

BP was successful in adding some acreage to its North Slope land map. As for ARCO, "We followed a simple producing axiom," a company executive said after the sale. "When you have an excellent position in an area, look ahead to new areas of exploration. Accordingly, we concentrated our bids on acreage representing new prospects. We mapped five such areas and got into four of them." ARCO had leased in four new areas on the Slope.

WHEN THE DUST CLEARED at the September 10 sale, the State of Alaska was richer by close to a billion dollars. The state had offered nearly half a million acres of four-section (2,560-acre) tracts and received bids on all 179 parcels. Tom Kelly rejected fifteen bids as below his minimum per-acre requirement. But for the 164 accepted tracts, covering more than 400,000 acres, the total paid to the state was more than $900 million.

Tom Kelly had predicted bids of $5 billion at the auction, but this public guesstimate had been partly wishful thinking and partly an attempt to stimulate higher bids. If the companies had actually submitted bids totaling $5 billion, the state should have ended up with about $2.5 billion from the winning bids. So Kelly had grossly overestimated how much the state would rake in. But despite this, most Alaskans were still taken by surprise at the great amount of money that filled state coffers thanks to the sale.

Bidders had to come up with 20 percent of their bid up front, so by the end of the day of the sale, the state had $180 million to deal with in the form of certified or cashier's checks. The state put the checks aboard a chartered United Air Lines DC-8 and whisked them to San Francisco for deposit in a special Bank of America account. On September 11, the day following the sale, the state began earning $45,000 in interest for each twenty-four hours the money lay in the bank.

An editorial in the *Anchorage Daily News* praised Tom Kelly, saying that the resources commissioner "may have made an extra half billion dollars for the state by his astute handling of the sale in the months preceding it."

"Kelly got rid of a lot of caribou pasture at some pretty high prices," the editorial said. "He played a tremendous poker game and won for the state all the way."

SPOTLIGHT

TAKING THE PRIZE

The work of British Petroleum crews on the North Slope translated into some major accolades. In 1970, Britain's premier engineering prize, the McRobert award, was given to BP's Alwyn Thomas, Sir Peter Kent, and Harry Warman, and they in turn shared the $75,000 in prize money with twenty other employees who played a role in the Prudhoe Bay discovery. BP's Geoff Larminie received the Order of the British Empire from Queen Elizabeth II for his part in the company's Alaska success.

BP liked to honor its employees, Larminie says. "BP had a rather pleasant old-fashioned policy of giving silver tankards to small groups of people to celebrate significant events in the company's history. . . . They gave a dozen silver tankards to those of us involved on the North Slope between July 1968 and March 1969."

British oilman Peter Kent was an early believer in the oil potential of the North Slope. He was a winner of Britain's McRobert engineering prize in 1970 for his role in the Prudhoe discovery, and a year later he received knighthood.

Marvin Mangus recalls that ARCO handled things differently. Mangus, an ARCO geologist at the time of its first Prudhoe discovery, says there was "never any gesture to compliment the scientists and engineers who found Prudhoe. That's still disappointing. . . . BP at least gave some of their people nice medals and monetary recognition.

"Hell, there wasn't one person in high management who ever said to us, 'You guys did a good job.' Henderson Supplee, former chairman of Atlantic, was the only one who wrote me a letter. There was a fine gentleman. The top ARCO people said there were too many involved in the discovery. What a crock."

Chapter 25
The Pipeline

The biggest order of business for the petroleum companies after discovering oil at Prudhoe was finding a way to get it to market. A pipeline across Alaska seemed to be the most practical method for moving oil from Prudhoe Bay, icebound most of the year, to an open-water port.

Representatives of the principal Prudhoe lease owners—ARCO, Exxon, and BP—met in Dallas as early as the first part of 1968 to settle on the route of a pipeline from the North Slope to an open-water port somewhere on Alaska's coast. With only cursory contact with state officials, they chose the shortest, least expensive route to Valdez on Prince William Sound, on the southern coast of Alaska.

They also debated the point where the pipeline would cross the Brooks Range. The longest, but probably cheapest, route over the range was through Anaktuvuk Pass. A shorter route, but higher and more difficult, was through Atigun Pass. By the time a pipeline agreement was signed by the three oil companies in October 1968, the Atigun Pass route was chosen.

Also that fall, the state selected land at Valdez for an oil pipeline terminal. Pipeline planners said they needed more land for the terminal site inside the Chugach National Forest, so the Forest Service gave a Special Land Use Permit to the state for the needed acreage. The pipeline company, said resources commissioner Tom Kelly, could build a terminal and tank farm at Fort Liscum

HARRY JAMISON

Edward Patton headed the outfit formed by the oil companies in 1969 to build the trans-Alaska pipeline. Patton's unequivocal statement that no pipeline could be built until Native land claims were settled helped push business leaders and the oil industry into uneasy support for the claims.

on Valdez Arm, as long as it paid the state $200,000 for a road right-of-way to the location and a dock site.

On February 10, 1969, ARCO, Exxon, and BP officially announced plans to design and build a 798-mile pipeline from the North Slope to a marine terminal site at Valdez. It was to begin at Pump Station No. 1 near the center of the Prudhoe Bay oil field, then traverse Alaska to the northernmost ice-free port in the United States.

Two months later, the pipeline owner-companies purchased 800 miles of 48-inch-diameter pipe at a cost of nearly $100 million from three Japanese companies. The cost of building the pipeline, exclusive of interest on borrowed capital but including ten pump stations, was estimated at $900 million.

Despite some problems, ARCO's Bob Anderson says that during the fall of 1968, the federal government had been processing the oil companies' pipeline papers as "just another right-of-way." Oilmen felt, says Anderson, that "it was a done deal."

Suddenly, Anderson says, Interior Secretary Stewart Udall and then-Governor Wally Hickel "fell out over something. Hickel was campaigning for Nixon, and he called Udall some names.

"The next thing we knew, Udall stopped the easement. We were almost grandfathered in, but Udall pulled a clever political ploy. While leaving office, he was thumbing his nose at Hickel. We were caught in a trap. By 1969, TAPS [Trans-Alaska Pipeline System] was a hot potato. No one wanted to touch it."

ENVIRONMENTAL CONCERNS and Native land claims were to delay construction of the pipeline for years. Pipeline builders needed rights-of-way across Alaska before they could proceed with the massive project. But the pipeline, along with all other land-use matters in the state, was on hold because of the land claims. Under the Statehood Act of 1959, Congress gave

Alaska the right to select 104 million acres during its first twenty-five years. Now, ten years after statehood, Alaska's Natives were lobbying Congress to be given all or a portion of the same land the state had tentatively selected.

These claims had prompted Stewart Udall's land freeze, which stopped further state selections and halted the issuance of federal oil and gas leases in Alaska. Everyone concerned with exploitation of Alaska's oil riches became increasingly nervous as the state and the Natives continued as land adversaries.

By early 1969, pipeline owner-companies were sending out their landmen and lawyers to acquire right-of-way easements from Natives over whose land the pipeline was to be laid. In exchange, Natives were being offered pipeline construction service contracts. Pipeline owner-companies were agreeing to employ Natives on construction jobs, granting them exclusive right-of-way clearing and tug and barge operation contracts, and leasing office facilities along the pipeline corridor from the Native groups. All the Native

STEVE McCUTHEON/ANCHORAGE MUSEUM OF HISTORY AND ART

Work began on the oil pipeline terminal near Valdez in the fall of 1970, although government approval for the full pipeline was still years away.

landowners along the proposed right-of-way corridor—except the Arctic Slope Native Association—executed right-of-way waivers.

Debate in Congress over the National Environmental Policy Act during 1968 raised the vexing question of whether drilling should be allowed to continue on the North Slope and whether a pipeline permit should be issued.

The pipeline right-of-way would cross 552 miles of federal public domain. Its width, by federal law, was limited to fifty-four feet. This wouldn't be enough. The 48-inch-wide pipe was to be laid in a deeply cut ditch, then backfilled with earth. Such an operation would require heavy equipment and huge cranes. A roadway would have to be built adjacent to the pipeline so supplies could be hauled in and so that cranes and tractors could operate.

On June 6, 1969, owner-companies applied to the Department of Interior—now under charge of former Alaska governor Wally Hickel—for a 100-foot-wide pipeline right-of-way. The companies said the additional width was needed to get to the proposed pipeline and its eleven pump stations. This 100-foot transportation easement, or "haul road" permit, from Livengood to Prudhoe Bay would also include rights-of-ways of from 200 to 500 feet wide for river crossings. In July, the department's Bureau of Land Management issued the state a permit and shortly thereafter the first 53-mile section of the haul road, from the gold mining community of Livengood to the Yukon River, was begun.

The Arctic Slope Native Association pointed out that pipeline permits issued by the federal government made no provision for compensating Natives in case of an oil spill on their land claims. This was particularly important, they said, if oil were ever to be spilled at the Yukon River crossing north of Fairbanks, at Valdez, or in Prince William Sound.

PRESIDENT NIXON signed the National Environmental Policy Act on January 1, 1970. The legislation would delay construction of the trans-Alaska pipeline, as would the Alaska Native Claims Settlement Act, and the time and energy it took during the early 1970s to deal with environmental issues and Native claims drastically altered oil development plans on the North Slope.

Three environmental organizations sued in federal court, charging Interior Department officials with failing to comply with the National Environmental Policy Act. They also argued that any pipeline right-of-way easement could not exceed the fifty-four-foot maximum allowed under the 1920 Mineral Leasing Act (a width determined back then to be sufficient to turn around a team of oxen for laying pipe).

Wally Hickel's successor as Interior Secretary, Rogers Morton, and Commerce Secretary Maurice Stans visited Alaska during the summer of 1970. They told Alaskans that though Morton had the authority to extend the land freeze, he had decided to wait for the federal court decision sometime in mid-September, at which time he would recommend to President Nixon that he authorize the pipeline right-of-way permit before the end of the year.

The oil industry organized a campaign called "Speak Up Alaska" in an effort to speed the pipeline permit process. The campaign nearly backfired when its chairman labeled Rogers Morton as "Public Enemy No. 1" for failing to administratively issue the permit.

Pipeline delay was seriously affecting most of Alaska. Oil-related employment in the state dropped to 3,300 by midsummer 1970. In 1967, a total of 2,500 oil people had been employed; a year later, after the Prudhoe

Lengths of pipe for the 800-mile trans-Alaska pipeline are stacked high on a barge. Oil companies bought nearly $100 million worth of the 48-inch-diameter pipe from three Japanese companies in 1969.

discovery, 8,400 had jobs. Now, oil employment dropped back to the pre-Prudhoe level. Only one exploratory well was drilled during 1970 in the entire state—at Union's Hemlock site on the Kenai Peninsula.

Local businessmen, expecting work on the pipeline to begin no later than 1971, had borrowed heavily and could no longer meet their financial obligations. Bankruptcies grew in number. Already concerned about the pipeline's delay, BP chairman Eric Drake suggested that crude oil from the North Slope might be taken to market by submarine.

Governor Keith Miller appointed a pipeline committee and hired the consulting firm of Harbridge House, Inc., to advise him on whether the state should attempt to own the pipeline. Would state ownership speed construction? In late 1970, Harbridge House advised that not only would state ownership not help solve the construction delay, it would add materially to it. The state lacked the people and money to carry out such a huge task, Harbridge said. And if the state owned the pipeline, Alaska would become "economically unviable, and the public risk was too great."

SEVEN OIL COMPANIES formed Alyeska Pipeline Service Company in 1970 as a separate outfit to coordinate construction, operation, and maintenance of the pipeline. Engineer Edward Patton, who had been in charge of building Exxon's huge Benicia, California, oil refinery, was hired as Alyeska president to oversee what was even then being called "the largest private construction project in U.S. history."

Patton, though he didn't know it when he began the job, was to spend his next three years shuttling between Alyeska headquarters in Bellevue, Washington; Washington, D.C.; and Juneau, negotiating with federal and state lawmakers, bureaucrats, and Natives. The environment, Native land claims, and a host of construction problems would occupy most of his time.

Speaking to the Anchorage Chamber of Commerce in September 1970, Patton made it clear to his business audience that there would be no pipeline right-of-way permits until Congress settled the land claims issue. Until that time, Patton said, neither the President nor Secretary of Interior would authorize the pipeline.

This unequivocal statement from oil's most visible spokesman in Alaska finally convinced state business leaders that the oil industry was in this thing together with the state and the Natives. Many businessmen thought the Natives weren't entitled to any land, but now that Patton had spoken, they were willing, reluctantly, to back a Native land claims settlement.

Patton was a sailing enthusiast, and before accepting the Alyeska assignment, he had insisted that he and his wife, Dorothy, reside where they could enjoy year-round sailing. Anchorage, or most anywhere else in Alaska, was not suitable. A more likely spot was on the shores of Lake Washington in Seattle. So in October 1970, Alyeska opened its headquarters office in Bellevue, east of Seattle, where fresh and saltwater sailing is always available.

> *Pipeline delay was seriously affecting most of Alaska. Oil-related employment in the state dropped to 3,300 by midsummer 1970.*

Alaska's businessmen felt that a project of this scope should be headquartered in Alaska. The decision to locate Alyeska headquarters in Bellevue hurt the oil industry's image in Alaska, but the headquarters remained where it was. Perhaps to ameliorate the hard feelings of many Alaskans, Alyeska's first project manager, BP's David Henderson, took up residence in Anchorage.

Ed Patton was given authority to spend tens of millions of dollars on his own. But as the pipeline delay lengthened, this financial carte blanche was slowly withdrawn, and he was put under direction of an owners committee.

Hugh Gallagher, then lobbyist for BP in Washington, says the three principal companies — Exxon, BP, and ARCO — "didn't trust each other. Phelan Hunter [president of Exxon's pipeline company] was like something from an old silent film comedy: his hat was too small, and he never seemed exactly clear about what was going on. What *was* clear was that he didn't think much of Alaska Natives, whom he referred to as the 'Frito Banditos.'" The owners committee was now demanding monthly reports and quarterly budget reviews from Patton.

The industry was now well aware that the federal land freeze had to be lifted before a pipeline right-of-way permit would be granted — and that the land freeze would not be lifted until Native land claims were settled. Consequently the major oil companies got directly involved with the land claims, organizing their own team to deal with Congress. In the fall of 1970,

Alyeska hired the former director of the Alaska legislative affairs agency, William E. Foster, as coordinator of its Native Congressional land claims support team.

The following January, I became a contract consultant for Alyeska, working directly with Harry Jamison, now in charge of Alyeska's government relations. I had been practicing law with Russ Holland and was publishing the new magazine *Alaska Industry*. After watching the magazine's profits being devoured by printing costs, we had hired *Anchorage Daily News* printers Don and "Bub" Van Cleve so that we could print the 12,000 monthly copies ourselves. But with still not enough money coming in for my salary, it was with some relief that I got an offer from Jamison, who was on loan to Alyeska from ARCO, to become the pipeline company's "government consultant." From January 1971 to July 1972, I represented Alyeska in Juneau.

STIFF REQUIREMENTS were now being placed on Arctic pipeline construction by the U.S. Geological Survey. The pipeline would be carrying high-temperature oil, and laying a "hot" pipe directly into the Arctic's permanently frozen ground was unlike laying pipe in the Southwest U.S. or other parts of the world.

> "The trans-Alaska pipeline . . . is a desperate necessity not only to Alaska but to the whole United States."
>
> —Vide Bartlett, testifying to Congress

In 1970, the state legislature allocated $500,000 for a new Department of En-vironmental Conservation. Appointed the following year as the department's first commissioner was Max Brewer, a permafrost expert and former director of the Arctic Research Laboratory at Barrow. Pipeline engineers had initially estimated that only one-sixth of the 800 miles of pipe would have to be elevated above the tundra. But partly because of Brewer's concerns about damage to the tundra and the underlying permafrost, more than half the entire pipeline would eventually be perched on steel pilings.

Federal officials publicly warned pipeline developers that their original construction plans were on the wrong track. And Russell Train, director of the U.S. Council on Environmental Quality, roasted the companies for seriously misjudging technical difficulties involved in laying a hot pipe into permafrost. They failed to grasp, he said, the significance of public concerns as ex-pressed in the new National Environmental Policy Act.

The oil companies and their pipeline organization were ill-equipped to deal with environmental issues. By the time the final environmental impact statement for the pipeline was issued in May 1972, court and Congressional hearings were a foregone conclusion.

The pipeline owner-companies pulled in some big names to impress Congress. Among the first to testify before the Senate Interior Committee at its pipeline environmental impact hearing on February 13, 1971, was Vide Bartlett, Senator Bob Bartlett's widow. In a speech written by former Bartlett aide and now BP lobbyist Hugh Gallagher, she pleaded to let the pipeline begin.

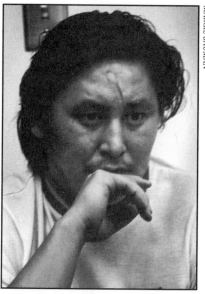

MARGIE BAUMAN

Testifying before the U.S. Senate in 1971, Alaska Native Charlie "Etok" Edwardsen, Jr., asked, "How can white men sell our land when they don't own it?"

"As a lifelong Alaskan, the trans-Alaska pipeline . . . is a desperate necessity not only to Alaska but to the whole United States, where we face a national emergency in the production of energy," she said.

After reciting the rigors of Alaska living and the hopes of early settlers for what statehood would bring, she said that "until the discovery of oil in 1957, we were still begging for our bread. We have always known that our hope for self-reliance lay in development of our natural resources. We must not be locked in a cavern of ice without the benefit of warmth from the use of our very own resources. No other state has been treated this way.

"Life in Alaska is not easy. It demands a fierce respect in exchange for a harsh grace. This is not all oil versus wilderness. There are real live people in this equation, with children, futures, and hopes. Do not forget them! Let's get on with the job."

One speaker purposely waited until all the VIP speakers had their turns. Then, stuttering in what seemed like a controlled scream, Charlie "Etok" Edwardsen, Jr., of the Arctic Slope Native Association rushed to the speaker's podium. His piercing, dark eyes glaring, his black hair cascading over his forehead, Edwardsen exclaimed:

"How can white men sell our land when they don't own it? How can they lease our land to oil companies when they don't own it? If the pigs want to use our land, then let the pigs pay the rent!"

Edwardsen was declaring that if oil companies weren't checked, they would destroy the Arctic and its people. He termed the pipeline environmental study naive, dealing with birds, not real people. Congress, he said, had neglected the Alaska Natives for one hundred years and was about to continue its old ways. Arctic Slope Natives were unanimously opposed to the pipeline, Edwardsen testified. His remarks, needless to say, were given nationwide media coverage.

Meanwhile, wrapping and coating continued on the hundreds of miles of 48-inch pipe then stacked at Valdez, Fairbanks, and Deadhorse. Preconstruction work proceeded on pump station design, and late in the fall of 1971, flow stations 1 and 2 were substantially completed. While the pipeline right-of-way permit continued to elude the companies, the cost of pipeline construction was escalating. The original $900 million estimate grew to $1.1 billion.

INSIDE STORY

WHAT THE OILMEN SAID

Hugh Gallagher tells some very revealing tales of the oil industry's early naivete about the political and economic complexities of doing business in Alaska.

"In the spring of 1969, Clive Hardcastle, the young president of BP North America, a real loose cannon, came to pay a courtesy call on the new senator [Republican U.S. Senator Ted Stevens]. Ted was held up on the floor and asked me to entertain Clive in the interim. Clive was the first oil president I ever met.

"Like all liberals of the day, I thought Big Oil was all-powerful. The pipeline had just been announced, to be completed as I remember in the next three years. I asked, 'How did you guys do it? How did you cut like a hot knife through butter to solve the land freeze and Native claims?'

"Clive looked at me: 'What are Native claims? What's a land freeze?' He had no idea. I wrote him a letter that night and he hired me [as a BP lobbyist] on receipt of the letter.

"Lord Strathalmond, Billy Frazer, came over from London to hire me officially and to be briefed. I had no office, nothing. On a yellow legal pad I wrote by hand a memo which said the pipeline will not and can not be built until (1) Native claims are resolved, (2) environmental requirements are met, and (3) real local hire is provided for.

"Years later, the last time I saw Billy before his death, he came through Washington. He pulled my old yellow memo, folded and creased many times, out of his pocket.

"'I thought you might like to keep this as a souvenir,' he said. 'I used it to brief the [BP] board of directors. It was the first we had heard of these things.'

"Billy told me once that, in those early days, [ARCO's] Robert O. Anderson said not to worry, he had talked to his friend Nixon and there would be no delay.

"It must have been that summer that [Exxon's] Ken Fountain—brash, pushy and smart—flew into town one night with the [pipeline] permit application. Phil Helmig of ARCO, John Knodell, and Quinn O'Connell had dinner with him. He said something like, 'The big boys have approved the schedule, we are ready to roll, and you guys have two weeks to get the pipeline permit approved.'

"I told him something like I did not think this would be possible. He replied, as I remember, 'I didn't ask what you think, this is an order from the top.'

"We tried to explain some of the obstacles: You can't ask Interior to approve the permit before you know anything at all about the impact oil shipments might have on the fisheries in Prince William Sound.

"It sticks in my mind so clearly that Ken replied, 'I don't care if every god-damn fish dies, get that permit in two weeks.'"

Gallagher went to London in 1971, at a time when the pipeline was being delayed by a court challenge, and met with the directors of British Petroleum. "The BP Board gave me a lunch in their private dining room," he said. "It was a big deal. They showered me with questions about the delay, Alaska, etc. I was at the head of the table; Sir Eric Drake [BP chairman], at the foot. At one point, talking about the legal case, Drake cleared his throat, fiddled with his fork, and asked, 'Is not there some way to, ahem . . . fix it with the judge?'

"I was stunned. Drake was a strange one, but he was, or at least was supposed to be, a gentleman. Very clearly, using my best Oxford intonation, I replied: "Oh, is that the way you do it here in England?'

"Drake got very red. All at once everyone at the table was speaking, desperately trying to change the subject."

Chapter 26

Looking Ahead

A month following the huge September 1969 sale, nine seismic crews were working on the North Slope. ARCO, Exxon, Texaco, Union, Amoco, Mobil, and Forest Oil had crews there, with four remaining throughout the winter. The two major lease owners at Prudhoe Bay, ARCO and BP, agreed to operate the Prudhoe oil field, BP on the west side and ARCO on the east. Dividing operations avoided unnecessary duplication. Airstrips, production pads, access roads, oil flow lines, and power plants could be handled jointly, or at least coordinated.

Resources commissioner Tom Kelly agreed that this division of responsibility could ensure more efficient production as well as maximum protection to the environment. Oil produced was to be shared among the companies according to their lease interest in the entire field; operating expenses were to be divided the same way. This process of negotiation ensured that the largest oil field in North America would be operated under the conservation laws of the state.

A network of thirty-foot-wide spine roads would be overlain by five feet of gravel, giving access to drill sites and other facilities. Six to eight wells were to be directionally drilled from each 55-by-270-yard gravel drill-site pad. The pads were somewhat similar in size to offshore drilling platforms, though the entire area each drilling site drained would be about 3,800 acres.

The wells, set about 100 feet apart on the tundra, would first have to be bored vertically through 2,000 feet of permafrost. Once through the permafrost, the bore hole would be drilled directionally 7,000 to 9,000 feet to the oil reservoir.

Drillers would have to take into account the effect on the permafrost and tundra of crude oil coming out of wells at temperatures around 180 degrees Fahrenheit. Sustained production of this hot oil could melt the permafrost for a significant distance from a well bore. If allowed to continue, it could not only erode the upper part of the permafrost, but might result in down-drag on the well's casing, possibly causing it to collapse.

The Prudhoe Bay oil field wouldn't look like fields in Texas or Southern California. There, surface pumps sometimes pull the oil from the earth. At Prudhoe, however, reservoir conditions would allow the crude to flow up through the well bore under its own pressure.

ARCO began building a 5,000-barrel-per-day refinery on the Slope to take off the higher ends of the crude to supply its vehicles. A two-story complex dubbed the "ARCO Hilton" was completed and occupied at Prudhoe airstrip. Its three-winged central building housed 210 men and could be expanded to accommodate up to 630. The building had Alaska's most modern water supply and sewage system, as well as self-contained, self-powered generation

JOE RYCHETNIK

A drilling crew works at a North Slope site in 1969.

equipment, enclosed vehicle storage, and a maintenance shop and warehouse. Prominent on the walls of the main room were signs that admonished: "No alcohol, No guns, and No women."

In the fall of 1970, Prudhoe Bay's West Dock, recently extended by anchoring four unloaded barges to the floor of the Beaufort Sea, was "christened" by the arrival of a 75-barge flotilla. Unloading the cargo had to wait for pack ice to retreat.

Down in Anchorage, a quiet man from Los Angeles hired Jack White Realty Company to acquire more than two dozen downtown lots (average price $20,000). The principal turned out to be Dallas oilman Bunker Hunt, now a Prudhoe player. Hunt acquired more than forty downtown Anchorage lots in all, eventually putting up the Hunt Building at Seventh Avenue and F Street. British Petroleum announced that by the end of 1971, it would complete a five-story office building several miles south of the Anchorage city center.

> *Down in Anchorage, a quiet man from Los Angeles hired Jack White Realty Company to acquire more than two dozen downtown lots. The principal turned out to be Dallas oilman Bunker Hunt.*

The huge investment by the Hunt/ Amerada/Getty consortium began looking good in April 1971 when Placid Drilling Company brought in a 2,000-barrel-per-day well on Tract 57—the one the consortium had paid $72 million to lease at the big 1969 sale. The following month, ARCO brought in a well capable of 1,300 barrels a day that discovered the West Sak oil field. (While the major oil companies concentrated on the Slope, bids by independents at the state's 24th sale—on May 12, 1971—showed that the smaller companies welcomed the chance to consolidate their drilling blocks in Cook Inlet without the usual competition from the majors.)

The gradual buildup toward full-scale production at Prudhoe continued in mid-1971 when the 28,000-ton Exxon tanker *Enco Gloucester* made a trip from Puget Sound to Alaska to study navigational requirements in Prince William Sound and the port of Valdez. ARCO christened the 70,000-ton *SS ARCO Prudhoe Bay* oil tanker and ordered three 120,000-ton carriers for the Alaska trade.

AS THE OIL INDUSTRY FORGED AHEAD, public policies regarding the state's newfound wealth were being debated. Governor Keith Miller hired A. D. Little Company of Boston to help him decide how Alaska should proceed. Not to be outdone, the legislature retained Walter J. Levy and Associates, of New York, to advise Alaska's lawmakers on petroleum policy.

Levy himself attended several legislative sessions during which his Kissinger-like voice and imposing presence lent an objective air to events happening in the outside oil world. Most legislators believed they lacked information about oil in Alaska, much less the "outside world," so the "real world" messages of Levy and his associate Milton Lipton were welcomed in Juneau.

Meanwhile, state Representative Gene Guess hired The Brookings Institution of Washington, D.C., to facilitate a Future of Alaska Conference. Guess was chairman of Alaska's Legislative Council, and he believed Alaska needed outside help in pondering the vast changes Big Oil was bringing. So in late 1969, after the September lease sale, 100 Alaska leaders— city slickers, Natives, bartenders, bankers, economics professors, merchants, political activists—found themselves seated side by side during two consecutive December weekends in Anchorage.

As delegates to the Future Conference, Guess tried to invite representatives of the varied lifestyles in Alaska. But delegate Arlon Tussing, a University of Alaska economics professor, told author Mary J. Berry (who wrote a book on the pipeline) that "a development for development's sake philosophy prevails. Almost everyone at this seminar shares that philosophy to one degree or another. But this is a set of attitudes peculiar to certain classes of people— businessmen,

JOE RYCHETNIK

In 1969, ARCO built housing at Prudhoe for its workers. Signs admonished residents: "No alcohol, No guns, and No women."

politicians and upper civil servants, economists and the like—exactly the kinds of people invited to these seminars and interested in the questions to which it is addressed."

One conference rule, enforced by facilitators, was that state lawmakers could listen but not speak. This opportunity for citizen-delegates to speak and not be interrupted by their elected representatives was unprecedented and greatly enjoyed. Politicians kept their mouths shut. The conference succeeded.

Foremost in every delegate's mind was what effect the huge North Slope discovery might have on Alaska's small population, fledgling economy, and varied life-styles. The economic value of the discovery became obvious after the September lease sale. But would oilmen "rape, ruin, and run," as some people were saying? Or would they, like gold prospectors, copper miners, and fish-trap owners of yore, take the money slowly from the state, not having to run? How much money would there be? And, most importantly, who was going to get it? And what would happen to Alaska's frontier way of life?

The wells at Prudhoe, set about 100 feet apart on the tundra, would first have to be bored vertically through 2,000 feet of permafrost.

Since statehood, the material standard of living for most Alaskans had increased only slightly, and much of that was due to income from Cook Inlet oil. However, the Slope discovery was a magnitude larger than Cook Inlet. Could this huge discovery and the powerful forces it unleashed actually jeopardize the hard-earned self-sufficiency that statehood had promised?

Conference opinions ran from fears that Big Oil would bring with it "population, pillage, and pollution" to "a feeling, at long last, of belonging to the United States."

The ten years of Cook Inlet oil development was generally accepted by conferees as being, along with statehood, the most important event in Alaska's past. Future priorities included more oil and gas exploration, settlement of Native land claims, and expansion of transportation, communications, education, and health services.

WHEN ALASKA'S LAWMAKERS convened in Juneau in January 1970, armed with the Future Conference recommendations—or at least with an idea of what a cross-section of development-minded Alaskans wanted—they could not have known the harsh economic impact that delay of the trans-Alaska pipeline would have on the state.

Governor Keith Miller expected to have a 1970-1971 fiscal budget of around $160 million. He anticipated receiving about $8 million from Swanson River royalties, a like amount from the state's oil severance tax, plus $19 million in royalties from offshore Cook Inlet wells. By the close of the 1970 legislative session, however, the state's fiscal budget had skyrocketed to more than $300 million.

Miller, a former IRS agent and legislator, seemed so overwhelmed by the state's top job that although the September sale had brought in $900 million, he could barely cope with the same issues faced by former governors Egan and Hickel: Native land claims and oil development.

The land-claims situation was heating up even more. Costs of building the trans-Alaska pipeline dramatically increased, and a delay loomed in building the pipeline's haul road. Local bankruptcies increased as businesses that had borrowed in anticipation of a pipeline boom couldn't meet their payments. The pejoratively named "Hickel's Highway" was generating a negative impact. The issues of oil spills and "local hire" became hot legislative items.

The 1970 legislature decided to look to the oil companies for more money. Most legislators were aware of the tremendous size differences between the production capacity of wells in Cook Inlet and those on the North Slope. Daily production from individual wells in these two areas differed by tens of thousands of barrels. Individual wells in Cook Inlet were producing in amounts similar to wells in California, Oklahoma, and Texas. By contrast, a North Slope well could produce daily volumes like those in Iran, Iraq, and Saudi Arabia.

The 1970 legislature decided to look to the oil companies for more money.

As a result, the legislature in 1970 amended the oil severance tax to make it attributable to production from individual wells rather than from an entire field. Levying the tax on each well captured a higher percentage of revenue from North Slope production. For example, either a North Slope or Cook Inlet well producing less than 300 barrels per day remained taxed at the minimum 3 percent. But wells producing more than 2,500 barrels a day would now be taxed at the maximum 8 percent rate—and such high-volume wells were found only on the Slope.

This "variable rate" tax would have little impact on the five producing Cook Inlet oil fields because most of these were already at or near the minimum production rate, but the new tax hit North Slope wells at the maximum rate.

The 1970 legislature also raised the natural gas severance tax from 1 to 4 percent. And legislators passed an oil tanker ballast law to regulate oil discharge from tankers in Prince William Sound.

SPOTLIGHT ▬▬
A WORLD VIEW

As the 1960s ended, consultants Walter J. Levy and Milton Lipton were lecturing their client, the state legislature, on how the international oil business works.

North Slope oil would be a part of the world oil picture, they said—but it would be big only by U.S. standards, not by the standards of OPEC. Levy pointed out that Saudi Arabia alone had hundreds of billions of barrels of oil, while Alaska would probably produce in the tens of billions.

The lawmakers soon gained a little perspective and realized that Alaska oil production—soon to be greater than that of any other U.S. state—would not greatly alter the total world oil picture.

Levy's world view, along with his acknowledgement of the tremendous impact Alaska's oil would have on the rest of the U.S., greatly impressed the lawmakers. Levy and Lipton also pointed the way to fresh ways of dealing with the oil industry. New ideas began to flourish in Juneau.

"You are now entering the big time," Levy told legislators, "so move slowly and cautiously."

Chapter 27

The Return of Governor Egan

ormer governor Bill Egan leaped back into the gubernatorial fray in 1970, soundly defeating Governor Keith Miller in the November general election. Many of the oil problems Egan had turned over to the Hickel administration in late 1966 were now handed back, along with some new puzzlers.

When Egan left office in 1966, there had been no National Environmental Policy Act, no $900 million cash from the North Slope, no Prudhoe Bay oil field. Natives claiming land had been active, but protests were only beginning. Now, Prudhoe Bay and the $900 million sale had made Alaska a major player in the world oil game. But Native land claims had halted federal gas leasing, state land selections, and work on an oil pipeline. The state's budget had more than doubled, but the pipeline delay meant the state couldn't start receiving the expected Prudhoe Bay oil royalties.

Bill Egan had always been cautious about the state offering its oil and gas lands for competitive bid without first knowing their "true value." Soon after Egan won the 1970 election, he was quoted by the local press as saying that leasing of all the state's previously unleased acres at Prudhoe Bay the previous September—the sale that had brought the state close to a billion dollars—"was one of the blackest days in Alaska's history." Some unleased acres, he said, should have been held back until after development drilling took place.

This way, the state might have known their true value before mineral rights were sold.

But in the aftermath of the September 1969 lease sale, everyone had a sense of their value, and it was high indeed. Oil and gas lease sales no longer brought in just tens of millions of dollars; they were now totaling hundreds of million. The possibility that billions of dollars would pour into the public treasury once oil began to flow through the pipeline created entirely new opportunities, entirely new problems.

JUST AS EGAN was being sworn in as governor in late 1970, President Nixon fired Walter Hickel as Interior Secretary. Hickel's 1969 letter to Nixon had been leaked—a letter in which Hickel decried the President's apparent insensitivity toward the escalation of fighting in Viet Nam. Hickel claimed America's youth were suffering a general malaise because of Nixon's Viet Nam policy.

Citing a "lack of mutual confidence," Nixon discharged Hickel. Hickel thinks the real reason he was fired was pressure on Nixon from oil industry executives still smarting from Hickel's tough stance toward Union Oil after the January 28, 1969, Santa Barbara offshore oil spill. Former Republican National Committee chairman Rogers C. B. Morton replaced Hickel as Interior Secretary, and Hickel returned to Alaska as a private citizen.

GOVERNOR EGAN put his cabinet together, asking Chuck Herbert to become resources commissioner and old friend Irene Ryan to be commissioner of economic development. Prior to the Prudhoe Bay discovery, Herbert served as deputy resources commissioner in the Egan administration and had taken a hand at trying to solve the Cook Inlet royalty pricing problem. In the first month of the Hickel administration, Herbert had helped persuade Hickel to hold a special sale of the top Prudhoe Bay leases.

Now, in 1971, Herbert could have expected oil exploration on the North Slope to increase. Instead, development drilling was dwindling to a virtual standstill. Some activity continued, such as the successful well on the tract leased by the Hunt/Amerada/Getty consortium. But delays in building the pipeline were stymieing full-scale efforts by the industry.

It seemed to Herbert that he was facing the same problems as four years earlier, such as the price of Cook Inlet royalty oil. In fact, his first act as resources commissioner in 1971 was to countersue Mobil Oil in response to the company's suit against former commissioner Kelly; Mobil was trying to prevent the state from setting only one price for all Cook Inlet royalty.

For attorney general, Egan named John Havelock, a product of Phillips Andover Academy, with undergraduate and law degrees from Harvard, who had arrived in Alaska in 1959. Havelock came to Egan's attention in 1970 when he managed Native leader Emil Notti's 1970 Democratic primary campaign for lieutenant governor. Havelock wrote many of Notti's land claims

NEVA EGAN

Bill Egan was back in the governor's chair in 1970, eager to campaign for ways to control the oil companies and to increase state oil revenue.

speeches; after Notti's defeat, Havelock drafted general election documents for Egan.

Egan's gubernatorial opponent, Keith Miller, argued that Native land claims were strictly a federal problem, while Egan acknowledged the state's financial responsibility. "The 1970 Egan-versus-Miller campaign was all about Native land claims," Havelock says. Egan received an overwhelming percentage of the Native vote.

Havelock found himself, as he says, "first among equals in Egan's cabinet." Most cabinet members and former associates called Egan "Bill." Havelock always called him "Governor." Havelock says he felt toward Egan much as Egan press secretary Will Lawson did: "Will worshipped the ground Egan walked on, sort of like father and son."

"Governor Egan had enormous and underrated intelligence," says Havelock. "And he had a mission of where the state was going."

"Egan was worried about the natural resource people," Havelock said, "from Chuck Herbert on down. The game was oil and gas, and Chuck was a hard-rock man. So the information Chuck was coming up with originated from [resources staffer] 'Easy' Gilbreth down in the boiler room, and Egan was paranoid about those people being overly influenced by the industry.

"Egan was always proud of the fact that he had better estimates of Swanson River than the state's bureaucrats. He always figured that there was more oil there, and that's the way it was. So he had no problem putting his judgment in place of theirs."

EGAN, NOW FACING a threefold increase in the state budget, began looking for ways to boost state oil revenues. Legislators are often seen as the big spenders, but governors spend money too. Even Republican governors Hickel and Miller had increased budgets, and Egan was simply trying to satisfy long pent-up needs of his constituents.

Faced with Native land claims and the pipeline delay, Egan resurrected an oil tax revenue bill that had passed the 1969 House but died in the Senate. By the spring of 1971, most lawmakers accepted the idea of some sort of minimum severance tax on all oil produced in Alaska; that is, a minimum tax to back up the existing severance tax based on a percentage of net oil value. For the state to receive a steady flow of oil revenue that could not fall below a certain minimum, Egan introduced a "cents-per-barrel" severance tax, setting a "floor" below the revenue stream.

> *Governor Egan, facing a threefold increase in the state budget, began looking for ways to boost state oil revenues.*

John Havelock explained the rationale behind a minimum tax at a time when drilling and geophysical work throughout Alaska had all but ceased, drill rigs once poised for work at Prudhoe were moving out of the state, and pipeline costs were rapidly escalating. "These costs were not merely a burden on the industry," Havelock said. "Quite the contrary. Costs were investments, since the industry expected its pipeline tariffs [charges] to be a percentage of all costs. The increased costs were a shift of profit-taking to the pipeline.

"But the state, since it was not an owner of the pipeline, looked with increasing consternation at rising costs. The revenue the state drew from the enterprise, whether in royalty share or in taxes, was based on value. So, as

310

transportation costs grew, the 'netback'—the value of the oil at the wellhead—shrank. So, even if the wellhead value shrank to zero, the industry would still make big money off transportation costs. State oil revenue could vanish to zero, because any percent of zero wellhead value was zero."

Havelock continued: "Thus the question of an alternative tax not based on value, but as a minimum cents-per-barrel tax on oil no matter what its value, became increasingly a driving force in shaping state policy. It also became a persuasive factor encouraging Egan's dream of state ownership of the pipeline."

Despite Egan's efforts, the 1971 legislature failed to pass a cents-per-barrel severance tax. But Egan used the proposal as a weapon the following year when he was being thwarted by the oil industry.

The 1971 legislature, however, did order the state to make loans to Alaska businesses harmed by delay of the pipeline. And a state-financed study of social and environmental impacts of the pipeline was conducted, including the question of why Alaska welders weren't being hired. The pipeline company was claiming that only welders from the welders' union in Tulsa had the necessary experience.

The oil industry became an increasing concern of the legislature. On the horizon for succeeding legislative sessions lay passage of a pipeline right-of-way leasing act, creation of a pipeline regulatory authority, "local hire" legislation, an oil spill liability fund, a ban on oil drilling in Bristol Bay, restrictions on oil exploration at certain times and in certain critical habitat areas, and legislation to stop further waste of natural gas.

SPOTLIGHT
WHO WILL CONTROL ALASKA?

Bill Egan's attitude toward the oil industry became more direct, more focused. To the governor in his third term, the question politically was how to control Big Oil. In the '60s, Egan had felt some comfort in the fact that Cook Inlet oil production developed in relatively small, incremental steps. But after the Prudhoe mega-discovery, the game had become: Who will control Alaska?

"Egan didn't trust the industry," his attorney general, John Havelock, said, "and figured it would hornswoggle the state after he was gone, and Alaska would be riding the tiger."

Fairbanks Representative Mike Bradner commented: "Egan had begun using the public's natural mistrust of outside industry to whip the legislature and dampen the oil lobby. He decided to ram laws adverse to the oil industry through the early 1970s' legislatures."

Egan sensed this was his last chance to keep the state from ending up "riding the tiger." This was a new Egan, and a new oil state. Would Egan's political skills be enough to harness the oil giants?

Chapter 28

Native Land Claims

T he 1960s brought change and unrest to the nation. As Prudhoe Bay development drilling was reaching a crescendo in the late 1960s, Neil Armstrong made the first moon walk, and the flower children massed at Woodstock; black Americans were pressing for full rights, and war protesters were on the march. Native rights were getting attention like never before as U.S. senators Fred Harris of Oklahoma and Ted Kennedy of Massachusetts stood up for the cause, Dustin Hoffman was a hit in the movie *Little Big Horn,* and Vine Deloria's book *Custer Died for Your Sins* became an instant best seller. In February 1969, a group of teenage Indians took over Alcatraz Island; Jane Fonda and eighty-five American Indians occupied Seattle's Fort Lawton Army base.

This climate of change reached up to Alaska, where the land claims of Natives, the needs of the oil companies, and the state lust for oil revenue were all converging.

BEFORE THE ALASKA FEDERATION OF NATIVES was organized in 1966, few Native groups had any direct dealings with oil companies. One group that did was the Tyonek Indians, whose 25,000-acre Moquawkie Reservation on the west side of Cook Inlet was the target of oil explorers.

In May 1961, the state offered leases, by competitive bidding, on land in the Cook Inlet Bombing and Gunnery Range adjacent to the western boundary of the reservation. This land drew high prices; Superior Oil bid more than $1 million for each of several parcels. Lawyer Stanley McCutcheon then advised the Tyoneks that oil-company drilling on the boundary parcels might result in draining oil from beneath the reservation. Superior Oil announced it would drill a well on the boundary near Chuit River. McCutcheon told the Tyoneks that in order to guarantee their control of reservation oil and to stop potential "encroachment," legal title to the Moquawkie Reservation had to be theirs.

President John F. Kennedy and his Secretary of Interior, Stewart Udall, were on record supporting Indian rights. This appeared a propitious time to move politically on behalf of the Tyoneks, so McCutcheon's good friend and fellow Democrat, Senator Ernest Gruening, personally introduced McCutcheon to Kennedy and Udall.

The executive order that originally created the Moquawkie Reservation in 1915 had left ownership of mineral rights unclear. Some said the Tyoneks owned them; others believed the U.S. Bureau of Education still owned the land and the mineral rights. Now, if Congress would grant clear title to the Tyoneks, they could lease oil and gas rights on the reservation to the highest bidder.

> *"There was no organized Native movement at the time. . . . The idea of being remotely involved in business or commerce, let alone oil, was the furthest from our minds."*
>
> —*Willie Hensley*

The 1962 Congress granted the Tyoneks title to the Moquawkie Indian Reservation. At the same time, it passed legislation upping the royalty reserved by the U.S. on "Indian trust lands" from one-eighth to one-sixth.

At their first oil and gas lease sale, in May 1964, the Tyoneks received nearly $13 million in cash. The money was heralded by Alaska media as a huge windfall for the Tyoneks, but this first competitive oil and gas sale by a Native group seemed to make little impression on other Alaskan Natives.

"There was no organized Native movement at the time," says Native leader Willie Hensley, of Kotzebue, who was then a student. "Most of us were still in school or fiddling around trying to survive. The idea of being remotely involved in business or commerce, let alone oil, was the furthest from our minds."

Most Native leaders were only vaguely aware of the potential of land claims. In the spring of 1964, the issue was still far from uniting them in a common political cause, though they could see that the Tyonek oil sale represented serious money.

Emil Notti was among the first Alaska Native leaders in the mid-1960s to urge united action by the state's Natives.

AFTER FIGHTING EACH OTHER for years as tribal entities, the Native leadership began to see that cooperation might pay big dividends. At a Bethel Village Chiefs Council housing conference in 1965, consensus started to emerge.

Among the first to recognize the need for united action was Emil Notti, then head of the Cook Inlet Native Association. In a *Tundra Times* editorial in early 1966, he called for all Alaska Natives to organize. Just that January, three Native residents of Barrow had filed a protest with the federal Bureau of Land Management against state land selections on the North Slope. By September, several Eskimo and Aleut groups began protesting all state land selections.

In early October, the Arctic Slope Native Association filed a lawsuit in Fairbanks District Court to enjoin federal and state government officials from disbursing revenues from any oil, gas, or mineral sales on the North Slope. The complaint argued that monies received for minerals on the Slope by either government should be placed in escrow until Congress settled land title.

Organizational costs of the Alaska Federation of Natives and its first conference, in Anchorage in October 1966, were underwritten by the Tyonek Native village. Albert Kaloa, Jr., the Tyoneks' young, charismatic chief, had been scheduled to speak, but he was killed in an Anchorage hotel fire. His death dampened convention enthusiasm, but it did not stop the newly formed organization's momentum.

Federal land-office records began showing protest notices by Native groups on land already selected by the state for its ownership. On much of the acreage, the state had already received tentative title approval from the Bureau of Land Management. The Kenaitze Indian Tribe filed a protest on the entire Kenai Peninsula. The Chugach Native Association filed for nearly all the uplands along the eastern shore of the Gulf of Alaska. Five Native communities north of the Brooks Range, including Barrow, claimed the entire North Slope. "From time immemorial," they said, "all of the Arctic land had been ours."

By the end of 1966, nearly one-third of the approximately 365 million acres in Alaska had been filed on or claimed by Native groups. And by this time, Interior Secretary Udall's land freeze had settled over the state. By halting "final action on any applications filed within areas where Native claims or protests had been filed," Udall halted further state land selections and federal oil and gas leasing. The freeze became a dominant reality in Alaska, forcing state officials, business leaders, and oilmen to work for resolution of Native land claims as quickly as possible.

The Alaska Federation of Natives now needed money to operate. Some organizational funds had come from the American Association of Indian Affairs, but most had come from the Tyoneks. Early in 1967, the Tyoneks' new chief, Seraphim Stephan, Jr., presented the Federation's first president, Emil Notti, a $100,000 loan. Meanwhile, the Tyoneks held another oil and gas lease sale, collecting $2.7 million in cash bonuses. Native leaders were beginning to put long-standing tribal differences aside, acting together in persuading federal and state officials to recognize their land claims.

DURING THE 1966 gubernatorial campaign, the Natives accused Governor Egan of failure to support their land claims. With Native backing, Walter Hickel became governor. Hickel created a Native Land Claims Task Force and appointed all twelve members of the Alaska Federation of Natives board of directors to be among its members. With each Federation director representing a separate region of the state, they could now travel to meet with constituents at state expense.

Hickel appointed his personal attorney, Don Burr, as state attorney general; Burr was an outspoken opponent of Native land rights. To soften Burr's

ALASKA STATE LIBRARY

Interior Secretary (and former Alaska governor) Wally Hickel (far left) meets with Alaska Native leaders. Hickel urged President Nixon to support Native claims for land and a cash settlement.

presence, Hickel had appointed Anchorage attorney Edgar Paul Boyko as his special counsel on Native affairs, and subsequently Boyko became Burr's successor as attorney general.

Hickel and Boyko preferred dealing with Indian claims in the more traditional way: they favored giving money rather than land. They feared that if Congress granted the Natives all the land they sought, there would be little desirable federal land left for the state to select as its own.

Hickel, however, told Native leaders he would support their claims against the federal government if they would not stand in the way of oil-lease sales on the state's North Slope acreage. And when President Nixon chose Hickel as his Interior Secretary, Hickel eventually won Native support by promising to extend Udall's land freeze and to support land distribution. Hickel later told Nixon that Natives should get 40 million acres in addition to a large cash settlement.

Nixon announced in the fall of 1970 that he favored "a just settlement of Alaska Native land claims." Shortly afterward, Wally Hickel's successor as Interior Secretary, Rogers Morton, extended the Alaska land freeze until July 1971.

"There was a big push on for the pipeline," Nixon aide John D. Ehrlichmann told Harvard University student Cliff Groh Jr. The administration wanted the pipeline; Native claims were stalling it. But it wasn't until April 1971 that Nixon finally became convinced that the Natives should get 40 million acres.

CONGRESS WRESTLED with a number of settlement scenarios in 1970 and 1971. During the spring of 1970, Alaska's Congressional delegation had reached agreement with "Scoop" Jackson's Senate Interior Committee on a bill that would give Alaska Natives 10 million acres and $1 billion in cash. Half the money was to go to a statewide investment corporation, with all Alaska Natives becoming shareholders, and the other half would go to regional organizations. Native villages would receive 6 million acres adjoining the villages; an additional 4 million acres would pass to individual Natives. Money and land were to be allocated to each region on the basis of population rather than on the basis of the amount of acreage claimed.

> **By the end of 1966, nearly one-third of the approximately 365 million acres in Alaska had been filed on or claimed by Native groups.**

This latter provision didn't sit well with the Arctic Slope Native Association, representing an area with lots of land but few people. The Arctic Slope share of land and money under the "population" formula would be substantially less than under an acreage standard. The Arctic Slope had only four of the state's 226 Native villages and a population of fewer than 4,000—about 5 percent of Alaska's Natives—in a vast geographical region. The North Slope Inupiats felt that Senator Jackson's proposal left them out in the cold.

Arctic Slope Native Association president Joe Upicksoun wrote to Jackson: "The State of Alaska wants to steal our lands. The Senate committee wants to buy our lands—56.5 million acres—and pay the other Natives of Alaska from them. The other Natives of Alaska are willing and happy to be paid out of our lands. The state is now rich from our lands. The oil companies want to build a pipeline by experiment over our lands. The United States wants to provide for its own security against foreign enemies out of our lands.

"We believe there will be 10,000 miles of pipelines and highways on the North Slope, some of which are built over our father's graves."

Upicksoun's strategy seemed to pay off, at least in part. By midsummer 1970, Jackson had floated an amendment that would give Arctic Slope Natives full ownership of 500,000 acres, including oil and mineral rights. The original bill had offered only surface rights to the half-million acres. Senator Fred Harris, Democrat of Oklahoma, tried to increase the acreage due all Natives from 10 million up to 40 million, but his amendment failed, 71 to 13. Jackson's bill then passed the Senate in July, 76 to 8, but failed to be taken up by the House of Representatives. Later that year three separate land-claims bills remained in the House.

> *"The State of Alaska wants to steal our lands."*
>
> — *Joe Upicksoun, of the Arctic Slope Native Association*

The two principal Native groups—now in conflict over how to divvy up lands and money—sought more funding. The Alaska Federation of Natives borrowed $225,000 from the Yakima Tribe of Washington state. The Arctic Slope Native Association received an $80,000 grant from the Presbyterian church and $10,000 from the Episcopalians.

BILL EGAN'S RETURN to the governor's chair in 1970 after defeating Keith Miller was due in part to the Native vote. Four years earlier, Native leaders had helped Walter Hickel defeat Egan. Later, the Natives felt alienated from Hickel's successor, Miller, on grounds he opposed any sizeable public monetary contribution to the Natives. Like most of his supporters in the business community, Miller believed that the Natives should get very little land from the state and that no land should be restricted solely for Native use. Egan's pledge to combat Miller's stance paid off for him at the ballot box.

Chuck Herbert says that, "Originally, Egan had the idea that the total acreage that would be given to the Natives was in the neighborhood of 5 million acres." Herbert recalls an incident involving Egan and Walter Hickel during the period before the 1970 election. "I was sitting next to him [Egan] in Washington when Hickel, as Secretary of the Interior, walked in and said: 'No, they ought to get 40 million acres.' Bill finally gave in. It was kind of a surprise. I don't know who advised him on that . . . From then on, that was the figure."

But the Natives now were asking Congress for 60 million acres. Egan was supporting a Nixon administration bill that would prohibit Natives from choosing land that had already been selected by the state. Egan was aware that the state's selection and leasing of parcels on the North Slope meant the Natives would not directly share in petroleum revenue from those lands. The governor wanted the Natives to be able to select land in federal parks and wildlife refuges, and he supported Native selections inside Naval Petroleum Reserve No. 4 (Pet-4) on the North Slope.

Herbert, Egan's resources commissioner, indicates that Egan showed some flexibility on the land-selection question. He says Egan helped solve one roadblock to a settlement when he agreed to Native selection of land already claimed by the state around existing villages. John Havelock, Egan's attorney general, says the governor instructed state officials to remain neutral among the Native factions and to act as moderators and facilitators.

SPOTLIGHT

OIL GIVES ITS OK

Desperate to secure a pipeline right-of-way—and aware the land-claims issue was standing in the way—pipeline owner-companies di-rected their Washington lobbyists to vigorously support some sort of Native land settlement. The Alaska Federation of Natives was now campaigning to receive 40 million acres plus $1 billion in cash.

Although ARCO's Bob Anderson later said "We didn't actively work at it," three oil lobbyists were working on the land-claims matter during 1970: Hugh Gallagher for BP, Washington lawyer Quinn O'Connell for the Alyeska Pipeline Service Company, and Exxon attorney John Knodell. These lobbyists were keeping track of the pipeline permitting process and trying to convince Congress that a settlement of the claims issue would be good both for the nation and for the oil industry.

They apparently impressed members of Congress from oil-producing states. William J. Van Ness, chief counsel to Senator Henry Jackson's Interior Committee, says these legislators "as a matter of course . . . don't tend to vote with Natives or Indians. It's just not a very natural thing for them to do. But they would think, 'If the oil industry says its OK, maybe it is the right way to go.'"

Cliff Groh, Jr., in a Harvard University thesis, quotes Native leader Don Wright as saying: "There would never have been a settlement without the oil companies."

Chapter 29
The Settlement

A final Native claims settlement bill worked its way through Congress in the second half of 1971.

In the House, the Interior Committee, chaired by Colorado's Wayne Aspinall, approved a bill granting 40 million acres to the Natives. Under this bill, Natives would first select 18 million acres adjacent to existing villages; then the state would select the 77 million acres still due to it as a new state; after that, twelve newly created regional Native corporations could select their final 22 million acres.

The Aspinall bill would permit Native selection of any federal land, including acreage in national parks and federal wildlife preserves—except that in Naval Petroleum Reserve No. 4, only selection of surface rights would be approved.

The idea of having a dozen Native corporations instead of a single statewide entity was a major change from the previous year's bill promoted by Senator Jackson. The concept of numerous corporations was considered more consonant with traditional Native cultural and living customs.

The Aspinall bill called for the federal government to pay the Natives $425 million over a ten-year period and for the state to pay an additional $500 million from its oil royalties.

The subcommittee bill was taken up in September by the full House Interior Committee, which tacked on a provision authorizing the Interior

MARGIE BAUMAN

Joe Upicksoun marked the signing of the Alaska Native Claims Settlement Act in 1971 with a speech warning that unless a "sense of order" is imposed on the oil "invasion," "subsistence living will be destroyed, and the discontent of our people will be worse." He called for creation of a North Slope borough with authority to tax oil.

Secretary to add acreage to national wildlife refuges in Alaska in an amount equal to whatever refuge land the Natives selected.

Conservationists persuaded representatives Morris Udall, Arizona Democrat, and John Saylor, Pennsylvania Republican, to try to amend the House bill so the Interior Secretary could set aside 50 million acres in Alaska as "a national interest study area." This provision, Udall said, would not cause further delay in construction of the trans-Alaska pipeline. Governor Egan, the Natives, and major oil companies opposed the amendment, which was defeated by the full House on a vote of 217 to 177. The House then went on to pass the settlement act, 334 to 63.

MEANWHILE IN THE SENATE, Scoop Jackson's Interior Committee passed a bill that would give Natives $1 billion plus 40 million acres to be selected from within twenty-five townships surrounding Native villages. The bill would create a comprehensive land-use planning commission and provide a corridor for the trans-Alaska pipeline across federal land from the Arctic Ocean to Prince William Sound.

On November 1, a Native claims bill— including a planning commission and a pipeline corridor—passed the Senate on a 76-to-5 vote. A Native Alaskan was defined as a person who is one-quarter or more Eskimo (Inupiat or Yupik), Aleut, or

Indian (Athabascan, Tlingit, or Haida). Natives residing outside Alaska would be given a share of the monetary compensation granted to Natives and would become members of a 13th Native regional corporation, headquartered in Seattle.

A conference committee of seven senators and ten representatives now went to work for nine continuous days to resolve differences between the House and Senate versions of the Alaska Native Claims Settlement Act. The committee included legislators who tended to support one side or another among the contending interest groups. Washington State Congressman Lloyd Meeds and Senator Mike Gravel of Alaska, both Democrats, spoke up for the Natives; Alaska Representative Nick Begich, a Democrat, and Alaska Senator Ted Stevens, a Republican, espoused views that reflected state interests and the oil industry; representatives Udall, a Democrat, and Saylor, a Republican, and Democratic Senator Alan Bible of Nevada were known as environmentalists.

The bill worked out by the conference committee gave Alaska Natives 40 million acres. Natives would first choose ownership to 22 million acres of land adjacent to villages; then the state would select its remaining 77 million acres; then final Native land selections would be made. All minerals on Native-selected land would be owned by the regional corporations.

The legislation granted Natives a total of $962.5 million in cash: $462.5 million from the federal government over an eleven-year period and the balance of $500 million from state oil royalties. There would be thirteen cultural and regional "for profit" corporations and a system of village corporations. Money would be allocated principally on a per capita basis.

> *The bill worked out by Congress gave Alaska Natives 40 million acres and $962.5 million.*

The bill also established a joint federal/state land-use planning commission and authorized the Secretary of Interior to create a pipeline corridor across Alaska. The Secretary was to withdraw up to 80 million acres of land in Alaska for study and possible inclusion in national parks or forests, wildlife refuges, or wild and scenic river systems. The land-use planning commission would recommend how to dispose of these lands.

The Alaska Native Claims Settlement Act passed Congress on December 14, 1971. President Nixon signed the act into law December 18.

That same day, delegates to a meeting of the Alaska Federation of Natives, meeting in Anchorage, were delighted to hear the voice of the President coming through auditorium loudspeakers praising them for their help in fashioning "a just and equitable" solution to the land claims. Ten days later, Interior Secretary Morton established a 100-foot-wide oil pipeline corridor from Prudhoe Bay to Valdez. Neither the state nor the Natives would be permitted to select land within this corridor. Without Congressional approval of the settlement act that granted 40 million acres and nearly a billion dollars to Alaska's Native people, there could not have been a trans-Alaska pipeline.

THE RIFT BETWEEN the Alaska Federation of Natives and the Arctic Slope Native Association didn't end with passage of the settlement act. Joe Upicksoun, president of the Native Association, was a speaker at the AFN meeting in Anchorage that was celebrating Nixon's signing of the legislation. Upicksoun delivered a memorable address, spelling out the demands of his North Slope people.

"AS WE PAUSE for a few days and one chapter ends in our fight for self-identity and self-respect and another begins, it is right and proper to take a look at the world.

"We from the north have led a happy life through the centuries. Yes, Western civilization sent its whaling fleets up here, one hundred fifty or so a year. Yes, our whales are gone. Once we had plenty of foxes, and just like the departed whalers, fur traders disappeared, too. Now we have the oil. One of our advisers has told us the average life of a pool is twenty years. . . .

"As I look at the world, I see some oil companies. I am referring in particular to Humble Oil and Refining [Exxon], Mobil, Atlantic Richfield, and British Petroleum. Do you know that these companies will not pay one penny in property taxes on the North Slope?

"What are taxes for? I will tell you. At Anaktuvuk Pass, Point Hope, Kaktovik, and Wainwright, there are no junior high schools. At Barrow there is no senior high school. We probably have fifteen hundred school children on the Slope. As they reach junior and senior high school age, we must send them from home to a different culture. Taxes pay for schools.

Eben Hopson won the election in June 1972 as the first chairman of the newly formed North Slope Borough, which includes the Prudhoe oil fields.

"In 1969, the state got $900 million from my land. Her budget for that year was $150 million. The next year, with the sale, her budget doubled to $306 million, and this year it is $296 million. Not one additional penny was returned to us for our children or for anything.

"And so, we have filed a petition for a borough so that we can tax the oil companies for schools. And do you know what Humble, ARCO, British Petroleum, and Mobil have done? They formally announced their determination to oppose our petition.

"Oil thinks that we have to live with them. They are wrong. Oil has to live with us. Oil has not yet learned the lessons of the OPEC countries. Just a few days ago, Libya confiscated British Petroleum's property there. When will people learn?

"We need a borough for another reason, for the protection of our subsistence living, because the borough would have the power of zoning. Not that we would zone out the oil companies. It is possible to be compatible. But I say to you, with the huge invasion coming in the north, there must be order. Without a sense of order up there, subsistence living will be destroyed, and the discontent of our people will be worse.

"I am not through yet. I simply have to talk about the pipeline, both the 48-incher and the feeder lines, possibly 10,000 miles of them. If a feeder line breaks, you won't be hurt, but we will be. And the risk of break magnifies by the more miles of line. As I said, we figure 10,000 miles of risk.

"We have, therefore, proposed that the oil companies pay us in case of a spill. . . . If, indeed, there is no risk of spillage, then oil could promise to pay us a million dollars per gallon of spillage. Since no spillage would occur, they would not have to pay a penny. Of course, the idea that there will be no spillage is silly. Of course there will be spills.

> *"Here we are, begging for some land."*
>
> —*Eskimo elder Alfred Hopson, Sr.*

"Our proposal was submitted to [Interior] Secretaries Hickel and Morton, and these guardians of ours dignified our request by silence. And not one person in this room helped either. All these thoughts are not new. I have said them before. It is now twenty months since [I wrote] these words:

"'The State of Alaska wants to steal our lands. The Senate committee wants to buy our lands . . . and pay the other Natives of Alaska [from them]. The other Natives of Alaska are willing and happy to be paid out of our lands. The state is now rich from our lands. The oil companies want to build a pipeline by experiment over our lands. The United States wants to provide for its own security against foreign enemies out of our lands.'

"You can obviously see that I am hurt and frightened and perhaps bitter. This hurt, fright, and bitterness have been caused by other Natives demanding more than their just share; by the state's being dishonorable in grabbing whatever she could; by the Congress's incompetence in not really understanding the problems and not trying to; by the oil companies stepping on us as if we were not people; by Western society's moving in on us and brushing us aside. . . .

"I now bid you goodbye."

THE IDEA OF A BOROUGH on the North Slope—a regional local government provided for in the Alaska Constitution—had been raised before. But in the January 9, 1971, *Anchorage Daily News,* a headline shouted: "Eskimo 'Borough' As Big As Oil Fields." The article by Stanton Patty reported that the Eskimos "are forming a borough . . . that will cover the entire Arctic Slope and give it jurisdiction over development of the Prudhoe Bay oil fields. They could tax the petroleum real estate and zone out developments that might threaten the area's ecology."

The article said the proposed local government would be about one-third larger than the state of Washington. Its primary purpose would be to build schools for students who now had to leave home to attend high school in southeastern Alaska or "outside" (in the Lower 48).

In 1971, Governor Egan named a young Native from Yakutat, Byron Mallott, as commissioner of regional and community affairs. Mallott's authority included approval or disapproval of petitions for local governments. Not surprisingly, Mallott approved a "first-class borough" petition for the North Slope.

The Alaska Local Boundary Commission held a series of hearings on the borough proposal, culminating in a session in Barrow on December 2, 1971. Four hundred residents were crowded into the school auditorium as Eskimo elder Alfred Hopson, Sr., spoke to the commission.

"Our people lived here before your ancestors ever came to the United States," Hopson said. "Here we are, begging for some land."

Oil's opposition to creation of the North Slope borough was spearheaded by the Alaska Oil and Gas Association, which argued that this area of "mostly uninhabited lands . . . is neither necessary, proper or desirable for a borough," particularly when the borough's seat of government (Barrow) would be two hundred miles from its principal tax base (Prudhoe). Creation of the borough, they said, would result in an unequal tax distribution system in Alaska because taxes paid by Prudhoe oil producers would go to only a few Alaskans instead of to all the state's citizens.

> *"Oil thinks that we have to live with them. They are wrong. Oil has to live with us."*
>
> —Joe Upicksoun

Fred Paul, a Native lawyer in Seattle, and Charlie "Etok" Edwardsen, Jr., sketched out a borough plan to tax and zone all property on the North Slope and to try to control development at Prudhoe Bay.

On February 23, 1972, the boundary commission certified the North Slope Borough petition, opening the path for a vote by Slope residents on creation of a local government. BP, Mobil, Amerada Hess, Amoco, Exxon, Phillips, and Union filed suit in Alaska Superior Court to stop the vote. Even if the borough was formed, the companies still hoped to limit its taxing power.

The lawsuit failed. After Superior Court Judge Eben Lewis refused to stop the June 20 referendum and election, oil lawyers appealed to the Alaska Supreme Court. Ruling shortly after the June 20 election, Justice Roger Connor said the vote should stand.

North Slope residents voted 544 to 29 in favor of forming a local government. They elected five members of the borough assembly and five members of the school board. Eben Hopson was elected the strong-executive-type borough chairman (later mayor), barely beating the strong write-in effort of "Etok" Edwardsen on a vote of 260 to 204.

Governor Egan was at first wary of the new borough government, fearing the oil companies might find a "tax haven" on the North Slope, with citizens elsewhere in the state cut off from the region's oil tax revenues. Egan eventually sought an accommodation. He agreed in November 1972 that the state should purchase $100,000 of the borough's 6 percent revenue anticipation notes to cover start-up costs, and he initiated negotiations with Eben Hopson over whether the borough could exceed the proposed 20-mill pipeline property tax cap. Eventually a revenue-sharing formula, lifting the cap for borough bonds for capital improvements, would be approved by the legislature.

PART IV:
RIDING THE TIGER

Alaska is a foreign country significantly populated with Americans. Its language extends to English. Its nature is its own.

— *John McPhee*
Coming into the Country

Chapter 30

Who Gets The Pipeline?

Governor Egan sent an intriguing telegram in October 1971 to the chief executives of all pipeline owner-companies. He asked them to meet him in Juneau on October 30 but gave no inkling what the meeting would be about.

At the appointed hour, eight oil company executives trooped into the governor's third-floor Capitol building corner office: ARCO's Thornton Bradshaw, Sohio's Charlie Spahr, Exxon's Tom Barrow, Phillips' William Martin, BP's Robin Adams, Union's Charles Briniger, Mobil's Richard Tucker, and Edward Patton, president of the Alyeska Pipeline Service Company. To the assembled officials, Egan revealed exactly what was on his mind: he wanted the State of Alaska—not the oil companies—to finance and to own the trans-Alaska pipeline. Egan's plan was to hire Alyeska to do the actual construction, but the state would pay for the pipeline and would own it.

THE PIPELINE PROBLEM, as Egan saw it, was elementary, though solving it was not. If the oil companies owned the pipeline, they would establish charges (tariffs) for using it; the companies would in effect decide how much to charge themselves for use of the pipeline they themselves owned. They would set tariffs as high as possible because every dollar they paid in tariffs could be deducted as transportation expense before paying royalties and taxes to the state. And the more the pipeline cost to build and operate, the higher the tariffs could be.

Egan knew that the expected high tariffs would decrease the wellhead value of Prudhoe Bay oil—the value on which the state's royalty and severance taxes were figured. The public would lose substantial oil income. Egan also believed the companies would inflate pipeline construction and operating costs. He pointed to the huge bonuses the pipeline owner-companies were preparing to pay labor union members in exchange for a no-strike contract.

Attorney General John Havelock had advised Egan that a federal agency, the Interstate Commerce Commission, would undoubtedly claim jurisdiction over tariff-setting. The ICC, Egan feared, would let oil companies set high tariffs in order to recover the needlessly high construction expenses, plus a profit of 7 or 8 percent. Federal courts would most likely support the commission's authority, Havelock said, because Alaskan oil would be marketed in other states—and Alaska's role in rate-setting would be merely advisory.

As state commissioner of natural resources in 1972, Chuck Herbert was an opponent of Governor Egan's controversial plan for state ownership of the trans-Alaska pipeline.

EGAN WASN'T ABOUT TO SIT on the sidelines. "Egan was serious about owning the pipeline," Havelock says. "He really believed he could achieve 100 percent ownership."

Irene Ryan, economic development commissioner at the time, says there were "serious discussions in the cabinet meetings on pros and cons concerning [state] ownership. I think Bill looked at the players he was facing. When he looked at the size of BP, ARCO, Union Oil, and the other corporate giants . . . only a very foolish person would not be very cautious, especially one charged with a trust, and he saw it as a trust."

Joe Henri, commissioner of administration, favored state ownership, as did Egan adviser Bruce Kendall, a former Republican legislator. Commissioner of Natural Resources Chuck Herbert did not.

"Nearly all commissioners endorsed state ownership, and it was difficult for me, because I didn't agree," says Herbert. "It was a brand new idea Egan was adamant about then and until the day of his death. He thought that it was the proper thing to do. I argued against it on the grounds that the state record of efficiency is always bad and there was inertia in state government in every state. You can't blame any person or administration."

Newly appointed revenue commissioner Eric Wohlforth also opposed state ownership. Wohlforth, former bond counsel with the New York City law firm of Hawkins, Delafield & Wood, had been in the Egan administration only three weeks before having to deal with the pipeline ownership idea. But once Egan announced his decision to the oil moguls, Wohlforth began scrounging up financial "experts" to support public financing of the pipeline. Havelock recalls many discussions with the governor and Wohlforth on how to bring the ownership idea off.

> *"Egan . . . really believed he could achieve 100 percent [state] ownership of the pipeline."*
>
> —**Attorney General John Havelock**

State Senator John Rader believes Egan wanted the state to own the pipeline "because the companies planned to make money off it, and he wanted the state to make the money instead. Besides, he thought other oil fields would be coming, and the state had to ensure reasonable pipeline rates."

Egan political aide Alex Miller says Egan adopted the pipeline ownership idea so "he could get it moving. He thought financing the pipeline by tax-free bonds rather than corporate funds would cut the cost of the project." No wonder Egan was pushing the idea; he believed that public financing could reduce costs, speed construction, limit tariffs, and increase the wellhead value of North Slope crude.

"Pipeline ownership is a most effective means of assuring that transportation costs stay low and the wellhead value of our oil remains high," Havelock would later testify at ownership hearings in Juneau. "Ownership simply and directly works to assure Alaskans they will receive what is due them for oil taken out of the state forever."

A DEBATE BEGAN between Wall Street bankers on behalf of the oil industry and an equal number of financial advisers for the state. Did state financing and ownership of the pipeline make financial sense? Egan had already decided that it made political sense. It would not be just another "public-versus-private" argument but would run much deeper. It was about who would decide Alaska's future. The consulting firm hired by Governor Keith Miller in 1970 had advised against state ownership. Egan disagreed.

In an article in the "Alaska Forum" section of the *Anchorage Daily News*, Egan cautioned Alaskans to be "mindful that the primary obligation of the companies involved is to stockholders and board rooms in New York, Los Angeles, and Houston. Alaskans must be vigilant and forceful in the protection of their own interests. The sheer size of the enterprise in Alaska demands effective public control or we will have an economic state, larger and more powerful than the political state which contains it."

> *"Efforts [of the oil industry] have been directed to convince us that the Constitution of the United States and the financial world constitute a steel box tightly fitting the status quo. Its view is that the state can do nothing."*
>
> — *John Havelock*

Pipeline owner-companies responded with uncharacteristic bluntness to the idea of state ownership. Sohio's Charlie Spahr called it "stupid." Alaska couldn't finance the venture, and state ownership would result in a "negative business climate." Even if Alaska could attract investment dollars, Spahr said, high construction costs would bankrupt the state. The simple message from Spahr and his industry partners was that the state couldn't finance the pipeline, but *they* could.

In another *Anchorage Daily News* article, on November 11, 1971, Egan said his pipeline ownership idea "isn't an anti-industry move . . . . But it's now or never if the state is to have ownership and knows what's going on with the production of crude oil. We must have full control and responsibility for moving that first huge volume of crude oil from Prudhoe Bay. The key is not whether the state would build and own future lines. It's that the first project is the important one. . . .

"No one from the oil companies has come to me, and said, 'Gee, we're glad the state made this decision,'" Egan said. "But I think we'll have a cooperative attitude from industry as we develop this thing. We'll have a case that is logical and I think the legislature will agree with us. I would expect some bipartisan support."

PIPELINE OWNERSHIP HEARINGS began at 8 A.M. on Monday, March 6, 1972. Legislators, staffers, lobbyists, and the general public crowded into the Gold Room of Juneau's Baranof Hotel to see the show.

Each day for nearly a week, with time out for lunch, the legislature's joint pipeline ownership committee met from 8 A.M. until 6 P.M. Committee co-chairmen Senator Ron Rettig, an Anchorage Republican, and Representative Dick McVeigh, an Anchorage Democrat, sat side by side. Also at the head of the room were committee members Senator Cliff Groh (an Anchorage Republican) and six Democratic House members. Rettig opened the hearing by asking for forbearance.

Attorney General John Havelock began his testimony by explaining the role the Interstate Commerce Commission played in the Lower 48 in setting pipeline tariffs. He noted that the state had no assurance that ICC-regulated pipeline rates would be "reasonable" or that there would be equal treatment for "all who might need access to the pipeline in later years for the shipment of oil."

"Customarily," Havelock said, "owners of pipelines, who may also be producers, agree among themselves as to the fairness of particular tariffs which the companies would charge themselves for putting their oil through their pipeline. They operate under an unwritten rule not to wash their laundry in public."

While the ICC took its time—probably four years or more—to set a value on the pipeline for tariff-setting purposes, the oil companies would set tariffs as high as they had been allowed anywhere else, Havelock testified. Depending on the ratio of debt-to-equity of pipeline financing, the pipeline's actual profit could be as high as 100 percent per year, he warned.

The state brought financial consultant Peter Temple forward to testify. Temple argued that if the industry owned the pipeline, the state would have to obtain separate data from each of the seven owner-companies in order to assess pipeline tariffs—an enormous bookkeeping task which the state did not have the personnel to carry out. "Shippers will be agreeing on rates with their own subsidiaries, making the task even more formidable," he testified.

In an attempt to discredit Temple, oil lobbyists leaked to the press Temple's unusual background: During the early 1940s he had been the original radio voice of "Jack Armstrong, all-American boy." Rather than discrediting him in the eyes of lawmakers, this fact seemed only to make him more interesting.

Temple cautioned the committee that the Interstate Commerce Commission normally allows the replacement cost of a pipeline to determine its value for tariff-setting purposes—despite the fact that "pipelines are seldom, if ever, replaced. Abandoned, yes, but not replaced." The result, he said, is that each partner in the building and owning of the pipeline would see an enormous return on investment. Temple predicted that if the oil company consortium was allowed to own the pipeline, and the ICC set rates, competition in oil exploration on the North Slope would be severely limited.

"Would state ownership delay construction of the pipeline?" Havelock asked Temple. "It would not," he replied.

To make public financing viable, would the oil companies have to guarantee they would use the pipeline, Havelock asked Temple. Probably, he replied.

Temple added: "I question whether the oil companies . . . fully understand the tension created within the state by this difference over transportation costs owing to the sensitivity of the royalties and severance taxes at the wellhead. I think the real issue is, do the people of Alaska want to play a game with their royalties and severance taxes. . . ."

Senator Don Young, Republican from Fort Yukon, was a naysayer, arguing that the sale of public bonds to build the pipeline would certainly delay construction. He also raised a startling scenario in a question to revenue commissioner Eric Wohlforth:

What if the oil companies, he asked, "find a cheaper source for world energy . . . and, therefore, decide not to produce Prudhoe oil?"

Replied Wohlforth: "Existing indications are that there is a need for North Slope oil that will continue."

Public finance consultant Tom Gildehaus, testifying for the state, said the state's general credit standing alone wouldn't be enough to float the bond money needed to build the pipeline—now figured at $3.5 billion, quadruple the original estimate. Oil companies would have to agree to pump a certain amount of oil through the line in order to assure bondholders that the state would have the income to pay off the bonds. The companies, Gildehaus said, "might agree to use the pipeline until its capacity was full before using any other source of shipment."

The Alyeska Pipeline Service Company could build the pipeline under contract to the state, Gildehaus said, with full performance and completion guarantees.

"Would the floating of $3.5 billion in public bonds affect normal governmental financing," Senator John Rader asked Gildehaus.

"I happen to believe that ownership of the pipeline will enhance the state's ability to issue general and revenue bonds," Gildehaus replied. "I think that ownership of the pipeline increases the security of the state's total income package, and . . . the state would be in a stronger financial position rather then a weaker financial position by owning the pipeline."

State Senator John Rader believes Egan wanted the state to own the pipeline "because the companies planned to make money off it, and he wanted the state to make the money instead."

At one point, Senator Groh asked Havelock whether the state had approached the oil industry directly about owning the pipeline. Were the companies willing to negotiate on the ownership question, Groh wanted to know.

"I could go and ask the attractive girl at the end of the hall whether she's willing," answered Havelock, "and I'm sure she'd tell me to go jump in the lake. On the other hand, if I invited her to dinner, I might get a good deal more information about whether she was willing. And if she started looking in store windows at furs and diamonds, I'd probably get a good deal more information. So, I think an old negotiator like Senator Groh is probably quite aware of the answer to his question."

"Mr. Chairman, I really do think I should correct my question," said Groh. "My question should have been, have you ever called?"

"We've talked with them hundreds of hours, yes," said Havelock.

"Did you ever ask them, 'Are you willing to sell?'"

"That was covered in the [news]papers quite fully," interjected co-chairman Rettig.

"The answer was no," said Havelock.

"Then what are we doing here?" asked Groh.

"He's still taking them out to dinner," Rettig said.

THE INDUSTRY'S FIRST WITNESS was Charles E. Spahr, chairman and chief executive officer of the Standard Oil Company of Ohio. Spahr said pipeline owner-companies "waited to see if the state could build the line without requiring the support of our credit" and had finally concluded that the state could not.

"There's only one reason why we want to build a pipeline and have a part in it," said Spahr. "That's to get that oil out of there to get it to market. . . . We've never built a pipeline in order to make money on a pipeline per se."

When Spahr first heard of Egan's pipeline ownership idea, he had called it "stupid." Now in Juneau, and upon reflection, he was trying to put his thoughts into more diplomatic language.

Spahr assured the committee that the Alyeska pipeline company would act only as agent for the owner-companies in design, construction, operation, and maintenance of the pipeline as a common carrier. Alyeska would have no ownership interest in the Prudhoe Bay oil field or the pipeline.

Oil industry witness Raymond B. Gary, managing director of the Wall Street investment house of Morgan Stanley and Co., also said the state couldn't finance the project on its own. The oil companies could afford to build the pipeline, he said, and would expect to recoup their investment plus a fair return.

Ed Patton made it clear that his Alyeska Pipeline Service Company wasn't happy with the idea of building the pipeline under contract to the state. First of all, he testified, "it would be impossible for Alyeska to bid a lump sum contract" because there are "so many contingencies and unknowns."

Couldn't the state negotiate a cost-plus contract with Alyeska, Senator Rader wanted to know, "auditing the costs as we go along?" This might be done, but the risks would still be too high for Alyeska, Patton claimed.

IT WAS A LONG WEEK at the hearings. The oil industry and the Egan administration were far apart. Sohio legal counsel Dick Donaldson recalls, in a 1977 magazine article, that, "We were treated with all the cordiality of hired killers! Governor Egan was, in effect, telling the oil companies: Fine, you finance and build the pipeline, but let the State of Alaska own it, run it, and take the profits."

342

Attorney General Havelock had his own version of the situation. In his summation to the legislative committee, Havelock said the "overwhelming impression from the argument of the oil industry is negative. Their efforts have been directed to convince us that the Constitution of the United States and the financial world constitute a steel box tightly fitting the status quo. Its view is that the state can do nothing. We cannot lease state lands as we propose. We cannot regulate it at all. We cannot own and operate a pipeline . . . .

"As one spectator remarked during a break yesterday, 'You know what I found out? Everything the oil companies don't like is 'unconstitutional.'"

PORTRAIT

CHANCY CROFT

One of the star players in the Alaska oil drama of the early 1970s was born and raised in oil country: Odessa, Texas. Chancy Croft's father was a geologist who worked with several Texas independents, and Chancy honed his attitude toward Big Oil around the Croft dinner table. He was impressed that the University of Texas paid its teachers well—thanks, he believed, to oil taxes paid by major companies for the use of university lands. During the summers Chancy worked as a rig helper for a small drilling operation and as a pipe-rock helper for a well-servicing company.

"Independents in Odessa were likely to be the local Chevy dealer," he says. "Major companies were constantly taking advantage of small operators . . . . Texas benefited from oil, but the oil industry controlled the Texas government."

In the early history of Texas as an oil state, Croft says, an independent oil-man "could get his fair share through powerful independents and royalty-owners' political associations. These forces were concerned with protecting individuals from unwanted state intervention." This opportunity for individual enterprise that Croft saw in his state's past was one of the lures of Alaska.

Chancy Croft drove up the Alcan Highway in 1962 with fellow University of Texas law school graduate Bill Bailey. Small towns in Texas were then suffering hard times, and the two freshly minted lawyers were looking forward to new opportunities in the Last Frontier. But by the time Croft arrived in Alaska, only a handful of Alaskans were oil royalty owners. The few Anchorage businessmen who owned royalty on producing leases near Soldotna on the Kenai Peninsula were the only successful "independents" in the state. A separate ragtag bunch of hardscrabble geologists, brokers, promoters, and hangers-on were eking out a living buying and selling federal and state oil leases, but none had any paying royalty share.

Shortly after arriving in Anchorage, Croft married Toni Williamson, the daughter of prominent Midland independent oilman J. C. Williamson, and during his first year in Alaska he filed for several federal oil and gas leases in the Copper River basin. At the 1964 federal lease drawing on the North Slope, he won two oil and gas leases, filed for him by my firm, Alaska Exploration. Like so many of us at that drawing, he made a handsome profit assigning the leases to major oil companies.

The tall, broad-shouldered Croft, once he became an Alaska legislator, was assumed to be an expert on oil. At a pipeline hearing in early 1971, his Texas-bred attitude toward major oil companies immediately influenced the proceedings.

"I think the oil companies have done an atrocious job by acting as though they had the right of eminent domain across federal property," Croft said. "Maybe it just never occurred to them that the federal government could say no to oil."

Chapter 31

Rival Schemes

As Bill Egan fought for his pipeline ownership plan, a political rival was promoting a different scheme to give the state control of pipeline tariffs. State Senator Chancy Croft believed he had found a way for the state to circumvent the power of the Interstate Commerce Commission. He called it "right-of-way leasing." Using the state's proprietary power and its inherent right to contract for use of its land and minerals, Croft believed the state might do indirectly what federal law prohibited it from doing directly.

DURING THE 1971 LEGISLATIVE SESSION, House Speaker Gene Guess and Senate President Jay Hammond appointed a pipeline impact committee to examine tariffs, marine transportation costs, environmental safeguards, and oil-related employment—and to formulate an overall state oil policy. As chairman of the committee, Guess and Hammond appointed Senator Croft, an Anchorage Democrat.

Croft, who had his own oil legislative agenda, dealt gingerly with Egan's pipeline ownership idea. In late 1971, however, he was quoted in the newspapers as saying: "For some time now it has been widely assumed, if not advocated, that whatever benefited Alyeska [pipeline company] benefited Alaska. Now that notion has been laid to rest. Whatever merits or pitfalls

347

exist in the governor's proposal to own the pipeline, at least Alaskans will be discussing the state's interest from now on, and not Alyeska's."

Croft knew that although the pipeline right-of-way would lie entirely inside Alaska, the oil being transported through it would be marketed outside the state, and thus pipeline tariff-setting would be preempted by the federal government. Because Prudhoe Bay oil would cross state lines, tariffs would come under jurisdiction of the Interstate Commerce Commission. The state of Alaska, home to the pipeline and owner of the richest oil lands, would be relegated to the sidelines. But Croft believed state legislation could be drafted to get around the problem.

Croft got his approach from Joseph Witherspoon, a professor at the University of Texas law school while Croft was a student there. Witherspoon's theories on the power of an "owner-proprietor" state argued that a state might contract (lease) its land for a pipeline right-of-way and, by the price it charged, in effect regulate pipeline tariffs.

Croft's right-of-way leasing scheme went head-to-head with Egan's state-ownership plan. Both proposals came before public hearings in the first part of 1972, meaning they would be coming down the legislative track at the same time. Both bills were designed to control pipeline tariffs, each in a different way. And both aimed at taming the oil industry so that Alaska wouldn't end up, as Bill Egan feared, "riding the tiger."

CHANCY CROFT'S plan got an airing at both sets of public hearings. During the March 1972 hearings into state ownership, the committee asked Croft to explain his right-of-way leasing concept. Croft obliged.

> **Croft's right-of-way leasing scheme went head-to-head with Egan's state-ownership plan.**

The pipeline would cross about 200 miles of state land on its way from Prudhoe Bay to Valdez, Croft said, and the state could charge a fee for this. The right-of-way fee would be formulated with the goal of bringing overall state oil revenue up to the same level it would have been if the state itself set pipeline tariffs.

The fee would be based annually on a percentage of the original pipeline construction cost or on a percentage of the pipeline's net earnings for that year, whichever was higher. High construction costs and high pipeline earnings could be expected to translate into high pipeline tariffs—which in the end would mean less money for the state from oil royalties. But Croft's self-adjusting right-of-way fee would counter the problem, in this way: If the oil companies spent a great deal on building the pipeline, the right-of-way fee could be correspondingly higher; if the companies' pipeline tariffs (and thus net earnings) rose, the right-of-way fee could rise.

In the final analysis, the right-of-way fee would regulate the effects of pipeline tariffs and, most importantly, control the state's revenue from oil.

Croft spelled out other details of his plan. The right-of-way lease would have a term of ten years, after which it could be renegotiated. The lease would give the state an option to acquire an equity interest

Chancy Croft wanted the state to impose right-of-way leasing fees on users of the oil pipeline. The plan promoted by State Senator Croft in 1972 clashed with Governor Egan's campaign for state ownership of the pipeline.

of about 25 percent in the pipeline. The oil companies would have to build and operate the pipeline as a common carrier and common purchaser, and they would have to agree to not transfer their interests in the lease without the state's consent.

Croft likened a pipeline right-of-way lease to an exploration lease. The oil companies were used to paying a percentage of production for the right to drill, so they would be familiar with the percentage fee structure in his bill. Right-of-way leasing, Croft argued, was better suited than state ownership of the pipeline to obtain the limited goal of state control over tariffs.

Sohio chairman Charlie Spahr made it clear at the ownership hearing that the oil companies didn't like Croft's plan any more than they liked Egan's. Sohio lawyer Joseph Cortez jumped on Croft's comparison of right-of-way leases and exploration leases. An exploration lease requires the state to "grant the lessee the right to market the oil," but a right-of-way lease interferes with that right. The right to market the oil, Croft responded, extends only to the boundary of the exploration lease and not beyond.

Apparently fearing that Democrat Croft's leasing bill would lead to union demands for more jobs, Ed Patton, president of Alyeska Pipeline Service

Company, opined: "I like to think you are not talking about a state policy furthering featherbedding, but the bill can be interpreted that way."

Testily, Croft replied: "I think that that is a very significant indication of an attitude towards this legislature, when we have sought in a very responsible manner to deal with that problem, to be accused, in effect, of having that goal in mind."

BILL EGAN'S PLAN for state ownership began to look doomed, while Chancy Croft's proposal gained support. In interviews with members of the legislature after the hearings, it was hard to find a good word for the plan.

Early one morning during the 1972 legislative session, Governor Egan placed a call to Senator John Rader. By this time, Egan knew his pipeline ownership bill was lost. It had been reported out of the Senate commerce and resource committees with a "do not pass" recommendation. Rader says that in their phone conversation, Egan asked him to vote for Chancy Croft's right-of-way leasing bill. Egan apparently believed that Croft's legislation was better than no legislation at all in the battle to control pipeline tariffs.

Rader told Egan he had serious reservations about the right-of-way leasing concept, because if Alaska in effect imposed its own tariffs on an interstate carrier through exercise of its contractual power, would not the U.S. begin to be balkanized, split into tiny competing units? Rader had philosophical problems as well with government ownership. Should a government own a project when experienced private enterprise was ready to do the job?

Rader was convinced that passage of either plan would delay pipeline construction—and that neither proposal would survive a court challenge. Why not simply tax the oil industry to control it, using the state's sovereign power to tax instead of owning the pipeline or charging right-of-way fees.

Rader repeated his concerns about state ownership. Might not $3.5 billion in public bonds impair local bonds? Where would the state get money to pay cost overruns?

"The private sector could operate [the pipeline] more efficiently," Rader told Egan. "Besides, the state lacks staying power—governor to governor, legislature to legislature—so the pipeline might in the future become a political football."

Rader finally told Egan that he would agree to vote for Croft's bill—but that if the oil companies refused to put the pipeline across state land because of the law, Egan should counter with an increase in the cents-per-barrel tax. No matter who owned the pipeline or what the tariffs, Rader said, such a tax, adjusted so the state could maintain its fair share at the wellhead, was a far better answer.

Sohio chairman Charlie Spahr made it clear that the oil companies didn't like Croft's plan any more than they liked Egan's.

AS EXPECTED, the Senate voted down Egan's ownership bill. On the 17 to 3 vote, his only support came from Democrats Willie Hensley of Kotzebue, Ed Merdes of Fairbanks, and Joe Josephson of Anchorage. After defeat of the ownership bill in both the Senate and House, an amended version of Croft's right-of-way leasing bill passed the legislature, and Egan signed it into law.

"At that point," says John Havelock, "there was a mad scramble to put together a policy in sixty days which called for massive changing of gears from the regulation/taxation approach we had been developing from the previous year. Even though Egan's policy team had a low opinion of the actual worth of Croft's proposal, we put the Egan forces to work to make Croft's right-of-way leasing package as prickly as possible so that we would still have position during the following year [in the event the oil companies sued to kill the law].

"This worked, the industry sued, and we had a new forum in which to work out an accommodation of industry and state interest."

Companion legislation to the right-of way leasing act that would have given the state 20 percent ownership of the pipeline was defeated. Had it become a part owner, the state would have been able to establish its own tariff. It could have made a profit by buying crude oil from small North Slope producers and shipping it in its own space in the pipeline.

Some legislators believed that by owning a part of the pipeline, the state would have a better chance of keeping pipeline management honest. But Egan wanted nothing to do with partial ownership. "It would be like getting into bed with the oil companies," Havelock recalls Egan saying, "and that was the last thing he wanted to do."

Croft's bill had passed, and Egan had suffered an ignoble defeat. A deep rift began to develop between the followers of Croft and those of Egan. Stung by defeat, Egan took to statewide radio and television to tell Alaskans they weren't getting their fair share of oil money.

"It would be like getting into bed with the oil companies," Havelock recalls Egan saying, "and that was the last thing he wanted to do."

Egan's figures showed that after production of an expected 15 billion barrels of North Slope oil over a thirty-year period, the companies would make a profit of more than $25 billion. In percentages, he said, this meant that nearly 45 percent of the North Slope's oil riches would go to the companies, some 36 percent would go to the federal government, and less than 19 percent would be received by the people of the state of Alaska.

INSIDE STORY

OWNERSHIP LOST

Republicans and Democrats alike had ganged up against Governor Egan's pipeline ownership scheme.

"Historically, America has been built and developed by industry," said Representative Keith Specking, a Republican from Hope, after the ownership hearings. "And to take it out of the hands of industry and put it in the hands of state government, to me is absolutely unthinkable."

"I am more against state ownership now than I was at the beginning of these meetings," said Representative Mike Colletta, Anchorage Republican. "As the Mafia is wont to say: 'Before you rob the till, make sure there's money in it.'"

From Senator Lowell Thomas, Jr., Anchorage Republican: "I feel that as long as private industry can and is willing to construct it, they should be allowed to do it."

It wasn't only the Republicans. "Had the Democrats stuck with him," says John Havelock, Egan's attorney general, "he would have had it."

Havelock says Egan "became very bitter with [Chancy] Croft, and that colored subsequent events. Because of Croft [being a political rival], he needed to get something distinctive, his own program. He figured that the reason ownership didn't go was that Croft and the Democrats submarined it."

With several of the state Senate's ten Democrats displaying a pro-industry bent, Egan's pipeline ownership bill never had a chance. "At one time, we counted five votes in the Senate, never more than that," says Alex Miller, Egan's legislative assistant in 1971-1972.

"We just couldn't get the votes," Miller says, "so there was no use making an issue of it. . . . We wanted the state to build the pipeline, and the legislature wouldn't buy it. The money scared them. They couldn't visualize the state doing it."

To the end of his days, Egan continued to believe the state should have owned the pipeline and hired the Alyeska Pipeline Service Company to build and run it. Pipeline ownership, he said, was "the only legislation in the state of Alaska that was really meaningful insofar as giving Alaska the full handle on what goes on . . . and really having control insofar as the people's interests are concerned."

Says Alex Miller: "It would have been the best thing that ever happened to the state if we had gone ahead and built it. We tried. We tried to convince them, but we couldn't get by Chancy Croft. Croft was the biggest opponent, the guy who really fought us."

Chapter 32

Give-and-Take

O il remained a pivot point for lawmakers in 1972 even after they ruled on the pipeline ownership and right-of-way bills. With state ownership a dead issue, Governor Egan reintroduced his old cents-per-barrel tax. If he couldn't own the pipeline, at least he could place a floor beneath the state's oil income.

Egan saw the tax as a mechanism that would smooth out the many price variables that affect Alaska's oil revenue—variables that were largely beyond the state's control. Alaska couldn't control the world oil price or Congressional changes in oil laws. It couldn't control pipeline construction costs, pipeline tariffs, tanker charges, or oil-company accounting methods. But a guaranteed minimum payment to the state for each barrel of oil produced, regardless of the oil's value, would assure a steady flow of money to the state budget. And this minimum cents-per-barrel tax would be a simple one to administer.

The tax would be a backstop to the severance tax already in effect. The existing tax was a percentage of the value of the oil; the new cents-per-barrel tax would be a minimum charge per barrel, no matter what its value. Oil producers would be required to pay whichever tax was higher. The idea was that if oil values plummeted below a certain point, the new cents-per-barrel minimum tax would kick in.

355

The cents-per-barrel bill was drafted to produce an income for the state no less than what it was already receiving from severance taxes. It would bring in no new revenue, but it would establish a floor beneath state oil income. This time around, legislators went for the concept, voting to establish a floor under the existing severance tax. The cents-per-barrel tax, with a credit for royalties paid the state, passed the 1972 legislature.

BILL EGAN ALSO WANTED to tap the oil companies for property taxes. With the state's economy on hold until the pipeline could be built, and with the state budget down, there was pressure to raise money for schools and municipal services.

Egan proposed a 20-mill property tax on "all oil field machinery, appliances and equipment" in the state. The tax would initially affect mainly the oil rigs, platforms, and pipelines of the Kenai Peninsula and Cook Inlet, but it would also fall on the Prudhoe Bay oil field and the trans-Alaska pipeline once they were in operation. Money from the property tax was to go right into the state's general fund—not to the local boroughs and towns where the oil property lay.

Part of Egan's strategy with the property tax was to undercut the Arctic Slope Native Association in its efforts to create a North Slope borough. The governor was concerned about creation of a borough that could siphon off oil property taxes. Egan's tax would prevent local governments from taxing petroleum drilling and transportation installations; only the state would have that right.

Egan reintroduced his old cents-per-barrel tax. If he couldn't own the pipeline, at least he could place a floor beneath the state's oil income.

But Egan didn't figure on the heated reaction from local governments in the path of the oil pipeline.

"Immediately, Fairbanks led the charge against 'taking the only tax base we'll ever have,'" says Mike Bradner, who was a state representative from Fairbanks. "The North Slope Borough was rather late in the game, actually. They woke up, and then Valdez. Egan really thought he could keep it all."

During the 1972 session, lawmakers narrowed the 20-mill petroleum facilities tax down to the pipeline only and introduced the concept of revenue-sharing with the communities through which the pipeline would pass. They devised a revenue-sharing formula based on the assessed value of land within those communities and on the number of residents.

The legislature put off final action on oil property taxes, however, leaving the issue to be taken up again later. But in 1972, Bradner says, "The idea of a state-take-all property tax couldn't even get started. Fairbanks, the Arctic Slope, and, finally, Valdez went to the trenches, with their eye on Anchorage. What were Anchorage legislators going to do?"

As mayor of the Greater Anchorage Area Borough in 1973, I testified at the regular 1973 legislative session that Anchorage didn't need a part of the 20-mill pipeline property tax but that a cap should be placed on the amount other local governments could claim. Anchorage wanted more money to be left in the state's general fund.

THE OIL AGENDA of the 1972 legislature seemed to go on and on. The legislature passed a Pipeline Regulation Act and created an Alaska Pipeline Commission to regulate tariffs on oil that stays within the state and to advise the Interstate Commerce Commission on interstate tariffs, common carrier rules, and other matters.

The legislature placed a marine restoration severance tax on oil produced on the North Slope so that any owner or carrier of oil who spilled it on Alaska's land or water would pay for the damages and cleanup. Lawmakers also banned oil and gas leasing in Bristol Bay and created several "critical habitat" areas in the state. They also dealt with how the oil companies should build a "hot oil" pipeline in permafrost and passed "local hire" legislation requiring the Alyeska Pipeline Service Company to hire Alaska residents.

Republican state senators Jay Hammond and Bob Palmer introduced a resolution calling for a study of an alternative pipeline route through Canada. The main interest of Hammond and Palmer was in protecting Alaska's waterways from environmental degradation. Hammond thought a non-marine route would be "the way to keep the oil away from the fish; in other words, no tankers."

Midwest political forces led by U.S. Representative Les Aspin and U.S. Senator William Proxmire, both Wisconsin Democrats, supported the Canadian route in order to bring oil to their area. National conservation groups also supported the alternative route, their motive being a desire to delay or kill the trans-Alaska pipeline. The legislature failed to approve the resolution.

SPOTLIGHT ▰▰▰▰
POLITICAL TURBULENCE

Bill Egan's political fortunes suffered a severe blow during the summer of 1972, as the legislature was in adjournment. The politics of the Viet Nam generation had arrived in Alaska. Young idealists, calling themselves "ad hoc Democrats," began organizing the state's Democratic precincts, setting up rap sessions in high schools and door-to-door campaigns. This movement eventually turned against Egan and his staid, old-time party regulars.

Teamsters leader Jesse Carr, the women's liberation movement, and the young "ad hocers" found themselves allied against Egan in an attempt to take over the Southcentral Democratic Convention in Anchorage in July 1972. This turbulent political period saw the beginning of efforts to revitalize Anchorage's neighborhoods through community councils, community schools, public transit, land use planning, greenbelts, and bike paths; I was elected Anchorage Borough mayor in October 1972.

During the 1972 Presidential campaign, George McGovern said many times: "I am not against the trans-Alaska pipeline." But in the November general election, with most Republicans and many Democrats, including Egan, expressing grave concern over McGovern's general anti-development attitude, McGovern ran far behind Richard Nixon in Alaska.

Hickel-appointee Ted Stevens won reelection to his U.S. Senate seat by defeating state House representative Gene Guess. No longer seen as Hickel's protegé, Stevens would soon help oil companies obtain a pipeline right-of-way through Congressional passage of the pipeline authorization act.

Republican state Senator Don Young won in a special election called to replace Congressman Nick Begich, who was aboard a charter flight from Anchorage to Juneau that disappeared on October 16, 1972. Twenty Democrats were elected to the forty-member state House of Representatives, and the make-up of the state Senate was now nine Democrats and eleven Republicans.

Chapter 33

The Companies Counterattack

During the 1972 legislative session, oil lobbyists had warned that passage of Governor Egan's cents-per-barrel tax or Senator Croft's right-of-way leasing bill would force their clients to sue. Now that Egan had signed these two bills into law, the oil companies, true to their vow, filed suit in September 1972. The suit was filed by ten companies: Amerada Hess Corporation, Amoco, BP Oil Corporation, Humble Oil (Exxon), Humble Pipeline (Exxon), Gulf, Phillips, Skelly, Sohio Pipeline, and Union.

This suit asked an Alaska Superior Court to void both laws. The cents-per-barrel tax placed a fixed minimum wellhead price on North Slope oil and the right-of-way law tried to regulate interstate pipeline tariffs, both in violation of the doctrine of federal preemption of interstate commerce regulation; thus both laws were unconstitutional, the suit alleged.

The companies claimed that rentals under the right-of-way leasing act would amount to at least $2 million a year, many times higher than California pipeline fees. And no pipeline, they said, determined right-of-way rental by reference to the net earnings of the lessee. The cost of building the pipeline and the assets of its owner-companies also should be irrelevant, they said. Finally, the oil companies said they felt certain that "the state employs no personnel with expertise in buying and selling crude oil on the open market and lacks the facilities necessary to engage in such business."

In a separate lawsuit on behalf of Mobil, the Anchorage law firm of Holland and Thornton not only asked the court to void the right-of-way leasing act but to grant a pipeline easement across state land.

Egan directed state attorneys to answer both lawsuits, consolidating them, but he believed the companies were simply trying to pressure lawmakers to repeal or rewrite the laws in question. The companies said the state was trying to unilaterally amend North Slope lease contracts.

The right-of-way leasing act was particularly vexing to the companies. Their legal action against the act was a "first impression" lawsuit, and if the U.S. Supreme Court upheld the act, an entirely new regulatory concept might become part of pipeline law. The oil industry much preferred leaving pipeline legal precedents undisturbed.

The companies claimed it might take four years for the case to work its way up to the Supreme Court and that work on the pipeline could not begin until the matter was resolved. Egan thought they were bluffing, but he couldn't be sure. He knew that if the pipeline continued to be delayed, his chance of reelection in 1974 would disappear.

UNBEKNOWNST TO EGAN, Attorney General Havelock arranged to meet with Sohio and Exxon attorneys in Washington, D.C., in late 1972. Havelock thought he might make progress by talking directly to oil lawyers.

When Egan heard of the meeting, he was not pleased. No one in his administration, he said—especially his attorney general—would have any further dealings with oil companies without his personal participation. During the remainder of Egan's term, all meetings with oil company representatives involving the 1972 oil legislation would take place in the governor's third-floor Capitol office.

Of his meeting with the oil attorneys, Havelock wrote Egan: "Payment of money to the state, as such, was not the biggest problem. If the state could obtain the same amount of money overall . . . without the inhibitions on management which obtain in the existing legislation [right-of-way leasing], they [the companies] would like an opportunity to discuss it privately in their various corporate headquarters."

Havelock warned the attorneys that the state might argue in court that the monopolistic aspects of the pipeline could raise the entire question of the legality of the original North Slope oil leases. "They were visibly agitated by the implication that the validity of their leases might be subject to challenge," Havelock said.

Havelock's memo to Egan sounded an optimistic note: "There is a considerable coincidence of interest between the state and the owners in assuring long-term industrial peace with economic justice to Alaskans."

As pipeline delay continued and constituent pressure grew, Egan gave Havelock the go-ahead in late February 1973 to begin serious negotiations with the oil companies aimed at a legislative solution. These negotiations began without consultation with key legislators.

Havelock seemed ready to swap the right-of-way-leasing act for the cents-per-barrel and 20-mill property taxes. Havelock had told Senator John Rader that the right-of-way leasing law might stand up in court, but privately he believed otherwise. The theories of Professor Joseph Witherspoon that Chancy Croft had used in devising the leasing law were "just plain wrong," Havelock said later. "You can't backdoor something in interstate commerce. We can't have little pieces of the dog swing the whole animal." In Havelock's view, the state couldn't build a stable regulatory policy on the leasing law. He believed that enactment of the property tax would raise as much money as the leasing act, with the added advantage of providing a steady stream of revenue to the state when it was most needed: immediately, before the first oil flowed through the pipeline.

JOHN HAVELOCK

During negotiations, Have-lock pressed for state ownership of the land on which the Valdez oil terminal was to be built. "If the state owns the terminal and storage facilities," he had written Egan, "it can more readily assure fair treatment of all producers . . . .

Attorney General John Havelock worked out a deal with the oil companies in mid-1973 to resolve lawsuits that challenged state laws and threatened more delays in building the Alaska pipeline. Havelock and Governor Egan then had to sell the state legislature on the agreement.

A move to high rates of return by the pipeline owners could meet retaliation in high terminal tariffs." But in the final negotiated package, the state agreed to sell the site to the companies.

"Any negotiation with an oil company is a long drawn-out affair," says Alex Miller, Egan's assistant at the time. "I don't think Egan knew at that time what the oil companies would agree to, but at the core of the package was the repeal of Croft's right-of-way leasing law."

> *No one in his administration, Egan said— especially his attorney general— would have any further dealings with oil companies without his personal participation.*

Havelock's talks with the oil companies were primarily about the level of the cents-per-barrel "floor" on state oil revenue. After a series of meetings, the Egan administration and the oil companies agreed July 20 on a 25-cents-per-barrel minimum tax and a 20-mill property tax—and all agreed that the right-of-way leasing law had to go.

After more give-and-take between the parties, the negotiators put together a final legislative package to bring before state lawmakers. The oil companies promised to drop their lawsuits if the package made it through the legislature. For its part, the state, according to Havelock, "would back off to an advocacy agency before the ICC rather than attempting direct tariff regulations."

By negotiating with the companies, Havelock says, he and Egan had been able "to trade off an untenable regulatory position for an oil tax policy that guaranteed a minimum revenue even if prices fell or if the cost of constructing the pipeline skyrocketed, which it did. Here was a policy that would endure for decades."

TO THE SURPRISE of most people concerned with the state's oil laws, Egan announced on September 23, 1973, that he was calling a special session of the legislature in mid-October to deal exclusively with oil matters.

This was the first time that Senator Chancy Croft realized Egan had negotiated an oil package designed to undo Croft's own right-of-way leasing law. Most legislators were surprised to learn that the oil legislation they had worked so hard to pass during the 1972 session had been turned on its head. It had been done by Egan, without notice to key lawmakers.

INSIDE STORY

THE MCGREW AMENDMENTS

Exxon oil lobbyist Vern McGrew came in for some special treatment during the legislature's 1973 special oil session. McGrew flew regularly into Juneau to warn Native legislators that if Governor Egan's original cents-per-barrel tax was allowed to stand, oil royalty payments going into the Native Fund under terms of the Native Claims Settlement Act would be in jeopardy.

McGrew's overheated warnings only offended the Native legislators and others. Reporter Andy Williams zeroed in on the situation in an article in the *Anchorage Daily News:*

"There is a theory among some legislators that oil lobbyists, at least those who fly in for a few days at a time from corporate headquarters, are not very bright. The theory goes that the oil executive is so used to dealing with public bodies corrupted by years of association with the industry that they don't know how to react to one that is young and proud of its sovereignty.

"This theory is probably too kind to the legislature and too unkind to the oil lobbyists. But the legislature is a representative body, and no one ever got rich underestimating the distrust many Alaskans have toward outside interests."

McGrew had so unfavorably impressed many lawmakers that the cents-per-barrel tax was boosted to make sure that the Natives would continue to receive royalty payments. The increase and future similar oil tax changes became known as "McGrew Amendments."

Chapter 34

The Oil Session

Alex Miller received a call in Fairbanks from Governor Bill Egan in late September 1973. The governor wanted his legislative aide to return to Juneau as his assistant for the upcoming special oil session.

"I told him it was a bad idea," Miller said. "He already had Bob Dittman down there and didn't need me. I had just gone to work for Neil Bergt [at Mark Air], and I didn't think it was fair to Neil. So, when I told Egan I couldn't do it, he said OK, and hung up. My feelings were actually hurt that he hadn't urged me to do it, you know.

"Then about a half hour later I get a call from Neil. 'Pack, you're on your way to Juneau,' he said. I said, 'Did the governor phone you?' and he said, 'Yeah. Maybe *you* can afford to say no, Alex, but I can't.'"

Tim Bradner, a lobbyist for British Petroleum at the time, recalls the 1973 oil session as "the toughest thirty days of my life." His brother Mike was a state representative from Fairbanks. The oil session, Mike Bradner says, "was an instance in Alaska's political history when the center moved. It became a thorough education of the entire legislature on oil issues." The session became one of the few times that the relationship between the oil industry and the state of Alaska changed in a significant way.

BILL EGAN FLEW INTO JUNEAU on October 16 from celebrations in Anchorage and Fairbanks of his fifty-ninth birthday. Those two northern cities had raised nearly $15,000 for his 1974 reelection campaign.

The oil session convened the next day. Before a joint session of the legislature, Attorney General John Havelock presented the oil package he had negotiated with the oil companies. The presentation was the high point of his public career.

Havelock told the joint session that while the state's objective had been to satisfy Alaska's financial needs, his negotiated settlement had not been designed to get "all the traffic will bear." He told lawmakers that resolution of the property tax issue left over from 1972 would go a long way toward resolving the pressure that legislators and the governor were feeling from local governments along the pipeline corridor. As to the lawsuits brought by the oil companies, Havelock said the state's chances of winning them in court were "less than 50-50."

State Senator John Rader (right) chose to side with Chancy Croft (left) at the legislature's 1973 oil session, provoking Governor Egan to call Rader into his office for a harsh dressing-down.

In fairness to the oil companies, Havelock said, legislators should not view them as a monolithic entity. And he had become convinced that they were willing to "meet us halfway."

The oil package was made up of several parts: the 25-cents-per-barrel minimum tax, the 20-mill property tax on pipeline facilities, amendments that would gut Chancy Croft's right-of-way leasing law, elimination of the tariff-setting authority of the newly established Alaska Pipeline Commission, a one-eighth-cent-per-barrel conservation tax, some increase in the 8 percent severance tax, a common-purchaser/common carrier pipeline bill, and provision for the pipeline owner-companies to purchase the Valdez terminal site.

A POLL TAKEN BY THE LOCAL MEDIA showed that a majority of lawmakers at the special session favored an out-of-court legislative settlement with the oil companies. But a majority of Democratic legislators said they thought Egan's oil package "favored the industry instead of the state." They would have to take a careful look at it before deciding how to vote. Most Republican legislators favored the package because it would move the pipeline forward.

Associated Press reporter John Greely wrote that legislators "have been shaking their heads over a common note sounded both by oil men and Egan's lieutenants." Egan's people, Greely wrote, were telling the lawmakers that "if they make 'substantive changes' in the negotiated settlement, the laws could be thrust back into court, possibly delaying pipeline construction."

> *"The toughest thirty days of my life."*
>
> — *Oil Lobbyist*
> *Tim Bradner,*
> *about the 1973 session*

Greely quoted an unnamed Democratic senator as complaining that Egan's oil package left them with "a sense of hurt pride. . . . In the 1972 legislature, we united with the governor against a common enemy; then we returned this time to find the governor was friends with the common enemy. They were together and we were on the outside."

Says John Havelock: "For some [legislators], the issues were simply too complex. They had not understood the daylong presentation I made to them earlier. With others, it was pride."

Egan had made little effort to stroke key Democratic legislators, and a week into the session Egan sensed his oil package was not generating the necessary support. Now he decided he should meet with legislators. After one such meeting, a lawmaker said: "I think the governor heard some things today that he's never heard before. The idea was to get his bill draftsmen to come down from their high horse."

But by then it was almost too late. Irreparable political damage had been done. Too many Democratic legislators had by then become alienated by Egan's silence and Havelock's perceived arrogance. Havelock and Egan were being accused by young Democrats of selling out to the oil companies.

Havelock assigned Assistant Attorney General Wilson Condon to brief Democratic senators, including John Rader, Chancy Croft, and Willie Hensley. "Everyone knew Havelock was planning to run for Congress," says Condon, "and he didn't want to risk alienating his fellow Democrats any more than necessary. So I was left to take the heat."

Condon also met frequently with key House members such as Bill Parker, Hugh Malone, and Willard Bowman. He believed that these Democratic "Turks"—who felt that *control* of the oil industry, not merely tariffs or taxes, was the fundamental issue—had the power to determine the fate of the oil package.

AS LEGISLATORS WRESTLED with the package of oil laws, the Arab-Israeli War of October 1973 was running its course. Arab nations cut off oil to the United States to protest U.S. military aid to Israel and began reducing their oil production. The world price of oil soared.

Havelock had made only brief mention of the effects of the war during his talk to the legislative joint session. He predicted that domestic fuel shortages would cause the price of gasoline to rise, and even as he spoke, the world price of crude moved past $10 a barrel. The average wellhead price of U.S. oil had been more like $3 a barrel.

Ironically, the huge jump in oil prices meant that at least temporarily, the cents-per-barrel minimum tax would be irrelevant to the state's oil income. The price of oil just wouldn't be dropping low enough for the foreseeable future to force the minimum tax to kick in.

Havelock confessed later that, "I sure wish I had traded that cents-per-barrel minimum for an even higher ad valorem [property] tax, but I was then too hung up on revenue stability."

THE KEY WITNESS for oil at the pipeline ownership hearings in 1972 had been Sohio chairman Charles Spahr. Now, at the 1973 oil session, Spahr warned that if Egan's oil package was not passed in its entirety—without substantial amendment—the pipeline would be further delayed and the oil companies would have to renegotiate their deal with the state.

Many legislators thought Spahr was bluff-

State Senator Cliff Groh worked to break a logjam in the House/Senate conference committee on Governor Egan's legislative package at the oil session. Groh's faction finally prevailed and the package was approved in 1972.

ing, but they couldn't be sure. Labor leaders and local contractors were more interested in getting the pipeline under way than in preserving the state's revenue base, so they supported Egan's proposed settlement.

Exxon lawyer Frank Heard testified that the negotiated package gave the state all the regulatory power it needed. To try to do more, he said, would make the legislation "unconstitutional."

"Silver-haired Frank was the perfect oil lobbyist," recalls Bill Parker, who was a state representative from Anchorage. "He wore suits which cost more than the mortgage on my home. He had us bumpkins mesmerized."

Rising in defense of the right-of-way leasing act was none other than Joseph Witherspoon, the professor whose theories had inspired Chancy Croft in devising the law in the first place. Witherspoon testified that abandoning the leasing law would leave the state vulnerable to "excessive tariffs and arbitrary use of pipeline services."

But the leasing law got no support from the legislature's chief oil and gas consultant, Walter Levy, who advised lawmakers to avoid new litigation at all cost. Levy said the state should demand an option to purchase up to 20 percent ownership in the pipeline. Levy, who seemed to be the only person other than Havelock who knew a war was under way in the Middle East, said the crisis with its sharp rise in oil prices would make the pipeline extremely profitable to build and to operate.

This option to buy 20 percent of the pipeline was actually included in the package of proposed oil laws, but the provision was dropped before the package finished working its way through the legislature.

THE TASK OF GUTTING the right-of-way leasing law was given to the resources and finance committees of both houses. It was in the Senate Finance Committee, however, that most of the important work was done. The committee minority argued that even if the leasing law was indeed unconstitutional, it should not be simply given away by the state without a final determination by the courts. Dissatisfaction with the idea of abandoning the leasing act was now being expressed by legislators in both houses.

Egan's oil package aimed to get rid of the leasing law by amending it to death. His proposed amendment would eliminate the essential pipeline tariff rental formula in the act and authorize the Alyeska Pipeline Service Company to condemn pipeline right-of-way by "eminent domain." Battle lines were drawn when the amendment came to the Senate floor, but it passed 17 to 3 after addition of a provision unequivocally requiring the pipeline to operate as a common carrier—that is, to allow all oil producers equal access to the pipeline.

> *"Silver-haired Frank [Heard] was the perfect oil lobbyist. He wore suits which cost more than the mortgage on my home. He had us bumpkins mesmerized."*
>
> —State Representative Bill Parker

The Senate and House approved a 20-mill property tax on oil and gas exploration, production, and pipeline assets, to be shared with local governments along the pipeline corridor. The local governmental jurisdictions through which the pipeline wended its way would now benefit financially from the property tax, although they were subject to a tax-ceiling formula and their share of the revenue would be in lieu of all local oil property taxes.

The Phillips liquified-natural-gas plant at Nikiski was exempt from the state property tax, and the facility would continue to be taxed by the Kenai Borough. Some legislators tried to have the property tax include known oil reserves in the ground, but this proposal failed.

Legislators also approved the 25-cents-per-barrel minimum tax.

Many lawmakers opposed sale of the Valdez terminal site to the oil companies, and the bill that authorized its sale was defeated in the Senate on November 2 by a tie vote, 10 to 10. However, Governor Egan convinced his old friend Senator Kay Poland, Democrat of Kodiak, that failure to sell the terminal site to the companies would delay the pipeline for at least an additional three months. Poland then changed her vote, and the bill passed 11 to 9. Egan's rationale for selling rather than leasing the terminal site was couched in terms of speeding construction of the pipeline. But what Egan was really afraid of was "breaking" the legislative package and allowing significant amendments to change the negotiated settlement.

The oil package originally provided for some increase in the top severance-tax rate, which was then 8 percent. But the legislature instead changed the production level at which the top rate would kick in. Now, the maximum 8 percent rate would apply to wells that produced more than 1,500 barrels a day, rather than the previous 2,500 barrels. Several wells in Cook Inlet would now have to pay the top rate. The tax was also incrementally increased on wells producing less than 1,500 barrels per day.

THE OIL-PACKAGE LEGISLATION now faced its final hurdle, the joint House/Senate conference committee. It was a "free conference committee," a term used to denote a conference committee whose compromise bill could only be voted up or down by the legislature as a whole, without change. Committee members were Republican Senators Cliff Groh (Anchorage) and Terry Miller (Fairbanks), Democratic Senator Chancy Croft (Anchorage), Democratic Representatives Hugh Malone (Kenai) and Dick McVeigh (Anchorage), and Republican Representative Millie Banfield (Juneau).

Croft, Malone, and Miller had agreed in advance on a conference committee strategy: make some small break in Egan's oil package so that substantial changes could be made later. One possible break could be the transfer of authority to approve enlargement of pipeline and storage facilities, now residing in the legislature, to the newly created Alaska Pipeline Commission. This was the issue over which the conference committee deadlocked.

As the impasse persisted, Egan aide Alex Miller suddenly appeared at the conference room door. It was near midnight. The committee had been meeting for many hours.

"Who's holding things up?" Miller asked Senator Groh.

"Well," Groh said, "Rader isn't helping."

> ### Egan's oil package aimed to get rid of Chancy Croft's right-of-way leasing law by amending it to death.

Senator John Rader had become a roadblock to final OK of the package. Offended by Egan's failure to advise him of changes in legislative strategy, Rader chose to support Croft in trying to preserve the right-of-way leasing law. Rader was even sitting in on the conference committee meetings that were trying to work out the final package; like Croft, he wanted to poke a few holes in it.

Alex Miller motioned to Rader, sitting to Croft's right, indicating that the governor wanted to see him. Rader got up and headed dutifully down the outside hallway.

"I walked into Egan's office, and he was sitting in the corner," said Rader. "You know how he used to rock back and forth, pulling up his socks. This motion was confusing, because people would see him rocking and, perhaps, think he was nodding assent or agreement. I walked in, and he was rocking back and forth in his chair, and I said 'Hi, what's up?' or something like that.

"He looked up and stood up, halfway crouching on the table, and he says: 'Why are you wanting to fuck Bill Egan?'

"I said, 'What?' In all my years dealing with him, I had never heard him use such language.

"He says,'Why are you wanting to fuck Bill Egan?'

"I said, 'What are you talking about?'

"And he said, 'That's all you do.' He said, 'You went to the press today, or yesterday, or something or other, and gave a statement. All you're doing is trying to destroy me.' . . .

"I said, 'What are you talking about?' And I really thought he was going to come around the table or over his desk and fight me. . . . He started screaming at me. It didn't make any sense. . . .

"After a certain amount of screaming, I began to get mad, and began to scream back. . . . I allowed that he expected me to be a part of the team. And I said I expected to be consulted before the team's position was taken, not afterwards. And if I wasn't consulted, I would assume I was free to go my own way. . . .

"I remember thinking that he was paranoid. . . . People were out to get him when people were not out to get him at all."

IN THE CONFERENCE ROOM, the committee continued to try to break the deadlock. To move out of free conference and onto the floor of the legislature for a final vote, a bill must receive affirmative votes from at least two committee members from each house. Somewhat shaky in his resolve, Senator Miller had agreed with Senator Croft and Representative Malone to try to break Egan's oil package. On the other hand, Senator Groh could count on firm support for the package from representatives McVeigh and Banfield. If he was to carry the day in favor of the bill, Groh needed a senator's vote.

The logjam broke after committee members lost track of the late-night time. After wrangling for hours over whether to transfer authority to the Pipeline Commission, the committee took a vote. Everyone was exhausted, and Croft unintentionally offered an amendment that could have the result of fatally weakening his right-of-way law. Seeing his chance to jump ship, Senator Miller immediately voted with Croft for his amendment. The amendment passed and, to Croft's dismay, effectively gutted the right-of-way law. The end result was committee approval of Egan's oil package, which then moved on to the legislature, where it passed both houses.

Bill Egan had won the battle of the oil package, but he would eventually lose the war. His push for the oil legislation made him a "sellout" in the eyes of some Democrats, and it crippled his reelection effort in 1974.

SPOTLIGHT

THE WARY LEGISLATORS

Anchorage Daily News reporter Andy Williams covered the pipeline ownership hearings and the right-of-way leasing bill's enactment into law in 1972. Now, following the special session, he tried to sum up the prevailing attitudes in Juneau. On November 10, 1973, he wrote: "It is obvious that when the legislature considers the agreement between the state and the oil companies, most members find more merit with the points favoring the state than it does with those favoring the oil companies.

"This comes as a surprise to a person who assumed that the legislature, as a matter of course, would become the well-fed and happy pet of the oil industry, panting eagerly to fulfill its master's smallest whim.

"It may happen yet, but right now the legislature does not appear to be playing dead.

"Legislators probably react differently in a special session than in a regular one. The fact that there are only eight bills focuses attention. No one has a pet bill for which he is willing to bargain. Legislators are more willing to vote their conscience.

"The fact that a sizable number of statewide candidates maneuvering for position also makes it tough on the oil industry. No candidate is going to make any points arguing for the oil companies' interests. If one candidate wants to raise the severance tax, another is going to want to raise it higher."

State Representative Willard Bowman had already exhibited the independent streak of some legislators. Bowman, Alaska's first black legislator, worked as a labor relations consultant in 1971 for the pipeline's coating contractor, Surfcote Northwest. His job was to keep track of the hiring of minorities and local residents.

In early 1972, Bowman gave a speech in which he criticized the hiring practices of the Alyeska Pipeline Service Company. He was promptly told by Surfcote that such public utterances might jeopardize its contract with Alyeska.

Bowman replied in writing: "Since I must be free to speak up or act when I feel it is in the best interest of Alaska to do so, and since this, in your opinion, may compromise Surfcote's present and future working relationships, it is best for us to sever our relationship."

From this resignation until his death on December 12, 1975, Bowman maintained his same independent stance.

Chapter 35

Victory For The Pipeline

T he pressure kept mounting to get the pipeline under way. Delay in construction was becoming an albatross around Governor Egan's neck. In a letter from Fairbanks resident John Clark, Egan learned how at least one hardheaded Interior Alaskan felt about the delay.

"It saddens me that the trans-Alaska pipeline will never be built, at least not in my lifetime," Clark wrote. "When I first came to Fairbanks it was a bustling mining community inhabited by a sturdy group of go-for-broke miners who represented the epitome of the free enterprise system. Now this community is supported completely by the taxpayers of some other community. The people race from one government agency to another looking for handouts. We have become so accustomed to this way of life that anytime we are refused some dole we become extremely incensed.

"I thought Adolph Von Hinkle [Walter Hickel] did everything he could to screw up construction of the trans-Alaska pipeline, but alongside Lefty Havelock [Attorney General John Havelock], Hickel is just an amateur."

NATIVE LAND CLAIMS had long hamstrung movement toward a pipeline. The Native Claims Settlement Act had cleared that roadblock, but environmentalist opposition continued. After the U.S. Supreme Court refused in 1973 to review an appeals court ruling that restricted the width of pipeline right-of-way, Interior Secretary Rogers Morton asked President Nixon and Congress to act.

During the summer of 1973, speeches on the floor of the U.S. Senate raised grave possibilities of a national oil shortage due to the impending Middle East crisis. Senator Scoop Jackson of Washington state told Nixon administrators they should prepare to print gasoline ration tickets. The Senate got serious about trying to expedite pipeline construction in order to tap the North Slope's vast new storehouse of domestic oil.

In June, Jackson's Senate Interior Committee took up consideration of a pipeline right-of-way act, and Alaska's two senators—Democrat Mike Gravel and Republican Ted Stevens—went to work, in different ways, to get it passed.

Stevens drew up a proposed amendment to the right-of-way bill that would prohibit the filing of environmental lawsuits against the pipeline, exempting it from further administrative or court delay. "I had a group of people come out to my house in Maryland," Stevens says, "and we spent several evenings going over what could be done. I was convinced from some of the work I had done when I was in law school that Congress had the power to close the courts to these demands. When I wrote the pipeline amendment, we did some pretty good background on the concept of closing the courts and leaving open only the question of the constitutionality of the amendment itself."

> *Congress authorized the Secretary of Interior to expand the right-of-way to whatever width was necessary to build the pipeline.*

Stevens got Gravel to agree with the proposed amendment. However, Stevens didn't plan to actually introduce the amendment in the Interior Committee unless necessary. "It was to be our ace in the hole," Stevens says.

But Gravel had other plans. "Gravel said it was going to be his amendment," Stevens recalls. "It was going to be known in history as his amendment." Gravel intended to run for reelection the following year, so despite opposition from Jackson, Stevens, and Egan, Gravel forced a vote in the Interior Committee on the amendment that would short-circuit legal challenges to the pipeline.

When Gravel's amendment got through the Interior Committee and was voted on by the full Senate on July 17, the vote was 49 to 49. Vice President Spiro T. Agnew broke the tie with a vote in favor. That same day the full

ANCHORAGE DAILY TIMES/ANCHORAGE DAILY NEWS

Democrat Mike Gravel (left) and Republican Ted Stevens both worked in favor of the pipeline authorization act that passed Congress in mid-November 1973 — but they disagreed on who deserved credit for the legislation.

pipeline right-of-way bill passed the Senate on a vote of 77 to 21. After approval by the House public lands subcommittee, right-of-way legislation was passed by the full House on August 2. A Senate/House conference committee approved the bill, authorizing immediate construction of the pipeline, and it passed the full Congress in mid-November.

Congress not only decreed that the oil companies had complied with the National Environmental Protection Act, but authorized the Secretary of Interior to expand the 54-foot right-of-way width mandated in the Mineral Leasing Act of 1920 to whatever width was necessary to build the pipeline.

The final authorization act made it clear that North Slope oil was needed close to home. The act forbade shipping of North Slope oil to any place other than the United States, Canada, or Mexico. Shipments anywhere else would require a Presidential finding that they were in the national interest. The authorization act also halted further consideration of any alternative pipeline route through Canada.

MIKE GRAVEL WOULD CLAIM most of the credit for passage of the pipeline authorization act, but Senator Stevens says the biggest thanks should go to Wally Hickel and Bill Pecora. "Wally created the Menlo Park group under Dr. Pecora, the head of the USGS," says Stevens, "to review all the claims filed by the environmentalists—how it couldn't be done and that kind of stuff. Pecora put this enormous base of scientists together and finally brought about the changes in the application for the pipeline and did the environmental assessment. He was able to tell Congress that he had reviewed all of the complaints, and that's why we were able to get it through. He set the stage for Congressional action."

> *Senator Stevens drew up a proposed amendment that would prohibit the filing of environmental lawsuits against the pipeline.*

Stevens says another key to Congressional approval was the surprise support of Nevada Senator Alan Bible, "one of the real environmental senators, dedicated to the National Park system.

"Alan told me, 'I understand what you are trying to do for your state. . . . I just want to know, I want to learn on this one.' So he sat there through whatever it was, three of four days of the debate. . . . It was the only time I know of that anyone sat on the Senate floor through all of the debate that didn't affect his own state.

"We lost two votes at the last minute," Stevens said, "and Alan came up to me and said, 'In my opinion you have made a good case and I'm going to vote with you.' And he did. A vote that we never expected. But he really listened, and he believed that we had done our work environmentally. It was the core of work that convinced him."

PRESIDENT NIXON signed the pipeline authorization act on November 16, 1973. Back in Alaska, the legislature's special oil session had just ended, and a few days later Governor Egan signed the package of state legislation into law. In January, Nixon and Egan jointly executed a state-federal agreement pledging cooperative surveillance of the pipeline.

With the federal handwriting writ large on the tundra, the Environmental Defense Fund and other environmental groups decided to forgo further legal challenges and concentrate on becoming pipeline watchdogs. And the oil companies began hiring. BP immediately advertised for petroleum production and drilling engineers, accountants, stenographers, a systems analyst, an attorney, and some stores personnel. The pipeline was ready to go.

PORTRAIT

JAY HAMMOND

Bearded bush pilot, big-game guide, poet, cracker-barrel philosopher, self-styled "bush rat."

This is Jay Hammond, as described by Gary Thurlow, Bill Egan's chief of staff in the early '60s.

"Above all," Thurlow writes in an unpublished book on Western U.S. politics, "he loved his home, Bristol Bay, and the Alaska outdoor life."

After serving as a Marine pilot in World War II, Jay Hammond came to Alaska from Vermont and attended the University of Alaska in Fairbanks. This future governor married Bella Gardiner, from the Bristol Bay village of Kakanok, and he worked as a pilot-agent for the U.S. Fish and Wildlife Service.

First elected to the state House as an Independent in 1958, Hammond served until beaten by Dillingham Democrat Joe McGill in 1965.

"I ran originally as an Independent," he says, "because I wouldn't dare go back home as a Democrat. Growing up in Vermont, I used to think that all the crooks, ne'er-do-wells, and no-good-niks were Democrats. But when you realize that that's all there is out in the bush . . . Democrats . . . they had the market cornered. There were virtually no Republicans."

Following his defeat by McGill, Hammond became part-time manager of the Bristol Bay Borough. In 1967, he beat Mount McKinley National Park manager Grant Pearson for a reapportioned Senate seat.

Recalling that election, Hammond says: "Mark Jensen of Juneau told me he would hold my filing papers until I made up my mind whether or not to run. The next thing I knew, I read in the newspapers that I had filed for the Senate seat."

Hammond ran as a Republican instead of an Independent. "The only way I ever got elected, quite frankly, was coattailing on Johnny Sackett" (a young Native from Ruby, Alaska, running for the first time).

"The bush at that time was about 6-to-1 Democrat," Hammond said, but the popular Sackett chose to run as a Republican. "Sackett helped me out enormously," Hammond said. "That's how I got elected."

In 1972, by an 11-to-9 vote, Hammond was elected Senate president. "One Democrat had crossed over; [Senator John] Rader was a statesman who had the public interest in mind." This kind of low-key humor and his consensus-style management generated strong personal loyalties among his followers. Hammond gave the impression to his political allies and administrators that he would gladly share the responsibility of governing with them.

Chapter 36

Egan vs. Hammond

The political fallout from the 1973 oil session of the legislature was very real, and it would last. "Legislators gained confidence during the special session," says Mike Bradner, a state representative then. "After that, they weren't afraid of the industry. They felt they knew what it was all about, and they realized that those guys—oil company lobbyists and employees—were having to check with their home offices, were fighting among themselves, were not all alike.

"People came to understand that the industry is divided on some major issues," Bradner said. "Like taxes. The industry was mired in bureaucracy, and generally, we, the state, weren't. We had small, fish-bowl politics that had the benefit of taking action quickly. That may not be the way it is now. In a way, the '73 session sunk the oil industry for the next decade."

The political fallout hurt Egan. "I think Egan's purpose in 1972 with pipeline ownership was to escape the taint of oil," Bradner said. "But at the end of '73 he had picked up some of it. The Democrats were trying to say that the Republicans sold out, but the administration picked up some of the flack, too."

"The new legislators were absolutely convinced that Egan sold out to the oil companies," says former Egan aide Alex Miller, referring to the oil-legislation package negotiated by John Havelock with the petroleum companies. "'Why do you say that,' I would ask them. And they really couldn't come up with a reason except that they, you know, basically those guys hated the oil companies."

Egan's relationship with the oil industry, forced on him by the need to gut Chancy Croft's right-of-way leasing bill and get the pipeline started, agitated Egan's normal calm. A year earlier he was head-on attacking the oil companies with his pipeline ownership idea. Now he was being accused of being in bed with them. He had won his legislative battle, but the political war wasn't going his way. Sadly, in the course of the struggle, political friendships had been badly tarnished.

Alex Miller sensed that most of the young Democratic legislators would abandon Egan in his 1974 reelection campaign, and he was right. Politically astute as Miller was, however, he couldn't have guessed in late 1973 that Egan's opponent one year later would be Bristol Bay's Jay Hammond. Former Senate president Hammond had been elected mayor of the Bristol Bay Borough. He and I would get to know one another as borough mayors, he in Bristol Bay and I in Anchorage. Though Hammond was an extreme long shot in the race for governor, the self-deprecating humor of this bearded "bush rat" made him attractive to those who saw themselves as independent, self-sufficient pioneers. Hammond's chances of becoming Alaska's fourth governor seemed remote, but change was in the air.

AS SENATE PRESIDENT during 1972, Jay Hammond had taken little part in the debate over Egan's pipeline ownership bill. "I voted against it because I didn't think it had a chance of passing," he says. On the other hand, he voted for Croft's right-of-way leasing bill, which he felt was one way to limit high pipeline tariffs.

Hammond was reapportioned from his Senate seat in 1973 and was not a member of the legislature during the 1973 special oil session. But he had plenty of strong opinions about the deal that Egan had cut with the oil industry. Hammond blamed Egan for placing the state in the position of having no alternative but to bow to the threat of a pipeline delay. He said Egan was forced to seek and spend oil money "because of a bloating bureaucracy."

Throughout 1973, in letters to the editor in the *Anchorage Daily News*, Hammond accused Egan of pushing his 20-mill property tax "so the state could pick the pockets of the North Slope Borough, even before the poverty-stricken North Slope could even acquire a pair of pants."

The state property tax, he wrote, "would be a net loss when state and municipal tax potentials are lumped together. Shifting money from local to state coffers does little to fatten us fiscally. Rather like attempting to stave off starvation by cannibalizing one's own hindquarters: temporarily sustaining perhaps, but likely to hurt in the end."

Hammond said he found it "hardly surprising" that the oil industry would support a 20-mill property tax rather than a potential statewide 30-mill local tax, because, "If it's a better deal for them, in all probability it follows, it's a worse deal for the state." If anyone was listening during late 1973, the 1974 governor's campaign had begun.

JOHN RADER

Issues that involved fishing were a principal point of difference between Jay Hammond and Governor Bill Egan as the 1974 gubernatorial campaign approached.

THE KACHEMAK BAY CONTROVERSY put the differences between Egan and Hammond into high relief. Egan told his resources chief, Chuck Herbert, to hold a competitive oil and gas lease sale for the offshore waters of Kachemak Bay, off the small fishing town of Homer in lower Cook Inlet. A petition signed by more than 300 Homer residents requested a public hearing. Fishermen wanted to express their fears about how oil drilling in prime crab breeding grounds around Anchor Point might damage their livelihood.

Chuck Herbert denied the request. "No specific issue or problems were raised," he said.

Objections to the lease sale filled the local newspapers for weeks. When the sale was held in December 1973 without a hearing, the fishermen became enraged. They blamed Egan for refusing to hear their pleas; now he would feel their heat.

Egan saw the Kachemak Bay issue drop right into his opponent's lap, and "fish-versus-oil" would shape and dominate the 1974 gubernatorial contest. Hammond vowed that if elected, the state would protect the bay's fishing grounds by buying back the leases that had just been sold to oil companies.

"Hammond really picked up and made the Kachemak lease buyback a campaign issue," says Herbert. "In hindsight, I should have held the hearing."

Hammond himself says that the lease buyback "was what killed Bill Egan in 1974."

FISHING ALSO WAS AT THE HEART of another sharp difference of opinion between Egan and Hammond. By 1973, Bristol Bay salmon stocks had reached near-record lows. That year a "limited-entry" fishing law passed during the regular legislative session, setting up a permit system for commercial salmon fishermen.

The state issued nearly 12,000 of the coveted entry permits, but not everyone who wanted a permit was able to get one. The value of the permits shot skyhigh as permit-holders sold them, and they came to be worth an estimated total of about $1 billion. Hammond says many Natives lost their fishing rights either because they sold a permit they had managed to secure or because they couldn't afford to buy a permit in the first place.

Hammond, a fisherman by avocation, had been representing the largest salmon-catching constituency in the world. He and the Bristol Bay fishermen opposed the limited-entry law, while Egan supported it as a way to control over-fishing. Says Hammond of the law: "Alaskans were crazy to allow only some Alaskans, and mostly nonresidents, to have exclusive right to commercially take one of Alaska's resources, salmon."

> *"The new legislators were absolutely convinced that [Governor] Egan sold out to the oil companies."*
>
> *—Former Egan aide Alex Miller*

When the legislature in 1974 passed an amendment supported by fishermen—requiring permit-holders to obtain a commercial license and to be physically present in Alaska — Egan vetoed it.

THERE WAS SOME FEELING OF UNEASE about the coming pipeline in early 1974. It was a feeling that this largest of all private projects might be too large for Alaska's small, sparsely settled population. Pipeline construction, it was feared, might cause another boom-and-bust cycle in the state. Against this background, Jay Hammond defeated Wally Hickel for the Republican nomination for governor and moved into a general-election battle against Governor Bill Egan.

State politicians were exchanging barbs about having "frittered away" the $900 million received at the September 1969 Prudhoe Bay lease sale. There was a mood of change, and Alaskans seemed to be crying out for new ideas.

Hammond recalls being kidded by Egan in late 1973 about polls which showed that only 3 percent of Alaskans knew who Hammond was. At the time, when asked if Wally Hickel and he were going to run against Egan and Lieutenant Governor "Red" Boucher, Hammond replied: "I don't think Wally could beat Boucher."

No love was ever lost between conservationist Hammond and developer Hickel. Hammond recalls laughing with Egan about their common nemesis.

> *Jay Hammond's chances of becoming Alaska's governor seemed remote, but change was in the air.*

When he announced he would run against Egan, Hammond says, his strategy was to "kill 'em with kindness." He says his 1974 campaign was basically anti-Hickel and anti-Atwood (publisher Bob Atwood).

Egan accused Hammond of being against the environment because he opposed an appropriation for the Department of Environmental Conservation. "That's like saying Egan was against higher education because he vetoed more money for the University of Alaska at Fairbanks," says Hammond.

During the campaign, the ruggedly handsome Hammond called for Alaskans "to slow down and see where we're going before we begin any new developments." Just as pipeline construction was about to start, he offered Alaskans a different kind of future.

Hammond could not have been more different from Egan when it came to oil. His principal interest in oil was to keep it from threatening fish or their habitat. When I interviewed him in 1990, his only expressed view toward the oil companies was a pragmatic "They'll do whatever is in their best interest. That's it."

JAY HAMMOND BEAT BILL EGAN in the November 1974 general election by only 287 votes. The state House was now composed of thirty-one Democrats and nine Republicans, while the Senate had thirteen Democrats and seven Republicans. Meanwhile, in the statewide general election, Mike Gravel beat Anchorage plumbing contractor and John Birch Society stalwart C. R. Lewis, a state senator, to retain his seat in the U.S. Senate, and Don Young was reelected to Alaska's lone seat in the U.S. House.

SPOTLIGHT

THE EGAN LOSS

John Havelock believes Governor Egan lost to Jay Hammond in 1974 because Egan wouldn't back down on his limited-entry fishing law. Egan assistant Alex Miller thinks Egan's record on the limited-entry law contributed to his political downfall—but a more important reason, Miller believes, was Egan's failure to appoint as head of the Alaska National Guard an Alaskan Native.

"Egan always carried the bush," says Miller. "Natives in every village got mad over that failure to appoint to the National Guard."

Instead of campaigning for Egan during the 1974 campaign, political rival Chancy Croft spent his time helping elect Democrats to the Senate. For his efforts, a year later he would become Senate president, heading what some would call the most liberal upper legislative body in Alaska's history.

Alex Miller says he asked Croft to support fellow Democrat Egan, but Croft replied, "I just can't do it. His philosophy and my philosophy are too far apart."

Publisher Bob Atwood had labeled Hammond the "no-growth" candidate.

"Without Hickel and Atwood against me," Hammond says, "I probably never could have become governor."

During his eight years as governor, Hammond never shook the anti-growth moniker, because it was partially true.

Chapter 37

Hammond Takes Over

O nce in office, Governor Jay Hammond carried out his campaign pledge to buy back oil and gas leases in Kachemak Bay. His attorney general, Avrum Gross, began negotiating with oil company lessees—including Chevron, which had paid more than $19 million for fifteen leases.

It would take two years before lawmakers authorized the Hammond administration to buy back the leases. Another year would pass before the state paid Chevron $12 million cash and gave it a tax credit for the balance. The state also repaid Texaco and several other companies the money they had paid, plus some predrilling and legal expenses.

During the 1974 campaign, Hammond talked about the "budget gap," claiming that Egan's profligate spending had put the state on the edge of bankruptcy. The flow of Prudhoe Bay oil through the pipeline had originally been expected to begin in 1974. Now it wouldn't be until some time in 1977. The oil beneath Prudhoe Bay was not generating income for the oil companies or for the state. In 1975, Governor Hammond felt something had to be done to close the "budget gap."

As his planning director, Hammond named Robert Weeden, a professor of wildlife management at the University of Alaska Fairbanks. He asked Weeden whether an offshore oil and gas lease sale in the Beaufort Sea might bring the state financial relief. Weeden concluded that a single lease sale would be just a "quick fix" and wouldn't generate enough cash to make a difference. Other options might be to sell general obligation bonds or to get more production from Cook Inlet oil fields or, once Prudhoe Bay oil production began, to sell state royalty oil to in-state refiners or outside buyers. The possibility of a corporate income tax on oil was also being discussed by some in the legislature.

> *Hammond was accused by his critics, and some of his own officials, of purposely trying to discourage oil exploration.*

Hammond knew that public bond debt financing would be as unpopular with citizens and lawmakers as a corporate income tax would be with the oil companies. He also knew that Cook Inlet oil production was out of his control and that royalty-oil sales were off in the future. Hammond turned to lawmakers and administrators to find a solution to the budget gap.

As commissioner of natural resources, Hammond appointed a man able to identify with Hammond's conservationist views, political science professor and lawyer Guy Martin. For the next two years, Martin oversaw a myriad of oil studies, including a survey of reserves at Prudhoe Bay. He examined joint federal-state oil and gas leasing on the Outer Continental Shelf, a proposed natural gas pipeline route through Alaska, the state's oil and gas leasing methods, and various plans to sell royalty oil.

The search for revenue led the Hammond administration and the legislature toward a host of possible ways to tap the oil industry. The tax consulting firm of Zeifman and Ainsworth took a look at the Alaska incomes of a sample of oil companies. The firm reported to the legislature that Alaska could bring in a great deal more in tax revenues if the state created a corporate income tax.

ANOTHER APPROACH to closing the budget gap—and one that had not previously been ruled out by the legislature—was a tax on oil still in the ground. This idea, now resurrected in the 1975 legislature and backed by Governor Hammond, was known as an "oil reserves tax." The proposed reserves tax would be levied on the assessed "market value" of the Prudhoe Bay oil as it lay many thousands of feet beneath the frozen tundra.

The idea wasn't a popular one among oil explorationists. It meant a significant tax on oil even before it was pumped from the ground and earned any money for its owners. It was a disincentive on oil and gas exploration. Rural legislators had supported several increases in severance taxes—taxes paid after oil has been pumped from the ground. But these legislators believed a reserves tax would threaten their own petroleum exploration plans. Native corporations wanted to explore for oil on their own lands, so they were poised to vote against the tax.

Sohio legal counsel Dick Donaldson led the industry charge against the reserves tax. Sohio, along with the other oil companies, wouldn't start making money from Prudhoe until the pipeline went into operation. Sohio was offering its corporate bonds on Wall Street to meet its pipeline financing obligations, but Donaldson said the bonds wouldn't be attractive to buyers if the reserves tax was enacted. He told lawmakers that unless changes were made to the proposed tax, pipeline financing would be jeopardized.

Donaldson's idea was to have the reserves tax expire in two years. And he wanted the oil companies to recoup their reserves-tax payments in the form of credits toward future royalties and severance taxes.

In other words, Donaldson wanted the reserves taxes to be simply a loan to the state. This was actually a fairly appealing idea to a state that was in a budget crunch but could see golden days ahead when the oil began flowing.

The reserves tax, in effect, gave the state a two-year, interest-free, $490 million loan.

Before the legislature finally voted on the reserves tax, Donaldson advised Senator Chancy Croft that his company had to be assured that future legislatures would not raise the tax, rescind its tax credits, or extend the time period that it would be imposed. Donaldson told Croft that with such assurances, the oil industry would support the legislation and the law would be "a done deal."

Lunching with Donaldson in Juneau, Croft wrote on a napkin the assurances Donaldson needed. He promised that the legislature would not amend the reserves tax; in exchange, Donaldson scribbled that the Prudhoe Bay producers would not challenge the tax in court.

Sensing the historical significance of this bit of luncheon tissue, Croft photocopied the napkin for Donaldson, Sohio, and its Wall Street bankers, and then gave the napkin to the state librarian in Juneau. Having thus assuaged Sohio and Wall Street, the reserves tax would not impede building of the pipeline. When rural legislators finally went along, the reserves tax law passed the 1975 legislature.

The reserves tax, in effect, gave the state a two-year, interest-free, $490 million loan. The companies would pay the tax on the estimated assessed value of the oil as it lay in the ground and recoup their payments in the form of tax credits once Prudhoe Bay began producing. The law called for the reserves tax to self-destruct no later than the last day of 1977.

WITH ALL EYES NOW TURNED toward building of the pipeline, no more state oil and gas lease sales would be held until the end of the decade, and then only jointly with the federal government. So few majors and independents remained active in Alaska that lease sales seemed unnecessary.

Hammond was accused by his critics, and some of his own officials, of purposely trying to discourage oil exploration, when in truth he left most oil decisions to his resource managers. His main concern was having enough money to run the state until the pipeline was finished.

Hammond named me as his deputy commissioner of natural resources in 1976, following my defeat in the unified City-Borough of Anchorage mayoral election in the fall of 1975. One of my first tasks after arriving in Juneau was to oversee a study of leasing strategies used by other oil states and nations. The study—conducted by Southern California economics consultant Mason Gaffney, who had been hired by the state—resulted in substantial changes in the state's leasing laws.

FEARS OF OIL SPILLS prompted the 1976 legislature to pass a comprehensive oil spill package creating a cleanup liability fund, similar to one in the Canadian Arctic, for pipeline oil spills. Navigational aids were specified for tankers traveling in and out of Prince William Sound, and tanker owners were to pay annually a risk charge based on the presence or absence of safety features. The legislature discussed but did not pass a requirement for double hulls on oil tankers plying Alaskan waters.

Later that year, Prudhoe Bay producers filed a lawsuit in federal court claiming the oil-spill law's key provisions were unconstitutional. The suit also said that because the oil would be carried in interstate commerce, tanker design and safety regulations in state waters were preempted by federal law.

ALASKA VOTERS overwhelmingly approved a state constitutional amendment in 1976 requiring that one-quarter of all oil and gas royalties, rentals, fees, and bonus bids be placed in a state "permanent fund." Four years later, an amendment doubled the percentage—and provided that an annual dividend from the fund's earned interest be paid to everyone who had lived in Alaska for at least one year. State lawmakers could no longer spend these oil and gas revenues without approval of the voters.

The fund's capital was to be invested to transform Alaska's nonrenewable resources—oil and gas—into "renewable" fish, agriculture, tourism, and the like. It was said that the fund would "create a sustainable, renewable source of income for future generations." Once the oil ran out, the corpus of the fund could be used to lessen the tax burden on future generations. "Nonrenewable" to "renewable" became another of the Hammond administration's policies.

INSIDE STORY

THE *OTHER* PIPELINE

El Paso Natural Gas said it would build a natural-gas pipeline from Prudhoe Bay to Gravina Point near Valdez or to Nikiski on the Kenai Peninsula. El Paso's "All-Alaska" natural-gas pipeline was touted by a local group called the Organization for the Protection of Alaska's Resources (OPAR).

OPAR was formed by such figures as Bob Atwood, Bill Egan, Wally Hickel, Tom Fink, and Bob Penney. The group had the support of Alaska's Congressional delegation.

In 1972, when then-State Senator Jay Hammond had asked fellow legislators to look into a Canadian oil pipeline route, OPAR's promoters became extremely upset. Now that Hammond was governor, they would have to deal with each other again, this time over natural gas.

"Bob Penney came into my office with a great big button that said OPAR," recalls Hammond. "He wanted to present this to me and engage my support for their organization, which stood for the Organization for the Protection of Alaska's Resources. 'Well, no environmentalist would object to that,' I said.

"'But,' I said, 'who's behind this?'

"'Wally Hickel and Tom Fink,' Penney said—and all sorts of people that I didn't view necessarily as friends of the wilderness.

"So I said, 'That's interesting. . . . Bob Penney, Wally Hickel, Tom Fink . . . that's funny . . . OPAR spelled backwards is RAPE-O.'

"The next time they came back, it was OMAR," says Hammond, which stood for Organization for the Management of Alaska's Resources. "Well, that's better, that's appropriate, that's RAM-O spelled backwards.

"I didn't do much to endear myself to the development interests, I'm afraid."

Meanwhile, Hammond's attorney general, Avrum Gross, hired the former chairman of the Kansas public utility commission, Jack Byrd, to draft several natural-gas sales contracts. Hammond officials decided to pressure Congress to allow El Paso Natural Gas to build its all-Alaska gas pipeline by selling all of its North Slope royalty gas to El Paso, Tenneco, and Southern Natural Gas. Sale contracts were executed, but nothing ever came of the scheme.

Chapter 38

Marketing Royalty

People close to the oil world could feel the pulse of the state quickening as 1977 dawned. The oil pipeline would be completed sometime this year and North America's greatest oil field would begin producing.

The state decided to go back into the oil-selling game to capitalize on the riches soon to pour from the Prudhoe field. As royalty owner of one-eighth of all Prudhoe oil, the state could take its royalty in cash or it could take it in oil. The idea of taking the royalty oil and then marketing it at a good price began to look more and more attractive.

Many legislators and administrators saw the idea as a way to stimulate local refineries and utilities. Direct in-state sales to these entities might decrease energy costs in the state.

And there was another strong motive. The state might make more money by taking its royalty in the form of oil and then selling it to the highest bidder. Many lawmakers believed that the oil companies in Cook Inlet had been paying the state far less in cash royalties than was warranted by the true market value of the oil. Why would it be any different at Prudhoe Bay?

Legislators questioned whether it was in the state's best interest to have pipeline owners—also owners of almost all the oil on the North Slope—simply pay cash royalties and thus own almost all the state's royalty oil. The state might do better by taking the oil and marketing it for itself. And if so, the oil companies might be forced to offer a higher royalty price.

Resources commissioner Tom Kelly tried this strategy in 1969 when he made a deal with Frank Cahoon to sell the state's Cook Inlet royalty oil to Cahoon's proposed new refinery. The refinery was built, and it began consuming all of the state's Cook Inlet royalty oil. But did the oil sales to the new refinery force the majors to raise the prices they paid the state for royalty oil? Probably not.

———

THE FULL MACHINERY to make Alaska an oil marketer was put into place. The 1974 legislature created the Alaska Royalty Oil and Gas Development Advisory Board to prescreen sales. The resources commissioner and this Royalty Oil Board were given authority to take the state's royalty in cash, or to take it in oil and then sell it.

If the commissioner and the board thought a sale was in the state's best interest, it could be made. The price would be determined either by negotiation or competitive bid. The oil could be sold to an out-of-state buyer if the commissioner ruled that it was surplus to the state's domestic needs.

As pipeline construction reached its peak during the fall of 1975, resources commissioner Guy Martin solicited royalty-oil purchase contracts from prospective buyers. He asked them to submit proposals to buy any or all of the state's nearly 150,000 barrels of daily royalty oil expected from Prudhoe Bay beginning some time in mid-1977.

Interest was high. By late 1975, more than 100 out-of-state companies and nearly all Alaska utility companies had submitted proposals. In-state refiners Chevron, Tesoro (the Cahoon refinery), and Mapco (which had a refinery near Fairbanks) asked for oil. The Prudhoe Bay oil producers also sent in proposals, preferring to continue paying the state the "fair market price" for its royalty oil. Prospective oil purchasers lobbied legislators, administrators, and Royalty Oil Board members; in-state organizations asked for preferential treatment.

Governor Hammond told Royalty Oil Board members at their early May 1977 meeting that the price for royalty oil and gas should never be less than the price already being received from the major oil producers. Any sale should prefer existing in-state facilities with no alternative source of oil or gas. Secondly, preference should go to companies that promise to construct or expand an in-state facility.

STEVE McCUTHEON/ANCHORAGE MUSEUM OF HISTORY AND ART

Petrochemical complex at Nikiski in 1973, 13 miles north of Kenai on Cook Inlet with offshore platforms in background.

Hammond wanted to create jobs and lower energy costs, particularly in the bush, and utilizing royalty oil in-state might be an answer. A portion of North Slope royalty oil and gas should always remain uncommitted to longterm sales contracts, Hammond told the board.

Decisions by the resources commissioner and the board to sell royalty oil did not require legislative approval. But because of political pressure, Hammond told lawmakers they could approve any sales of North Slope royalty oil.

To a question concerning a proposal to build a refinery and a large-scale petrochemical plant at Valdez to process all of the state's North Slope royalty oil, Hammond answered rhetorically: "Do I favor a refinery in Alaska? My answer has always been, yes, I favor a refinery in Alaska as long as it pays its own way on a net basis and is environmentally sound."

This "pays its own way" phrase would become Hammond's stated public policy throughout his eight years as governor. It gave little guidance to administrators dealing with Alaska's resource extractive industries.

THE FIRST BUYER of North Slope royalty oil turned out to be the Golden Valley Electric Association, a utility company located along the pipeline route near Fairbanks. In April 1977, several months before the pipeline began delivering oil, the state approved a sale of 2,000 barrels a day to Golden Valley. The hope was that this direct in-state sale of oil would help reduce energy costs in Fairbanks and in bush communities while bringing a good price to the state.

The state decided to go back into the oil-selling game to capitalize on the riches soon to pour from the Prudhoe field.

But first, the state had to lay down the law to Golden Valley. The utility's attorney, Robert Hartig, told the Royalty Oil Board that his client planned to pay the "average price" for royalty oil. Revenue Commissioner Sterling Gallagher replied: "Once you step off the highest price, it creates an endless series of nuances." The only policy the board had at the time to guide its decision was that royalty oil must be sold at the "highest price as set forth in the competitive lease."

Resources commissioner Guy Martin had left Juneau in the spring of 1977 to become an assistant secretary in President Carter's Interior Department. I was deputy resources commissioner at the time, and with the royalty oil issue particularly hot, I served as resources commissioner briefly at the time the Golden Valley sale was made.

To succeed Martin as resources commissioner, Hammond chose the former director of his office of policy and planning, wildlife biologist Bob LeResche. Dartmouth-graduate LeResche set forth his personal view of Alaska's resources in a talk to a coal conference in Juneau shortly after his appointment.

"We [the citizens of Alaska] still own most of the store, and our shelves are fully stocked with most of what the world wants. The days of great Alaskan fire sales, loss leaders, and giveaways are over now that Prudhoe has been discovered." To several Texas oilmen in the audience, LeResche's words were construed as being distinctly "anti-development."

BILLION-DOLLAR DECISIONS were now being made. In early May 1977, ARCO filed papers with the federal government proposing that ARCO pay a tariff of $6.04 per barrel to move oil through the pipeline. Other pipeline owner-companies filed individual tariffs, lifting the weighted average charge to more than $6.20 a barrel.

The amount of the tariff would have a direct bearing on how much Alaskans received in royalty and in severance taxes from North Slope oil. In general, the higher the tariffs, the lower the royalties and taxes. The tariff charges would be paid by the oil companies to the pipeline company, which they themselves owned. The oil companies would then charge the tariffs as a transportation expense and deduct it from the wellhead value of the oil. Royalties and severance taxes were a percentage of the wellhead value; the lower the wellhead value, the lower the royalties and taxes.

The proposed tariffs of more than $6 a barrel drew immediate fire. The state of Alaska, U.S. Department of Justice, Interstate Commerce Commission's Bureau of Investigations and Enforcement, and the Arctic Slope Regional Corporation filed protests with the ICC.

Prior to the Alaska rate case, the Interstate Commerce Commission had heard just four oil pipeline rate cases. Because the Alaska case appeared unique, the federal courts had instructed the commission to reexamine its rate-base valuation methodology.

> *"Do I favor a refinery in Alaska?*
> *My answer has always been, yes, I favor a refinery in Alaska as long as it pays its own way on a net basis and is environmentally sound."*
>
> —*Governor Jay Hammond*

In late June, the commission suspended the Alaska inception tariffs, dropping the tariff average from above $6.20 to $4.68 and $5.10 a barrel, depending on the company. The commission (renamed the Federal Energy Regulatory Commission later in 1977) said it would investigate "just and reasonable rates." But eight years would pass before any significant decision would be forthcoming. When the suspension of the inception tariffs expired in June 1978, the average Alaska pipeline tariff climbed back to the even higher level of $6.25 a barrel.

THE COST OF MOVING Alaska's oil to market was the key factor in another difficult economic issue facing the state.

The natural market for Prudhoe Bay crude was in the Puget Sound region, San Francisco, or Los Angeles, and sales to refineries in these areas normally determined the price of oil. But changing market demands meant that close to half of Prudhoe's crude oil would be shipped to the Gulf Coast or the East Coast, rather than the West Coast. The oil companies were estimating it would cost them $2 to $3 per barrel more to ship Prudhoe Bay oil to the Gulf or East coasts. The net-back wellhead price of a barrel of this far-traveling oil, therefore, would be $2 to $3 lower per barrel, and the state's royalty and severance-tax income would be correspondingly lower.

ARCO decided to take advantage of this situation despite the fact that it owned refineries on the West Coast and actually planned to send only about 10 percent of its Prudhoe Bay crude to the Gulf or East coasts. ARCO claimed it was entitled to a wellhead price that was the same as if it had shipped *all* of its oil to these areas.

BP, on the other hand, said it would not deduct any additional shipping costs. BP owned no West Coast refineries, and the company planned to sell or trade most of its Prudhoe crude. Though it planned to ship some crude to the Gulf and East coasts, BP said it would not deduct transportation costs to either area. BP was therefore prepared to accept a wellhead value some $2-a-barrel higher than its Prudhoe Bay co-operator ARCO. As it had earlier in Cook Inlet, the state was again faced with trying to untangle a conflicting web of oil values claimed by the various companies.

INSIDE STORY

A LEARNING EXPERIENCE

During the late 1970s, the Hammond administration asked major petrochemical companies to help Alaska transform itself into a world-class petrochemical production center. Lieutenant Governor Terry Miller led the administration's effort.

To that end, in June 1978 the legislature awarded a 27-year contract to the Texas-based Alaska Petrochemical Company to sell it 150,000 barrels of oil a day—nearly all of the state's North Slope royalty oil. But just three years later, a bankrupt Alaska Petrochemical simply walked away from its contract, still owing the state nearly $60 million.

"Alpetco was a learning experience," Hammond said later, stating that even at the time, "I knew it couldn't be put together. I used to tell my environmental friends who were castigating me . . . : 'If you hold [Alpetco's] feet to the fire on many of the things you're concerned about and compel them to do a good business deal for the citizens of this state collectively, they'll fall flat on their face. Because all kinds of people who could care less about the dickey-birds will get uptight if you control them, and they are going to lose money in the process.'"

Chapter 39
"The Best and Brightest"

oming down the homestretch toward opening of the trans-Alaska pipeline, the state and the oil people were still miles apart on how to put a price on the state's royalty oil. The state owned one-eighth of all the oil soon to come out of the ground at Prudhoe, but what was it worth? How should a price be set on it?

Neither Governor Hammond nor his attorney general, Avrum Gross, seemed personally very interested in details of the pricing and marketing of oil. Gross turned petroleum matters over to his deputy, Wilson Condon, a former Stanford University crew coach, who had been active in the earlier Cook Inlet royalty litigation and had helped negotiate Bill Egan's 1973 oil-legislation package with the oil companies.

Condon appointed an oil task force of the state's "best and brightest" young lawyers, who met regularly in Juneau during the spring of 1977 just as the pipeline was nearing completion. Their focus was on pipeline tariffs and on the value of royalty oil.

Assistant attorney general Fred Boness told his fellow "oil lawyers" he was certain the state's legal department lacked the firepower to deal with these sticky issues. He expected North Slope oil producers to file a royalty valuation lawsuit soon. And they were bound to complain about the new severance tax regulations just presented to them by Tom Williams of the Department of Revenue. The 1977 legislature had raised the oil severance tax from 8 to

12.25 percent and voted to allow reduction in the tax on marginally profitable oil fields. Wouldn't this be the time to hire outside lawyers?

ON JUNE 19, 1977, the first day Prudhoe Bay oil entered the pipeline at
Pump Station No. 1, lawyers for the oil producers met in San Francisco. They
were sitting down to decide how much their clients would pay the state for its
Prudhoe royalty oil. Former state assistant attorney general John Reeder, who
represented the state in Cook Inlet pricing litigation in 1972, now worked for
BP and took the lead for the companies.

Reeder was well aware that the state objected strongly to receiving different
royalty prices from the same lease from joint lease owners. But Reeder and the
other oil lawyers also knew their North Slope clients intended to use the same
royalty valuation calculations that had upset the state in Cook Inlet. By filing
separate pipeline tariffs and billing separate tanker charges, each company

BRITISH PETROLEUM

Endicott Field in 1981 with Sag 7 in foreground and Sag 8 in background.

would be able to report different prices for oil, as they had in Cook Inlet. And they planned to keep deducting upstream field costs.

Reeder got on the phone to Tom Williams, head of the state's royalty pricing negotiating team in Juneau. Williams was director of the division of petroleum revenue in the state's Department of Revenue. "What price does the state expect to receive for its North Slope oil," Reeder asked Williams. "That partly depends," Williams said, "on the exact point at which the oil is valued." Williams said the state would accept royalty payments during the first few months of production on a "transactional basis."

Williams acknowledged to Reeder that language in the state's lease forms on field-cost deductions was ambiguous. But according to Exxon lawyer Tom Krueger, Williams volunteered that "political pressure" would keep the state from allowing deductions for "upstream" field costs, at least at this time.

The oil companies and the state had generally agreed that "downstream" costs—mainly transportation costs from Pump Station No. 1 at Prudhoe to the refineries in the Lower 48—could be deducted in arriving at a wellhead price for oil. But the state didn't want the companies to deduct the expenses of getting oil from the well to Pump Station No. 1—the "upstream" costs.

Meanwhile, Fred Boness, who had been appointed deputy resources commissioner, sent a memo to members of his Juneau oil task force. He said he expected the Prudhoe Bay producers to stubbornly begin taking substantial field-cost deductions in figuring their royalty payments. If the companies failed to pay what the state believed the royalty was worth at Pump Station No. 1, he said, the state should sue.

ON JULY 12, oil company lawyers and state oil officials met on the royalty pricing matter in the Juneau office of state revenue commissioner Sterling Gallagher. The state was planning to sue the oil companies, but the two sides couldn't have been more cordial about it. Tom Williams and Fred Boness took notes.

Deputy attorney general Wilson Condon began the meeting by framing what he considered the basic legal issues.

"Knowing the complexity of the Cook Inlet pricing case," Condon said, "it seems that an earlier resolution means a less complex mess to litigate." He made the state's point that the market price or value of the state's royalty oil was to be made at Pump Station No. 1. No deductions for upstream field costs would be allowed.

Condon recalls that all parties at the meeting agreed that costs of transporting oil from Pump Station No. 1 to the refineries—the downstream costs—would be deductible in figuring royalties. What those costs were, and whether they were "reasonably incurred," remained to be determined.

Condon told oil lawyers that because pricing data was not yet in, it was too early to discuss the royalty's actual market price or value. He said the producers could have until the end of the year to gather pricing data, and the state would wait until then to accept the companies' interim royalty payments.

Exxon's Tom Krueger reported to his management after the meeting that Condon had assured him that "the state is not going to play the game the lessees did not pay enough royalty so default notices would be issued. Condon sees the lawsuit as based on conceptual legal issues with little or no questions of fact so it should go rather quickly."

Krueger said Condon stressed the "responsibility on the part of the state administrators to show that by working the cost-netting problem quickly, they are vigilant and, in general, doing a good job. Condon explained that the state considered litigation on the cost-netting inevitable and preferred that the matter be settled at an early date before it becomes an unmanageable mess."

Phillips attorney Tom Blume also reported to his employer. "All the Alaska officials are relatively young attorneys," he wrote. Blume said these officials were careful to say that their position on field costs was an expression of opinion and not "an order from which appeal would have to be taken."

> **The state was planning to sue the oil companies, but the two sides couldn't have been more cordial about it.**

"It is unlikely that a compromise can be reached without litigation," Blume wrote, "as any such compromise would have to be extremely favorable to the state for its officials to take the political risks of approval. The Alaska officials were cooperative in their recognition of the bona fides of our dispute and their willingness to seek resolution in an orderly manner."

After the July 12 meeting, Sohio lawyer John Lansdale visited Condon in his office in Juneau. Lansdale said he believed that Sohio's merger partner BP might consider selling the state its 16 percent share of the pipeline. Rather than fighting over tariffs, BP might want to get entirely out of pipeline ownership. Would the state be interested in buying BP's share?

The proposal went nowhere. Condon told Lansdale that he didn't believe the state had the "capacity to digest" the purchase but would discuss the matter with Attorney General Gross and Governor Hammond. Hammond later said he didn't recall being advised about the matter.

> *"It is unlikely that a compromise can be reached without litigation."*
>
> —Phillips attorney
> Tom Blume

ON JULY 18, the state's ten-page oil royalty report forms were mailed to Prudhoe Bay producers. The forms were accompanied by instructions from Fred Boness, telling producers to "describe how your reported value of oil production is derived, who purchased the oil, the volume, gravity, full consideration, point of sale, and transportation costs."

Two days later, assistant attorney general Bob Maynard faxed BP and ARCO the draft of a memorandum of understanding between the companies and the state, covering interim royalty payments until litigation was complete. The memorandum included an assurance that the state wouldn't file its suit against the companies until after September 1.

On August 1, in a memo to Governor Hammond marked "confidential," Bob Maynard predicted that Prudhoe Bay leaseholders would pay the state prices ranging from \$2.93 to \$7.70 a barrel for royalty oil. Mobil would pay the former and Getty the latter, said Maynard. He said the companies could also be expected to deduct—despite the state's protestations—field costs ranging from 66 cents to \$1.11 a barrel. Maynard's important memo was hand-delivered to Hammond by Attorney General Gross and deputy Wilson Condon.

On August 26, Governor Hammond authorized Gross and Condon to file the state's royalty-pricing lawsuit against the North Slope oil-producing companies. The suit was filed September 2.

"There was a two-part reason for filing the lawsuit," Bob Maynard later recalled. "One was simply litigation over the value of royalties in the past and the principles for determining the value in the future. The other was that the state did not have any good database for determining what was going on in the marketing of oil. We had a tremendous amount of historical information spread all over the place. That's why Wil Condon's there, to build that database for the future." (Wilson Condon's firm handled the royalty lawsuit for the state.)

The problematic language of the state's leasing regulations was heading into the courts. Such simple-sounding phrases as "at the well" were being debated and scrutinized for meaning. A decade later, the case was still unresolved.

The lawsuit demonstrated that in the late 1970s, the state of Alaska seemed no better prepared to deal with oil pricing than it had been ten years earlier. The same calculations were to be used by North Slope oil producers as had been used in the mid-1960s in Cook Inlet by some of the same companies. These pricing methods would inevitably lead to the same underpayments and delays the state complained of before; meanwhile the companies had use of the cash they otherwise would have had to pay to the state. But unlike the tens of millions of dollars involved in the Cook Inlet dispute, at issue this time were billions of dollars.

Chapter 40

The Oil Flows

Oilmen initially believed the 800-mile trans-Alaska pipeline could be built with construction methods used in other parts of the world. Arctic permafrost and government environmental regulations taught them otherwise. Instead of burying the pipe in the ground, they eventually had to suspend 420 miles of it on stanchions above permanently frozen ground. Only 380 miles were buried where the tundra was not frozen.

The pipeline crosses 600 streams and rivers, traverses three mountain ranges, and travels through several seismically active areas. Where the pipeline crosses the Denali Fault, builders placed operable block valves on either side of the pipe to isolate it in case of an earthquake.

ARCO president Thornton F. Bradshaw confessed at a Congressional hearing that in the early planning of the pipeline, "We did not know how to make an environmentally safe line." But the many delays, caused mostly by environmental concerns, "taught us some lessons."

Vice President Spiro Agnew's "yea" broke a Senate tie vote in late 1973, opening the way to passage of the pipeline authorization act. Construction of the pipeline's access road—known as the "haul road"—began in earnest in April 1974, and by that September, more than 350 miles had been completed. Work on the pipeline continued for three very full years.

Beginning in the spring of 1974, pipeline workers from outside Alaska began inundating the state. At peak construction, more than 28,000 workers were drawing pipeline wages. Local high school students earned more than $5,000 a month doing menial tasks. Government employees left their jobs for higher-paying work on the pipeline. Fairbanks boomed, its airport filled day and night with mostly transient males. One couldn't complete a telephone call in Fairbanks because the phone system, along with other public utilities, was hopelessly overloaded.

At one point, Teamsters Local 959 had 23,000 dues-paying members. The union built a multimillion-dollar Anchorage headquarters. Teamsters boss Jesse L. Carr had use of a Lear jet and two Merlin turboprops to ferry him from Anchorage to wherever he cared to go.

I recall standing next to a local labor leader, Bob McFarland, as the Teamsters headquarters was being dedicated in early 1974. I had been invited to attend as Anchorage Borough mayor, and as Teamsters honchos Dave Beck and Arne Weinmeister dedicated the building, McFarland turned to me and said, "I'm sure glad I won't be here when this place falls down."

Jesse Carr's empire did collapse after pipeline construction ended in late 1977 and union membership plummeted. At one time during the '70s, however, Carr came as close to controlling the state as Bill Egan envisioned oil companies might have done several years earlier.

The pipeline was an extravagantly expensive undertaking. The oil companies claim that it cost almost $10 billion.

ALYESKA PIPELINE SERVICE COMPANY

A workman lines up a section of the trans-Alaska pipeline in preparation for welding. (1976 photo)

OIL ENTERED THE PIPELINE at Pump Station No. 1 on the North Slope at 10:05 A.M. on June 19, 1977. The inaugural passage of oil did not go smoothly as the pipeline shut down several times during the first weeks because of

JOE RYCHETNIK

Trans-Alaska Pipeline on the North Slope in 1978.

YESKA PIPELINE SERVICE COMPANY

The last portion of pipe installation in 1976 was in the northern section of the trans-Alaska pipeline in the Brooks Mountain Range, where the line was installed through Atigun Pass, elevation 4,800 feet.

leaks and cracks. Crude oil spraying from one pump station started a fire and resulted in the death of a worker. It took until the end of July to get the pipeline running well.

The 800 miles of 48-inch pipe slowly filled to its 9-million-barrel capacity. Oil passed over 4,800-foot Atigun Pass at a speed of 7.35 miles per hour and later glided over Thompson Pass and flowed down to the tiny town of Valdez on the shores of Prince William Sound.

The first oil through the pipeline reached the terminal at Valdez at 11:02 P.M. on July 28, 1977. Three-quarters of a century of wildcatting and exploring, of speculating and scheming, had led to this day when Alaska began exploiting riches that Earl Grammer and the other oil pioneers could scarcely have imagined. Several days later, this first oil was loaded into the ARCO *Juneau*, bound for the refinery at Cherry Point, Washington.

CLARK JAMES MISCHLER

The Trans-Alaska pipeline crosses three mountain ranges on its 800-mile route from the Arctic Ocean to the Gulf of Alaska. (1992 photo)

EPILOGUE

Some sort of indigenous, recognizable culture had been growing . . . in Western towns and even Western cities. It is the product not of the boomers but of the stickers, not of those who pillage and run but of those who settle, and love the life they have made and the place they have made it in.
— Wallace Stegner
Where the Bluebird Sings to the Lemonade Springs:
Living and Writing in the West

WITH THE PIPELINE, Alaska's financial future seemed assured. No longer dependent on Uncle Sam for its economic survival, Alaska would become self-supporting. With statehood and Prudhoe Bay, economic independence and freedom had finally arrived. No more waiting for outsiders to tell us what to do to develop our resources.

That's what we thought.

But today, our capital projects, loan programs, highways, and schools depend on checks from BP, ARCO, and Exxon. Decisions concerning timing and pacing of almost all oil exploration programs in Alaska are now made in London, Los Angeles, Houston, and New York. Not unlike the earlier days of economic domination by mining and fishing interests, we wait for financiers and executives in far-off capitals to decide whether exploration in Alaska is worth it. And we continue to send Alaska's outmatched "best and brightest" into battle with oil industry lawyers over taxes and royalties.

The two decades since completion of the pipeline have seen a struggle between state and industry lawyers and accountants. The battle is over money: pipeline tariffs, royalties, taxes, and of course the big overall question: What is the state's fair share of oil income? It's a constant campaign to avoid being overwhelmed by the oil business and by the oil companies; to avoid ending up, as Bill Egan had feared, "riding the tiger." The ghost of Bill Egan, ever the cautious protector of Alaska, still hovers over state officials as they make decisions involving oil.

ONCE PRUDHOE BAY DOLLARS began flowing, state lawmakers looked for ways to spend them. Demands accelerated for public housing, education, social programs—all the pent-up "needs" and desires of constituents. With the golden deluge of money, many of these desires could now be financed.

Beginning in the late 1970s, the elderly, the young, and the disabled received public subsidies; loans went to local businesses; grants were made to local governments, many of whom repealed property and sales taxes. After Anchorage voters in 1980 rejected a bond issue to build a convention center, sports arena, performing arts center, and library, the legislature handed the city $200 million to build the projects. New schools, libraries, and gymnasiums appeared in the bush. The North Slope Borough increased its public bonded indebtedness to over $1 billion—more than $200,000 for each of its 4,500 residents. Every community could now set its sights on having gleaming new projects like those in Anchorage.

THE FLOW OF OIL DOLLARS wasn't automatic; it meant constant legal bickering and frequent tinkering with oil taxes so that Alaska got its "fair share." The battle over changes in the corporate income tax is an illustration of the jockeying for position that continues to occupy the state and the industry.

Lawmakers amended the corporate income tax in 1978 to provide for something called "separate accounting." Oil company income from production in Alaska would henceforth be treated in three separate and distinct ways, and income earned outside Alaska could no longer be commingled with that earned in Alaska for corporate income tax purposes. The changes were advantageous to the state.

ARCO, Sohio, and Exxon counterattacked with a lawsuit that claimed the tax violated their right to equal protection under the U.S. Constitution and unfairly burdened the unearned portion of the federal windfall profits tax.

Republican legislators promoted a new corporate tax amendment in 1981 that had the blessings of the oil industry and that, the lawmakers claimed, would be "revenue neutral"—that is, it wouldn't reduce state income. As oil lobbyists waited—their company jets parked side-by-side at Juneau International Airport—the amended tax law passed.

Jay Hammond was governor at the time. "I agreed to the corporate tax amendment on the basis of [Deputy Attorney General] Wil Condon's argument that we were so vulnerable that we were likely to lose lots more than we did," Hammond says now. "Frankly, that was not good counsel. On the other hand, you had to go on the best advice you had at the time, and Wil was not alone."

And not everyone believed the new law would really be "revenue neutral." To offset any drop in state revenue, the 1981 legislature increased the oil severance tax from 12.25 percent to 15 percent. In this and a dozen other critical matters, government and Big Oil practiced a one-upsmanship seemingly designed to always keep one another off balance.

IN 1978, WALLY HICKEL—former governor, former Interior Secretary, developer extraordinaire—was back for another try at the governorship. Four years earlier, Jay Hammond beat Hickel for the Republican nomination. He did it again in 1978, but by only 98 votes, and Hammond went on to defeat Democrat Chancy Croft in the November general election.

One of the campaign issues in 1978 was a proposal to sell state oil to a Kenai refinery. Hammond says the issue "probably dramatizes more than anything the point of departure between Wally's attitude and mine. . . . Hickel and I were on totally different wavelengths. Hickel wanted to create 400 jobs by discounting the royalty $1.25 a barrel to a Kenai refinery. That would be $96 million a year in public subsidy."

In Hammond's view, a refinery shouldn't be a ward of the state. But Hickel's attitude, as Hammond tells it, is that "any growth is good if it creates jobs for Alaskans."

THE PRUDHOE MEGA-DISCOVERY was by no means the end of possible major oil fields in Alaska. Two years after the pipeline opened, oil companies leaped back into the bidding at a joint state/federal competitive lease sale for areas in the Beaufort Sea northwest of Prudhoe. Twenty-seven oil companies plus two dozen individuals and associations bid at the December 1979 sale on seventy-one tracts covering 341,000 acres.

For the first time, the net-profits bidding method was used. Bidders promised to pay the governments a percentage of net oil profits. Amerada Hess bid as high as 93 percent on some tracts, and Chevron bid as low as 2-3/4 percent.

Several Native groups protested the sale because potential oil-platform "blowouts" would injure waters and wildlife, while several other Native groups bid in the sale with British Petroleum. BP's strategy was to have Natives participate with them to counteract Native protests and gain support for North Slope exploration. BP asked only the North Slope Natives to join in bidding, but Native leader Willie Hensley insisted that all twelve in-state Native regional corporations be given the same opportunity.

Four regional corporations bid with BP, putting up $1 million for a 1 percent interest in the leases. They are still waiting for their investment to pay off.

THE STATE'S OIL RICHES brought all sorts of unexpected repercussions, including repeal of Alaska's individual income tax. Jay Hammond says he opposed the repeal as governor because "the public needed to be able to say, 'What are those idiots doing with our tax dollars.'" He says he signed the legislature's repeal legislation in 1980 only because he assumed a public initiative would repeal the tax if he didn't.

Legislators, fervent to bring oil dollars back to their constituents, fought Hammond over control of the new money. After tense negotiations with House and Senate leaders, Hammond finally agreed that each legislative body would have the sole authority to decide how to spend a third of the state's capital-expenditures budget. Pork-barrel lawmaking carried the day.

In November 1982, former Sears appliance salesman and millionaire Alaska hotel owner Bill Sheffield was elected governor. I was in Sheffield's Anchorage home, standing next to Bill Egan, when Sheffield's victory was announced. To no one in particular, as I recall, Egan said: "Well, at least he's a compassionate person."

After eight years of Hammond's personal benign neglect of the oil industry—unless it had to do with fish—Sheffield felt he had to try to resolve disputes with the oil producers. As the self-styled chairman of the state's board of directors, Sheffield settled several important oil lawsuits, most notably the pipeline tariffs case. In so doing, his critics painted him as too close to the oil industry. It didn't help when, as one of his first acts as governor, he took his attorney general and resources commissioner on a political fund-raising trip to Texas.

Sheffield tried to break up the budget deal he inherited from Hammond in which the state House and Senate had won control of two-thirds of the state's capital-expenditures budget. All he got for his trouble was more trouble.

On July 2, 1985, a Juneau state grand jury charged Sheffield with "a serious abuse of office," accusing him of directing a Fairbanks state office lease to a political crony. The Senate later voted 12 to 8 against impeaching Sheffield, but his wings had been severely clipped.

In early January 1986, the Sheffield administration reached a severance tax settlement with ARCO in which the company agreed to pay $243 million in back taxes. Sheffield told the public he couldn't disclose terms of the agreement because it would mean revealing ARCO's "proprietary marketing information." State law permitted tax settlement data to remain confidential, but Alaskans' unflattering perception of Sheffield at the time made them suspicious of his failure to disclose.

THE DISPUTE over pipeline tariffs was one of several that have kept the state and the oil industry in the courts almost continually. The state likes to see these tariffs, or charges, for sending oil through the pipeline kept low, because oil producers deduct the charges from the value of oil before paying royalties and taxes. The oil companies that own the pipeline, on the other hand, benefit by keeping tariffs high.

Governor Hammond's top legal and revenue officials advised him in 1981 that even if tariffs were found to be unlawfully high, collecting refunds was highly unlikely. So Hammond proposed a settlement covering tariffs to the year 1994, but the Senate rejected the proposal as too vague.

After Bill Sheffield became governor, Assistant Attorney General Bob Maynard was put in charge of settling the pipeline tariffs lawsuit that the state had filed. From 1975 to the early 1990s, Maynard worked for three governors, six attorneys general, and five resources commissioners.

"Each oil company has a different personality," Maynard says. "For example, you had to be very careful in dealing with ARCO, because it would sell other companies down the river. When Exxon and Sohio [BP] learned of what ARCO did . . . they were mad as hell."

What ARCO did was agree on its own to settle the tariffs dispute. In late 1984, much to Maynard's surprise, ARCO accepted the state's latest settlement offer.

"Each company negotiated differently," Maynard says. "ARCO gave the most local authority. Exxon had to have engineers involved. BP didn't use lawyers; it used businessmen. BP's people would be very friendly and superficially accommodating, but when you analyzed what they seemed to have agreed to, you realized they hadn't moved a bit."

After settling with ARCO and other pipeline owner-companies, the average pipeline tariff went the state's way. It dropped by almost half—from just over $6 a barrel to about $3.20 a barrel.

BOB MAYNARD OFFERS some perceptive insights into dealing with oil companies. "The state . . . always knew," says Maynard, "that if we sued and lost, we could always exercise the state's 'sovereign power.' . . . We could tax. The companies will wait until you walk away to see if you are serious. Then they will deal. We tried not to have the negotiation sessions [on pipeline tariffs] at our place. You can't walk out of your own office."

Maynard says there is "a tendency in the state to go from 'pals of the industry' to its 'enemy.' Sometimes we have similar interests and sometimes we are adversaries. There's a kind of healthy mutual distrust, but it doesn't mean that you are enemies.

"You can't distrust oil people because you think they're dishonest" Maynard says. "They're like you or I, and they believe their rhetoric. They have kids. They're interesting people. It's not a question of distrusting them, or that they're liars. They just clearly have a different viewpoint. They're not out to protect the state; we are."

Former ARCO chairman Bob Anderson weighs in with a skeptical insider's view of modern oil-industry executives. They're overly conservative, he believes. "Most of today's CEOs . . . they're fifty-five or so . . . they really get the seat, the power, and the reins. They've got ten years to go, a great retirement plan, great stock options, their focus is only from here to the finish line. Unfortunately there aren't many people making long-term decisions. Major oil company managers believe order and process are the keys to success, while leaders champion their visions and step on toes."

THAT OIL EXPLORATION IS A GAMBLER'S GAME was proven in a big way by British Petroleum in 1983. BP drilled a wildcat well that year in the Beaufort Sea northwest of Prudhoe Bay. It was thought the giant structure of this area might hold reserves as large as those at Prudhoe.

As the drama unfolded, I watched BP geologist Roger Herrera and other BP employees strain to keep their excitement and optimism under control. It was clear they expected great things from the Mukluk well.

About a month before the well was expected to reach target depth, oil geologist Marvin Mangus spoke to my oil-history class at Anchorage's Alaska Pacific University. Mangus told the students he didn't expect the Mukluk well to produce oil. Water; perhaps gas; but no oil.

Mangus was right. The hole was dry. Drilled at a phenomenal cost of $2 billion, it was the most expensive well in history. Oil had probably been there tens of millions of years ago but since had seeped out.

"It was amazing to me to observe the level of confidence BP people had concerning that prospect," says geologist Gil Mull. "In exploration, one has to have confidence in a play, but one must also be a realist. One would think that someone in BP should have been bothered by the fact that some of the other companies—ARCO and Exxon, and I think others—did not even bid on the Mukluk tracts. That should have been a clue . . . ."

ALASKA'S IMPOTENCE in the face of international oil developments was never more obvious than in the mid-1980s, when Saudi Arabia boosted its oil production. Saudi production jumped from 4.5 million barrels a day to more than 6 million barrels, causing the world price of crude oil to drop during the fourth quarter of 1985 to about $8 a barrel. At one point in mid-July 1986, the wellhead value of a barrel of Prudhoe Bay crude at Pump Station No. 1 fell below $3.50.

Alaska's economy, particularly the Anchorage real estate market, plunged precipitously. The state general budget fell from $4.5 billion to $2.5 billion. Of the eleven Anchorage banks in 1986, only five remained three years later.

In January 1987, Fairbanks lawyer Steve Cowper succeeded Bill Sheffield as governor. In his inaugural speech, Cowper bemoaned Alaska's subservient position in the oil world.

"Blameless though we may be for these events, today we find ourselves helplessly hoping for the success of OPEC in enforcing an agreement which, if it were in this country, would be illegal conspiracy in restraint of trade," he said. "When they [the OPEC oil countries] cheat on each other and produce more oil, our school districts in Alaska go bankrupt and our workers lose their jobs. For Alaskans, continuing this craven dependency is unthinkable."

Cowper spent most of his four years as governor fighting to keep the legislature from lowering the corporate income tax on North Slope oil production, and an oil disaster in Prince William Sound allowed him to succeed.

ON MARCH 24, 1989, the Exxon Valdez, under command of Captain Joseph Hazelwood, was traversing Prince William Sound outside of the normal shipping lane, trying to avoid icebergs calving off the nearby Columbia Glacier, when it punctured eight of its oil tanks on Bligh Reef. Eleven million gallons of crude oil spilled into the waters of the sound.

Countless marine organisms, seabirds, and mammals were killed. Delicate intertidal zones along hundreds of miles of coastline were severely damaged. It's still not clear whether salmon or other commercially important fish species suffered long-term damage. Exxon spent an estimated $2.5 billion on spill cleanup and settlement of some 12,600 related claims. Exxon paid the state and the federal government $125 million toward restoration of Prince William Sound, with another $900 million to be paid over ten years.

"The spill caused a lot of people to reevaluate what they most treasure about Alaska," Steve Cowper said. "Is it oil wealth or is it the country itself that is at stake?"

"The oil companies went instantly from being 'angels of economics' to 'demons of destruction,'" says Jay Hammond.

One major side-effect of the Exxon Valdez spill was to delay exploration on the coastal plain of the Arctic National Wildlife Refuge (referred to almost universally as ANWR, pronounced "Anwar"). The refuge's coastal plain—a mostly flat, treeless, 120-by-15-mile strip in the northeast corner of the state—sees about 200,000 caribou each summer come to calve.

One oil well has been drilled by Chevron and BP in ANWR on land owned by the Arctic Slope Regional Corporation near the Native village of Kaktovik, but information from the well remains confidential. Congress has yet to decide whether to allow drilling on non-Native lands in the reserve or how much oil revenue will be shared with the state if drilling takes place.

"I'll be very surprised if ANWR is drilled before the year 2000," says oil industry veteran Harry Jamison. "ANWR is like the pipeline. The Natives are out of the way, but the environmental lobby is effective."

"ANWR will come along," says Bob Anderson. "More importantly, you've got something certain at West Sak and Ugnu [oil fields near Prudhoe Bay]. If we don't produce these, we're going to have gasoline lines again.

"The West Sak field will require twenty to thirty wells to equal what one Prudhoe well produces. But the West Sak field will produce for at least fifty to sixty years. And the Ugnu on the North Slope will begin with steam injection in twenty to thirty years and will produce for more than a century."

Anderson says he probably made a mistake in his days at ARCO in not pressing for a permanent new community near the Prudhoe oil fields. "While preservationists won't like it," he says, "I think more people are going to want to visit the Slope, and inevitably a motel like a Holiday Inn will probably be located at Deadhorse, possibly built by a Native corporation."

WALLY HICKEL regained the governorship in 1990, succeeding Steve Cowper. With a stated motto of "Alaska's common resources for the common good," and with veteran trial lawyer Charlie Cole as attorney general, the new Hickel administration settled several major oil lawsuits—most significantly the Amerada Hess suit that had been filed on September 2, 1977.

The Amerada Hess suit had charged that the oilmen were massively short-changing the state on royalties. The oil producers were making unauthorized deductions of field costs upstream from Pump Station No. 1 before settling on the value of the oil, the state claimed. They were also manipulating downstream prices and deducting unreasonable tanker costs. Deputy Attorney General Condon had thought he would get a quick resolution of the case, but nearly a decade and a half passed as parties to the suit spent hundreds of millions of dollars on legal fees.

The lawsuit was settled by Charlie Cole and Wally Hickel in early 1992, more than fourteen years after it began. A trial had been scheduled that spring in Juneau to determine what the producers owed the state for the billions of barrels of oil pumped from the North Slope. But only weeks before the trial date, the last of the Big Three defendants settled out of court. ARCO had agreed in late 1990 to pay the state $285 million; BP agreed in 1991 to come up with $185 million; now Exxon would pay $128 million.

The Hickel administration called the settlements "fair." Had the case gone to trial, hundreds of depositions from "experts" and rooms full of documents—about 3 million pieces of paper—would have been summarily dumped into the jurors' laps.

The settlement came up with a formula for setting the value of North Slope royalty oil. But it didn't cover royalty obligations on gas liquids and natural gas, and under certain circumstances either side can reopen this vexing valuation question.

Democrat Tony Knowles followed Republican Hickel as governor in 1994. The Knowles program of "partnering" with industry will, perhaps, bring more exploration activity and jobs. New laws providing for the leasing of large tracts of state land, such as Roscoe Bell envisioned three decades earlier, and royalty reductions for "marginal" fields, similar to the "discovery royalty" granted before Prudhoe, may give the industry the incentives it needs to remain in Alaska.

The Knowles approach may work if it also reflects the idea that laws and regulations should encourage competition, not just jobs. Usually the greater the competition, the better protected is the public interest.

DESPITE THE LONG DELAY in approving the pipeline and despite Bill Egan's "in-your-face" politics of pipeline ownership, the major oil companies remained in Alaska in the '70s. When the state sought more taxes and tightened regulations during the 1970s and '80s, the majors stayed. The companies might occasionally call Alaska "politically unfriendly," but the oil of Prudhoe has calmed most of their concerns.

Oil companies make exploration and development investments when geologic prospects are good and when resources and technology make solid profits likely. And wherever the companies explore, they seek political stability. Alaska is a political safe haven for Big Oil, compared with some of the foreign venues that oil people must deal with.

Though Alaskans sometimes worry that the major companies will leave Alaska for better foreign prospects, this isn't likely. The oil is still here, and there's more to be found.

Partly by design, and partly by good luck, the North Slope leases won in 1964 and 1965 by ARCO, BP, and Exxon brought them great wealth. In the first ten years of Prudhoe Bay production, these three companies recorded after-tax profits from oil production of $29.1 billion and from pipeline tariffs of $12.4 billion. Since then, the Big Three have taken in additional billions and now dominate Alaska financially. Other companies exploring for oil on the Slope must deal with them, and the overwhelming advantage of their existing infrastructure and pipeline control makes true competition difficult if not impossible.

At the same time, the state has received billions of dollars that it has used for schools, cultural and recreational facilities, and public support programs that make living in the Last Frontier much less harsh than before.

SINCE MY ARRIVAL IN ALASKA in 1954, great change has taken place. Less freewheeling in entrepreneurial spirit, we now seem to be stuck riding the oil-industry "tiger." Some of the exploration urge remains—witness Stewart Petroleum's 1991 discovery in Cook Inlet—but the dominance of ARCO, BP, and Exxon has slowed what might have been a more diverse and lively oil business.

If Alaska's oil had been allowed to develop more slowly—say, with a series of Swanson River-size oil fields in many of Alaska's geologic basins— "little guys" in the image of Earl Grammer and Locke Jacobs might still be here. They played an important early role in one of this century's great oil dramas, and other "little guys"—maybe Native corporations or oil independents— could still appear, though perhaps not with the enthusiasm and certainly not with the persistence of Earl Grammer.

Oil has brought many material benefits and talented people to Alaska. Prosperity has forever changed the Alaskan lifestyle, though not always for the better. Most Alaskans hope the multinational oil companies here prosper.

The oil people will explore in the state for decades to come because vast new reserves remain to be discovered. "Alaska," says Bob Anderson, "has the underpinning of economic development and jobs for the next hundred years." With the money will come more of the challenges and the upheaval that have both plagued and enriched all of us who call Alaska home, and that will follow our children and their children after them.

Can you blame us if we have mixed feelings about the storehouse of natural resources that is ours?

APPENDIX

Oil exploration personnel active in Alaska during 1950s and 1960s — (partial list)

MAJORS

Amerada Petroleum Corporation, Tulsa
R. O. Williams, Jr., landman

American Petrofina Company, New York
Guy Patat, petroleum engineer
Henri Pierard, T. R. Russell, geologists
E. L. Singletary, Norris C. Bakke, Jr., landmen

Amoco (then Pan American Petroleum
Corporation), Tulsa
Ross W. Craig, Dist. super.
Art E. Piper, Dist. prod. super.
William Van Allen, B. E. Shaw, William Easton, C.
L. Conrad, J. H. McKeever, geologists
R. B. Jones, O. J. Gross, geophysicists
Don L. Simasko, E. A. Watlington, landmen

(The) Atlantic Refining Company, Philadelphia
(now ARCO)
W. B. Moore, John M. Sweet, Richard W. Crick,
Marvin D. Mangus, Thomas B. Patrick, Jake
Thomas, geologists
C. H. Hightower, L. L. Brantley, Jack H. Carlisle,
geophysicists
John Marston, Robert M Parks, Roland Champion,
Gordon Davis, landmen
Norman Shear, scout

BP Exploration Company (Alaska), Inc., London
T. A. D. W. Hillyard, John O. Zehnder, Michael J.
K. Savage, Edward C. Mees, R. J. Stephens, Alwyne
N. Thomas, local representatives
Jim Spence, Laurie O. Gay, Roger Herrera, geologists
R. J. S. Sherwin, geophysicist
D. W. Gough, landman

(The) British-American Oil Producing Company,
Dallas
Robert M. Kenyon, Dee Beardsley, geologists
John D. Mohrle, landman
John J. Freeburg, geophysicist

Cities Service Company, New York

Continental Oil Company, Houston
Roger M. Dungan, Billy C. Osborn, John V.
Trailkill, Kenneth G. Smith, George C. Soronen,
geologists
Donnell O. Wells, landman

Exxon (then Humble Oil & Refining Company),
Houston
Joseph F. Homer, prod. supervisor (Bear Creek)
Perry Frederick Sollars, Regional geologist
Ben Carsey, H. G. Graham, Dean L. Morgridge,
geologists
A. C. Winslow, paleontologist
Robert J. Walker, Jr., landman
Carl R. Jamison, scout
J. R. Jackson, Area explor. manager
O. K. Fuller, Jr., geophysicist

Gulf Oil Corporation of California, Houston
James R. Wylie, geologist

Hunt Oil Company (also Placid Oil Company),
Dallas
E. W. Tynes, Warren Gray, geologists
W. O. Bazhaw, C. G. Dahm, geophysicists
James W. Beavers, Jr., landman
Paul Scott, production

Husky Oil & Refining, Ltd., Calgary (also Bristol
Bay Oil Company)
J. C. Scott, geologist
Robert Strother, landman
G. A. Peschke, production

Kerr-McGee Oil Industries, Inc., Oklahoma City
Breene M. Kerr, exploration

Marathon (then The Ohio Oil Company), Findlay
Richard W. Shoemaker, Thomas Wilson, Jr., geologists
W. J. Nowlan, M. L. Lowman, landmen

Mobil (then General Petroleum Corporation), Los Angeles
E. R. Orwig, Joseph Harvey, John A. Forman, E. R. Bush, geologists
Daniel W. Richardson, geophysicist
Jack D. Swafford, William H. Cook, Jr., Bob Gallison, landmen

Occidental Petroleum Corp., Bakersfield

Phillips Petroleum Company, Bartlesville
S. P. (Phil) O'Rourke, Henry T. Herlyn, Don W. Buelow, Robert O. Dunbar,
Keith W. Calderwood, A. W. Schlottman, William C. Fackler, L. L. "Vern" Vigorin, geologists
Robert I. Swetnam, landman

(The) Pure Oil Company, Chicago
Robin A. Saunders, Joseph L. Borden, M. Charles Durfee, geologists
Robert Harlow, geophysicist
Frank L. Shogrin, Garth M. Armstrong, landmen

Richfield Oil Corporation (now ARCO), Los Angeles
William C. Bishop, G. Ray Arnett, Les D. Brocket, Leo F. Fay, Harry C. Jamison, Ben W. Ryan, Jr., Charles G. "Gil" Mull, Garnett "Gar" Pessel, geologists
Jim M. Clinton, Charles H. Selman, John G. Sindorf, geophysicists
R. J. Misbeck, engineer
Graham P. Stewart, Jr., Armand Spielman, landmen

Shell Oil Company, New York
Max Birkhauser, R. L. Blocher, James Kennell, Donald M. Robinson, Herb Lang, C. A. Barkell, geologists
Charles W. Barnes, Richard Freeman, Roger A. Chaffin, Thomas S. Cate, landmen
J. R. Cheney, geophysicist
Earl David, Jerome Sager, scouts

Sinclair Oil & Gas Company (now ARCO), Tulsa
Zed Grissom, Ross R. Gahring, Clarence Unruh, Ernest R. Bush, geologists
Vic H. Howard, geophysicist
J. R. Lodle, Richard Porter, William A. Armstrong, landmen

Skelly Oil Company, Tulsa
Joseph E. Morero, Donald D. Bruce, geologists
A. L. Cashman, landman

Sohio Petroleum Company, Cleveland

Standard Oil Co. of California (now Chevron), San Francisco
P. W. Gester, Expl. superintendent
Jack T. Crooker, C. V. Chatterton, Prod. superintendents
William E. Whitney, engineer
Allen B. Scouler, Charles E. Kirschner, geologists
Robert Brace, geophysicist
B. L. Price, Charles W. Hagans, Paul F. McAndrews, Robert W. Killen, landmen

Sun Oil Company, Philadelphia

Sunray Mid-Continent Oil Co. (Sunray DX), Tulsa
E. W. Pease, Richard A. Eckhart, geologists

(The) Superior Oil Company, Los Angeles
George Y. Wheatley, W. W. Hagist, W. G. Binkley, geologists
Eugene J. Wentworth, landman

Teikoku Oil Co., (Alaska Petroleum Dev. Co. and Alaska U.S.A., Ltd), Tokyo

Tenneco Oil Co., Houston
Donald Trimble, landman

Texaco, Inc., Los Angeles
Wayne M. Felts, L. B. Freeman, Gerald Ganopole, J. W. Bedford, Donald C. Hartman, W. J. Hughs, geologists
Claude H. Brown, landman

Tidewater Oil Company, Los Angeles
H. H. Neel, Explor. manager
Robert Dyk, geophysicist

Union Oil Company of California, Los Angeles
John C. Hazzard, Senior geologist
Charlie E. Smith, Operations manager
Russ Simonson, Harold M. Lian, Lum C. Lovely, E. H. East, Richard A. Lyon, geologists
Joe Dockwiller, scout
Duncan B. Robinson, John Clark, geophysicists
Ed P. McLeod, C. W. Dunham, drilling & production
William E. Thompson, Homer L. Burrell, Jr., Kenneth Robertson, landmen

Western Gulf Oil Company, Pittsburgh
O. Lee Wix, landman

INDEPENDENTS

Alaska Consolidated Oil Company, Inc. , New York
(also Alaska Oil & Mineral Co., Inc.)
John Zappa, Pres.

Alaska Exploration Corporation, Anchorage
John R. Roderick & Gerald Ganopole

Alaska-Gubik Oil & Gas Co., Fairbanks
Paul Elbert, Chm.

Alaska Gulf Oil & Gas Development, Inc., Bakersfield
John "Tex" Scarbrough and Chester Ashford

Alaska Oil & Gas Development, Anchorage
C. F. Shield and William O'Neill

Ambassador Oil Corporation, Ft. Worth
F. Kirk Johnson, Pres.

Anadarko Production Company, Houston

Anchorage Gas and Oil Development, Inc., Anchorage
George H. Tucker & Ralph D. Peterson

Apache Oil Corp., Minneapolis

Belco Petroleum Corporation, New York

*(Paul G.) Benedum, Pittsburgh
Paul G. Benedum, Jr., geologist

Colorado Oil and Gas Corporation, Denver
D. G. Benson, geologist
C. E. Titus, landman
J. R. Coleman, production
Donald Meek, Superintendent (at Yakutat)

(The) Cortez Oil Company, Denver
(also Polaris Oil Company and The Alaska Company)
John J. King, Pres.

**Fairbanks Oil and Gas Co.
Dr. Hugh Fate, Pres.

(The) Freemont Petroleum Company, Denver

Great Basins Petroleum Co., Los Angeles
R. G. "Scotty" Greene, Pres.

Halbouty Alaska Oil Co., Houston
Thomas E. Kelly, geologist
Ted E. Dobson, petroleum engineer

Home Oil Company, Ltd., Calgary
R. A. "Bobby" Brown, Jr., Pres.

Hondo Oil & Gas Company, Roswell
Robert O. Anderson, Pres.

Honolulu Oil Corporation, San Francisco

King Oil, Inc., Wichita Falls

Louisiana Land and Exploration Co., Houston

(John W.) Mecom, Houston

Monterey Oil Company, Los Angeles

Newmont Oil Company, New York

Northern Development Co., Tacoma
Ben Gellenbeck and William T. Foran

Northlander Oil Company, Denver
Graham P. Stewart, Jr. and Frank L. Shogrin

Pan-Alaska Corporation, Houston
(also Global Exploration Company - Raymond M. Thompson)

(Neville) Penrose, Inc., Ft. Worth

Penzoil, Inc., Houston

Plymouth Oil Company, Pittsburgh

Reserve Oil and Gas Company, San Francisco
Signal Oil and Gas Company, Los Angeles

Skyline Oil Company, Salt Lake

(James H.) Snowden, Ft. Worth (also Aledo Oil
Company)
Waring Bradley, geologist

Sun Oil Company, Philadelphia

Territorial Development Co., Seattle
William T. Foran and Tom A. O'Connell

TULM - Tennessee Gas Transmission Company,
Union Oil & Gas Corp. of Louisiana, Lion Oil Co.
and Murphy Corp.

Union Texas Petroleum, Houston

Wallace Mining Company, Inc., Anchorage

Yakutat Development Co., Washington, D. C.
Nathanial Ely

* Participants with Benedum drilling at Nulato in
the Bethel-Koyukuk basin in the early 1960s were
Ambassador Oil Co., BP Exploration Co. (Alaska),
Inc., El Paso Natural Gas Co., Michel T. Halbouty,
Claud B. Hamill, Kenwood Oil Co., Northern
Natural Gas Producing Co., Pan-Alaska Co., Peake
Petroleum Co., Peerless Oil & Gas Co., Texas Gas
Exploration Corp., Texas National Petroleum Co.,
Tex-Star Petroleum Cp., Robert Uihlein, Woodley
Petroleum Corp. and Union Carbide Corp.

**F. Kirk Johnson (Ft. Worth) and Brooks-Scanlon
Oil Company (Minneapolis) filed leases in 1954 in
the Kateel River area with Texas-Yukon Oil
Company and Kivalina Oil Association of
Fairbanks.

LEASEBROKERS

Allen, Monte J.
Barnes, Charles W. (Ivy, Inc.)
Burglin, Clifford, Fairbanks
Campbell, Alexander P., Los Angeles
Catron, Ed, Casper
Davis, Walter J.
Devine, Ed (Pappy), Glenallen
deGinzburg, Francois, Denver
Erickson, Jean
Fahrny, D. L. "Pinky"
Fricks, Pat and Claudia, Fairbanks
Gellenbeck, Ben G., Tacoma
Glaisyer, Roland
Grammer, L. E.
Grimes, George S.
Hagen, Alfred, Palmer
Hillman, Loren, Los Angeles
Hines, Leroy, San Francisco
Honsinger, Lloyd E.
Jacobs, Locke, Jr. (Western Lands & Leasing Corp)
Jenks, Robert, Delta Junction
Koslosky, Harold
Ledbetter, Charles
Link, Don R., Denver
Malcolm, William T.
Noey, L. W. (Tex) (Alaska Oil & Gas Leasing
Service)
Novosel, Frank
Pickrell, Daniel, (Pexco, Inc.) San Francisco
Roderick, John R.
Rowlett, John R., Fairbanks
Shogrin, Frank L., Denver
Simasko, Donald L.
Stevenson, Albert, Los Angeles
Stroble, Donald L.
Walker, Jack V.
Zamarello, Peter

CONSULTING GEOLOGISTS

Andresen, M. J., College (Geonomics)
Bradley, Waring
Calderwood, Keith W.
Church, Richard E., Fairbanks (Geonomics)
Fackler, William C.
Folk, Stewart H., Houston
Folta, William
Foran, William T., Seattle
Ganopole, Gerald
Gardner, R. C., Pasadena
(L. F.) Ivanhoe, Beverly Hills
Lovely, Lummie C., Jr.
Mangus, Marvin D.
Marshall, Thomas R., Jr.
Neighbors, Glen R., Houston
Rowlett, John T., Fairbanks
Ryan, Irene E.
Schmidt, Ruth A. M.
Taylor, Earl F., Houston
Thompson, Raymond M., Englewood
Willis, Dr. Robin, Los Angeles
Wylie, James R., Aptos
Zaegel, William

INDEX

439

442

McVeigh, Dick, 339, 373, 375
Meeds, Lloyd, 327
Melville Sound, 263
Merdes, Ed, 248, 351
MGS field. SEE Middle Ground Shoal.
Middle Ground Shoal No. 4, 181
Middle Ground Shoal, 140-141, 164, 181-182, 191, 240
Miklautsch, Tom, 175
Miller, Alex, 97, 337, 353, 364, 367, 374-375, 385-386, 388, 391
Miller, Glenn, 59, 62-63, 65-66, 76
Miller, Keith, 235, 255-256, 278, 290, 300, 302, 307, 309, 338
Miller, Terry, 373, 407
Mineral Leasing Act of 1920, 21-22, 27, 289, 381
Mobil, 27, 39, 54-56, 179, 181, 186, 223, 243, 249, 267, 279, 297, 309, 328-329, 332, 335, 431. SEE ALSO General Petroleum Corp.
Monterey Oil Co., 433
Moquawkie Reservation, 315
Morgan Stanley and Co., 342
Morgan, Frank, 73
Morton, Rogers C.B., 289, 308, 319, 328, 330, 380
Mount Becharof, 22
Mount St. Elias, 42
Mukluk well, 425
Mull, Charles G. (Gil), 136-138, 188-189, 200, 211, 217, 220, 425
Murkowski, Frank, 210

N

Nagley, Willard, 62
National Environmental Policy Act, 288, 293, 307, 381
National Iranian Oil Co., 123
Native Claims Settlement Act, 365, 379
Native claims settlement legislation, 325-332
Native Land Claims Task Force, 257, 318
Native land claims, 180, 204-205, 209-214, 234, 254, 256-258, 286-288, 290-291, 294, 307, 309-310, 313-323, 325-332, 365, 379-380
Naval Coal Commission, 40
Naval Petroleum Reserve No. 4, 40-41, 125, 135, 156, 163, 322, 325
Nenana (Alaska), 67
Newmont Oil Co., 433
Nielsen, Sig, 102-103
Nikiski (Alaska), 119, 207, 247, 249, 372, 399, 403
Nixon, Richard M., 234, 253-254, 286, 288-289, 295, 308, 319-320, 322, 327-328, 359, 380, 382
Noatak area, 41
Noey, Tex, 158

Nominee system, 127-128
Noncompetitive bidding, 100-101, 105, 161-162
North Slope Borough, 329-332, 356
North Slope lease sale, 267-271, 275-281
North Slope refinery, 298
North Slope, 20, 40-41, 71, 73, 85, 92, 112, 122, 124-125, 127-131, 133-145, 147, 151-163, 167-189, 195-196, 199-205, 109-210, 215, 217-226, 233-235, 237, 244, 249, 255-257, 261, 264, 267-271, 275-281, 285-286, 288, 297-303, 305, 307-308, 317-319, 322, 328-332, 340, 345, 356-357, 361-362, 381, 399, 401, 403-405, 407, 409, 411, 416, 426-427, 429: map, 122
Northern Development Co., 42-43, 433
Northlander Oil Co., 433
Northwest Passage, 262-263
Notti, Emil, 309, 316-318
Novosel, Frank J., 181
Nulato (Alaska), 53
Nushagak Peninsula, 87-88

O

O'Connell, Quinn, 296, 323
O'Neill, Bill, 49
O'Rourke, Phil, 43, 47-48
Occidental Petroleum Corp., 72, 432
Ohio Oil Co., 61, 431. SEE ALSO Marathon.
Oil Bay, 21, 33
Oil Creek, 22-24, 33
Oil exploration personnel, 431-435
Oil in pipeline, 415-417
Oil Point, 21
Oil seepage, 20-24, 27
Oil session (legislature), 367-375, 377
Oily Lake, 43
Oldman's Bay, 147
OPEC, 305, 426
Operation Statehood, 257
Organization for the Management of Alaska's Resources, 399
Organization for the Protection of Alaska's Resources, 399
Osborn, Alan, 276
Ownership (Trans Alaska Pipeline System), 335-343, 347-353

P

Pacific Oil & Commercial Co., 24
Pacific Steam Whaling Co., 37
Palmer, Bob, 357
Palmer, David, 276
Pan Alaska Corp., 433
Pan American Petroleum Corp., 127, 163, 182, 431. SEE ALSO Amoco.
Paradiso, S.J., 76
Parker, Bill, 370-372
Patton, Dorothy, 291